Heino's *Liebe Mutter* . . . EMI Columbia. Album cover credits: photos: Trawinski.

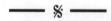

Publishers/Editors: V. Vale/Andrea Juno
Production Manager: Elizabeth Borowski
Staff Photographers: Robert Waldman, Olivier Robert
Production Staff: Mindaugis Bagdon, Maria Coletsis, Nicole Frantz, Mason Jones, Mary Ricci, Ken Sitz, Marian Wallace
Book Design: Andrea Juno
Communications Director: Chris Trela
Chief Consultant: Ken Werner
Special Thanks to: Rex Doane, Tom Guido, and everyone else we couldn't interview who sent us tapes and suggestions—you know who you are!
Publicist/Foreign Rights: Ira Silverberg, NYC, Tel.: 212-226-6580

BOOKSTORE DISTRIBUTION: Consortium Book Sales & Distribution, 1045 Westgate Drive, Suite 90, Saint Paul, MN 55114-1065. TEL: 612-221-9035 or 800-283-3572. FAX: 612-221-0124.
NON BOOKSTORE DISTRIBUTION: Last Gasp, 777 Florida St, San Francisco, CA 94110. TEL: 415-824-6636. FAX: 415-824-1836.
U.K. DISTRIBUTION: Airlift, 26 Eden Grove, London N7 8EL, England. TEL: 071-607-5792. FAX: 071-607-6714.

Send SASE for catalog: RE/SEARCH PUBLICATIONS
1232 Pacific Ave
San Francisco, CA 94109
(415) 771-7117

Printed in Hong Kong by Colorcraft Ltd.

Photostat service: Northern Lights, San Francisco

10 9 8 7 6 5 4 3 2

Front Cover Albums:
Music Out of the Moon—Peace of Mind, © Capitol Records, Inc. Music featuring the Theremin, themes by Harry Revel. Album cover credits: cover posed by Virginia Clark of Earl Carroll's Theatre, Hollywood. Photograph: Paul Garrison.
Space Escapade by Les Baxter, © Capitol Records, Inc.
Electronic Hair Pieces by Mort Garson, A&M Records. Produced by: EmGee Productions. Album cover credits: art director: Tom Wilkes, photography: Jim McCrary
Music to Work or Study By by The Melachrino Orchestra, conducted by George Melachrino. © RCA Victor.

——— ℁ ———

Back Cover Photo (of Jello Biafra): Robert Waldman

CONTENTS

Incredibly Strange Music, Volume Two, continues the exploration of the territory spotlighted in *Volume One:* mostly out-of-print vinyl recordings from the '50s-'70s which do not fit into the already critically scrutinized genres of rock, jazz, and classical music. (See the introduction in *Volume One,* which need not be repeated here.) As in *Volume One,* we have included collectors who have remapped their own musical aesthetics (taking chances on records for a quarter or a dollar at garage sales and thrift stores). We also interview original artists responsible for some of the most unusual and imaginative recordings since the invention of the 12" LP: Bebe Barron, Juan Garcia Esquivel, Robert Moog, Ken Nordine, Korla Pandit, Yma Sumac, Elisabeth Waldo, and Rusty Warren.

This is not a completist's volume: there are thousands of undocumented recordings which have yet to be unearthed and appreciated—many of which were produced and distributed only locally. A record may be worth owning if it has just *one* outstanding track, or perhaps just beautiful, provocative cover art-

work (especially if it's cheap). A universe of unusual 45s awaits an encyclopedic overview, not to mention countless vinyl records from other countries. Readers (and travelers) are encouraged to have fun inventing their own categorizations and collecting specialties as they uncover an "incredibly strange" sonic past they never knew existed, and which yet awaits rediscovery in the garages, attics and storerooms of the world.
—V. Vale and Andrea Juno

The Vampires' Sound Inc., *Psychedelic Dance Party,* Mercury International.

Balsara & His Singing Sitars' *Great International Hits*, World Record Club.

Sensuous Women & Men Together, Audio Stag Records.

The Stanley-Johnson Orchestra's
Have Harp Can't Travel, Liberty Records.
Album cover credits:
cover design: Pate/Francis & Assoc.,
color photography: Garrett-Howard.

Percussive Jazz, Audio Fidelity. Album cover credits: cover art: Irving Sloane.

The Braillettes' *Our Hearts Keep Singing*, Heart Warming Records.
Album cover credits: cover photo: Jack Chinn.

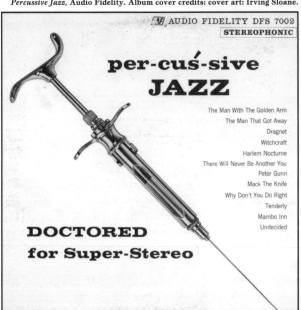

5

JELLO BIAFRA

Jello Biafra is a self-described "cultural terrorist" who debuted as singer for the punk band Dead Kennedys in 1978, as well as a songwriter, spoken word activist and collage artist. While releasing numerous recordings, he has sustained a long history of societal provocation—and suffered a major arrest and "obscenity" trial in the '80s over the inclusion of an H.R. Giger painting in a Dead Kennedys LP (he was acquitted, of course, but had to pay enormous legal bills). Biafra was the first person in American history to be put on trial over a record! He founded Alternative Tentacles (dedicated to keeping the independent recording scene alive), and since the '70s has collected unusual vinyl from Brazil, the former U.S.S.R., Europe, Africa, and the Pacific Rim while touring the planet. Biafra's contact address is PO Box 419092, San Francisco CA 94141.

♦ **VALE: *You were heavily involved in the censorship controversies of the 1990 election year, which have come and gone, supposedly—***
♦ BIAFRA: Total bullshit—not at all! It's getting worse and worse. Now the religious right has near-veto power behind the scenes over a lot of TV programming. Ben Bendikian's book, *The Media Monopoly,* details corporate buyouts of TV networks, newspapers, major record labels—you name it—and the dumbing-down effect this has on all kinds of culture. Tabloid journalism has now devolved into *tabloid politics.* Bendikian and the group Fairness and Accuracy in Reporting show how so-called news programs contain less and less actual news. Even the President can't get anyone to tune him in unless he goes on a talk show like Larry King. One of the worst forms of censorship going on today is: depriving people of basic *information* so they can make informed decisions about what to do with their lives and everybody else's lives.

For example, only now is it coming out that one of the most polluted places on earth is the former Iron Curtain—in places like Poland, the water's so bad that people won't drink it because it has who knows how many types of crankcase oil in it. In Czechoslovakia the Bohemian forest is dead because of air pollution. There are toxic dumps everywhere, especially around military bases, and a lot of this wouldn't have happened if the corporate media hadn't censored all environmental impact study information for so many decades. The horrors of what that has led to over there are only just beginning to come out. Meanwhile, more and more information about how it's collapsing *here* is just being pulled out of the news. All three of the major networks have closed their environmental bureaus in the past year! None of them bother making documentaries anymore. This is just one example of how we're deprived of information. People are now conditioned to worry more about a Marine getting his dick cut off than the societal collapse we're seeing all around us.

The papers never talk about what the hole in the ozone really means. Sure, Reagan's secretary of the interior said, "No problem—people should just wear sunglasses." But what are all the *animals* going to do? By the year 2001 we won't be sending spaceships to Jupiter; we'll be figuring out how to find something to eat once the plankton are gone and all the animals have gone blind and died.

♦ *V: I've read that in Antarctica, which is the nearest to that hole in the ozone layer, fish are already going blind.*

♦ B: So are livestock and who knows what else in the southern part of South America. They keep wandering into ponds and drowning! Australia's now the skin cancer capital of the world. People cover themselves Islamic-style as the atmosphere turns into Swiss cheese. There's two holes now—there's one above the North Pole, too.

With corporate media designed to keep people obedient and asleep, who's left to tell people what's really going on? Artists! Musicians. So naturally music censorship is getting worse. On my records I've detailed

Photo: Robert Waldman

the impact of having "Parental Advisory" stickers on them, which hasn't led to the censorship people backing off—*now* state legislators are pushing for making Tipper Gore's "Parental Advisory" stickers the legal equivalent of an x-rating, so stores can be prosecuted for selling them to minors or even selling them at all. The state of Washington passed the worst music censorship law in the country, banning all so-called "erotic" music.

Meanwhile, it appears as though the Catholic hierarchy and the christian religious right have finally made peace with each other—at least forming a marriage of convenience in hopes of banning abortions, free speech and turning America into even more of a theocracy than it already is. With almost a *fundamentalist* christian majority on the Supreme Court, Rehnquist has come out and said the wall of separation between church and state should be "frankly and explicitly abandoned"! Clarence "Uncle" Thomas goes to the same holy-roller church that Oliver North attends, where people roll on the floor and speak in tongues. Clinton's justice, Ruth Bader Ginsberg, voted

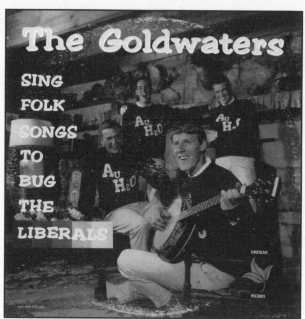

The Goldwaters' *Sing Folk Songs to Bug the Liberals*, Greenleaf Records.

with Thomas a majority of the time when they were both on the U.S. Court of Appeals. Scalia is extreme rightwing Pat Buchanan school of Catholic, so you can bet you're probably going to see school prayer and a lot of other stuff rammed back down people's throats by law within a few years.

So this unholy alliance means that rather than working *separately* to try to censor things like films and books, they're working together now. Cardinal Mahony in L.A. came out with a demand that movie studios revert back to the early versions of the Hays Office code from 1934, including a ban on "lustful kissing."

♦ V: *What about this Washington state law?*

♦ B: Luckily a court threw it out; at least for this time. The irony is: this happened when Seattle was being hailed as the new rock'n'roll capitol of America, with tons of popular new bands including Nirvana who the governor praised for all the dollar bills they'd brought to the state of Washington. But under this law he signed, their records were classified obscene in their home state!

The religious right is also out to crush the environmental movement. Everyone from Pat Robertson to Jesse Helms to Sun Myung Moon's Unification Church as well as James Watt are behind a new, orchestrated, fake "grassroots uprising" in the Northwest called the "Wise Use" movement. *Their* idea of wise use is: clear-cutting forests, strip-mining, oil drilling everywhere, and making national parks available for dirt bikes, jeeps, motor boats and even theme parks! They smear environmentalists as "devil worshipping pagans more interested in trees than people." After all, we should strip the planet of what's left as fast as possible because Jesus will replenish it all when he returns. Creeps like Watt actually believe this! So if you're on god's side, you're supposed to support this "wise use" move-

ment and cut off all dialogue with your neighbors on the other side, thus erasing the middle ground and fanning hostilities in dying Northwestern logging towns.

Another example of media manipulation is Operation Desert Scam: not just whipping draft-age people into a frenzy and getting older people to forget Vietnam and support it with yellow-ribbonism—they even hit the little kids this time with Operation Desert Storm bubble-gum cards! Here's one of a Tomahawk missile painted bright penile red—it looks just like a flying vibrator! What kind of mutant children are we going to get when *they* reach draft age, growing up on "sports heroes" like Norman Schwarzkopf? There's even a high-fashion sunset shot of carpet bombing, complete with a "batting average" on the back telling little kids how it works and what *fun* it is.

The urgent question isn't, "Who killed JFK?" but "Where are they now?" The answer, of course, is: they're running things! All those militant kids in suits and ties who attended the *Young Americans for Freedom* conventions in the '60s and worshipped Richard Nixon and Barry Goldwater are now in charge and getting revenge on any sort of consciousness that came out of the '60s . . . by the way, does anyone have any Y.A.F. sing-along records? They had a whole set of anthems, with lyrics like "Back to back, belly to belly/ Burn their bodies with Napalm Jelly/Put the goo on every left-winger, Joan Baez was a real torch singer." I

I was inspired by the music critic of the *Denver Post*—he was so square! When he trashed somebody like Black Sabbath, he'd go out of his way to compare them to other bands he loathed, thus giving me that many more names to look for.

have a rightwing folk-song LP of *The GOLDWATERS Sing Folk Songs To Bug The Liberals.* Four geeky guys with the chemical symbol for gold knitted into their preppy sweaters, sing about how great Barry Goldwater's going to be, and how evil the commies, Castro, and welfare cheats are. On this alleged "live" album, the same canned laughter track intrudes at inopportune times. The humor is back-stabbing; you can easily find the seeds of Republican dirty-tricks campaigning in this frat-boy recording from '64.

♦ V: *How did you start collecting records like that?*

♦ B: By mistake! From early on I developed a sense of humor about records and music that weren't necessarily "cool." In some cases I would remember a record because I thought it was the worst thing I'd heard in my life—but that would keep me going back to it and eventually I'd decide that I liked it—this was when I was in junior high school and listening to *Black Sabbath.* Examples of records that I first laughed at but later liked a lot include HANK WILLIAMS and the RAMONES.

The Ramones—instead of long guitar solos and operatic heavy metal singing, there were these one-and-a-half minute songs with lyrics like "Beat on the brat with a baseball bat—oh yeah!" Me and my friends would sit and laugh at the Ramones for hours. Then I saw them live and my whole life changed. They were so powerful, yet so simple.

♦ *V: You probably thought, "Oh, I can do that—"*

♦ B: Of course! Some of us went to see the Ramones figuring, "This'll be a good yuck." They were opening for an L.A. record company band called Nite City which included Ray Manzarek and Nigel Harrison before he was in Blondie. Me and my friends went early and sat in the front row, and out came four guys in black leather jackets and torn jeans. Behind us were row upon row of the Denver-Boulder, Colorado country rock glitterati . . . women had flowers in their hair because that was what Joni Mitchell was wearing. The guys looked like Kenny Loggins, with muslin shirts and scattered "power ties." One chord from Johnny Ramone's guitar let us know it was going to be a helluva lot *louder* than we'd thought—I turned around and noticed the look of utter terror on the faces of almost everybody in the club and thought, "Yeah!" The Ramones were not only the most intense band I'd seen in my eighteen years, but part of their beauty was: they made it look so simple: "Yeah, I could do that, too. Why not? I think I *will.*" And the rest, as they say, is sordid history. Myself, Wax Trax Records, Angst, Ministry, The Nails—we all grew out of that show.

I come from Boulder, Colorado, which in some ways was a great place to grow up, but then turned into a miserable place. My earliest memories are of a sleepy college and mountaineering town—one of the main streets, Canyon Boulevard, was then called Water Street: four lanes of gravel with oil trucks you'd get stuck behind, and trains running down the middle. The babysitter used to take me horseback riding on what later became the first shopping mall in town, called Crossroads. Then the hippies discovered Colorado and came in droves. That was when they were considered very dangerous: "Don't go down on The Hill, Eric, you might run into some *hippies.*" Of course, that was where I went!

By the time I was coming of age in junior high and high school, where I could really start to immerse myself in this culture, the culture was gone. It wasn't the '60s anymore, it was the '70s, and people were just beginning to realize how stupid and boring it was to be eighteen in 1975. People weren't into rebellion any-more, the music was much more salable, respectable, and had been slowed down and watered down—they had figured out how to take the rebellion of everybody from Bob Dylan to Steppenwolf (yes, Steppenwolf scared people at one time) and water it down into Bad Company, Lynyrd Skynyrd, and worst of all, country rock and disco.

Country rock ruled in Boulder. That and jazz-fusion was pushed to the gills by media and record stores. Some L.A. country rock mafia had moved to Colorado and lived around Boulder, so you'd also have these pre-yuppie moneyed hippies swaggering into town: "Hi, I'm Rick Roberts (Firefall)—give me a free meal!" "Hey, I'm Steven Stills—get the fuck away from that pool table!" Things like that, which I hated—although one dude made the mistake of doing that to the real Rick Roberts! But one thing saved me: starting in the ninth grade, I got so fed up with radio that I began buying records just on the basis of which *covers* looked the most interesting. The first one I tried was *Tyranny and Mutation* by Blue Oyster Cult. Didn't quite dig it at first, but it turned into my favorite album for a year. About that time I discovered the used record stores, including Trade-A-Tape (R.I.P.) where you could listen before you buy. During my sophomore year in high school I went through every record that looked interesting in the *whole store,* and scoured the 25-cent bins and especially their free box—anything they didn't think they could sell, they'd throw into the free box. Being the curious type, I just took every free record every day for three years! Looking back, this was the advantage of living in a country rock town: STOOGES for a dime, MC5 for a quarter, 13th FLOOR ELEVATORS, NAZZ and Les Baxter for free . . .

Les Baxter's *Ritual of the Savage,* Capitol Records. Album cover credits: cover illustration: William George

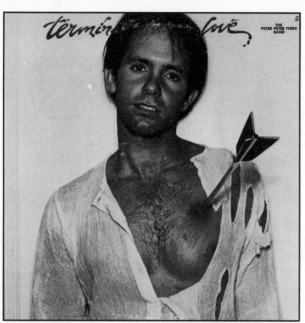

The Peter Peter Ivers Band's *Terminal Love,* © 1974 Warner Bros. Records Inc. Album cover credits: art direction and design: Lockart, photography: Steve Silverstein.

I was also inspired in a weird way by the music critic of the *Denver Post,* Jared Johnson (who now only writes a bridge column). He was so square! He claimed that Paul Simon and the BeeGees were the greatest composers of the twentieth century—we were not on the same wavelength. Yet he seemed to have obsessive and detailed knowledge of music he *didn't* like. He'd go on and on trashing Alice Cooper, saying, "He could write pretty ballads if he *wanted* to!" When he trashed somebody like Black Sabbath, he'd go out of his way to compare them to other bands he loathed, thus giving me that many more names to look for—that's how I found out about the MC5 and Kim Fowley. Usually he would do capsule reviews of 5-10 records every week in the Sunday Denver *Post.* Only rarely would he devote an entire column to one record. Just imagine my sense of accomplishment when he devoted an entire scathing column to Dead Kennedys' *Fresh Fruit for Rotting Vegetables!* Boy, did I feel proud that he seemed to hate my record more than Alice Cooper and Black Sabbath combined.

Two examples of "bad" records that later turned into "good" include SPARKS. At first their warbling falsetto vocals were unbearable—the worst I'd ever heard! Then I saw them on *In Concert,* an ABC TV show at the time (unlike stupid lip-synched MTV videos, they shot all the bands "live" in the raw in front of a real audience). Seeing that and Alice Cooper kindled my Walter Mitty desire to become a singer. Far from just unbearably schmaltzy warbling, SPARKS on TV did high-energy performances with Russell Mael as extrovert front-man and his brother Ron—a piano player with slicked-back hair, a Hitler moustache and a tie who looked utterly disgusted at the camera every

time it came his way. I've heard claims they were both little boy underwear models in Sears catalogs when they were kids. Later, they even brought four go-go dancers dressed in Nazi uniforms on Don Kirshner's *Rock Concert.* As far as I know that was their last television performance for some time!

The Sparks album I'd take to a desert island is *Indiscreet,* where they dropped a lot of the glitter rock guitar and replaced it with big band horns and orchestra arrangements in a deliciously obnoxious way, with probably the most intricately cruel lyrics Russell Mael ever wrote. He was a main influence on my lyrical style—he's very wordy but wields a very sharp blade when he wants to. He suited my verbose style better than, say, IGGY POP.

Another big influence was *Terminal Love* by the PETER IVERS Band. The album cover has the title written in dripping blood, above a guy with a horny look on his face and an arrow sticking out of his chest. Musically, Ivers had an even more obnoxious singing voice than Russell Mael of Sparks; so nasal it reaches inside you and tickles. At first I didn't realize that he must have put a lot of work into honing such a unique instrument. Being cursed with a nasal voice myself, I thought, "Aha! This may not be what I want, but if I develop this style it'll sure *penetrate.*" Ivers made his living as a session harmonica player but was also Harvard-educated and a great songwriter. Later he resurfaced as host of *New Wave Theater* (which Rhino has released on video). This was a cable TV program for underground and independent bands in the pre-MTV '80s. Ivers was the host who would end each show with a rapid-fire rap about what he felt was going on in the world. Even if you could only catch

Another album I'd take to a desert island is *Think Pink* by the Pink Fairies' drummer, Twink. It's spacey but piercing psychedelia—this record surrounds and attacks you with delicious musical acupuncture.

snippets it was very thought-provoking and subversive. He was *brilliant!* In early '83 he was found beaten to death in his apartment in L.A., and the killer was never caught—all the stranger, because even though he was a very gentle soul, he was a martial-arts expert. Some people feel it might have been a disgruntled lover, or the mob, or even the LAPD, because what he said on the show threatened a lot of people. New Wave Theater was just about to break big before he was killed—that ended the show.

The female equivalent of Peter Ivers would have to be GENEVIEVE WAITE's *Romance Is On The Rise* LP—she probably only got to make a record because she was hooked up with Hollywood's number one celebrity dope dealer, John Phillips of the Mamas & Papas fame. It's sly, almost '20s or '30s crooning music, but delivered in such a magnificently obnoxious way that it's a classic in its own right. Her voice is completely unique; I wonder where she is now.

Another album I'd take to a desert island is *Think Pink* by the Pink Fairies' drummer, TWINK. It's spacey but piercing psychedelia complete with a groaning woman on a track called "Fluid." Instead of a mantric trance to swim in, this record surrounds and attacks you with delicious musical acupuncture. There's great guitar by Paul Rudolph of the Pink Fairies, and this has been an all-time fave for fifteen years.

♦ **V: Who steered you into picking up more than rock music?**

♦ B: The SCREAM-ERS! They were my fa-

Photo: Robert Waldman

vorite of all the early West Coast punk bands. No guitar—just an Arp Odyssey synthesizer on milk crates, fuzzed electric piano, drums, and a trained mime for a singer who could startle a whole audience just by lifting an eyebrow. Their live shows were dynamite—not just the powerful visuals, but—their music took more twists and turns than anyone I knew then. It's the ultimate musical tragedy that they held out for the big major record deal that never came, and wound up not being properly recorded at all. Only a bootleg single and the Target video survive. No one has sound-ed anything like them since. If they'd cracked Europe, 15 years of synth-pop and techno-dance dreck might never have happened! So being in a band myself, I wondered, "How did they create this?" At a party, singer Tomata du Plenty recommended JOHN BAR-RY to me, and off I went in search of his James Bond soundtracks. That of course spun into more things, like *exotica* music.

My father had a fascination with ethnic music from all over the world. My favorite album when I was four was a Japanese album by the AZUMA KABUKI Musi-

The Azuma Kabuki Musicians, Columbia Masterworks, Columbia Records Inc. Album cover credits: cover art: Marion Zelenko.

cians on Columbia Masterworks. I've never heard any Japanese music which could top this one—it has more driving rhythms and all-around intensity than, say, Indian music. Some of the rhythms sound like another all-time favorite, HAWKWIND. I often wonder where psychedelia would have gone if people like George Harrison had gotten into Japanese kabuki music with its overtones of pain and violence, instead of Indian music which is more blissful. One of the few kabuki-influenced '60s albums was the first LP by MAD RIVER, with spiny, piercing guitars and vocals. If you listen to it back-to-back with Television's *Marquee Moon,* there's a lot of similarity.

In my sophomore year, my high school Spanish teacher played us some examples of music south of the border. She put on *Voice of the Xtabay* by YMA SUMAC, and I thought, "Wow, man, she sounds like Robert Plant!" I excitedly filed her name away, and a couple years later got my own copy from the free box at Trade-A-Tape. I saw her in *Secret of the Incas* (1954) which also featured Charlton Heston, and that was an incredibly racist movie—even by Charlton Heston standards. Years later I got to meet Yma Sumac in L.A. That album was produced by LES BAXTER, and after I got a copy of Baxter's *Sacred Idol,* I realized that his own music reminded me of the composer CARL ORFF (who did *Carmina Burana),* as well as the *Mekanik Destructiv Kommandoh* LP by the French band MAGMA, the most violent progressive-rock band *ever.* Unlike that classically-trained *Osmonds*-like Yes and Genesis dreck, this was totally extreme.

MAGMA was run by Christian Wander, who like Frank Zappa went through various members whom he worked very hard and fanatically. Supposedly he was a child prodigy on classical and jazz piano, but in Mag-

ma he mainly played drums. He wrote all the parts, and was a megalomaniac to the extent of inventing his own language for the lyrics, and a planet with an ongoing science-fiction plot to explain the existence of the language (detailed on the liner notes). His alphabet resembled Russian cyrillic, and Magma's logo was unforgettable—one of the most sinister symbols this side of the swastika. Even when they did jazz-rock, it was the total opposite of sedative-fusion: a brutal, intense roller-coaster ride through purgatory and below.

♦ *V: How have your record-collecting aesthetics expanded in the past few years?*
♦ B: The same way as always: *magic accidents!* Especially for someone who's trying to make their *own* music, roots are not enough—why not explore the *roots* of the roots? There are plenty of garage and surf-instrumental bands who never ask themselves: "What were the people who created the *original* music listening to?" The worst offenders are post-1980 punk, hardcore and metal bands who only listen to early "genre" bands—consequently, the songs are not as interesting. When I first came to San Francisco it was an unspoken edict: if you want attention don't hide behind formulas; every band must be *different.*

The Screamers were my favorite. No one has sounded anything like them since. If they'd cracked Europe, 15 years of synth-pop and techno-dance dreck might never have happened!

Thrift-store singles broadened me even more. I looked for '60s punk obscurities and got surf instrumentals by mistake. Then I looked for instrumentals and wound up with rockabilly and rhythm-and-blues. It just mushroomed from there, and my tastes continue to widen. Now, my record-collecting has gotten out of control; whenever I come home from a trip it's like *Citizen Kane* coming back from Europe: all these records follow me home! I struggle to keep life's chores at bay and carve out time to listen to them all.

♦ *V: How do you write your music?*
♦ B: I guess I'm a mutant form of singer-songwriter. Unlike most songwriters, I don't play any instruments. I've always been a real bumbler with my hands—making friends with a guitar is completely beyond me. I make up the melodies for my songs in my head and then I sing them to people. If I were writing *Dead Kennedys* songs, I would listen to anything *but* punk

Modern Sound Six, Riversong Records.

music, looking for that left-field idea that would make a song different from what everyone else was doing.

♦ **V: *Expanding the gene pool—***

♦ B: Yes, plus I was raised on classical music; my dad played Carl Orff a lot. Both method acting and a classical music influence from my parents gave me a sense of orchestration that a lot of my fellow bands at the time didn't have. I didn't like classical after I found out about rock'n'roll, but later that influence crept back in. LYDIA LUNCH once told me she had no musical influences, but I, on the other hand, have *thousands* of musical influences! Why else would there be tango horns in the middle of my punk song, "Terminal Preppie"? If I'd stuck to trying to compose music on a guitar, I doubt I would have come up with nearly as many unexpected quirks and diverse-sounding songs. Anyway, I was such a bad guitar player that Klaus Fluoride (in *Dead Kennedys*) finally said, "Oh, forget it, Biafra—just sing it to us and we'll figure it out." I thought, "Aha—I'm a free man!" Then my songs got more interesting. I keep expanding and discovering more and more sounds; I blunder into new things.

♦ **V: *Don't you discover a lot of interesting musical hybrids in your travels?***

♦ B: Sure, but not nearly enough. Besides television, the major villain responsible for eradicating unique cultural differences has been rock music. It used to be that if you found a punk rock or new wave album out of an Eastern Bloc country like Hungary or Yugoslavia or even East Germany, it wouldn't sound anything like a Western band. Even the early Finnish punk bands had melodies and rhythms derived from a uniquely Finnish pop/folk dancing music I heard on the radio there. (Then they heard *Discharge* and that all changed.) I crave native music and rhythms blended with really

wild rock'n'roll. Hybrids and blends are the most intriguing, especially when they're unintentional. In the next few years South African music is going to be dynamite: an audio culture-clash stew, as apartheid fades away.

♦ **V: *You were in Brazil around the time of the Earth Summit. What did you discover there?***

♦ B: A lot! In Sao Paulo there was a great used record store where I looked for records by early Brazilian psychedelic bands. Unfortunately, the "psych" records were mostly gone—the word had gotten out. But there were still earlier garage band recordings from the early-to-middle '60s. In Rio, I bought an original Gene Vincent album from somebody selling records on the street and thought, "Aha—there have to be more!" I started literally running from store to store, and found one bargain record store where, due to the economy, LPs were 30 cents apiece. I went haywire, especially because I could listen before I bought the record. I found a copy of ESQUIVEL's *O Piano, As Vozes E O Som De Esquivel*, which came out in Mexico under the title *Esquivel 1968*.

Many of today's most popular Brazilian artists sustain a strong sense of dissent. Lyrics are very important there; Brazil is a bit ahead of us in the sense that the mass media are so tightly controlled that it's up to the musicians to tell people what's really going on, and be political activist-minstrels. A lot of the artists on David Byrne's Brazilian compilations have this spirit, but he's just scratched the surface.

I'll just give brief descriptions of some Brazilian records. MODULO 1000 is a brilliant psychedelic space-rock band, but the rhythms and some melodies are unmistakably Brazilian. They were heavily persecuted by Brazil's military junta and their album and concerts

Trio Elétrico, Dodô E Osmar, Continental.

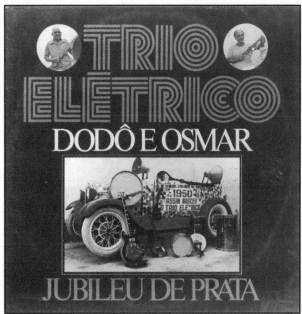

were all done in secret. Someone played me this record; it was too rare for me to find ... Zdoes Bahian folk music blended with psychedelic rock, and dub-mixed! One of the band members, J. Z. Ramalho, is a mainstream pop artist who turns up on David Byrne albums ... A totally unknown Brazilian '60s garage band is the MODERN SOUND SIX, who apparently were engineering students from a little town outside Rio trying as hard as they can to look degenerate; one of two guys slumped in a bathtub is wearing bad-ass wraparound shades, while another has plastic glasses shoved down his nose. Their version of "Born To Be Wild" features a wicked electric-razor fuzztone guitar. Guess they couldn't figure out the English lyrics—they just slur all the words! They also do this to Nielsen's "Everybody's Talking." In the middle are some straight Brazilian wedding songs—are they trying to be All Things To All People?

OS NOVOS BAIANOS, a commune sort of like Stephen Gaskin and the Farm in this country, produced hybrid Brazilian/rock music. They even had their own soccer team! They collaborated with TRIO ELETRICO people among others, and have produced dozens of albums. The most fiery and unique music I found in Brazil came from Trio Eletrico: rapid-fire picking by 3 or more people dueling on miniature electric guitars. Even the drums are inhumanly fast and tight. I guess I'd describe this as bluegrass-gone-Latin—at 78 rpm! There's a festival each year in a northern town in Bahia where Trio Eletrico combos come from all over and play to throngs in the town square on the backs of multi-colored trucks—all playing at the same time! Talk about vertigo ... Another spacey-acid Brazilian/folk record is by FLAVIOLA: *o bando do sol* ... LAMMA has huge dreadlocks and sings in the streets of Rio, selling his albums. In terms

Sergio Ricardo's *A Noite Do Espantalho*, Continental Records.

of completely over-the-top craziness he can be compared to the Legendary Stardust Cowboy, with very little rhythm or structure but a lot of ranting.

Psych-ploitation done Brazilian style is absolutely amazing—the best I've ever heard, such as on this movie soundtrack, *A Noite Do Espantalho* by SERGIO RICARDO. The front cover shows a Peter Max-ish screaming hippie; you flip it over and see people wearing spiked World War I German helmets riding motorcycles with giant insect wings attached to their backs! I found a record with an astrological chart on the front; all it says on the back is KRISHNANDA. It's on the Brazilian CBS label, and blows all those Sidewalk movie soundtracks away! It's like *Astro Sounds From Beyond The Year 2000* gone Brazilian ... I found a Brazilian Crown Records-style *Music From Barbarella* which blows the original version out the door; it really rocks ... This generic-cover *Meet The Gang* by FRANK & THE TOP TEN is another Davie Allen & The Arrows contender. It has titles like "Hippie Happening," "Beach Bunny," "Bad Girl," "Dirty Trick," and "Double-Face"—do they mean two-face? ... LEE JACKSON (oddly enough, this is the name of a group, not a person) put out a tribute to Elvis Presley: an entire album of his hits done *samba*-style!

When I was in Rio the safest part of the city seemed to be the slums up on the hill; the neighborhoods police themselves because if you cross your neighbor, you might not wake up in the morning. So people just go down into town and rob the rich people instead. Up in the hills I saw a samba concert attended by all ages. I'm told poor people in third world countries see rock music as a bourgeois, middle-class thing—they want something that means more to them. So rock music hasn't really caught on in third world slums—*until* death-metal. There's a huge death-metal scene in Bra-

101 Strings' *Astro-Sounds From Beyond The Year 2000*, Alshire Records.

zil, Columbia, and it's catching on in Cuba, Moldavia, Indonesia and Singapore—no form of rock music has penetrated third world countries like this. Why? Is it because it's so simple to make a great racket? The violent imagery? The pen-pal network is the tightest in the world. People into death-metal in Norway know what's happening in Malaysia. Some death-metal bands include Brujeria (which we released; all their graphics are cut out of *Alarma* and *Alerta*—pretty scary), Exit 13, Disrupt and Napalm Death; early ones include Venom and Slayer. A lot of the songs have armchair satanic, horror movie and splatter movie lyrics, and some songs are political, too.

Here are some miscellaneous Brazilian records I like. Out of thousands of Brazilian drum records, *Brazilian Beat* by CIPO & His Authentic Rhythm Group features great hammering sensual hypnotic percussion that would make Crash Worship proud. It's much more fully recorded than most *macumba* albums . . . JEAN-PIERRE & HIS ROCK PLAYERS' *J.P. Teaches You To Rock* is a '50s 10-inch that sounds like a big band attempting to be Bill Haley—a metronome audible through every song is what makes it unique . . . In the '50s or '60s, a popular genre was "Drink Music," and I found two examples by DJALMA FERREIRA on the Drink Discos label—the packaging features beautiful gatefold photos promoting alcohol consumption.

♦ **V: —look at that unusual electric bass. Have you ever sampled from your record collection?**

♦ B: I'm good at imitating other people's voices so I don't need a sample bank. I do things myself and nobody can sue me. Anyway, I'm more into the emotional side of music than the "let's tinker around with it for days on a computer" mentality. Why sample

somebody else's music, when I can make up my own? I'm not against sampling, especially when the sampled artist is reimbursed—I'm *grateful* Ice-T paid me for sampling a spoken word track from my *Freedom of Speech* album; it financed my *Tumor Circus* album. I make photo-collages for my covers—this is the visual equivalent of audio sampling—so I don't exactly have the moral high ground to object to sampling. I don't want to end up with the mentality of Polygram Records; they have a full-time employee whose job is to listen to every rap record, hoping to detect a James Brown sample so they can sue.

Psych-ploitation done Brazilian style is absolutely amazing. On *A Noite Do Espantalho* by Sergio Ricardo, the front cover shows a Peter Max-ish screaming hippie; you flip it over and see people wearing spiked World War I German helmets riding motorcycles with giant insect wings attached to their backs!

♦ **V: Now you have a huge record collection—**

♦ B: But I didn't intend it that way. I don't want to possess records for the sake of possessing records ("Ha ha, I have this and you don't") or because "they're worth money"; I don't have time for that. I'm a *scavenger* more than a collector. I go after a record because of a hunch that it might have something interesting on it. I used to go through frat-house dumpsters on the way home from grade school, and picking up old auto and machine parts to hook into Lego toys—as well as bottle caps and matchbooks—probably gave me the graphic design sense I now use in designing my album covers.

♦ **V: You had a major arrest and censorship problem when you included an H.R. Giger painting in an album. Has the censorship situation improved under President Clinton?**

♦ B: Well, it may not be as up-front and in-your-face, but both Tipper Gore and Hilary Clinton re-endorsed censoring records through labeling, in a recent interview in *Family Circle* magazine. Then Mr Bill himself told *TV Guide* that his favorite show is Donna Reed (!) and called for a movie-style rating system for music and records. Quayle or Pat Robertson could never have gotten away with that, but from an uptight yuppie liberal it's accepted. Now that Clinton is in, the attitude seems to be, "Okay, everything's fine. Just shut up

Lee Jackson's *Tribute to Elvis Presley,* Underground Records.

and shop." When Ice-T was booted off Warner Bros for "Cop Killer," close to a dozen rappers also got axed—not for saying "bitch" and "ho" or graphic gangsta gunplay songs, but for bad-mouthing the police. Warner Bros dropped GWAR over a song called "Baby Dick Fuck"—something they wouldn't have objected to pre-Clinton. So now, especially when you see Bush's feudalistic NAFTA and GATT treaties rammed through by an allegedly Democratic president, we have New World Order Lite! Which makes it easier for our multinational overlords to get away with more.

♦ ♦ ♦ EXOTICA ♦ ♦ ♦

♦ **V: Let's get back to music—what exotica music have you discovered?**

♦ B: With exotica music, a lot of people prefer Martin Denny. What I like about LES BAXTER is his overkill orchestration in the fine tradition of Carl Orff, Busby Berkeley and Magma. A quiet five-piece cocktail number by Denny will, in Baxter's hands, become a full orchestra with dozens of deep baritone voices singing *ooh* and *ahh* choruses to create the mood of the jungle. If Les Baxter decides to do a folk album, he won't use one person with a guitar—no, he'll use eight guitars and a banjo player *plus* his orchestra! Move over, Kingston Trio—here comes the whole King Family! He also did the great *Passions* 10" with Bas Sheva, a Jewish singer from Philadelphia with Yma overtones, who also recorded a great album of exoti-fied Hebrew folk songs, *Soul of a People.* The *Passions'* liner notes imply that this is Baxter's attempt at being viewed as a "serious" (as in classical) composer—and what a fractured symphony it is. *Vertigo*-style suspense violins; Bas simmers, growls and suddenly screams—all interspersed with familiar Christmas and children's song melodies . . . I know one person who never quite for-

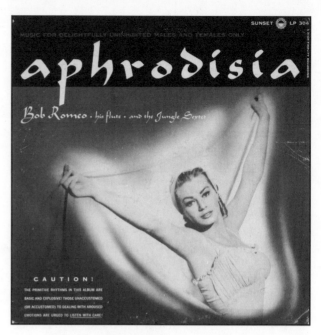

Bob Romeo & the Jungle Sextet's *Aphrodisia*, © 1957 Sunset Records. Album cover credits: cover girl: Anita Ekberg, photograph comes from *Hollywood Or Bust,* a Hal B. Wallis Production for Paramount in which Dean Martin and Jerry Lewis are starred.

gave me for forcing her to listen to the *Passions* during sex! Liner notes say Baxter traveled all over the world for inspiration (hell, maybe he never left Hollywood), and subsequently released dozens of albums including *African Jazz* (which has a *white* woman with "native-style" face paint on the cover). This is one of his better records, and it also has sax-and-flute-legend Plas Johnson on it. Back then, people didn't travel that much—they stayed home and let the world come to *them.* Although . . . even Les Baxter didn't record the exotic sounds of Cambodia or Vietnam; nobody did back then.

I didn't fully appreciate Les Baxter until I went home one Christmas, put on *Sacred Idol* and realized he was inspiring music in my head. So I'd play it, take the needle off, start singing and improvising into my tape recorder, and change parts into my own song. I didn't rip off any melodies or riffs directly, but made up my own harmonies or changed the beats and added fat, nasty guitars. Sometimes they'd fit perfectly with other music I already had in my head and *voila:* a song is born! So in that sense, Baxter has played a key unseen role in my music, particularly *Plastic Surgery Disasters.*

♦ **V: What are some other exotica favorites?**

♦ B: I'll just list a few. WEBLEY EDWARDS is another arranger with a Baxter angle, especially on *Fire Goddess.* Another arranger who tried to cash in on the Baxter-Denny exotica craze was FRANK HUNTER, who did *White Goddess.* I never found any other album by him to be even remotely interesting, but that one is amazing. The same goes for GENE RAINS' *Lotusland* on Decca—much more consistently "out there" than

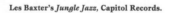
Les Baxter's *Jungle Jazz*, Capitol Records.

most Denny albums, and none of the Lawrence Welk-type filler that mars certain Baxter LPs. SHORTY ROGERS came up with "Wuaya-canjanga" on his *Afro-Cuban Influence* LP, a long track even more amazing than the *Voodoo Suite* he did with PEREZ PRADO—which, contrary to some opinions, *is* fantastic. And my favorite mambo album is *Mambo* by the great YMA SUMAC; even without her voice the backing tracks are much more infernal than any Perez Prado album I've heard.

When I realized Martin Denny was basically taking lounge and cocktail jazz and spicing it up with exotic percussion and bird calls, I decided to investigate further back into atom-age lounge music. When looking at records by people you've never heard of, the song titles furnish a clue as to whether the album might be "exotic." Even Lawrence Welk's accordionist, MYRON FLOREN, put out an album that included "Quiet Village," "Calcutta," "Miserlou" and "Taste of Honey." If "Caravan" is included, the record might be interesting—the THREE SUNS did an especially strange rendition of that, complete with jews-harp. Florida lounge organist JOE VENTO, accompanied by a primitive metronome-drum machine, recorded very Denny-esque versions of "The Godfather" and "Yellow Bird." And his '70s polyester-grotto sleeve art is hilarious.

In the "avant-garde meets exotica" genre, *ATTILIO MINEO conducts Man in Space with Sounds: for the*

Jungle Exotica, Strip Records.

Besides television, the major villain responsible for eradicating unique cultural differences has been rock music.

Seattle World's Fair is experimental classical music which the producer tried to package for a pop audience. Note the astro-cover on the front, contrasting with his sinister appearance in the back cover photo ("Even . . . *you* can commit mur-der . . ."). One avant-garde composer who seemed closer to exotica than to John Cage-style experiments was HARRY PARTCH, whom Iggy Pop credited as "the original inspiration for the Stooges." He was quite melodic, and he also made his own instruments with their own scales. An attempt to take Partch-type ideas further into the mainstream was the "concept" album *Speed the Parting Guest: Hi-Fi Bull in a China Shop* by JIMMY CARROLL. He uses "seven tympani, five cocktail shakers, four marimbas, four huge gongs, thirteen timbales, one toy drum, one wind machine, one celeste, four military snares, assorted tambourines, one buzzimba, one quadihead horn (courtesy U.S. Coast Guard) and nine musicians." This was put out by Cook Laboratories in Stamford, Connecticut—why, I don't know.

♦ *V: Can you talk more about the record labels themselves?*

♦ B: Okay. Some people worship the PHASE FOUR series on London—they have vivid gatefold covers—but I've never found much good music in them. MERCURY, whose house orchestra was directed by DAVID

The California Poppy Pickers, Alshire Production.

CARROLL, also had vivid gatefold covers. They put out a number of Middle Eastern belly-dance orchestral cash-in albums including *Percussion Orientale*—Carroll's version of "Caravan" is really good.

There were other low-budget labels who put out records that were sold at bargain prices in grocery store racks: besides CROWN, there's WYNCOTE, SUTTON, GUEST STAR, and SOMERSET. You take any category, be it cha cha, bagpipe, rock'n'roll or whatever, and they would have a whole series probably recorded in an hour and in the stores by that evening. Often they repackaged the same recordings over and over. Some tracks appear on fake exotica compilations, fake surf instrumental comps, hula records and psychedelic records—*those* have a few spooky reverb sounds dubbed in. Many pseudo-psychedelic records can be traced to Crown or Somerset, and at one point Crown packaged BB King and Jimmy Beasley as "twist" artists! Sometimes when somebody made it big, they would unearth some demo tape and release an album with two tracks on it by that artist and get somebody off the street to record eight more songs to fill out the record. You'd see "Johnny Rivers Sings!" in big letters and then notice "Plus So-and-So" who would sing eight or nine of the other songs. But they're still worth looking for, because in the case of Johnny Rivers, Trini Lopez, Otis Redding and many more, their most rocking tracks *ever* are the demos that were unearthed and reissued on Crown. If you want to hear Otis Redding during his Little Richard phase, that's where you'll hear it. The best FIREBALLS' instrumental tracks are on Crown, when the label was trying to cash in on the success of "Sugar Shack." CROWN was the worst offender: they'd take a '50s rock'n'roll instrumental and do a rock'n'roll house party record with it,

a surf record (some of their surf tracks are recycled hula recordings from their exotica cash-ins); some of their rock records will be two rock songs plus Lawrence Welk-style orchestral numbers; etc.

LIMELIGHT was a label devoted to "exotica spilling into avant-garde electronics." Some of it was stuff like *Moog Espana*, with synthesizers playing flamenco tunes, but *Song of the Second Moon* by Tom Dissevelt and Kid Baltan has enough of an ethereal '50s sci-fi mood to be called *avant-electronic-exotica*. There was even a top-notch San Francisco psychedelic rock band with avant-synth mixed in: 50-FOOT HOSE.

In a similar vein (although not on the Limelight label) is *Atlantis Revisited* by ELECTRONIC MUSIC RESEARCH, INC from Las Vegas, of all places! And from Mexico comes JORGE REYES's album (which he did with Antonio Zapeta), *A la Iziquierda del Calibre*. This is the most direct missing link I've heard between Les Baxter and Tangerine Dream! And the only *exotica-psychedelic-lounge* record I've found is by the KAPLAN Brothers: there are Spaghetti-Western riffs all over the place that even Morricone would envy.

♦ **V: In the late '50s-early '60s a lot of companies released "percussion" records—**

♦ B: —and percussion-*exploitation* records like "The Sound of Hawaii" by the Percussive Pineapples. Unfortunately, that contains nothing but schmaltzy versions of tunes like "Hawaiian War Chant," which is neither Hawaiian nor war-like *nor* percussive. Almost anytime you see "Hawaiian War Chant" on an album, that's a dead giveaway that you're dealing with the bottom of the barrel in ethno-exploitation ... The *Wild Stereo Drums* sampler has a jungle drum-exotica treatment of Sandy Nelson done by DICK HARRELL.

Almost anytime you see "Hawaiian War Chant" on an album, that's a dead giveaway that you're dealing with the bottom of the barrel in ethno-exploitation.

That led me to his album, *Drums and More Drums*—a great romp through *rockin'* exotica that *Swing For a Crime* album fans would love. *Jungle Drums* by the SHANGAANS contains my favorite version of "Taboo," but there *is* a problem, as the liner notes reveal: "The fusion of conventional Western world melodies and lyrics pulsating with African tribal rhythms as perfected by South Africa's top group"—guess what color they are?! The cover shows all these African drums in front of white guys—you can bet the South African government and audience wouldn't dare listen to what was actually being played by the people who made the instruments. "Taboo" has rock guitar in it, as does their song "Voodoo Drums"—voodoo is actually Haitian, but here it's applied to Africa as well.

Vanilla Ice is the Pat Boone of rap! Those same major labels never would have pushed so hard to package the "grunge" trend if they weren't so desperate to steer that huge white suburban twenty-something audience away from political black music.

Sorcery! by SABU and His Percussion Ensemble, on Columbia's Adventures in Sound series, shows a white woman with Oriental eye make-up. Dig these liner notes: "In the old jungles, strange ache-hungry birds watch from trees that wilt and hang. Small loinclothed men step through overgrown verdure . . . Here a mating call and a death rattle uttered by separate and independent beasts combine into a peculiar and haunting chime. The whine of a mateless mammal and the ticking of some hundred tiny pests occur haphazardly together to give an *orchestra of blood and friction*"— what a great name for a band! "This is the rhythmic magic of birth and rot . . . corpses and genes well-mixed in a great stew of fertility, reproduction and decay. Sabu has heard all this, and *much, much* more." But from listening to this record, it sounds like "Sabu" was just some bow-tie session musicians hired to cut a cash-in ethno-exotica record—and be quick about it!

Here's an aside: an example of racial segregation *today,* just like there was in early rock'n'roll (where Little Richard couldn't get a song on the pop charts unless Pat Boone covered it), is the massive push behind Vanilla Ice, and earlier, The Beastie Boys. It's a way of taking young white people's interest in hip-hop and transferring it to white "stars" who won't say the kind of *content* that Public Enemy and Ice-T speak. They haven't found their BeeGees yet, but give 'em time. They found their Pat Boone—Vanilla Ice is the Pat Boone of rap! Those same major labels never would have pushed so hard to package the "grunge" trend if they weren't so desperate to steer that huge white suburban twenty-something audience away from political black music.

One of my favorite guitar instrumentalists is ALVINO REY, the orchestra conductor for the King Family

in his earlier days, who could play about any stringed instrument you can name. He invented the blow-bag guitar made notorious by Peter Frampton and Joe Walsh, where you stick a tube in your mouth so your guitar has that twoinky hollow kazoo-like sound. On his *Greatest Hits* album (featuring re-recordings on *Dot),* his version of "Tiger Rag" must be heard to be believed, and there's half-hula, half-country steel guitar with lyrics that would drive Tipper Gore up the wall if re-interpreted into today's lingo.

I heard some great guitar instrumental music at a Chinese restaurant, but they wouldn't (or couldn't) tell me who it was by. Then I found an album by a Hong Kong band led by a guy who looks to be a bit of a hunchback, TEDDY ROBIN & the Playboys. All but one song is nasal Chinese chirpy Herman's Hermits-type Merseybeat, but in the middle is one of the most rip-roaring biker-flick guitar instrumentals I've ever heard, called "Teddy's Tune." He later made a great psych album. I've heard he's still alive.

♦ *V: There are some great cassette tapes as well as B-movie videos available from Indian, Vietnamese, Thai, Middle Eastern, Chinese, Hispanic and Filipino stores. You have to wade through a lot, though.*

♦ B: Exotica-influenced rock is alive and well. Exotica never died, it just keeps infecting new hosts. Besides Dick Dale's Middle-Eastern surf instrumentals, there's tons of jungle-sax and spy-movie/rock singles that never turn up on compilations. Too weird for surf purists, I guess. One example would be ERKIN KORAY from Turkey, who's been blending his native music with psychedelic rock for at least 25 years. He's way more rock and deliciously Mid-Eastern than someone like Dissidenten. He'll still throw in something like a SAM THE SHAM cover on an album. Hound

Terauchi Takeshi's *Blue Jeans Golden Album,* King Stereo.

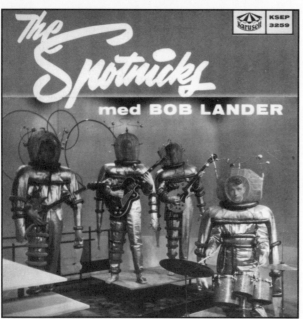

The Spotnicks, Karusell Records.

those Turkish import shops! At his best he reminds me of a male DANIELLE DAX. Dax is an English electronics genius and multi-instrumentalist who produces her own records and designs the covers. She used to be in the Lemon Kittens and is on United Dairies comps. She's becoming Top Forty but still retains a lot of what's cool about her. Her voice is 1920s slithery-sultry, like Marc Bolan's voice on the first two acoustic TYRANNOSAURUS REX albums. Other recommendations for Danielle Dax fans would be MAY EAST from Brazil, and an Israeli album by EHUD BANAI and the Refugees. There's even the *Turkish Delight* CD—a wall-of-guitar hybrid of Turkish music and Killing Joke or Big Black, done by an immigrant in Berlin.

An Egyptian guitarist named OMAR KARSHID produced belly-dancing albums which occasionally included cover versions of tunes like "Apache." After producing at least a dozen albums, he died during what the moneyed Egyptian elite indulge in: drag-racing to the pyramids! Another Lebanese musician, ELIAS RAHBANI, recorded some interesting records, and the DEVIL'S ANVIL produced some strange hard-rock from the Middle East. But the definitive blend of Rock/Middle-Eastern happened in the late '60s in Israel: a band called the CHURCHILLS. Their LP sounds like the first Pink Floyd album with SYD BARRETT, but played on Mid-Eastern instruments—it's *that* good and is one of my all-time favorites.

Some of the European space rock of the early '70s had a distinct *exotica* feel, aside from having some of the most mind-blowing covers ever designed: like BRAIN TICKET from Switzerland (reissued on CD) or GILA from Germany. Basically, this represents the missing link between electronic avant-garde and psychedelia. The legendary OHR and BRAIN labels

launched a lot of these records. This was a huge scene, and it led to bands like *Nurse with Wound* and *Legendary Pink Dots* later on. A lot of the originators are New Age mello-drones now.

◆ ◆ ◆ **JAPAN** ◆ ◆ ◆

Here I'll mention the kabuki-rock blend album I always hoped someone would do: *Benzaiten* by OSAMU KITAJIMA. If anybody knows of more Japanese recordings like this, by all means flood my mailbox immediately! In Japan, where to this day the VENTURES remain very big, you can buy entire albums of the Ventures covering Japanese pop tunes and traditional folk songs—albums that were only released over there. The Ventures inspired native bands to do a lot of great twangy guitar, rock, and instrumental versions of Japanese folk songs. I have an LP by TAKESHI TERAUCHI and the BLUE JEANS, and it's one of the best instrumental albums I've ever heard. Terauchi is seen as *key* in the development of this kind of music in Japan.

Japan seems to have the most extreme hardcore bands, the most extreme metal bands, the most extreme noise bands, the most extreme industrial bands, and the weirdest pop music. Sometimes the same people move between different categories. The BOREDOMS (released in the U.S. on Shimmydisc, but now they're on Warners—ick!) give a whiff of all that is extreme in the Japanese underground. Other favorites include GISM (hardcore and metal) led by Sakevi, who put out a full-color book totally devoted to death: interviews with a PLO terrorist, articles on diseases, the mandatory interview with Genesis P-Orridge, etc; and the ultra-brutal pounding noise to primal scream of ZENI GEVA (now on Alternative Tentacles). Some of these hardcore-noise bands not only distort the

The Iron Curtain is still great for finding records that break the mold, although I don't know how long that will last: "You play tuba? Join the band!"

guitar, but the bass as well. Finally a band called LSD thought, "Why not distort the *vocals,* too?" The pinnacle of sonic attack that hardcore and noise has reached, has come out of Japan. Now Seattle's gotten the Gism/Zeni Geva treatment in the form of the Cop Ass Grinderz—I love what some of these bands do to the English language! One band modestly called GOD put out an 8-inch (yes, 8-inch) record titled "Get Down Valis, I Want to Flapple and Train."

If you like Shonen Knife, brace yourself for PAPA-

YA PARANOIA: five women in geisha-girl garb with a few punk necklaces plus spiked heels who are classically trained; they sound somewhere between the B-52s and No Means No with a good dose of FETUS thrown in, and with vocals ranging from a chirp to a scream. In the '60s, some Japanese musicians recorded a hard-psych album in Hollywood under the name EAST (on Capitol); it has a lot of Japanese ethnic influences rarely found in psychedelic rock records.

When the drugs, the consciousness-expansion and the rebellion began being expressed by bands, the record companies were at a complete loss: they asked, "How do we keep the 'happy' side of flower power, but leave out the drugs and revolution?"

♦ ♦ ♦ IRON CURTAIN ♦ ♦ ♦

♦ V: *What are the strangest records you have from behind the Iron Curtain?*

♦ B: The Iron Curtain is still great for finding records that break the mold, although I don't know how long that will last: "You play tuba? Join the band!" Soviet New Wave is really mutant. One band even tried to be the Stray Cats, complete with Confederate flags, and their music is so crude that today's deliberately lo-fi "trashabilly" crowd couldn't sound like this if they tried! Rock is most interesting in these places right before Western non-culture avalanches in. Not only do native folk melodies creep into punk and psych, but sometimes the way they interpret precious tidbits of Western sounds is really bizarre, especially if the government's involved. Lately I've been fascinated by Soviet New Wave—not Russian, *Soviet*. For a USSR band to record (or even exist) they had to be government-approved and certified "professional." You were either "professional" or you couldn't play. To keep youth at bay they had to let Western rock'n'roll in—but only *so far* (Blondie, Talking Heads). Needless to say, these "New Wave" government musicians never quite got it right.

A Soviet band called ARERA has produced totally weird, mutant lounge music; I consider them "the band at the circus at the edge of the world." They even do a mariachi medley . . . One of my favorite guitar instrumental albums is *Romanian Pop Music II* (1965) which is very happy-go-lucky twanging guitar instrumentals, like a schmaltzified SPOTNICKS or middle-of-the-road VENTURES. But what makes it eerie is imagining Ceacescu in the background gloating, "This

is what you will like as 'pop music'—you will be happy and sedated, *or else.*" I *have* to get more Romanian music—that, and the uniquely Carpathian progressive-rock of PHOENIX, are the only ones I've found so far.

KOLA BELDY (singer, backed by WHITE ISLAND) produced a record which is unclassifiable; the vocals sound like Native American chants over the more trance-like material on the POP GROUP's first album, but with the percussion subtracted. Kola is a singing *Eskimo* crooner in full arctic garb! . . . I have a record by a Russian heavy metal band, CRUISE-1, and even though they look as ridiculous as any commercial American band, the "Volga Boatmen Song" influence is very prevalent in their sound—I'd call it "Cossack Metal." They're very promising indeed. I have a horrible fear that this is all going to be lost soon, as Western music floods in. Country by country, the other great dumbing-down of world culture is caused by (besides television) rock'n'roll—particularly hardcore and metal. From Hungary to Columbia to Malaysia to South Africa to Huntington Beach, you can find hardcore and thrash-metal bands that sound *exactly* alike.

Once we got a letter from Hungary asking for records, so I sent them a record with a note, "Send a Hungarian record back." What did I get but *Hovalett* by NAGY FERO, backed by the band BIKINI. Apparently Nagy Fero was the leader and singer of a Hungarian Sex Pistols-equivalent called BEATRICE. Beatrice was banned from recording, but the government grudgingly agreed to let Fero make an album with session musicians, and what he came up with is possibly the most unclassifiable punk album ever made. Everything from CRASS and Ritchie Blackmore to Chinese pop music, violin solos, industrial synthesizer

Kola Beldy

and ska can be found on one record—sometimes in the same song!

Even dwarfing him, in some ways, is VAGTAZO HALOTTKEMEK (VHK for short) which translates as "The Galloping Coroners." They've been together for about fifteen years (meaning, pre-punk) and have a history of some serious government persecution, simi-

The kings of mutant rock packaging come from the French-Canadian scene of the mid-'60s. Every member of Les Classels had their hair dyed not just blonde but silvery-white, with white suits to match—an entire group of Men From Glad!

lar to that of the Plastic People of the Universe in Czechoslovakia, and Brazil's Modulo 1000 (mentioned earlier). They were banned from performing for eleven years. Their main acknowledged influences are Hawkwind, Yma Sumac, and Amon Duul I (the cacophonous predecessor to Amon Duul II), and the visuals at their live shows in Budapest are like BUTT-HOLE SURFERS with GWAR-size props, dancers, and a tympani player. At one of these extravaganzas they even had people on cables high above, dropping meat on the audience! Their singer, Attila Grandpierre, is an astrophysics professor by day. He's fascinated by Native American shamanism, which he studies to find ways to better hypnotize and affect the minds of the audience! Their ambition is to play on an American Indian reservation. A nuclear physicist plays bass, and they are literally a band of mad scientists. They really do have a hypnotic effect, and reportedly have put people in trances . . .

◆ PSEUDO-PSYCHEDELIC & PSYCHEDELIC ◆

Now it's time to move to pseudo-psychedelic, like the Lemon Pipers and the Grass Roots. When the drugs, the consciousness-expansion and the rebellion began being expressed by bands, the record companies were at a complete loss: "Do we dare touch these people or not? What do we try to sell in their place?" Since there was so much going on in fashion (meaning: a baby-boomer crop to buy lots of clothes) they asked, "How do we keep the 'happy' side of flower power, but leave out the drugs and revolution?" Before long, old Hollywood jingle writers and retreads had Beatle wigs and checkered bellbottoms. Everyone from the Mamas and Papas to the King Family had flower-psych album graphics! HOMER & JETHRO released *There's Nothing Like an Old Hippie,* with songs like "Hillbilly Hippie," "I Crept into the Crypt and Cried,"

and "World's Oldest Teenager." And let's not forget *The Crewcuts Go Longhair.*

In a similar way in the past, the record industry had gotten singers like Tennessee Ernie Ford to do rhythm 'n' blues songs but strip away the sexual innuendo, so that songs like "Catfish Boogie" or "Blackberry Boogie" really *would* be about fishing or picking blackberries! Capitol released *The Happening: Adventures in the Strange New Mind-Manifesting Music* by FIRE & ICE, LTD. Basically, through two sides of a major label album some people try to do a beatnik vocal jam and fall flat on their faces. This is the sort of thing I would have expected from Crown, not Capitol.

More than Crown, the kings of pseudo-psychedelia have to be the ALSHIRE & SOMERSET labels, who churned out loungey-schmaltzy versions of "Hair-Aquarius," "Yellow Submarine" and "Back in the USSR" suitable to play for mom. The cover of this LP by John Bunyan's Progressive Pilgrims shows 1965 miniskirt go-go girls (but in 1970!) with the caption, "The sound that sent the pilgrims on a trip!" Somerset/101 Strings did *Astro Sounds from Beyond the Year 2000* which was a serious psych-out album with moog and guitar. The 101 Strings even put out pornographic novelty singles, as well as an endless line of albums like *The Young Sound '68: Out of Sight Hits for the Now People* (like "San Jose" and "MacArthur Park"!); *Crystal Blue Persuasion and Other Sounds of Today* by the ORANGE GROOVE; *Sock It To Me* by the NOW GENERATION; *Blockbusters* by the Young Sounds of Today; *Organ Freakout* by The MUSTANG . . . and all the covers are from the same photo session. In particular, ANIMATED EGG has a strong track or two. *Call*

The 18th Century Concepts' *Off On A 20th Century Cycle,* Sidewalk Records. Album cover credits: cover photo: Capitol Photo Studio, Dick Brown.

Les Classels' *Spectacle*, Production Franco-Disque Inc.

It Soul by HAIRCUTS & The IMPOSSIBLES has some strong tracks, too. But after awhile I noticed that the strong tracks sounded familiar, and discovered that the label had recycled (retitled and repackaged) the same instrumental tracks over and over! Some are "Astro Sounds" tracks minus the 101 Strings.

Even the COMMAND label got into the pseudo-psych act with The HELLERS: *singers, talkers, players, swingers, and doers.* The members are listed as Hugh Heller, Marie Antoinette, Adolf Hitler, Edsel Ford, George Custer, Bonnie Parker, and Benedict Arnold! Another psychedelic exploitation label was DESIGN; they released *Out of Sight* which had some early LOU REED recordings under the name The BEECHNUTS. They put out the Love Machine's *Electronic Music to Blow Your Mind By,* which is neither electronic nor mind-blowing: it's a surf instrumental album with a few spook effects dubbed in a reverb chamber. *Sitar & Strings* by the Nirvana Sitar and String Group on MISTER G Records is pretty good, as well as this record by the Cajun in-house back-up band for Gold-band Records—they jumped onto the pseudo-psych bandwagon under the name SATAN & THE DECI-PLES. Musically, this is one of the stronger albums in this genre, with great kitschy occult lyrics. AUDIO FIDELITY even jumped onto the bandwagon with *How to Blow Your Mind and Have a Freakout Party* by The UNFOLDING (which is musically on a par with Crown's *Light My Fire* by The Electric Firebirds)—that has some decent fuzz-psych originals on it. And CHARLES RANDOLPH GREAN, who recorded the *Dark Shadows* music, jumped on the pseudo-psych bandwagon with *What's Happening?* by The MIND EXPANDERS. Again, it alternates between schmaltz and occasional decent psych-exotica flashes.

Even biker-flick soundtrack legend MIKE CURB got into the pseudo-psych act with his albums by the 18th-Century Concepts—all these older people in pow-dered white wigs and 18th century royal court garb on motorbikes (!) doing baroque-classical versions of "Eleanor Rigby," "Light My Fire," "Penny Lane," "I Was Kaiser Bill's Batman" (?!) and more. He claimed to have been vacationing in Bavaria where he encoun-tered a group of school teachers playing this music for their own enjoyment—a likely story.

Mike Curb could legitimately be labeled the King of Psych-ploitation (as opposed to pseudo-psychedelia), along with cohorts like Kim Fowley and Ritchie Pod-olor. Psych-ploitation is several steps higher than pseu-do-psych. It was Curb who took the Ventures' twang and surf instrumental sound one step further into fuzzy psychedelic instrumentals used as soundtracks for biker flicks and drug-exploitation films, mostly performed by all-time greats DAVIE ALLAN & The ARROWS. I think some of the Arrows were on the CHOCOLATE WATCHBAND album; Watchband pro-ducer Ed Cobb forbade them to play their own mu-sic—as well as instruments—and instead had session people play—one more reason not to sign with a major label . . .

♦ **V: Tell us about Mike Curb's political career—**
♦ B: On *Teenage Rebellion*, Mike Curb had these hilar-ious moralistic narratives a la Jack Webb putting down prostitution and the gay teenager. After his psych-ploitation days and before he ran for governor, he was appointed the young whiz kid head of MGM Records and Verve. Bragging that it was done to please Richard Nixon and get into Republican politics, he purged MGM of Frank Zappa, the Velvet Underground and the Seeds, among others, and instead concentrated on

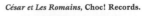

César et Les Romains, Choc! Records.

the Osmonds—this is the mentality Mike Curb is under today. He then got elected lieutenant-governor twice by waging very dirty smear campaigns. But when he ran for governor the tables finally got turned against him when at a press conference, one of his opponents trotted out a lifesize blowup of the label to the *Mondo Hollywood* psych-ploitation soundtrack, and pointed with a pointer to Mike Curb's writing credits as creator of the soundtrack of this allegedly pornographic film—after Curb had denied having anything to do with that whole scene—specifically, those records!

Quebec produced some of the most twisted '60s recordings, all in *French* and very regional. The Quebecans feel like a people without a country, because when they go to visit the motherland in France they don't fit in there either. In the '60s after the Beatles and psychedelia came in, they created their own especially weird pseudo-psych, including the album by LES MALEDICTUS SOUND. In between the schmaltz are numbers like "Monster Cocktail"—some of the most screaming exotica-psych I've ever heard in my life. They followed that up with *L'Experience Nine,* described as "Freakout Total" on the back (which didn't even bother listing the song tracks) and *Reels Psychedeliques, Vol. 1 & 2,* which are—believe it or not—psychedelic square dance albums!

The kings of mutant rock packaging come from the French-Canadian scene of the mid-'60s. Every member of LES CLASSELS had their hair dyed not just blonde but silvery-white, with white suits to match—an entire group of Men From Glad! Later they straightened out and tried to get a little more Sgt. Pepper-ish in a leisure-suit way, but by then it was too late . . . Another "unique" image was presented by CESAR & THE ROMANS, who dressed in togas and roman

Mutantes, Polydor Records.

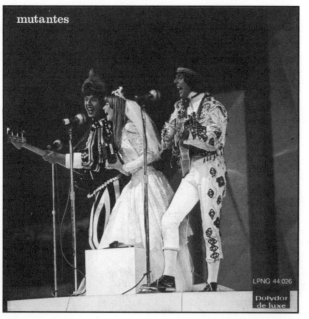

sandals onstage—I have a video of them performing on a TV show to prove it.

♦ **V: *What about American pseudo-psychedelia?***
♦ B: All over the country, lounge bands got into the psychedelic act. The SILHOUETTES, out of Pittsburgh, had been around since the '50s, but "didn't feel they were ready to record until recently." So on their

The record industry had gotten singers like Tennessee Ernie Ford to do rhythm 'n' blues songs but strip away the sexual innuendo, so that songs like "Catfish Boogie" or "Blackberry Boogie" really *would* be about fishing or picking blackberries!

first album you get straight cocktail lounge mixed with a couple of killer psychedelic space tracks titled "Funky First" and "Lunar Invasion." Another LP taken seriously by psychedelic collectors came out of Nashville: *In the Hands of Karma* by The ELECTRIC TOILET. Even major labels got into the act: *Mesmerizing Eye Plays Psychedelic* was a session-man job done by Hank Levine on the Smash label. Mercury's budget label, WING, came out with *Guitar Explosion* by The ELECTRIC UNDERGROUND, which was actually country session musicians like Jerry Kennedy trying to make a quick psych record to compete with Crown's bargain-bin market, and do it in a day or less. Some of the ballpark-organ-through-reverb-chamber and other effects have Les Baxter written all over them . . . The best of the SMASH records was *Come and Have Some Tea with the TEA COMPANY.* It has a great rap toward the end of side two: "They call us hippies, but we know better"—it's a hilarious period piece about society putting young people down, and the music is good, too.

Here, a few odd '60s records that deserve mention include The MONKS: American soldiers stationed in Germany with their heads shaved into monk haircuts. The opening track is about how much they hate being in the army. They even have an electric banjo player in the band, and it works—this is actually an incredible album which may be reissued on Matador. Another '60s group that's a link between the Limelight label and Walter Carlos-type electronics is THE SILVER APPLES, who made two albums, *Contact* and *Silver Apples,* on Kapp. They had a drummer and a guy who called himself "The Simian" who bought all these oscillators in a navy surplus store and built his own instrument. It's pulsating, driving trance electronics—I'd call them the mid-'60s version of *Suicide;* powerful and hypnotic. They merit some serious study; for starters, what happened to "The Simian"?

OS MUTANTES, from Brazil, put out an album I would describe as "Sgt. Pepper flower-psych as played by a demented cartoon orchestra." Intentionally or not, a lot of Spike Jones dynamics are at work here. Their singer was an American named RITTA LEE who to this day still makes records in Brazil. One of OS MUTANTES' leaders was quite distraught after breaking up with Ritta Lee, and he made a totally cracked psychedelic-folk album called *Singing Alone.* It's has the same "trying to crawl out of a great abyss" vibe as *Oar* by SKIP SPENCE, who was the drummer for Jefferson Airplane and Moby Grape before he allegedly attacked a band member with a hatchet while stoned. Spence made his LP as part of therapy to get himself released from a mental hospital, and Columbia actually put it out! (It's been re-released on CD under the name Alexander Spence.) The songs are sparse and very beautiful, in a way, but obviously they're the product of somebody who's been through a *lot.*

A psych-ploitation album that stands up to the best of Davie Allan & the Arrows is *Distortions* by BLUE PHANTOM—it combines elements of the Arrows and James Bond soundtracks, depending on the cut. It was probably a quickie job—but what a great one! The cover painting shows the artist's theory about the evolution of life: a ray of light is destroying the earth, while giving birth to a baby! "All through the seeing-eye, from life before birth through conception, evolution, construction, resurrection and destruction—in all, a total experience." As the years went by, psychedelia got more and more crazed, but because there was little distribution, many of these records never got past the band's local audience. Some of the singles have been released on compilation albums.

Dora Hall was the heiress to the Solo paper cup fortune and spent her money trying to make herself a serious singing star. She is somebody who cannot sing to save her life. You can still get Dora Hall's albums and even *videos* if you save enough Solo cup proof-of-purchase coupons!

The CRO-MAGNON album that came out on the ESP label has some of the most grating, growling sounds of the '60s. They did a couple songs which, if they came out on the Amphetamine Reptile label today, people would think they were by a Midwestern noise band. And one of the most all-time crazed psycho-rock

recordings is the "Good Times" single by NOBODY'S CHILDREN. It had the most negative lyrics around until G.G. ALLIN hit the scene: "Well, I watch TV til it goes on the blink/Spend all night listenin' to water drippin' in the sink/Rusty old stove leakin' gas everywhere/Strike a match, it blasts my face an' burns off my hair/Good times?!? *Ha ha ha ha!"* For a '60s band to be completely disgusted with everything (as this band is) is very rare indeed ... The BUGS, from Boston, did a single about Albert DeSalvo (the Boston strangler) and the B-side featured a New York DJ impersonating Albert, singing a country ballad about being a "Strangler in the Night." They had a bass player in her '40s who is now in her '70s and still playing bass. The BUGS actually did a reunion awhile ago, complete with their bumble-bee striped suits.

♦ ♦ ♦ JOE MEEK ♦ ♦ ♦

Finally, a recent '60s favorite is JOE MEEK, the first successful, fully independent record producer in the U.K. He was barely known in this country, but was an unseen hand in ruling and shaping pop music pre-Beatles in England on a scale the size of Phil Spector—except that his taste was weirder. As a producer, not only did he not play any instruments, but apparently he couldn't sing very well either ... yet he was very exacting in getting the sounds he wanted out of musicians. He not only sang the notes to a keyboard person, but was very specific as to *how* he wanted the keyboard to sound. He was fascinated with Outer Space, and one of his songs which is best-known in the U.S. was the TORNADOS' "Telstar" instrumental; it has an organ sound like no other. And as soon as he found a skiffle band with Hawaiian guitar, there was no stopping him. Remember, "Exotica" was an America-only phenomenon. The only English Martin Denny release I've seen had a generic ocean photo, probably xeroxed off a Mantovani album. Yet here was someone pursuing the same outer reaches, but from a completely different angle!

His fascination with sci-fi and ethereal sounds and other-worldly female voices and Outer Space is so unique—you can tell a Joe Meek record a mile away. He recorded the instruments way into the red so that even drums distorted; he used all kinds of wild echo and reverb. I read that not only did he use everything but the kitchen sink—he even recorded *in* the kitchen sink the sound of running water, blowing bubbles, drinking straws, and half-filled milk bottles played by spoons! He also used the teeth of a comb across an ashtray, electrical circuits shorted together, etc. He had problems getting along with mainstream music industry powers, but eventually got his own studio together above a leather store. It was on three floors, so some instrumentalists would literally be playing on different floors, with the console on the third floor.

Joe Meek also recorded a full-on electronic exotica album called *I Hear a New World,* credited to THE BLUE MEN, and he also recorded SCREAMING LORD

Mrs Miller's *Greatest Hits*, Capitol Records.

SUTCH (whose autobiography *Life As Sutch* was published in 1991). The British equivalent of early Alice Cooper, Sutch ran for parliament as a candidate for the National Teenage Party in 1963, and has done numerous pranks, outrageous live shows and records—well worth reading about.

There's a book out, *The Legendary Joe Meek,* by John Repsch. Meek was obsessed with Buddy Holly—to the point of trying to communicate with him on a ouija board, asking for guidance when he recorded. Apparently he got caught in a mini-version of the Michael Jackson scandal; in those days it was scandalous to be gay. He became very paranoid, and near the end of his life was even questioned about the dismemberment murder of a boy he apparently knew, which led him to believe the cops were out to frame him. In '66 he shot his landlady to death and then turned the gun on himself—on Buddy Holly's birthday. There was a BBC documentary on him, and now a number of his CDs have been re-released. A favorite is "Have I The Right?" by The HONEYCOMBS, which sounds like no other record. A later record by The BUZZ is absolutely stunning for its sinister atmosphere.

♦ ♦ ♦ **DO-IT-YOURSELF** ♦ ♦ ♦

♦ *V: Tell us about some eccentric, one-of-a-kind recording artists—*

♦ B: One of the most notorious examples of what can happen when *anybody* is allowed to make a record is MRS MILLER. She was an old woman with a warbly, operatically-trained voice who had a nasty habit of veering out of time and off-key. Somebody recorded her singing Petula Clark's "Downtown" and it was a huge hit! Then Capitol released an album with her own unique versions of "Those Boots Are Made for Walkin'," "Hard Day's Night" and "Chim Chim Cheree"

from *Mary Poppins,* among others. For a few months she was all over TV, and then she disappeared.

Another example is the Pia Zadora of the '60s, DORA HALL. Much older than Pia, she was the heiress to the Solo paper cup fortune and spent her money trying to make herself a serious singing star. On one of her albums she covers "Hang On Sloopy," "Satisfaction" and "Boots," and once again she is somebody who cannot sing to save her life. She made her own TV special, too, with quality guests like FRANK SINATRA, JR and Oliver, and for whatever reason, you can still get Dora Hall's albums and even *videos* if you save enough Solo cup proof-of-purchase coupons!

LADY JUNE's *Linguistic Leprosy* featured a British poet with a deep, gravelly voice who looked a little like a hippied-out Phyllis Diller on the back cover; the front cover features a mind-blowing collage of her own creation. She reads twisted surreal poetry against a sparse, almost exotic backing—possibly the first record Brian Eno ever played on. I've never heard anything remotely like it, except possibly the MOPSIE BEANS album from Australia.

From the late '60s til the late '70s when punk happened, there was not much of an independent music distribution network. Nevertheless there was a slew of independent records produced. Many of the best ones, by people whose minds are not of this earth, are either priced so high it's downright evil, or they turn up in thrift-stores. If their reputation grows, they even get reissued, like this classic first album by D.R. HOOKER. The cover shows a blissful blonde guy with a beard dressed in a robe, standing with his guitar on a hill overlooking a city. It was actually *20 degrees* outside when the photo was taken, and musically the record is a psychedelic-rock masterpiece. For every

Lady June's *Linguistic Leprosy*, Caroline Records.
Album cover credits: cover art: Lady June, photograph: Trevor Key.

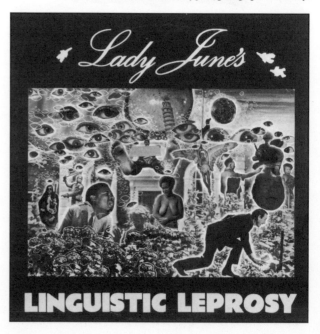

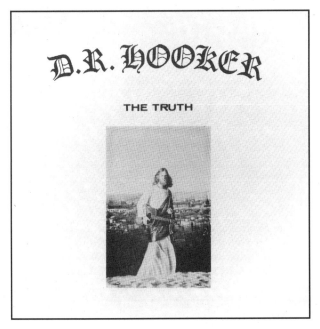

D.R. Hooker's *The Truth*, Here Music Pub. ASCAP.
Album cover credits: cover photo: Jon Fischbach.

Skip Spence who got released on a major label, there's at least 3 or 4 dozen like him who made albums in their home town that nobody ever bought.

My current favorite has to be this double album by The CORILLIONS. It's basically the vision of one man, Marlin Wallace. He's from Springfield, Missouri, and was very exacting as to how he wanted the singers to sing the songs—which may explain why the phrasing is consistently off-time. But the real attraction here is the liner notes. In the fine tradition of Dr Bronner's soap they *cover* the back of the record: "My mother was against communism, but she was badly deceived by *concealed* communists around her. When she died of heart trouble, I attributed her death to the Red conspiracy. For two years while I had stayed at her house, the Reds had tortured me with invisible radiation attacks. There was nothing to prevent the Reds from using lasers and microwaves on my mother ... The Reds began using lasers on me as far back as 1961 ... My sex organs, rectum, head and liver have been consistently hit with different kinds of lasers. The pain from these attacks can be almost unbearable ... The Reds have been stealing my music and ideas for years. It began over twenty years ago when I first started writing songs ... The Reds are not only stealing ideas from my conscious mind, but they are also pilfering information from my *subconscious* mind when I am asleep." Now, what does he sing about on his record? "Abominable Snow Creature" (here, at least he's not sexist), "Little Green Men," "Head Hunters," and also a Martian song. There is one song about the Russian Bear, but the rest is straight country music. I feel sorry for Mr Wallace—obviously he's in such pain and torture from all these communists.

A record that's both touching and eerie is a 45 I found in a Stockton thrift store: "David's Song" by TARIANNE & ELIZABETH GOTELLI. It was put out to raise money for the "David Smith Fund" in Stockton. David Smith was a football player who was paralyzed during a high school football game. That's one of the things they don't publicize about school sports: over a dozen kids each year get paralyzed for life playing high school football—and that doesn't include gymnastics and wrestling which take several more. So in this case, the song is about how "you'll always be scoring touchdowns in our lives—keep up the spirit!" etc. It's very "hickoid" in an eerie way. [reads] "Dave, a high school football player, was paralyzed from the *neck* down" (christ, I hope they sued the fuckin' coach) "in a football game October 21st, 1977. Many people joined together, all for one, in a spirit of compassion and generosity to support David spiritually and financially." I knew people who remembered the incident and they just shrugged their shoulders and said, "Oh yeah, everybody visited him for awhile, but a year later they'd forgotten all about him." But the record lives on—the front cover shows a patch with his number on it. Now insurance rates are so high, there's *finally* talk of dropping high school football and replacing it with soccer. Takes a lot less equipment in the age of shrinking school budgets. I'm hopeful ...

In the "Anybody Can Make a Record" category, the number one front-center is ROBBIE the Singing Werewolf, a folksinger from Santa Monica who in the early '60s recorded *Live at the Waleback*. The graphics re-

Tarianne & Elizabeth Gotelli's *David's Song*.

DAVID'S SONG

PRIDE OF TOKAY

34

DAVID SMITH

ALL FOR ONE

semble modern compilations like *Sin Alley*. I'm amazed the CRAMPS never covered any of these—particularly songs like "Vampire Man" (which is a parody of a folk song of the day, "Greenback Dollar": "I don't give a damn if the victims holler/drain 'em fast as I can") and "The Streets of Transylvania" (a parody of "Streets of Laredo": "You can see by my coffin that I am a vampire/And if you had pneumonia you'd be coughin' too!")—that's a great one. Then there's "Tiptoe through the Wolfbane," "Rockin' Werewolf," "Frankie Stein" and the *tour de force,* the ending number where the sound gets crazier and crazier with more and more reverb on guitar and voice, to the point where it really *does* sound like a CRAMPS song—Robbie's just banging on two guitar chords singing, "I am Count Dracula" while letting out this Bela Lugosi laugh ("heh-heh-heh") over and over. Whatever happened to him? He was a great guitar player and obviously a monster talent (no pun intended).

Dora Hall isn't the only person whose wealth could allow her to indulge her musical fantasies. In the late '70s, SMITHFIELD FREEMAN put out an album showing himself with red ink on his hands, and maidens crawling out of gravestones toward him. The back cover shows him in front of his mansion with a Rolls-Royce and three dogs, and a '70s gangster moll-looking woman beside him . . .

Parents with money must have indulged their teenage-son when they produced the JEFF GRAY album, which is just vocals and Jeff playing a drum, sitting on the shores of the Great Salt Lake. On the cover, his face is obscured by cymbals as he plays the snare drum with a fly-swatter! The liner notes say: "Jeff, the man and his music, is where genius begins. Like that wise saying: 'Beat your wife, black her eyes, kick her in the

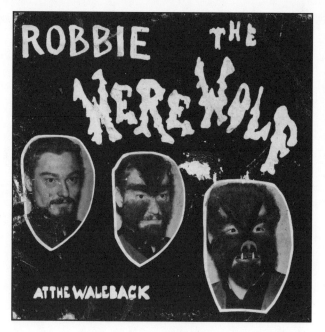

Robbie Robison's *Robbie The Werewolf.*

shins, break her arm, and you'll end up having to get your own dinner,' now climb on board our musical chain-letter and whisk yourself beyond the bounds of reason." With records like this, it's not how close they come to "greatness," it's how they fuck things up that opens new doors of dementia.

I'm sure LUCIA PAMELA thought she was making perfect sense on *Into Outer Space* . . . The liner notes claim she has hobnobbed with celebrities throughout her life and visited the moon several times. She plays a movie theater organ souped up with horns and pipes, and sings original tunes. I know someone who actually found her at a bingo parlor in Fresno, and she still insisted that her pink Cadillac travels to the moon. She said, "There's lots of Asian people there—I don't know why." A CD is available now.

The most deranged "rich person do-it-yourself" album is *All That I Am* by KIT REAM, heir to the Nabisco cookie fortune. According to someone who knew him, he dropped tons of acid in the '60s and wound up in a mental hospital where he spent six months staring at his own reflection in a mirror. Eventually the acid wore off, he was deemed "cured" and let loose in society, whereupon he decided to become a guru and make a record. From his maniacal expression you can see that this is a man who has seen it *all* and knows that he has "the answer" (note the psychotic paintings behind his head). The songs are light beatnik jazz mixed with pseudo-psychedelia; he chants lines like "Don't be so holy, poly, over my soul-y." [laughs] As far as I know his cult is still vastly outnumbered by Maharaj Ji, Rajneesh and the Moonies.

Another notorious D.I.Y. example is Dallas's own PALMER ROCKEY: *Rockey's Style.* Musically, some of his album resembles the stripped-down eerie folk-style of NICODEMUS. But mostly he's the disco lounge

Kit Ream's *All That I Am,* Creative Records.

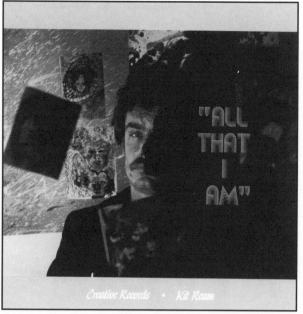

lizard from hell. He looks "straight," particularly in the glamour portrait on the back, where he resembles a TV detective-star of the late '70s. But that weirded-out grin on the front cover is closer to the Palmer Rockey of legend. His main claim to fame is a film which he spent ten years making; you can see a dog enter the room as a puppy and in the next cut the dog is ancient, about to keel over—it took him *that* long to finish the film. Allegedly, the movie was shown once—then it vanished after Palmer Rockey skipped town. All the rich Dallas widows he'd hit up, claiming he was a "movie producer" as he drove around in a Cadillac convertible wearing polyester suits, all began talking to each other and realized he'd bilked them for more than a million bucks! But he's not the only guy like that who's made a record—remember GLENN W. TURNER, the pyramid-scam king of the mid-'70s? Turner promised: "Any man with a hare-lip can make it in this world if you just have enough desire to. Just put your money in the right place." He was right in the middle of building his answer to San Simeon when he was arrested for ripping off hundreds of investors!

Ability, by the HIGH HOPES BAND, is in a class by itself. The liner notes proclaim: "A musical group formed at Hope School carries their message of 'Don't judge me by a label; look at the ability, not the disability.'" These were all mentally-retarded teenagers doing cover versions of John Fogerty tunes!
♦ *V: There's also a CD by retarded kids titled The Kids of Widney High.*
♦ B: RAYNE, four brothers from Louisiana who supposedly still live together, made an album, decided they didn't like it, and used most copies for skeet-

shooting practice. At least a dozen survived, and the LP has some very dark, violent, anti-social lyrics. I heard their chorus of "Paint the Day Red" right after the Stockton schoolyard massacre—that was eerie. Musically, it's a cross between Bubble Puppy and Son of Sam. At least two more unreleased albums are rumored to exist.

Lucia Pamela claims she has hobnobbed with celebrities throughout her life and visited the moon several times. She said, "There's lots of Asian people there—I don't know why."

Going to the Dogs by CHARLIE, BILL and STEVE gives new meaning to the term "back porch" or "home-spun" recording. Their LP was a fund-raiser for the Fidelco Foundation to raise money to train seeing-eye guide dogs for the blind. At one point one of the wives walks into the yard while the tape's rolling and asks, "Oh, are you *recording?* Should I turn the dryer off?" The tape just keeps going, and they left this on the record! Musically, it's fairly decent back-porch guitar instrumentals. This sort of "real people" honesty-leading-to-unintentional-originality is one of the true outer frontiers of kink.

Another one-of-a-kind: poet BUCK WARNER recorded an entire spoken-word album about how much he loves O'Hare Airport in Chicago! . . . And a 1984-ish album by "ZING" attacks both racial supremacy and abortion, linking one to the other: "How you live or die in the year 2020 is being decided right now . . . In the year 2020 social security recipients and unproductive people will be considered an unnecessary burden to those who remain productive. What will society do with unproductive people? Who will *you* be in 2020? Will your life end naturally, or will someone else choose?" In his case, the buyers chose . . .

And here's a LOUIS FARAKHAN *disco* single! It shows him posing in front of a fake sunset remarkably like the fake sunsets found on HEINO album covers. He croons in Barry White-style, "Let Us Unite" with the same "unity or else" mentality of early *Agnostic Front* skinhead lyrics . . . JOAN BAEZ is also not immune to this sort of embarrassment; her debut album on Fantasy (not Vanguard) had her attempting acoustic covers of R&B songs like "Annie Had a Baby," "La Bamba," and even "Young Blood" where she tried to do the different voices of the original Coasters' version—and didn't exactly succeed.

Louis Farrakhan's *Let Us Unite,* © 1984 A.V.C. Music, Inc. Album cover credits: art direction: First Impressions Group Inc., Rubin A. Benson, album jacket concept: Abdul Akbar Muhammad, photography: Austin Studios.

One of the best "real people" records comes out of Fremont, Ohio, by the WUZZ BAND. They cover everything from "I'm Henry the Eighth, I Am" to "Strychnine" by the SONICS. Almost every song has the same one-two drum beat. They'd been together fifteen years when they recorded their first album, and they have a real down-home charm to them. Their press release says it all: "Somewhere south of Toledo lies the town of Fremont, Ohio, where the smoking lamp is always lit and there's always a party going on somewhere. The folks put groceries on the table either working the midnight shift at Whirlpool or making those Ginsu steak knives you see on TV. When the weekend comes around, it's time to go grab the paycheck and party. There's only one band you can see to get down and party-hearty with, and that's the Wuzz Band. The Wuzz Band plays that kind of loud animated crazy-style rock'n'roll that hardly ever finds its way into the *real* world anymore. They don't give a damn about trans-chart positions, videos and certainly not nostalgia." Can't argue with that! This was produced by Cub Koda from Brownsville Station—he's also a collector of weird records. KING USNIEWICZ, whom Norton Records reissued, is one of his "discoveries."

Here's one from Denver: *The King's Loft Presents the Billy Thompson Show:* "Billy Thompson is unparalleled in his flexibility to please his most discriminating listeners. To add spice to his already showy group, Billy has the ever-popular Katie Jean (Mrs Thompson) on vocals." He's actually a pretty rip-roaring country guitar player, but in the tradition of the High Hopes Band you see what appears to be a mentally retarded person in the group—normally you don't see that. The cover's autographed, too.

The Wuzz Band's *Loud, Fast and Wild*, Stomp Records. Album cover credits: front cover photo: KC DC Productions, album design: George Keller & The Wuzz Band.

King James Version, Jaro Recording Company, Seattle. Album cover credits: photography: Carl Brandt, cover artistry & print: Jo Copland

Another unclassifiably twisted band in the *lounge-dementia* department is KING JAMES VERSION, in drop-dead late-Elvis and miniskirt-with-white-Beatle-boots outfits. They have these eerie looks on their faces (would you leave your child alone with *any* of them?), and the liner notes are very pompous, which you can read while you listen to their Blood, Sweat and Tears-y versions of songs . . . BRUTE FORCE's *Confections of Love* (on Columbia) shows him looking like a Tom Jones-type. He's holding out roses, with flowers at his feet, but you'll notice he's standing in the middle of a landfill! On the back he's holding up a cooking pot for no reason. His forceful, up-tempo croon-tunes include "To Sit on a Sandwich," and "Tape Worm of Love."

Here's a definitive D.I.Y. album by the WILLIE WALL Trio, photographed in front of their Winnebago. The liner notes have that typical lounge mentality: "The choice of the selections took many hours. They are contemporary, and each has inspirational appeal for all ages . . . Early in 1968 Willie and Mike formed the Willie Wall Trio, and the three performers have been providing delightful music at the Rooster Tail Restaurant on Route 2, South Burlington, Vermont. It is my considered opinion that with the release of this album, the response from the public will be instantaneous, and the demand for further albums will be inevitable—[signed] E.O." (Note that whoever wrote the liner notes only gave their initials.) A final product credit: "The Winnebago coach pictured on the front of this jacket is furnished by Suburban Distributors of South Burlington, Vermont." Some of the most interesting lounge records were ones people put out themselves, and were probably only sold at shows.

Another of the more crazed recent D.I.Y. records is *The One That Cut You* by REV. FRED LANE of Tuscaloosa, Alabama. The cover shows a grinning guy with a handlebar moustache, glasses that magnify his eyes and bandaids stuck on his face, plus strange drawings and sayings on both front and back. Song titles include "Fun in the Fundus with You," "Danger Is My Beer," "I Talk to My Haircut," and "Oatmeal." Musically, I'd say he's the Butthole Surfers of Big Band Music! This got re-released on a Shimmydisc CD. He put out a second, more countryfied album, *Car Radio Jerome*, with songs like "The Man with the Fold-Back Ears" and "The French Toast Man" who gives out his wares to happy kids: "Then mom takes the French Toast/ From the kids to examine it more closely/It has green mold growin' right outta the crust/And it smells like something awful/She throws it into the garbage can/A rat comes along and eats it up/And falls right over, dead/And his stomach busts open and his liver pops out/Then the French Toast Man/Comes from right around the block/And puts it in his French Toast sock." He's better known in the South as an award-winning sculptor.

Even exercise records are not immune to the mutant factor—meet SLIM GOODBODY, looking a lot like Jeff Goldblum turning into *The Fly*. He's wearing a jumpsuit with human organs painted on, including intestines, liver, heart and veins. He calls his album *The Inside Story,* and some of the songs are hilarious, especially "Your Mouth Is a House" and "Hair" whose lyrics go "Hair, Hair, My Beautiful Hair!" It comes complete with a full-color "activity" poster and a lyric sheet . . . New Age-style snake oil didn't start in the '70s or '80s; I found a 78rpm album called *Deep Relaxation* on Mind Power Records (!), put out by the Cambridge Institute.

Going to the Dogs by Charlie, Bill and Steve gives new meaning to the term "back porch" or "homespun" recording. At one point one of the wives walks into the yard while the tape's rolling and asks, "Oh, are you *recording?* Should I turn the dryer off?"

Even though everybody knows about it, probably few people have listened all the way through *Lie* by the ever-trendy country-rocker CHARLES MANSON. A lot of it sounds like an off-key, Okie James Taylor. In retrospect his titles are amazing: "Ego," "Mechanical Man" (remarkably similar to DEVO's "Mechanical Man"), "Look at Your Game, Girl," "Garbage Dump,"

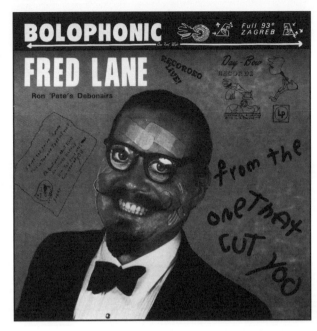

Fred Lane's *From The One That Cut You*, Day-Bew Records.

"Don't Do Anything Illegal," "Clang Clang Clang Goes the Big Iron Door," "Eyes of a Dreamer," "People Say I'm No Good" (!) and "Home Is Where You're Happy." And if Manson had gotten the record contract that Dennis Wilson had supposedly promised him—! DAVID BERKOWITZ and JOHN HINCKLEY have also apparently written songs, but I don't think they were recorded.

◆ ◆ ◆ **SINGING POLICEMAN** ◆ ◆ ◆

A disaster area all its own are SINGING POLICEMAN records, especially COPS, LTD. from Yakima, Washington. Their album is titled *Old Play New* (or *Play Old New,* depending on how you read it). The back cover shows them standing in incredibly dorky poses in a locker room trying to look like Fonzie from *Happy Days*. One of them wields a switchblade he probably took from a *real* delinquent earlier in the day. Their names are Gary Grease, Shoes, Romeo, Square and Kinky (the one holding the knife). Without a doubt, these are the worst cover versions of "Roll Over Beethoven" or "Bony Maronie" ever recorded! I'm sure nobody had the nerve to tell them just how horrendous they really were.

From Jacksonville, Florida, where Herschell Gordon Lewis made those lovely movies, comes The GREASEMAN album: *What it must be like to be a real lawman?* The cartoon on the cover shows a fat cop beating up a hippie. This LP features a wild, over-the-top, screaming deejay telling police-brutality jokes from the *cop's* point of view! He describes raiding an adult bookstore, dropping the bottom half of one's uniform and shaking down teenage girls at Lover's Lane (a la *The Bad Lieutenant*)—jokes like that. The cops who beat up Rodney King probably laughed at jokes like these in their spare time. This record is one of the best arguments around for freedom of speech. In Germany

Greaseman, © 1978 Jack Holeman Productions, Lard Gutt Records.
Album cover credits: art work: Chris Armstrong.

it's illegal for neo-Nazis to publish, but what if that had happened to David Duke? He could have gotten away with denying all his Klan and racist connections when he ran for President (like he tried to), but people were able to nail him because of the books he'd published. I'd much rather have this stuff out in the open so people can counter it, than hidden behind closed doors and passed down from parents to children, like it was in East Germany.

Here's a sample from the *Greaseman* album, where the cop gets a call to transport a hippie prisoner picked up on a local college campus. Forget those TV shows like *Cops*—here's the real story: " 'Damn!' you scream.

'I gotta put another one of them flea-bitten suckers in the back of my clean patrol car? Probably all full of shootin' up that marriage-a-juana.' You drive over to get him and sure enough he's ugly as the day is long: all kinds of sores on him, ain't had a haircut since Day One, but it's kinda handy 'cuz you forgot your handcuffs when you left home this morning, but with that long hair, though, you can kinda slam it in the door so he can't go nowhere—aha! You're driving him down to the station and he says, 'Officer, I think I'm gonna be sick.' You say, 'Wait a minute—don't you go getting sick in my clean patrol car.' He says, 'Oh, you better stop; I'm gonna be sick.' So you squeal over to the side of the road before the creep can heave his guts out; you open the door and he takes off running . . . You walk around to your trunk, you open it up as the kid gets smaller and smaller in the distance. You pull out your pump shotgun. The wood feels good against your cheek. You start to salivate a little bit at the thought of pulling the trigger. You get almost a *sexual stimulation* as you caress that long cold steel barrel. The kid's got hope in his eyes now; he thinks he's beaten you—the creep thinks he's gonna get away. You shift the lever one time and BAM—you shoot his legs out from under him! Only now when you pick him up he's bleedin' too bad to put in the car, so you strap him to the bumper . . . you get to the jailhouse . . . you laugh out loud as you scream, 'Book him!' " And people think that the Geto Boys and Snoop Doggy Dogg are too violent?! If Greaseman were black, he'd be hanging from the nearest tree, courtesy of these kind of cops. Instead, he has just signed with Howard Stern's agent and he's going national, folks.

♦ ♦ ♦ **SINGING WRESTLERS** ♦ ♦ ♦

There's a long tradition of singing wrestler records, and the best known is FRED BLASSIE's "Pencil Neck

Front & back covers of Cops Ltd. Album cover credits: album design: Terry Rosenberry, photos: Dave Minic, Baumgardner Studios.

Geek" on Rhino, written by Johnny Legend who coordinates Rhino's film reissues and has a rockabilly band. Another one was released by an Oregon wrestler named BEAUREGARDE, showing him riding a unique three-wheel motorcycle. The backing band later became The Wipers.

♦ ♦ ♦ BIKER ♦ ♦ ♦

As fun as biker flick soundtracks are, they're very different from records made by *real* bikers! Like *The Burnt River Band Recorded Live at the Carlton Harley-Davidson Annual Swap Meet,* Mantua, Ohio. The photos on the back (similar to the photos in *Easy Rider)* say it all: women lifting their shirts. Song titles include "Harley Ridin' Man," "Drunk Again," "Pussy-whipped Again," and "Electra Glide in Blues." Here's why they don't play regular rock clubs: "One, they won't hire us because of our reputation. Two, all them creepy mothers want to hear is sissy-fag sh-t anyhow." [laughs] "We enjoy our music and we enjoy our friends to the max. I think that we have more excitement on a Friday night than a lot of citizens have their entire lives!" The usual modesty . . . Unfortunately, the music to that one, as well as that of MILWAUKEE IRON from Shell Beach, California, is not as hardcore as the attitude—it's more in the beer-boogie vein.

The BOYZZ: Too Wild to Tame, is a lot more rockin'—it's the last good pre-punk hard rock album, before punk made '70s hard rock obsolete. The singer-songwriter Dirty Dan Buck is posing like Marlon Brando on the cover, and the back shows an even more gnarly-looking band, and when you pull out the insert there's a whole gang taking over the town with their babes, ready to fight—then you flip it over and they *are* fighting!

Most extreme of all in music and attitude was PUKE, SPIT & GUTS from Southern California—their album was subtly titled *Eat Hot Lead.* They're none too subtle about how much they hate having to play with punk bands, even though they sound like them. In L.A. they even had a run-in with an original D.C. hardcore band, The Teen Idles (Ian MacKaye pre-Minor Threat; Henry Rollins was their roadie). Seems Ian borrowed their bass amp and blew it up. P.S.& G. chased them all over the parking lot outside Madame Wong's [a punk club]! "Kick and Kick and Kick and Kick" is one of their "classics," as well as "Scratch 'n' Sniff," "Kill for Kicks," and "Who Needs a Queer Cut?" (about guess who). Their names are: Captain Worm, Donny Death, Marie Manslaughter (pin-up photo available for $2.98), Dick Head (with an autographed beer gut), and the totally straight-looking Stu Icide on drums . . . Another barroom bonehead band from Austin, Texas who got to the meat of the matter calling themselves ROKKER obviously didn't like punk rock. They recorded a song: "Who's a Punk? Your Mother," and "What You Doing To My Sister?" about a father who's a child-molester. "Pigeon Hole Wankers" seems to be a critique of punk-rockers: "You get no thanks from Pigeon Hole Wanks/

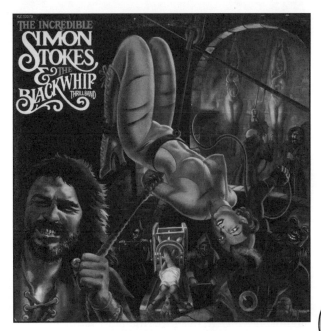

Simon Stokes & The Black Whip Thrill Band, Spindizzy Records. Album cover credits: album design: Pacific Eye & Ear, cover illustration: Joe Garnett.

Garbage Bag Punkers and their cosmic septic tanks/ I'm talking about You, You Wanks." But musically they were 3-chord garage punk, not a '70s Skynyrd bar band.

The ELMER CITY RAMBLING DOGS from New Jersey recorded songs like "Hot Prison Love," "Spitball King," "Silly Putty Sweetheart," "Little Floozy," and "The Prowler." The cover is a cartoon drawing that looks like a '70s country-rock band sitting around the cabin, but if you look carefully the mushrooms growing in the ground are penis-shaped, one of the dogs with a human head is pissing on the side of a building, and two dogs are fucking upstairs while a bird is shitting on the roof nearby. Their earlier album, *XXX,* is said to be more hardcore.

A disaster area all its own are SINGING POLICEMAN records, especially Cops, Ltd. The back cover shows them standing in incredibly dorky poses in a locker room.

The most brutal biker music on a major label was by SIMON STOKES. He was first on MGM as Simon Stokes & the Nighthawks, and later on Nils Lofgren's Spin Dizzy label as Simon Stokes & the Black Whip Thrill Band—the cover painting depicted a torture chamber with women in rather politically incorrect

positions. Stokes was no lightweight himself—he has an instantly recognizable rip-throat gravelly voice and *very* violent lyrics—especially unusual for the time. There are numerous descriptions of fights, plus the graphic depiction of a biker who committed murder being fried on the electric chair. "Waltz for Jaded Lovers" describes a knock-down, drag-out family quarrel, the likes of which even splatter-rock bands like W.A.S.P. or Carcass would be hard-put to upstage today.

Like right-wing '60s folk, there is such a thing as *right-wing garage bands:* here's the BLIND TEETH VICTORY BAND from Houston. They're older guys with beer guts, and one of them is wearing a '70s leather jacket. They titled their album *Kill a Baby, Save a Dog*—about how much they hate animals rights activists who are pro-choice! Other songs include "Ravioli on Your Shirt" and "If You Are a Christian . . ."

♦ ♦ ♦ TRUCK DRIVIN' SONGS ♦ ♦ ♦

Several labels put out truck driving compilation albums, but STARDAY's are the most hardcore, with songs like "Convoy in the Sky" (which I cover on my new album with Mojo Nixon, *Prairie Home Invasion),* "Girl on the Billboard," "Long Haul Weekend," "Truck-Drivin' Son-of-a-Gun," and a song about a trucker who loses all his money to that wicked demon "Pinball Machine." *Diesel Smoke, Dangerous Curves* is a good anthology of classic truck tunes. Another good song is "Gear-Jammin Buddy" by JIMMY LOGSDON—the more LPs you find, the more you get sucked deeper and deeper into a culture that is more twisted than first meets the eye. No song is complete without coffee and a waitress. The covers are amazing: a beehive woman in tight capris looking up longingly at the mighty trucker in his rig, a trucker getting out of the cab ogling the waitress by the jukebox. On the back of

Diesel Smoke, Dangerous Curves & Other Truck Driver Favorites,
Starday Records.

That's Truck-Drivin', there's a pointy-chested, beehive woman staring in awe at a buzz-cut trucker as he plays a pinball machine—that's a *man's* job. There's even a *woman* truck-driving record from the '60s, *Wheels and Tears,* featuring "Little Pink Mack." *Songs of the American Trucker* is a more recent D.I.Y. comp from all-singing truckers (including a *Playboy* model), rather than Nashville studio musicians writing trucker novelty songs. There are photos of everyone *except* George "Wildman" Rawls, the only black trucker.

Two album covers by the WILLIS BROTHERS featured on-the-road truckin' encounters, like helping out the poor lady in her scarf and Volkswagen convertible who needs a tire change. Another great truck song writer is JOHNNY BOND, who also did the original "Hot Rod Lincoln" as well as "Sick, Sober and Sorry" and "Ten Little Bottles."

Of course, a lot of trucker songs deal with the problems truckers have with "Smokies"—the cops. ROCKY JONES figured out how to bridge *both* sides of the fence with *I'm Smokie Trucker*—driving rigs *and* giving out tickets! A later, more guttural country-novelty singer is JIM NESBITT, who sang "Truck Drivin' Cat with Nine Wives" and "Tiger in Your Tank"—brimful of sexual allusions.

♦ ♦ ♦ THE SINGING LOGGER ♦ ♦ ♦

The "real people" phenomenon includes singers singing about the working man who knows his trade. Here we don't just have singing truckers, we have singing loggers—specifically BUZZ MARTIN. His first album is the most hardcore: *Where There Walks a Logger, There Walks a Man.* He sings about how much he loves his logging truck and his chainsaws and hates the forest service and environmentalists. You can learn

Jim Nesbitt's *Truck Drivin' Cat with Nine Wives,* © 1968 Chart Records.

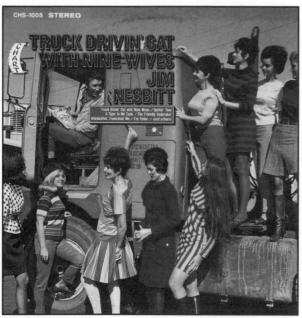

a lot of loggin' lingo from songs like "Whistle Punk Pete," "Cat-Skinnin' Gyppo," "Two High on the Stump," and "Since They Repossessed My Used Log Truck." His album *The Old Time Logger: A Vanishing Breed of Man* has a photo of Buzz, and speaking of vanishing breeds, just look at the size of that tree he's cutting down! The liner notes say it all: "Buzz Martin is a different breed of man. A logger once himself, Buzz Martin demonstrates the safe handling of chainsaws and discusses the ways of the woods, with the hundreds of people who attend trade shows and fairs such as chainsaw and lumber equipment sales conventions where he performs." But the funny thing is: he can't sing to save his life! He just tells—no, *mutters* the stories.

Buzz has a fairly powerful song about being stuck on unemployment, which of course is happening to many loggers now, but not for the reasons they think. My favorite is a tearjerker about a depressed logger who can't pay his bills and sees no way out, so he just saws a tree a certain way and lets it fall on top of him! We'll never be able to hear Buzz's comments on the spotted owl—he was killed in a powerboat accident a few years ago.

Buzz Martin's *Where There Walks a Logger, There Walks a Man,* Ripcord Records.

◆ ◆ ◆ COUNTRY ◆ ◆ ◆

Ain't nothin' like a country tear-jerker. There's the kind that really hit you: when Hank and Patsy do 'em right. Then there's the other kind where you almost wipe out in your car 'cuz you're laughing so hard! KENNY STARR's "Blind Man in the Bleachers" is the tear-jerker of them all, about a blind man who holds a radio to his head: he wants to hear his son get to play in the high school football game (and hopefully not wind up like David Smith!). He waits for week after week, year after year, and then it's the last game and

they finally let the son play because they've given up all hope of winning. Of course, he scores the miracle touchdown! But his father doesn't *know* that, because he'd died in the stands of a heart-attack a few minutes earlier! For country tear-jerkers, this one takes the cake . . .

COUNTRY MUSIC FROM OTHER COUNTRIES

CANADA: STOMPIN' TOM CONNORS is the Canadian Hank Williams. All his songs are about Canada, e.g.: "Muk Tuk Annie," "When You Mention Manitoba," "Sudbury Saturday Night," and "Roll On Saskatchewan." He even quit performing for a decade to protest being billed under Americans at festivals. But now he's back, singing about how heartsick he is that Canada's slowly splitting apart [low voice]: "The most important thing in life should be your country. If not, you should leave." He even did a TV special with K.D. Lang.

His fans are fanatical. He's called Stompin' Tom because he stomps on a piece of plywood to keep time, so his fans have him autograph pieces of plywood! His abandoned, broken-down van is still a roadside shrine in his main "stompin' grounds" in Southern Ontario. Canadian schoolchildren will one day be singing his songs, if they aren't already. You can learn a lot of Canadian geography and history from his down-to-earth, simple, old-style songs—as far as I'm concerned, he's one of the all-time great country songwriters. He's featured in a '70s movie called *Across This Land*.

He's so fiercely patriotic he won't let his records be released in the United States! I heard he threw a public shit-fit when he discovered a truck stop he ate at was using hashbrowns from a mix instead of good *Canadian* potatoes! I'm waiting for him to do a song about his native Prince Edward Island, where the growers are

Rocky Jones' *I'm Smokey Trucker*, Ripcord Records.

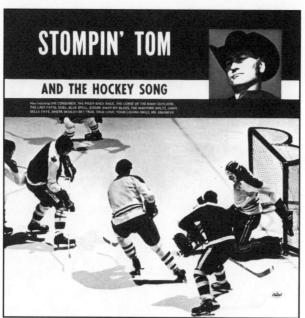

Stompin' Tom & the Hockey Song, Capitol Records.

now forbidden to grow potatoes because there's an indigenous weevil or worm that eats tobacco plants there, and American tobacco growers don't want this pest imported. So they've exerted pressure to forbid an entire island of farmers from growing their own food and making a living!

AUSTRALIA has come up with some classics too—I'm kicking myself for not picking up Australian trucker song compilations when I was there—they call them "truckies" there, not truckers. Surfers are called "surfies," and bikers are "bikies"—don't call a Hells Angel that in *this* country! *The* Australian country-western singer has got to be SLIM DUSTY, whose hit was "A Pub with No Beer"—he's made tons of albums.

♦ **V: Also, early '70s ROLF HARRIS records contain some great cuts. According to Rolf Harris-collector Mick Dillingham, "Sunarise," "Tutankhamun" and "Click Song" are epic tracks.**

♦ ♦ ♦ **GERMANY** ♦ ♦ ♦

♦ B: Half the fun of playing "incredibly strange" records for people is seeing the look on their faces! And of all the records I subject people to, *no one* is neutral about HEINO—he is *the* most quintessentially hideous recording artist . . . a kind of blonde-wig Aryan combination Mitch Miller-Tom Jones. I've heard that older hausfraus throw underwear at him during his concerts. His music is German oom-pah, with huge Abba-esque sensurround backgrounds behind his Bryan Ferry baritone—he can sing really high, too. He's the definitive crooner for the Bavarians in the south of Germany who never apologized for the war. In Bavaria, badmouthing Heino is like bad-mouthing Sinatra in Little Italy.

If there's any bloodcurdlingly schlocky production move to be made, he'll do it: he'll have saws on one

song, children's choir on another, and hula guitars . . . I think Heino's animal magnetism extends to South America, where he may have a large audience among a certain population that moved there. Almost every album has these Latin Lover songs like "Carnival in Rio," "Karamba Karacho Ein Whiskey," "En Einer Bar in Mexico," and even "Komm In Meinen Wig-Wam" (sung in German, of course). Can you imagine being enticed into a wigwam and finding Heino inside?

I have HEINO's Great Hits #5, which has his hula song, plus his cover of "Paloma Blanca" and "Spanish Eyes." He's wearing black leather and rectangular black plastic sunglasses (it's rumored he bought the company so no one else could have the design). On another he's sitting on a fencepost with an obviously fake sunset in the background. His packaging comes in many different flavors: Macho Heino (posed with two German Shepherds), Lysergic Heino (sleeve shaded acid-pink with him holding two poodles), Nosferatu Heino, Heino In Space, and even an entire album of Mother's Day songs. Here he's in a skintight black turtleneck with this wicked *Village of the Damned* grown-up-child look on his face, holding a bouquet of roses you swear are about to explode. There's something so sinister about him—that's partly what makes it all work. Look at those hands! His song about the Ponderosa Ranch must be heard to be believed, and all his songs are sung in booming Teutonic German. Gaucho cowboy music filtered through Heino is—well, priceless.

You can empty *any* party (or evict annoying roommates) just by putting his records on . . . For a two-year period or so we used to play Heino over the P.A. before every Dead Kennedys show, to annoy the fans

Heino, *Seine großen Erfolge 6*, EMI Electrola.

Heino

ing he was the *real* Heino. Then they'd do butcher jobs on Heino songs, making fun of him. Heino *sued,* claiming exclusive rights to the name, the songs, the shades and the look—he cannot be parodied. To prove that he didn't have exclusive rights to the look, Die Totenhosen packed the courtroom with fans all dressed as Heino! This proved somewhat humiliating, and Heino withdrew and refused to talk to the press about this.

Now, after years of being somewhat out of favor, apparently he's back on top with a song celebrating the reunification of Germany, after his rap and acid house singles didn't do so well. He almost seemed washed up until the Berlin Wall fell—suddenly he had 20 million more fans! Erich Honecker's communist dictatorship had actively suppressed his music, so Heino had become a cherished underground cult figure inside the DDR—a symbol of *rebellion,* even! I heard that he also has a *nightly* TV variety show which is filmed in a phony bier-garten. Where does he find his guests? One amateur-hour Chris Montez and Debby Boone after another!

◆ ◆ RELIGIOUS, CULT & OCCULT ◆ ◆

Even thrift-store religious records are worth looking at. There's a record by Dr DANNY HART with a generic sundial cover, and in the middle of straight church music is a song, "Those Funny Little Saucers in the Sky" with lines like: "So round, so firm, and yet so high/Even the Great Big Dipper is breathing a jealous sigh." Of course, many charlatans and gurus have made records; while still in Indiana, JIM JONES put out a quite-hip preaching record full of '60s radicalism.

There was a local guru named BUBBA FREE JOHN who moved to the Fijian island of Naitauba in 1983, which he bought from a group which included Raymond Burr. In 1985 he was sued by a former "sex

who just want to hear punk records. In Hamburg the Mohican studded-leather jacket types at first broke into traditional German folk dances as a joke, but when they realized they were getting more than one Heino song, they threw everything they could find at the sound booth until he was turned off.

I actually saw Heino live in a huge San Francisco auditorium, and every seat in the house was filled. Me and the people I went with were the youngest people in the audience by at least 25 years, except for kids who'd been forced to attend with their parents—they looked utterly miserable. But once Heino hit the stage—in an admiral's uniform, no less—it was sheer mania. *Everybody* knew all the words, and all these people swished and waddled back and forth in their seats in unison, singing and clapping. Finally he brought onstage his wife Hannelore, who was wearing a teenager's pink prom dress, and she was 17 from the neck up and Reagan from the neck down (you could tell where the facelift ended) with this eerie crocodile smile on her face the whole time, waving to the fans and singing a duet *mit* Heino. I thought of an LP cover I'd seen in Germany, which had him running through an alpine field, jumping up in the air in lederhosen clicking his heels, waving an acoustic guitar while all these young Tyrolean fraulein maidens chased him with outstretched arms. Anyway, at the end of the concert, Heino and Hannelore came out to autograph postcards, and it was like Beatlemania—all these elderly Germany hausfraus charged the stage waving their postcards and jumping up and down an inch-and-a-half off the ground.

There's a German band named DIE TOTENHOSEN (a popular, funny punk band a la The Dickies) who as a gag had one of their friends come onstage dressed as Heino, complete with the shades and blonde wig, claim-

Bubba Free John's *The Gorilla Sermon,* Dawn Horse Records.

37

slave" charging him with ordering sect members to sexually abuse her. Allegedly he staged orgies and humiliation rituals, and had nine wives. His album, on which he displays a very sly, untrustworthy smile, contains "The Gorilla Sermon," about the radical nature of spiritual life. A quote on the back says, "The guru is not a gentleman. I couldn't care less about being a gentleman. I have come to make an absolute demand, so you should not approach me if you are not willing to be *undone.*" [!] The titles of his talks include "Dancing With The Guru In Public," "The Dog Costume," "The True Yogi Is A Bastard," and two sides of this double LP are taken up by "Garbage and the Goddess." In his "Yogi" speech he says, "As soon as the Lord makes contact with you, he rips you off. So if I approach you I'll ask you for this; give me this, give me that . . . I'll ask you for *everything.* You must yield yourself in your body; your *cells* must yield."

♦ **V: Well, he's laying all his cards out on the table, so to speak.**

♦ B: A cult classic is this album by BARBARA THE GRAY WITCH, featuring a blonde in hot pants and knee-high laced-up boots with her arms outstretched on the front cover. On the back it says, "Witchcraft has never looked better." Right off the bat she tells you that "the modern witch is not the old cackling hen with a wart on her nose. It isn't even necessary to have long black stringy hair to get into the witches' guild. And even if she were possessed of these qualities, she'd probably have a face job . . . The modern witch also doesn't ride a broomstick. She may not even own a cat, black or otherwise, who in private life could be her lover. [?!] . . . You just blew a lot of money on this album, but at least it's probably the first time you've been screwed by a witch."

Barbara, The Gray Witch, DEA Records.
Album cover credits: cover photography: John Brooks,
art direction: Bob Klein.

Another album is by a Hare Krishna-ite, HANSADUTTA, born Hans Carey in West Germany in 1941—wearing highway patrolman mirror shades on the cover of *The Vision.* It's attempted celestial folk music but he is so off-key that he sounds like a more wasted Skip Spence instead . . . Another LP by a person who is not of this earth is MOLLIE THOMPSON's *From Worlds Afar.* This D.I.Y. record came out on Asteroid Records in the early '60s: a woman in England singing to space aliens in her backyard! And another cracked record that ended up on a major label was JONATHAN ROUND's LP, complete with a round cover! He does a growly-voiced hellfire-and-brimstone version of "Sympathy for the Devil," with Arthur Brown theatrics . . . A band calling themselves SALEM, MASS (from a tiny rural town in Idaho, of all places) put out a strange MAGMA-sounding album, with a burning witch on the cover.

♦ *V: Are there recordings by David Koresh available?*

♦ B: There are a lot of tapes tied up in litigation. Now there's a bootleg CD! He did release one single, ironically titled "Mad Man in Waco"—about his predecessor (the guy he got in a shooting match with, who was even nuttier than he was and is now in a mental hospital. He tried to prove he could wake the dead better than Koresh could by digging up graves, bringing the corpses into the compound and trying to bring them to life).

MERRILL WOMACH was an undertaker in Spokane, Washington who was badly burned in a plane crash. He made all these records thanking jesus for sparing his life (and his operatically-trained voice) and

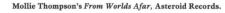

Mollie Thompson's *From Worlds Afar,* Asteroid Records.

he *flaunts* his burn scars on the cover of every record! His liner notes say it best: "Despite horrible burns covering most of his body, he remained conscious—in fact, he started to sing as they headed toward the hospital. In the hospital, as the attendants peeled his charred clothing from his body, he continued to sing . . . The flames had practically devoured his face—swollen, within a few hours, to the size of a basketball, his face was a charred mass. There were at first no openings for his eyes, so great was the swelling. And still he sang!

"He sang while they rushed him to surgery, and sang when he recovered"—that would make a pretty out-there movie, wouldn't it? Well, Merrill thought of that, too, and he made a soundtrack album as well: *Happy Again* (the movie is titled *He Restoreth My Soul*). Open up the gatefold and it says, "Nearly 50 surgeries! God's ways are best!" Hard to tell if his family *wanted* to play themselves or not. There's a close-up of his head made-up to look charred, and if that picture were used on a heavy-metal or rap album, Tipper and Hillary would jump on that in no time, especially with the caption next to it: "It looked as if someone had taken a marshmallow and left it in the fire too long." I'm trying to find the video—if someone finds it, *please* send it to my PO Box. Apparently Merrill did very well with his career, cornering the market on funeral home music as he owns the largest recording studio in Spokane. I also found an album, *My Song—The One Man Chorus,* that came out *before* the plane crash, and it had 42 pictures of his face (count 'em) on the front cover.

Other religious favorites include *LSD: Battle for the Mind,* released by Bible Voice, Inc, and supervised by WILLARD CANTELON . . . Great confessional preach-

Merrill Womach's *Happy Again*, New Life Records.
Album cover credits: cover design: Roger Koskela Agency.

er records include one by JOE LEE KIRKPATRICK: the front shows his prison mug shot, but the back shows him recovered, with his beehived, cat-eyeglasses wife who in a sharp bayou twang reads a poem written by an actual heroin addict: "Miss Heroin." . . . *Million Dollar Monkey On My Back* is a wild mumbling black preacher record . . . Epic Records (of all people) released a "rock-jazz cantata" by the SYNANON CHOIR. Synanon was a self-help group for alcoholics and drug addicts that crossed the line and became a full-fledged cult. Some predicted they'd be the first to

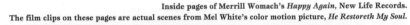

Inside pages of Merrill Womach's *Happy Again,* New Life Records.
The film clips on these pages are actual scenes from Mel White's color motion picture, *He Restoreth My Soul.*

LSD: *Battle for the Mind*, Bible Voice Inc. Supreme Recordings, Inc. Album cover credits: cover photo & design: Alpha Omega.

follow in the path of Jim Jones. They fell apart around the time their leader, Charles Dederich, fell off the wagon and some of them were busted for the attempted murder of a Marin County D.A.—by sticking a rattlesnake in his mailbox! Earlier, there was a movie about Synanon; the soundtrack LP cover shows Chuck Connors shooting up!

Possessed by Demons shows a black person being possessed, next to a large double-knit white person. It's by Reverend R.W. Shambach, no less—in *Re/Search #11: Pranks* (a book by RE/Search Publications) I talk about the time I faked being healed by him. There's plenty more, like *Flight F-I-N-A-L,* the nonstop supersonic service to the New Jerusalem (a christian euphemism for death): "Your pilot is the lord jesus christ; I am your stewardess, the angel of mercy." . . . I think this one's a Mormon recording: *Youth Against Drugs Presents 'Drugs and What Your Own Child Won't Tell You'*—side two features interviews with "actual marijuana addicts." *Where Are The Dead?* shows a morbid graveyard cover, but is this a heavy metal satanic death-rock album? No, it's Jerry Falwell!

The Addicts Sing is now well-known, but did you know that one of the members was John Gimenez, a big wheel in the Reconstructionist Movement who were in tight with Reagan. They want to bring back strict interpretations of old testament biblical law, and some of them believe that unless America is turned into an Iranian-style theocracy with clerics deciding what you read, what you know, and who lives and who dies, then Jesus isn't going to come back for the second coming, so we better get this theocracy going as soon as possible, complete with executions for witchcraft and heresy, and seizure of all property of non-

believers . . . after all, zero tolerance laws are already in place for suspected drug dealers and pornographers. Falwell, Randall Terry, Pat Robertson and the California school voucher crowd have all endorsed this! Some of these people have even endorsed the death penalty for unruly children (while they're still anti-abortion, of course), the death penalty for gay people, and much more.

The Sacred Saxophones by The Royal Heirs is hands-down the most miserable, depressing collection of dirges I've ever heard. They always talk about how "uplifting" religious music is supposed to be, but not the Royal Heirs! Suicidal teenagers beware—you're much safer with Ozzy or Judas Priest! Of course, many local churches pressed their own records, like San Francisco's People's Temple. *He's Able,* by the People's Temple Choir, shows Mrs Jim Jones with piled-up hair singing off-key *Godspell* songs, a lot of hallelujah-ing people, plus about a hundred little kids—one wonders: where are they now?

Rightwing moralizing records can be hilarious. We all remember "We Love You, Diane," by Art Linkletter, released after she dropped acid and jumped out the window, and before Art went on his campaign to stop drugs and promote contour chairs (he narrates a PMRC video, by the way). An even funnier one is VICTOR LUNDBERG's *Open Letter to My Teenage Son.* With patriotic music in the background he goes on and on about how we have the freedom and the right to do this and that—"but if you burn your draft card, I will have no son." He's got some interesting thoughts on "the long hair," too.

Christian heavy metal is another genre perversion: at their concerts STRYPER threw bibles out to the

Youth Against Drugs presents *Drugs and What Your Own Child Won't Tell You,* © 1971 Youth Against Drugs, Inc.

Dr. Jerry Falwell's *Where are the Dead?*, Thomas Road Baptist Church.

crowd. One album shows them posing with bombs painted to match their striped spandex pants and sporting Farrah Fawcett '70s wigs and eye makeup. I wonder if the *Charlie's Angels* cast realized their most lasting influence would be on heavy metal wig-styles! Some fundamentalists like Jimmy Swaggart and JACK T. CHICK (famous for his apocalyptic, giveaway christian comic books) are down on christian rock. They feel that because it has satanic rhythms handed down from the druids, it's still satanic music—therefore groups like Stryper are either knowingly leading children to hell, or unknowingly are under the influence of druids and satanists. But that doesn't deter people like the MESSIAH PROPHET BAND, who do "Rock the Flock"! There's also christian *rap,* by the RAP'SURES: "You Must Be Born Again" and "Break Out for Jesus."

Some of the loopiest "Real People" records come from christians, such as this album by the GUITAR ENSEMBLE from Las Vegas, New Mexico, "sponsored by Pino's Mobile Service, Las Vegas Barber Shop, and Graham's Medical Arts Pharmacy." Some of it is quality lounge garage rock. However, it's dwarfed by my favorite christian of all, JOHN YLVASAKER—check out his album, *Cool Livin'.* He does garagey '60s folk-rock with very theatrical vocals, and sometimes he'll add instruments nobody was working with at the time: flute, violin, etc. *But* ... did he rehearse the band ahead of time? Hell no! Occasionally the musicians come in at different times, and it's like fire-and-brimstone SHAGGS ... Harder psych-rock is done by GLENN SCHWARTZ & The ALL-SAVED FREAK BAND: this is more hippie-christian music—actually not that bad. Carole King is thanked on the back—*uh oh* ... On an opposite note is an equally passionate

Neil Young-type song from Canada by MILL SUPPLY: a totally serious "thank you" tune praising satan!

◆ ◆ ◆   **CHILDREN'S**   ◆ ◆ ◆

When major labels aimed rock'n'roll records at kids, the music would often be much wilder than what they'd aim at adults or even teenagers. The Collins Kids on Columbia, the Bantams on Warner Bros—their screaming version of "Suzy Q" would put the Yardbirds to shame. Those monster records by Frankie Stein & the Ghouls are nonstop great sleazy rock instrumentals—there are no ballads filling out the albums, like the record company would expect a "serious" artist to do. And cartoon music can be wild—I loved the music for the *Spiderman* cartoons when I was a kid.

Like those tasty Coronet instructional films, children's records made in one era often have very different interpretations in another. For example, guess whose lyrics these are: "What do you do with the *mad* that you feel, when you feel so mad you could bite? ... What do you do: do you punch a bag? Do you pound some clay or some dough?" Is that Black Flag or Henry Rollins—no, it's MISTER ROGERS! (The song is titled "Let's Be Together Today.") Or take *Spin Spider Spin* by PATTY ZEITLIN and MARSHA BERMAN: one of the songs is "The Little Bird Is Dead." That could be the title of a Nick Cave album!

The two weirdest children's albums I know were both by BRUCE HAACK, who is better known for a particularly sinister electronics album called *Electric Lucifer* on Columbia. He disappeared from that scene, but for years he's been making what he calls "psychedelic children's records" where some of the sinister overtones remain. *Together* by JACKPINE SAVAGE (Haack's pseudonym) features a booming, overpower-

Kimbo, The T.V. Koala, Fidelis Records.

ing voice (like, threatening to destroy the Starship Enterprise): "Now you must stop thinking." Later, this same voice goes, "Now you can think again." Because he mixes in psychedelic rock music, the album is not only clever but musically enjoyable. Judging by the cover art for *Bite*, Bruce Haack is still as anti-social as ever—he just decided to penetrate minds at an earlier age.

A really warped children's record is *KIMBO the TV KOALA* from Australia—it looks as if they took an actual skinned koala and stuffed it! This ventriloquist sings high-pitched wheezy songs like "Laugh Like the Kookaburra" and "I'm a Little Football Fan"—it's the *voice* that really gets you. And leave it to the christians to come up with the most demented children's records I've ever seen: by LITTLE MARCY, another religious ventriloquist who dressed like Jackie O in a pillbox hat, and had a doll to match. A *Triumph of the Will*-type cover photo shows all these little kids willingly submitting to this weird-faced tiny doll that looks like a female Howdy Doody on acid, chirping songs like "When Mr Satan Knocks at My Heart's Door," "I'm in the Lord's Army," and "God Has Blotted Them Out." People who grew up believing this stuff are now trying to rewrite our laws!

♦ ♦ ♦ **BLACK COMEDY** ♦ ♦ ♦

In the early days, the infamous BLOWFLY had this cookin' band which would do novelty cover parodies of soul hits of the day; e.g., "Sittin' on the Dock of the Bay" became "Shittin' on the Dock of the Bay (watching my great big turds float away)." Other song titles include "Prick Rider," "Panty Line," and the intense "Twelve Signs of the Zodiac." He put out other people's records like this, too, such as *Six Thousand Dollar Nigger* by WILDMAN STEVE. I would say there would

be no Two Live Crew if it weren't for Blowfly. Apparently he's a practicing minister who's had several straight hits under his real name, Clarence Reid. He put down Two Live Crew for trashing women, saying that all *his* songs were about *love*... Other nasty black comedy records include a recent compilation album titled *Shaftman*, with "Check Me, Baby" by Willie Tomlin and "Shorty the Pimp" by DON JULIAN & the LARKS; "Groovy Gruntin' by the GRUNTIN' GROOVER; "Do the Football" by ACRES OF GRASS, and much more.

Of all the records I subject people to, *no one* is neutral about Heino—he is *the* most quintessentially hideous recording artist . . . a kind of blonde-wig Aryan combination Mitch Miller-Tom Jones. I've heard that older hausfraus throw underwear at him during his concerts.

♦ ♦ ♦ **BLACK PSYCHEDELIC** ♦ ♦ ♦

♦ *V: Were there other groups like* **Funkadelic** *or* **Parliament** *who didn't get famous?*

♦ B: It may be a bottomless pit. Records that looked soul or disco may actually have been black psychedelic rock. Originally, the OHIO PLAYERS were very strange; their early single "Funky Worm" sounds like a Limelight attempt at recording the Legendary Stardust Cowboy. Another good album is by PURPLE IMAGE on the mysterious Map City label, which also released an excellent post-'60s punk album by YESTERDAY'S CHILDREN. Black or urban psych doesn't have a lot of "Let's bliss out into higher consciousness, man" lyrics; the opening track here is "Living in the Ghetto"—more street-wise "struggle" and "depression" content. Other black-psych LPs include MAGNUM, WARLOCK, WOLF MOON, BLACK MERDA (Jimi Hendrix-esque) and NEXT MORNING—highly regarded by Blue Cheer fans, and released on Calla Records which put out old Bob Marley material— possibly without royalties being paid. Calla was Roulette's black label, and the intense soul singer J.J. JACKSON was originally on that. This "black psychedelic" sound has come back recently via LIVING COLOUR and their organization, the Black Rock Coalition. Another band, STRESS, have a CD out on Reprise which is very spacey indeed. I forgot to mention the pioneering forerunners of rap today: THE LAST POETS. They put out a lot of great albums, and they're still active.

Marcy Sings, Word Records. Album cover credits: cover photo: Alpha Omega.

Hendrix/P-Funk-style guitar-playing has survived in the BODY COUNT album, which I think is great. Body Count is Ice-T's rock band (as opposed to his hip-hop band; he's the only rapper who has recorded in both genres). The lyrics open a window on a world that has been graphically documented in hip-hop but never before in rock form; "Cop Killer" is the best example. Ice-T deleted that song from his repertoire when cops began calling in death threats to Warner Bros executives at home (nonchalantly reported as perfectly acceptable behavior in the straight press). Also, he saw Republican sharks circling around him thinking, "Aha—we've got another Willie Horton here." "Cop Killer" had been played for a *year* before the cops made a big public issue about it. After the Rodney King episode made them look bad, the cops were fishing for something to get public sympathy back on the side of the police. It was better than a rap song about killing cops, because it was a powerful rock'n'roll song that had 20,000 people a night singing along to it at the Lollapalooza Festivals that year. This was before the political conventions of 1992.

Of course, for years previously there had been songs about killing cops by MDC (Millions of Dead Cops) and the CRUCIFUCKS . . . as times get nastier and life gets cheaper and more people get beaten up, that emotion is going to turn up in song more and more. People whose plight is not featured on the straight media can only show what's going on through music and art. Again, the reason the major labels suddenly pushed grunge music so hard is: they thought it was their last chance to push a generation of suburban white teenagers away from political rap music; if they didn't know that the world that rappers describe existed, they'd be less likely to want to change it. Many of the bands being promoted the most (as part of the grunge and post-grunge hoopla) are ones whose lyrics mainly deal with feeling sorry for yourself: "Boo hoo—my baby left me." NIRVANA and L7 have shown some political inclinations that their record companies were perhaps not prepared for. The danger that originally was in punk is alive and well in rap; punks can be so rigid and musically conservative nowadays, with little understanding or communication with the outside world, so their message goes unheard.

♦ ♦ CELEBRITIES GONE WRONG ♦ ♦

My favorite is *Leonard Nimoy Presents Mr Spock's Music from Outer Space.* Nimoy made a number of albums as a crooner, but this particular one includes a butchery of the *Star Trek* theme and Nimoy reading Vulcan poetry with lines like "Twinkle, twinkle, little earth." At the end he beams down to a planet where all is destroyed except for one survivor who dies in his arms, talking about how the planet once had plenty, but everybody wanted *more*—of course, it's *earth* after a nuclear war.

I'm sure she doesn't appreciate this, but there are several albums about PATTY HEARST, including *Song*

Two Sides of Leonard Nimoy, Dot Records. Album cover credits: photography: Wm. R. Eastabrook/Grant Photography, Del Hayden, design: Sandy Dvore.

for Patty by SAMMY WALKER, who later made a straight folk album for a major label. I also have the *Patty* soundtrack, featuring a bad Patty Hearst look-alike on the cover, and mainstream '70s funk songs like "Love For The People" and "Gotta Get A Gun."

In *NASCAR Goes Country,* all the famous bad-ass stock car drivers (Bobby Allison, David Pearson, Richard Petty, Buddy Baker, Darrell Waltrip) are singing country tunes. These guys have fearsome reputations; they didn't get to the top of the stock-car world by being nice guys. But on this record they all have these wheezy, high-pitched Wally Cox voices that can barely hold a tune. The closest it comes to working is Darrell Waltrip's "I Can Help."

Lee Harvey Oswald Speaks: Recorded Live, is a radio interview from New Orleans where he's trying, in a coherent level-headed way, to defend Castro. He must have had a very lonely existence in those days . . . Right after that movie *Blaze* came out (about Governor Earl Long of Louisiana falling in love with the stripper Blaze Starr), what do I find in a thrift store but an EARL LONG spoken word album, *Last of the Red Hot Papas:* "Humor and philosophy; his best story-telling from pea-patch to mansion." He looks a lot like Nikolai Ceacescu on the cover.

♦ ♦ RIGHT-WING FOLK SONGS ♦ ♦

As the draft-age audience saw through the Kingston Trio, and anti-war protest songs caught on, the entertainment arm of the military-industrial complex tried to counter it with *right-wing* folk and protest songs, such as the famous right-wing alternative to left-wing folk songs by Sgt. Barry Sadler, "Ballad of the Green Berets." On the album, some other songs hit you like Lou Reed's *Berlin:* he goes straight into the mind of the

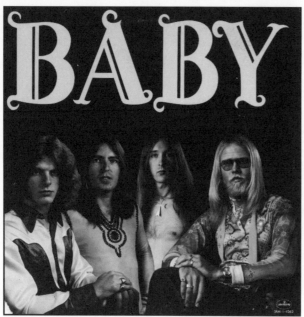

Baby.

women left behind, and the guys not knowing whether they'll get shot or whether they'll make it home. He had a real feel for that sort of thing. He couldn't control himself, however; later he got away with shooting either his wife or his wife's lover—something like that. Another famous right-wing song is "Dawn of Correction" by the SPOKESMEN—a rebuttal to Barry McGuire's "Eve of Destruction." A seethingly racist pro-war single titled "Ballad of the Yellow Beret" was the first-ever record by Bob Seger.

◆ ◆ PACKAGING GONE AWRY ◆ ◆

Both unintentionally demented artwork and "packaging ideas gone wrong" appeal to me, like the covers of The SPOTNICKS. They produced schmaltz-twang guitar instrumental rock albums, and (along with the SHADOWS) were the European VENTURES. They were huge, and as far as I know are still playing. This cover shows them not just in spacesuits, but spacesuits with extra arms, weird mosquito netting and screen-door material on their space helmets, with wires going from helmet to helmet. That's how they could hear each other onstage.

I'm sure the cover of the first JUICY LUCY album (of a woman covered with sticky fruit—some of it drooling out of her mouth), was not necessarily sensuous or good for sales. It's a shame, because this is a good recording featuring a great steel guitar player, Glenn Ross Campbell (ex-Misunderstood), who can make the instrument scream. It's got some DR JOHN "gris-gris" overtones, too. This is a long-time favorite album.

The "Worst New Wave Sleeve Award" belongs to BLIND DATE, the only new-wave cash-in band put out on John Denver's Wind Song label. It shows a glitter-suited, shaved-head mermaid with her skin dyed

green talking on the phone, just like a 1-900 ad . . . Another dyed-skin cover is by PIOTR FRONCZEWSKI from Poland. *Na Progu Raju* is a fairly straight record, but for some reason on the cover he had to be green-faced with maniacal eyes. Musically, he's trying to be a more rocking version of Peter Allen or Billy Joel, but with a bit of the ol' beer-hall swagger. For communist government record company packaging, this is truly out-to-lunch.

SILVER BLUE, from the disco era, shows a sleazy Barry Manilow-meets-the-Mafia man holding the reins of two scantily-clad blond twins sporting dog-collars. On the back he's kindly letting one of them off the leash. Probably *the* most sexist artwork was found on '70s disco albums—I remember one that showed nothing but a woman's butt, plus a wind-up key sticking out of her back.

Warner Brothers did a somewhat famous mispackaging of RON NAGLE's *Bad Rice* album. Nagle was a hot singer-songwriter-former MYSTERY TREND member from San Francisco; now he's a world-class ceramicist. Warner Bros gave him a big promotional push, but instead of putting a Jackson Brown-type sensitive artist photo on the cover, they put the words "Bad Rice" above a pile of rice, and on the back, a truly wasted-looking mug shot of Ron Nagle with one of his teeth missing! What they were expecting to accomplish, I don't know. Somehow it's not as yuppie-friendly as a smiling Jimmy Buffett. This is especially sad because the album is a masterpiece. It really rocks and has well-written lyrics, some of them written from an interesting blue-collar angle. "Marijuana Hell" is about people falling under the spell of pot, and there's a song about somebody becoming crippled from arthritis—which most rock'n'roll people were *not* writing songs about!

Another one-of-a-kind: poet Buck Warner recorded an entire spoken-word album about how much he loves O'Hare Airport in Chicago!

Examples of GENDER-MISPACKAGING include MICHAEL FENNELLY. He tried to become a '70s heavy metal star, but his career seems to have ended after *Stranger's Bed* came out. You don't push an awesome macho rock star by showing him curled up seductively on satin sheets in a bed! . . . A shit-kickin' Southern Rock band of the day was . . . how did they expect Lynyrd Skynyrd fans to go for a band calling themselves *BABY*? A few years later another band

Front cover of Mama Lion.
Album cover credits: design: Fred Marcellino, art direction: Bill Levy.

Inside cover Mama Lion.
Album cover credits: inside photo: Maria Del Ré.

called themselves BABY ROCKER; the cover shows a baby doll with a cigar in its mouth, beer-tab earrings, safety pins, and (dare I say it?) a piece of gum stuck on the bottom of a baby shoe . . . A German hard-space-rock album by BRAINSTORM called *Smile A While* showed hairy German hippie guys posing in corsets and girdles. Needless to say, it didn't quite work—too much gorilla hair for foundation fetishists, I guess.

The original version of DANIELLE DAX's first album, *Pop Eyes,* disappeared quick. Now she has "exotica-goddess from the jungle depths" packaging, but the original cover of *Pop-Eyes* showed cut-up slices of body organs and meat! . . . Another example of blatant meat-marketing was from a Minnesota metal band called CAIN: their album *Pound of Flesh* literally showed a pound of oozing flesh protruding from a tin can . . . tongue-like jelly fingers of *undetermined* origin.

LYNN CAREY was a songwriter with a powerful Janis Joplin voice who wrote most of the music for *Beyond the Valley of the Dolls.* Surprisingly she neither sang on the record nor (considering her looks) appeared in the film. But that didn't stop her from using her cheesecake appeal, under the influence of Canadian transplant letch Neil Merryweather; he repackaged her as a serious blues singer, MAMA LION. The front cover shows her behind the bars of a lion cage, and if that isn't enough to offend today's feminists, open up the "cage" and Mama Lion is suckling a lion cub with one of her ample teats. The thing is, she was a really good singer—where is she today? Merryweather disappeared for awhile and resurfaced as the Svengali behind the revived career of ex-Runaways guitarist Lita Ford.

Another packaging job gone wrong: '60s punk leg-end ALAN FRANKLIN made a somewhat legendary live album in '69, but hardly anyone knows about his '70s comeback album. Rather than present himself as a heavy raw blues-garage musician from the other side, he had himself photographed in bed with a "Come hither" look—there he is under the covers with seemingly no clothes on, a copy of *High Times,* and a huge wad of hundred-dollar bills on a tray along with a bottle of Chianti. On the back he's posing in Tarzan bikini briefs somewhere in the Everglades. Leave it to Florida . . .

MEXICO has been responsible for some incredible packaging. Their early rock was uniquely latin-tinged and very badly recorded, thus making it more fascinating. ORQUESTA FANTASMA is one of my favorites: it shows these guys in Mexican wrestler garb and KISS makeup posing with a mutilated body in a graveyard—I suppose it's half-Kiss and half-King Diamond, but I think it predates King Diamond. Musically it's like a cool crude fuzz-guitar version of Santana.

Comparable to SPARKS in terms of high-voiced glitter rock was the most popular Australian band of their day, the SKYHOOKS. They were one of the first to flaunt their "Australian-ness" and become popular for it in Australia. Their Russell Mael-like lyrics, which trashed the trends of the day, gave a very cynical look at '70s singles-bar stupidity. Their outfits were incredible: part glam, part children's fairytale robes, with occasional Banana Splits fur. The main songwriter, Greg Macainsh, was quite witty, and I'm amazed that he only produces TV shows today.

For the teenybopper market came MILK 'N COOKIES, led by Ian North from New York who supposedly had an attitude a mile wide—all the funnier consider-

ing how wimpy his band was. His voice was an even more breathy/cutesy version of Russell Mael or Peter Ivers. The cover shows one member holding an over-size football, and off to the side a cheerleader is fixing her hose.

THE STARZ were groomed by KISS's manager to succeed them, but they went into a drastically different direction economically! Their only good song was a morbid heart-thumping dirge called "Pull the Plug"— I think it was about Karen Ann Quinlan . . . Another unique band of the time was PAVLOV'S DOG, produced by the same people who did Blue Oyster Cult and the Dictators. David Surkamp's freak, pain-drenched vibrato voice was higher than either Russell Mael's or Peter Ivers', and it warbled clear up to Japanese kabuki standards—his voice could literally stick its needle-like fingers around your spine and pull. The songs weren't so special, but that voice was one-of-a-kind and never equalled. They did two albums and Columbia refused to release the third, so they ended up having to bootleg themselves in their hometown under the name of ST. LOUIS HOUNDS.

On the surface, CRACK THE SKY was a sophisticated, slightly poppish rock band. All of the members seemed to be picked for their looks, except for John Palumbo who just happened to be the one who wrote all the songs. A song titled "Surf City" had the refrain "Surf City, here come the sharks!" But instead of going into really mean, humorous put-downs (like Russell Mael does) of people in stupid social trends, he writes penetrating songs about loneliness and growing up in isolation; e.g., "Robots for Ronnie," which is about a fat little boy who has no friends. The boys think he's queer and the girls stay away, so what Ronnie needs is

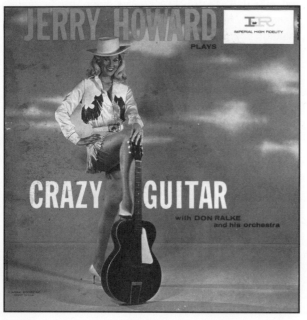

Jerry Howard's *Crazy Guitar*, Imperial Records.

some stainless-steel chums: "a boy and a girl; maybe an aluminum cat."

Then Palumbo left Crack the Sky and went for the Barry Manilow market; *Innocent Bystander* shows him standing in a black suit by a white piano and looking a lot like a Manilow or Neal Diamond type, but one thing got in his way: he couldn't stop writing such hateful, depressing lyrics. For example, in a string-drenched '70s pop-dreck way he'd croon, "It's okay to die." [laughs] "When Raymond comes home tonight he'll crack up on his bike, fracture his skull, and he will die. Mummy and dad will be so very sad; they'll be so very sad they will cry," etc. John Palumbo, the singer-songwriter from hell!

In the "Anybody Can Make a Record" category, the number one front-center is Robbie the Singing Werewolf, a folksinger from Santa Monica. "You can see by my coffin that I am a vampire/And if you had pneumonia you'd be coughin' too!"

Seventies crotch-rocker Rick Derringer was finally on the brink of the arena-stardom he'd geared his whole life for when "Rock'n'Roll Hoochie Koo" was a hit single. But instead of following up with a kick-ass hard rock album, he handed his fans *All-American Boy*, featuring hilarious, sappy, tear-jerker ballads like "The Airport Giveth; The Airport Taketh Away." That was in cut-out bins for years afterward. That wasn't nearly as big a disaster as the deserved retribution incurred by Robert Stigwood. After *Saturday Night Fever* and the BeeGees and *461 Ocean Boulevard*, he sunk all his profits into a movie of *Sgt. Pepper's Lonely Hearts Club Band* with the disco BeeGees playing the Beatles and Peter Frampton as the 4th member. This double LP was supposed to be Stigwood's crowning moment, bigger than *Saturday Night Fever,* and it shipped triple-platinum to the stores. Shortly thereafter it shipped triple platinum *back* to RSO Records. This was the *Heaven's Gate* of the recording industry! Stigwood was never quite as powerful again. Another project on the drawing board was John Travolta starring as Jim Morrison—I'm glad *that* never happened!

Of all the people like IGGY POP and ROKY ERICKSON who were revived by punk, one great gaping hole remains: whatever happened to THIRD WORLD WAR? They were a '70s band from England who had much more of a raw garage-y tone than most bands of their day—as powerful as the Pink Fairies. What set them apart was their political angle: as left-wing, Communist working-class brawlers. They put out two albums on major labels, and how did they get away with this—their first album had lyrics like "Waiting on the rooftops, looking for a sign/Pull your hand-grenade pin, I'll pull mine/Power to the people, when we rise/ Power to the poor, when we rise . . . There's people out of work here/There could be a riot here/Very soon, you know, there could be a riot *everywhere.*" On their second album, the song "Hammersmith Guerrilla" goes: "I've got just the thing for you, a real cop beater/A sawn-off twelve-gauge, five-shot repeater/Get your arse along down to Hammersmith town/Join the urban guerrillas, take up arms against the crown." Another song was titled "I'd Rather Cut Cane for Castro"! They were were dead-set about armed struggle against the British monarchy: "Let's free the working class/We're tired of licking the government's ass," etc. I wonder if they're in jail now. The graphic style on the sleeves has early Stiff Little Fingers written all over it—but five years before punk!

For all-time great packaging jobs we must move back to San Francisco for ZOLAR X, a glitter-rock band who wore Spotnicks-type space helmets and spacesuits onstage, complete with paste-on pointy ears. They came and went, and Lenny Kaye's *Rock Scene* magazine described them as "Pink Floyd crossed with Black Sabbath." Finally in the early '80s they reached vinyl in the form of a bootleg that came out in L.A., and it's astoundingly powerful—sort of the missing link between CHROME and the STOOGES, complete with electronics effects. Their guitarist used a theremin-sounding device operated with a steering wheel! In their waning days they played a few early Mabuhay punk shows. Then they broke up and their singer, Zori Zenith, became a born-again christian. Now he's an anti-rock preacher under another name.

From Italy is DEATH S.S. ('77-'84), a spacey occult metal band. They wore lots of make-up, and were led by Paul Chain who later renounced the occult and started making christian gothic metal albums—he remains as dark and sinister-sounding as he was before. The cover of his first solo 12" showed him with a very Manson-esque look in his eyes. Musically they were great. Visually, years before *Spinal Tap,* Death S.S. were putting little plastic crosses and gravestones onstage—except that underneath their white makeup they were serious. The bass player wore a mummy suit from head to toe.

ANGELINE first surfaced on the Baby Blue single out of the Masque punk scene in L.A. '77—she has a chirpy bird voice and sings catchy girl-group songs— what a voice and what an image. Apparently she had a wealthy husband who financed an enormous boob job for her; he paid for billboards promoting her and produced a number of later records including picture discs. Her song titles include "Loony Bin," "Sexy Stranger," and "Dracula." She drives around L.A. in a

Lucia Pamela's *Into Outer Space*, Gulfstream Records.

pink Corvette and gets on talk shows just because she's Angeline and she knows she's a star. JOHN WATERS was taken by her and tried to interview her, but finally decided that even though she was ridiculous (to the point of having a huge portrait of herself painted on the side of a multi-story hotel), she had no sense of humor about herself and took her trip totally seriously. She even said, "Jayne Mansfield learned everything she knew from me," although Angeline was probably 10 years old at the time Jayne died!

◆ *V: And almost none of the above are on CD—*
◆ B: One more reason why CDs suck! Digital sound is so sterile—it takes away so much of the earth, presence and soul, unless it's mastered very, very carefully. Sure, every nuance and cymbal tingle is crystal clear, but is that *ambience?* Is that rock'n'roll? There are so many reasons not to depend on a CD player for your musical needs. If you really want to get into the weirdest of the weird, you have to take chances, and the vinyl jungle is where it's at.

I've had two turntables for years; one is for scratchy records only. When I started getting into singles, I couldn't judge them by the cover anymore—they didn't have one! So my hunches depended on other clues. If key words like "death," "voodoo" and "murder" are in the title, it's probably worth checking out. I'll also take chances on records from small, remote countries— that's how I found out that *Iceland* had produced one of the darkest, grimmest and most brutal psych records I've ever heard: ICE CROSS. At times they even remind me of the early MEAT PUPPETS, especially their song, "1999." One of my all-time favorites is a band called TRAFFIC SOUND from Peru. They produced a mix of psychedelic rock and Andean folk music; you could imagine being at Machu Picchu look-

PG101 stereo

PETER GRUDZIEN
ALBUM NO. ONE
(in two sides)
THE UNICORN

Peter Grudzien's *The Unicorn*, © 1974 Peter Grudzien.
Album cover credits: Peter Grudzien.

ing out over the clouds while stoned. When psychedelia hit Central and South America, there were a lot of mutated results, partly due to kooky recording equipment—fuzz guitars in South America could be very fuzzy indeed.

Part of the reason I search for weird rock-ethnic-experimental musical hybrids is: they inspire me to come up with new material. I get aggravated by people who spend their life trying to sound like their chosen formula over and over again, and wind up sounding inferior. For example, I'd rather listen to a Ramones or Hüsker Du album than the hundred or so Hüsker Du clones who've flooded our mailbox with demo tapes. So when I'm trying to write new songs, I hardly ever listen to any music that sounds like my own—I listen to everything else instead! The more bent and unexpected, the better—you never know what you may find, and what sort of catalyst/inspiration it could be. And *magic accidents only happen to those open enough to not expect them!* People have complained to me that their favorite thrift store watering holes have dried up after *Incredibly Strange Music,* Vol. One came out. So what? Dig deeper. Burn new borders and let the mind fly. For those who stay curious, there are always new frontiers . . .

BIAFRA &
PAUL MAJOR

BIAFRA interviews record collector PAUL MAJOR on the underbelly of DO-IT-YOURSELF & RELIGIOUS Records. For information on Paul's record label, send a

SASE or 4 IRC's (International Reply Coupons) to Parallel Worlds, 332 Bleecker St #27D, NY NY 10014.

◆ ◆ ◆ **DO-IT-YOURSELF** ◆ ◆ ◆

◆ *BIAFRA: One of the beauties of searching for completely unknown, home-made records is: sometimes you find somebody whose outlook on the world is so bizarre, you wonder how they ever managed to get it together to record their own record, let alone release it. This 1974 LP by PETER GRUDZIEN, The Unicorn, is a psychedelic equivalent of Hasil Adkins in terms of his story, the number of songs he's written and his completely out-there angle on life in general—*

◆ PAUL MAJOR: In the '50s as a teenager in the Bronx he was nuts about bluegrass and country music. He went to Nashville and recorded a lot of authentic-sounding Johnny Cash trio-type rock'n'roll-bluegrass-country music—except the lyrics were completely twisted, like "Don't Come Feelin' Up My Doorknob Anymore." Back in the *fifties* he recorded a song about wandering around in the desert eating mescaline. He mixes together chopped-up Wagnerian choruses, bluegrass, a gay sensibility (double-entendre references involving unicorns, etc), with imagery like "when the pieces of my nerve-ends come crawling up your stairs," Catholic religious themes, Gregorian chants, and early experimentation with sound effects. The whole LP sounds like madhouse hillbilly from the *Twilight Zone*—

◆ *B: I would call it a low-fi basement Donovan from the* Twilight Zone. *He had titles like "Broken Bottle Glass Sidewalks," "Queen of All the Blue-Eyed," "Satan's Horn"—*

◆ PM: And he had lyrics like "You're a white trash hillbilly trick/I'm going to give you my jelly roll because I like your hotcross buns." Or, "The eyes leave my head/The zombies are dead/We'll change all the old into new."

◆ *B: You managed to track him down—*

◆ PM: —In a downtown drag bar. He was like something out of the Addams Family: really tall and skinny in an obviously-slept-in tuxedo; about 55 years old. He wanted me to go out to his car and listen to the song he'd recorded the morning before, and when we walked down the sidewalk in Greenwich Village, every head turned on both sides of the street! I got into the car; it was covered with cigarette stains and grease and smelled strongly of gas—I was afraid that when he turned the key in the ignition to play the tape deck, the car would explode. He turned out to be a walking encyclopedia of early country music; he had met a lot of big country stars.

◆ *B: How does his sexual orientation figure into his music?*

◆ PM: He's probably the only gay person to play with Johnny Cash in 1957. He recorded an album to commemorate the Stonewall Riots.

◆ *B: How many songs has he written?*

◆ PM: I know of 300, and he says he's written at least

The Singing Psychic

triple that number.

♦ **B: My runaway favorite space-folk artist is a Detroit-area biker named NICODEMUS, who uses a lot of hand percussion—**

♦ PM: —Played by his brother "Matchez, the Congo Kid"—

♦ **B: He has four albums featuring very aggressive acoustic guitar-playing—driving and hypnotic—and an instantly recognizable voice that'll send chills down your spine. The music is like Ennio Morricone Western soundtracks plus an American Indian folk music influence. Again, he has a very weird outlook on life, with song titles like "The Word of Parrot," "Heads and Brains," "Rubber Spiders," and "Long Finger of the Flaw." Later he had a rainbow tattooed on his forehead. He has gravestones and sinister-looking artworks displayed in his apartment.**

♦ PM: It's easier to get your record together if you don't have a band and are a one-of-a-kind folksinger. This brings us to the mysterious RIN ERIC album which I found in Denver. This could be the only copy; it's a white-label test pressing with a magic-marker cover: "The Soundtrack to *The Movie In Your Mind.*" This came with a 50-page booklet, and the first song has lines like "That Chevrolet is a molecule/The smog above, pavement below." The over-the-top melancholy refrain goes, "I found my double/You've popped my bubble."

♦ **B: The booklet contains page after page of xe-roxed calligraphy, strange drawings (which would have a psychiatrist calling the police in a matter of minutes), plus lyrics like "Every time I see you our souls lock/Sometimes in the tick of tock." Heavy, man . . .**

♦ PM: Another record, which can still be ordered [from Paul Major], is *Attic Demonstration* by a New Jersey country singer, KENNETH HIGNEY. His mu-

sic is disjointed, sinister and negative, yet he seriously expected Nashville to buy his songs. He doesn't seem to like getting parking tickets: "No heavy trucking, no heavy parking fines/I've got one gallon left in my metal tank, I can't go anywhere/my windows are closing/my fuel lines are frozen/I guess I'll sleep right here."

♦ **B: If they found that in the tape deck of those kids who gassed themselves in the garage in Jersey, Higney would be in as much trouble as Ozzy Osbourne!**

♦ PM: There's many more regional records like this one: MIKE WALKER, from Eastern Washington, around Yakima (same town as the Cops, Ltd. record) is trying to be straight country-rock, but something else comes through, especially on the opening track, "Mr Pruitt's Apple Farm."

♦ **B: Folk and country lyrics are supposed to be heavy, bare-your-soul hard truths. But when some of these people try for a Dylan, Ochs or Guthrie anthem, things like this happen: "Have you ever worked in an apple orchard/and thought you were tortured/because of the blisters on your hand?/Man, you got to make a stand: 'Sorry Mr Pruitt but I ain't gonna do it today/I'm sick and tired of being wired to the basket on my shoulder/I'm gettin' much older'/hey hey, got to get away from Mr Pruitt's apple farm."**

♦ PM: The next example is when someone like this blunders onto a major label—Canadian, in this case. HYDE (the cover shows his weathered-looking face) writes passionate lyrics like, "If there's ladies in the park who'll attack you when it's dark, you got troubles, man." The liner notes say, "This is an artist of dedication with the scars to prove it. Think about your

Orville Andrews' *The Songs of Ranger Andy*, Cobble Brook Records.

own dreams and what you're on to as you listen . . ."

♦ B: Another semi-acoustic album with twisted lyrics is the first (disavowed) album by WARREN ZEVON, Wanted Dead or Alive—the only record officially dedicated to KIM FOWLEY.

♦ PM: In a thrift store I found this album by Eugene DeLuca of Philadelphia; there's no cover and it may have been one of those records made by studio hacks who, for a fee, advertise to "set your lyrics to music" and record them. The titles include "Boink—I'm a Lover" [pretty catchy], "Interspace Man," "Candy and Vintage Wine," and "Twilight Zone."

♦ B: On another topic, the ultimate "Lounge Lizard Gone Wrong" award would probably go to JOHNNY ARCESI—

♦ PM: He started in the '40s as a big band singer on the East Coast. Then he went to San Francisco and Los Angeles in the late '60s, took a lot of acid and when he was 52 years old made an astonishing album titled Reachin' that's full of Twilight Zone '50s weird lyrics, psychedelic Doors and Blue Cheer-type music, fuzz basses that sound like rubber bands, rain effects—

♦ B: All topped off by booming operatic lounge-singer vocals that absolutely do not fit at all—

♦ PM: —in a "bust a blood vessel" style of delivery. One song details an angel lifting its wing and gassing everyone in the room! I probably wouldn't have gotten the album if his style hadn't alienated the previous owner.

♦ B: . . . What happens when stage parents force their children into a recording studio and force them to produce a record? The most famous example is the SHAGGS album by the three Wiggin sisters. They barely had command of their instruments, yet their father took them into a studio, and the result was classics like "My Pal Foot Foot." The Shaggs are cited as a primary influence on HALF-JAPANESE. A far more obscure album from Oklahoma is JUNIOR & HIS SOULETTES's Psychodelic Sounds—the Shaggs of Soul! The oldest member of the band is Harold Moore Jr, age ten—he's quite a guitar player. Venita Marie plays keyboards, Denise Moore plays drums, and Jacqueline (age six) plays "waw-waw organ," and is also the vocalist of the group—she began playing at the age of three. Song titles include "Thing, Do the Creep," "Momma, Love Tequilla," and even "Pimp." The music sounds like uptown soul played on toy instruments—

♦ PM: But very competently. Actually, it sounds like strip-joint go-go organ music; one organ has a wah-wah, and every song is played in the key of C so they don't make mistakes—they sound like they've been playing clubs for 40 years! Their uncle recorded the album in his garage which was full of puppet theater props, stolen phone booths, mad scientist lab equipment, etc. The song "Momma, Love Tequilla" apparently was about their own mom—the uncle took care of the kids. Another great song is "Rock'n'Roll Santa." Most of the albums were shrink-wrapped on a relative's meat-packing machine; as a result the vinyl is usually melted. When my friends met the uncle, he answered the door wearing a sock with two buttons on it over one hand and asked, "You wanna meet my snake?"

♦ B: Here's the YEA'S AND NAY'S album from New Jersey: three guys and three women in a war-between-the-sexes concept album. "Dawn" [one of the women] is described as "cool, poised and velvet-voiced. Might blow your mind with a word or phrase. Free and easy onstage, her acting training comes through! Soulful and sex-sational. Hubba hubba! . . . Al plays lead guitar, writes some groovy arrangements and goofs off a lot. Definitely dily-gaf" (that's a slang term I never heard before). The leader of the band is "F.D.," which stands for Fat Daddy. Some songs are great full-on '60s punk, while the girls' songs are more hokey "put your daughter in front of a microphone and see what happens"—

♦ PM: —real sincere prom dress music.

♦ B: Here's the J ANN C TRIO At the Tan-Tar-A (a resort in the Ozarks, Missouri). "J" is shown with a bass guitar; she has a voluptuous body in a tight dress and spiked glitter heels, and the drummer looks old enough to be her father—he's sitting in a semi-lotus position with a snare drum. They do great versions of "Hey Bo Diddley," rockabilly songs, and an original called "Voodoo Doll" with a hypnotic torch voice on top—

♦ PM: —that's surf-psychedelic. They cover "Funnel of Love" by Wanda Jackson, and do a nice version of "Night Train." . . . Here's a record by RICK SAUCE-

Jr. and His Soulettes' *Psychodelic Sounds*, Harold M. Moore Publishing Co. BMI

Artie Barsamian's *The Seventh Veil*, Kapp Records.

DO, "Heaven Was Blue," which sounds like the psychedelic side of the BYRDS. On the back cover he thanks his dog "Satan" for back-up vocals! Today he's an Elvis impersonator who won't acknowledge his past; I know someone who sent him $400 for a wholesale quantity of records and he just kept the money.

♦ **B: On to The MUZZY BAND—**

♦ PM: —featuring a greasy Jersey hipster comedian with longish hair who played bars like The Playpen, The Jolly Smuggler, and The Headliner where a lot of albums were recorded. The vocalist, Rose Marie, blows everyone out of the water with her drunken scat-singing. The double-necked guitar-player tells the most insulting ethnic jokes imaginable. In New Jersey, Italian comedians over *Godfather*-type music are a whole sub-genre.

♦ **B: Rose Marie, the singer, is described as "Miss Energy. We love her for herself, and her talent is endless." If only she could sing on-key—then that might be true! "Billy Batistan, the drummer, is sheer power all around."**

Now we come to a record by a SINGING FLIGHT ATTENDANT(!) in L.A.: TANGELA TRICOLI, *Jet Lady*. One of her songs is called "Stinky Poodle"; another is "Space Woman." She's posed seductively on her Jaguar, which has a "Jet Lady" license plate, and her singing is spectacularly *off*—as if Wanda Jackson had turned into Mrs Miller.

Even high school talent show records occasionally provide something eye-opening, like a great garage-rocker tune. Here's *Context '70* from Queens, New York, with contributions from various high schools. I especially liked the spoken word poem by Marjory Rudman: "Seagulls walking down the beach explore the sands for remnants of a Saturday morning/One

with horrifying screech lands on the Boardwalk rail above a bench-sitting woman/She, astonishingly, takes the seagull by his flimsy legs and salts him and eats him . . . a pitying bystander begs her to stop her eating/She wipes her mouth pleasurably and points to the bath-house roof/A safe falls and kills him."

♦ ♦ ♦ **RELIGIOUS** ♦ ♦ ♦

Paul's nomination for the most demented record of all time is another religious singing ventriloquist record: JIGGER's *Story Time* from Anaheim, California.

♦ PM: I think it's a Firesign Theater-type parody of a christian record. There are subtle clues scattered throughout, like gay sexual overtones, and when they're talking about taxes, Jigger puts in crazy Bronx-accent wind-up whistling noises.

♦ **B: But why would anybody make something like that? I think it was designed for parents to sit down and listen to with *their kids, reminiscent of the era Pat Robertson wants to bring back. There are jokes to keep the adults interested, as well as the kids—the dialogue must be heard to be believed.***

♦ PM: Another religious find is XENOGENESIS #1 from Florida. The artwork shows an intricate galactic painting with a Star of David and an endless circle of cracked eggshells with apple-eating snakes. The liner notes throw all kinds of words, symbols and signs together (like swastikas and peace signs) mixed with phrases like: "equating equilibrium gamma rays of christ-crystal clear new-nuclear energy of-revelation 22:1-and he showed me a river of the everlasting water of life clear as crystal coming forth from the throne of god-seat of nuclear reactor power-within the nucleus of an atom . . . The pyramid-triangle-trinity laws that bear witness on earth-of matter for the numeral four-the holy spirit-neutron-five the water-electron-six the blood-proton-these three are one, therefore this is lim-

J Ann C Trio's *At the Tan-Tar-A*, Burdland Records.

Sheldon Allman's *Folk Songs for the 21st Century*,
High Fidelity Recordings, Inc.

itless sexual love law of 69, cancer, milky way of time-space existence, continuum of immaculate virgin conception . . . revert to a carbon 666 atom of recycle reincarnation. Now in order to obtain your Xenogenesis #2, please send me the price of a carbon 666 atom: $6.66. I'm not going to kid you or beat around the bush; I need a lot of money and workers in order to help everyone on this planet earth since you use money here. Considering there are about 3-1/2 billion people here, can you imagine if each of you only gave me one dollar? That would be approx. 3-1/2 billion dollars. I ask sincerely, humbly: would that be enough if I in turn spend that same one dollar on each of you?"

♦ **B: He does hot and heavy sexual breathing, with chants similar to the liner notes. But his voice sounds like Richard Simmons!**

♦ PM: The American Lutheran Church in St Paul, Minnesota, aimed its "Silhouette" series of records at wayward youngsters. One cover, showing a girl in a tiger-striped mini-skirt, proclaims, "It's Rock! It's Religious! It's a Revelation!" The record combines very well-done psych-ploitation movie soundtrack music with religious narrations and guest appearances by everyone from Marvin Gaye to Paul Revere & the Raiders to Peter Tork of the Monkees. The producers had a certain understanding of '60s teen pop culture; a lot of money must have gone into this.

Then there's *The CLICK KIDS Are Comin'*, another D.I.Y.-for-Jesus job out of Oregon—

♦ **B: —same stompin' grounds as Little Marcy! What is it about Oregon that creates these people? Oregon hillbillies are a unique breed.**

♦ PM: Here they are, all brothers, standing on top of their psychedelic-painted van that says "Jesus Is A

Soul Man" on the side, along with the phone number of their manager, Electric Norm. The music's just a half-step up from the Shaggs—

♦ **B: With "Go Tell It On The Mountain" fervor thrown in—**

♦ PM: And songs like "Run, Samson, Run/Delilah's Gonna Getcha" (as she chases him with a pair of scissors!). They also croon, "We're Happy Christians," and "Why Must I Be A Fugitive From God?"

♦ **B: The world's about to end, so why not put out your own end-of-the-world record with low-budget heavy-metal skull graphics? This album is by RON DILULIO & JAMES E. KERR, The Death of the World of Now, produced by "the Creation Factory, Inc. in association with astral projections." [?] DiLulio does the music; it's '60s experimental electronics that would fit well on a Limelight Records release, except this was recorded in 1978. Over eerie, echoey screams and sound effects James Kerr narrates: "A canyon began where man ended, and ended where the moon had stopped . . . Satan stood on a shelf of rock that shut out over the gorge and surveyed the aftermath of God's destruction. His laughter roared across the depression and echoed off the far walls washing back like waves over the sea of dead . . . thousands of flickering fires flurrying upward in a luminous background of red and blue. Cyclops monsters and creatures of the inferno swirled in the conglomeration of chimeras and hallucinations as they whirled around the fires, whipping themselves into a fitful fury of an orgy. Now and again a shout of laughter would shatter the night as a reptilian creature heaped the flames of a fire with the deformed body of a slave . . ." If Ken Nordine had turned into David Koresh, he would have made a record like this!**

The Click Kids' *Jesus Is A Soul Man*.

APPENDIX

S&M GIRL SINGERS: GINNY ARNELL was a little more like Lesley Gore, but what an angle on the world; her most famous line is "I'm a Dumbhead, Dumbhead, Stupid Little Girl . . . Won't somebody beat my head against the wall?" Another low-self-esteem "classic" is "I Wish I Knew What Dress to Wear"—even though she knows nobody will dance with her at the prom.

The Dream World of Dion McGregor: he was a talent agent from the '50s who had a habit of talking in his sleep. He recorded these loopy, what would have been called "acid-damaged" monologues if they hadn't happened a decade earlier. A long-time cult classic.

SOUNDTRACKS: *Taking Off,* a movie by Milos Forman, is a soundtrack album featuring songs written and performed by female teenage runaways. It's much darker and rougher than most folk music of the time. It also contains an early Carly Simon track and a song by Buck Henry.

GAY RECORDS: I like the all-gay male novelty versions of songs like "Wild Thing" and "Strangers in the Night" on *You Silly Savage* by TEDDY & DARRIL . . . GLENN MEADMORE's music is more cow-punk now, but check out his first LP, *Chicken and Biscuits.* It mixes hard-cracking drum machine and loud violins. In a deliberately obnoxious voice that Peter Ivers would be proud

Watkins Glen, Pickwick International, Inc.

of, he sings songs like "Lovin' In My Oven" and "Bun Boy" . . . PANSY DIVISION's *Undressed* album (on Lookout) is also well worth getting . . . An earlier example from '75, PAUL VANASE's *The World of Baby Bones,* has songs like "Cosmic Orgy," "Hopeless Case," "Sissy" and "Sticking Needles Through Paper Doll Eyes." Paul has a giant Fu Manchu moustache that dips four inches below his chin, glued-on felt triangle eyebrows that arch over the top of his shaved head, and wears a silver lounge suit cut into Flintstone-points at the bottom.

JACK TURNER: "Nightmare." Aside from having the most psychedelic-sounding steel guitar of the '50s, it also has surreal Dali-esque Hitchcock dream vision lyrics—the CRAMPS should cover this one.

BLACK PSYCHEDELIA: The cover of *LOFTY'S ZZEBRA: Original Afro-Fusion Music* shows Lofty wearing striped platform boots up to his knees, a chapaleta over one arm and loud polyester vest and matching pants, standing amidst some trees gesturing fairly angrily at the gods. Musically, the opening cut is bluegrass! . . . Another experimental black record out of Detroit is this one by DAMN SAM THE MIRACLE MAN (a former nursing-home choir director from Selma, Alabama) and The Soul Congregation. It opens with "Give Me Another Joint," and has rather puzzling, elliptical liner notes.

SATANIC FOLK MUSIC: FRED KUEHN & LIGHT recorded *Song of Gods Gone Mad.* You've heard of satanic heavy-metal, but how about *this* genre?

PSEUDO-PSYCHEDELIC: *NEW LIFE Sings The Sidehackers* (Ameret) blends rock, psychedelic plus a full orchestra. They had the nerve to title an eerie, long Hitchcock scare piece "Psychedelic Rape." . . . After Woodstock, a Crown-type label released a fake Woodstock album, *Watkins Glen,* which covered songs like "Whipping Post" by the Allman Bros, "Up on Cripple Creek," and other pseudo-*Nuggets* complete with rock-festival crowd noise dubbed in. Another all-time wonderful Crown atrocity is *Outa Space!* by TOBY REAN & The Common People. The cover art is psychedelic but the record has nothing to do with psych or space. After butchering a Billy Preston hit, the band plays all country-western, ending with a hilarious weeper about a Vietnam Vet who returns home just as the baby he's never seen croaks from crib death!

STRAND Records, who put out a lot of ethnic material, released RICKY VALE & His Surfers. The cover, which shows three prepubescent kids, claims this is the band, but the LP sounds like space-psych-jazz jams on surf tunes. It only has three songs per side, but each is double the length of most rock'n'roll instrumentals. Very ethereal

and well-done. A great sex record!

BELL Records: *The Electric Piano Playground* by THE PSYCHEDELIC SEEDS may have been intended for children; it's Ferrante and Teicher piano experiments put through various effects. They cover "Psychotic Reaction" and "Tobacco Road," among others.

OUTER SPACE: *Spaceship* by HALL & REASONS, two dorky-looking guys in polyester '70s shirts, is a NASA tribute. The music is fairly decent heavy-psych, but the packaging must be seen to be believed.

MILITARY: BULL DURHAM's *Songs of the Strategic Air Command* includes "Happy SAC Warrior," "Hang Down Your Boom, Ross Cooley," "Home on the Pad," and many more.

EXOTICA-PLOITATION had not quite died in '73: The INCREDIBLE BONGO BAND released "Bongo Rock," "Dueling Bongos," and "In-A-Gadda-Davida." The man behind this was Perry Botkin, Jr. who plagued us with "Nadia's Theme" later on . . . An example of *exotica-folk-rock* is *Song of a Gypsy,* released by a gypsy singer, DAMON. For blending atmospheres, this is an all-time great! . . . In Southern California in the late '70s, BOBBY BROWN, a blonde guy who built all his own instruments, put out at least three albums which revived the '50s exotica feeling. He claimed to have a 6-octave voice and recorded many of his pieces outdoors. He'd be playing one instrument with his hands while playing another with his feet. His best one is titled *Enlightening Beam of Axonda.*

DEMENTIA: One of the more demented bands I've seen in recent years is the GOD BULLIES—especially their singer, Mike Hard, who's a cross between Lux Interior and Renfield the fly-eater in *Dracula.* I've seen him stop a show to rant and rave about the Freemasons while slowly tearing pieces of his leisure suit off. Their music is head and shoulders above that of most so-called "noise" bands—it's like Flipper meets Link Wray. When I met them, their van was loaded with dozens of crackpot lounge and preacher albums they'd picked upon the road. See what diverse influences can lead to?

WHISTLING: Out of Kalamazoo, Michigan, comes a religious whistling record by EVELYN EVANS. Over an organ accompaniment, she produces warbly, yodeling effects.

TUCSON, ARIZONA produced *Two Sides of Bob Garrett.* The cover shows him in a fringed prom suit and bow tie posed between hanging slabs of meat. Songs include "Foldout Teenage Queen of Puberty," "Think I'll Become a Nark," "You Can Take Love and Shove It Up the North End of a Gila Monster Heading South," etc.

CALIFORNIA's Central Valley produced this D.I.Y.:

Overdose: album and game, © 1970 Nanticoke Publishing Co.,
Manufactured by Radnor Records with Nanticoke Pub. Co., Inc.

WILD 'N' TENDER's *Righteous Folk-Rock (in a stone groove).* Musically, it's like Del Shannon singing with Joe Meek's Blue Men on the dark side of the moon. Judging from their *Mannix*-villain '70s cowboy garb, I doubt this was intentional. This was recorded by Don Ralke, an early '60s pop producer.

ORGAN: A grim, sinister, solo organ record was made by DON BRADSHAW-LEATHER, *Distance Between Us.* On the cover he looks like he's covered his face, hair, everything, with blackish-gray makeup.

DRUG-PLOITATION: Not only were pseudo-psychedelic records produced, but this production possibly tops everything: *Overdose: album and game* (!), credited to Lumbee, on a Philadelphia label. It's a hip monopoly game for drug dealers, and places you can land include Sunset Strip, a crash pad, an overdose place, and Saigon. The cards you might be dealt (all of which show a skull with crossed hypodermic needles Jolly Roger-style) include "You ate the evidence," "Get out of jail free," "Pay off fuzz $200," "Overdose: go to crash pad, miss one turn," "Advance to Indian reservation—get wrecked on peyote," and my favorite: "Your friend dies from overdose—you inherit his dope and collect $100." The music is more Sergio Mendez-like, but what a game!

SITAR: My sitar-rock collection includes five brilliant sitar-rock albums by Ananda Shankar. My kitsch favorite is by BALSARA & HIS SINGING SITARS, produced by a mail order label in Perth, Australia. The highlight is a rockabilly version of "These Boots Are Made for Walking" played on sitar! "Tequila" and "Strangers in the Night" are given a sitar interpretation as well. A TONY RANDALL LP from the '50s has a spaced version of "Nature Boy," complete with drug-flick sitar!

♦ ♦ ♦ INTERNATIONAL ♦ ♦ ♦

GREEK-Psychedelic: GEORGE ROMANOS released *Two Small Blue Horses,* a fusion of Greek folkdance music and psychedelic rock ... Another Greek band, ANNA BOUBOULA, released (on Shanachie) an album reminiscent of Danielle Dax: a blend of ethnic music, sultry female vocals, and modern electronic rock.

MIDDLE-EASTERN: In America there's a lounge circuit for Middle-Eastern musicians, some of whom produce some great rock hybrids. VARTEVAR ANTOSSIAN, from Canada, does some good Middle-Eastern stringed-instrumentals. A straight guitar-bass-drums-piano quartet, WAYNE BEDROSIAN & The Immigrants, do revved-up Bee Bumble & the Stingers-like versions of "Holiday in Greece," "Delilah," "Zorba the Greek," plus a medley of "Chopsticks" and "Sabre Dance." Out of nowhere they end up with their version of "Aquarius." Their generic pressing-plant sleeve shows a photo of a mailbox overlaid with green polka-dots! ... GANIMIAN & His Orientals' "Come With Me to the Casbah" is both great Middle-Eastern belly dance and a hot rock song as well; it's from an album on Atco ... OUDI HRANT's *Turkish Delights,* on the Prestige label, is a beautiful blend of Turkish music and jazz. On the same label as both OMAR KHARSHID and ELIAS RAHBANI, is ASSAD KHOURY who does fleet-fingered Middle-Eastern belly dance music on a fancy electronic organ, using all those astro-effects that early Farfisas had.

NATIVE AMERICAN music fused with electronics: JACKALOPE, a Native American-Chicano duo from Arizona. Available on vinyl from Canyon Records, who maintain a gigantic catalog of Native American music. Most of it is strictly traditional, but a few recordings try to break the mold. Write: 4143 N. 16th St, Phoenix, AZ 85016.

MEXICO's demon-lounge contribution is EXODO. One of the singers thinks he's Louie Armstrong, and does a belting gravelly-voiced version of the Beatles' "Yesterday." Dig them *horizontal*-striped bellbottoms!

CHILE: GRUPO ZOOM produced very exotic cocktail lounge music mixed with rock. I don't know if this is early '70s or a *fake* '70s psych "rarity" pressed in the '80s and sold to collectors.

EUROPE: More great pseudo-psych albums from Europe: the *Vampires' Sound Incorporation; Free Pop Electronic Concept Presents a New and Exciting Experience*—this is for fans of *Astral Sounds From Beyond the Year 2000.*

GERMANY: '80s psychedelic rockers like The DIZZY SATELLITES released *Crisis In Utopia*—a much more driving version of the B-52s recorded underwater. In fact, the opening track is called "Underwater Love."

HOLLAND: an otherwise forgettable progressive rock band, EKSEPTION, did a great rock version of "Sabre Dance" on their first album.

SIBERIA: I've heard five cassettes by YANKA—very intriguing. The songs have a Danielle Dax feel and vocals plus *Hawkwind* guitars mixed deep into a reverb chamber. Stunning. Unfortunately, Yanka committed suicide.

SOUTH AFRICA produced a pseudo-psych record that gets right to the point: *Hip-o-crit* by The HIPPIES (featuring Richard Smith!). No comment.

From HONG KONG here's an image for you: CHANG LU [sic], a catwoman in a kitty-cat mask with a pistol. She does weird Chinese pop nasal-voice renditions of "Ghost Riders in the Sky" and "Shakin' All Over." A pseudo-Chinese LP cover from Britain is self-explanatory: *Red China Rocks,* showing Mao Tse-Tung in rockabilly gear!

NIGERIA: Recently I discovered *Phase Two* by BLO, a balls-out psychedelic African guitar band. It's the closest thing I've heard to a Central African *Blue Cheer.* I also found a '72 album from Polydor, *Brown Rain,* by VICTOR BRADY—it's a very intricate psychedelic steel drum rock record. The title track is amazing. He's one of those people who bother me—I wonder, "What the hell could have happened to this guy?" It's to steel drum what OSAMU KITAJIMA is to blending kabuki and rock.

Dane Sturgeon's *Wild 'n' Tender,* Stur-Geon Records.

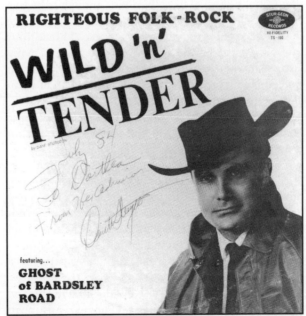

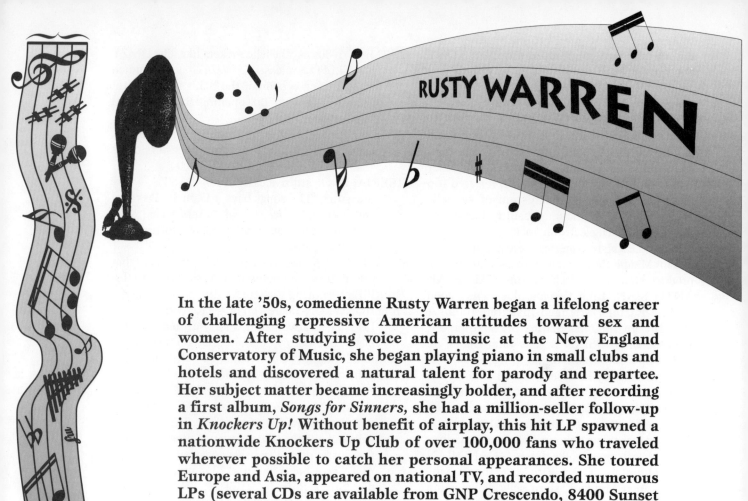

RUSTY WARREN

In the late '50s, comedienne Rusty Warren began a lifelong career of challenging repressive American attitudes toward sex and women. After studying voice and music at the New England Conservatory of Music, she began playing piano in small clubs and hotels and discovered a natural talent for parody and repartee. Her subject matter became increasingly bolder, and after recording a first album, *Songs for Sinners,* she had a million-seller follow-up in *Knockers Up!* Without benefit of airplay, this hit LP spawned a nationwide Knockers Up Club of over 100,000 fans who traveled wherever possible to catch her personal appearances. She toured Europe and Asia, appeared on national TV, and recorded numerous LPs (several CDs are available from GNP Crescendo, 8400 Sunset Blvd, Hollywood CA 90069 (213) 656-2614. A video of a live concert, *Rusty Warren Does It Again,* is also available).

♦ RUSTY WARREN: I'm 1) curious and 2) flattered that I finally seem to have lived long enough to be in a volume called *Incredibly Strange Music.* I was strange in the '60s; I guess I'm just as strange now! I read your interview with Eartha Kitt—we were friends many years ago when we toured together . . . How did you find out about me—did you enjoy the concept of sexual comedy I did in those years?

♦ *ANDREA JUNO: Of course. We discovered your records in thrift stores . . . Tell us how you built up your career—*

♦ RW: Mostly by word of mouth—people would buy an album and share it. In 1959 I received a contract to produce my first album with Jubilee Records—they had put out the famous *Bloopers* albums by Kermit Schafer. My manager had sent them audio tapes of my shows which had been compiled into *Songs for Sinners,* and the company liked it so much they gave me a contract.

At that time those records were not sold in stores. I was constantly touring in cities and towns, working in little lounges. After the show people would come up and I'd sell them an album, take a card and put them on a mailing list—SOPHIE TUCKER taught me how to do that. I had a mail firm in Detroit, and I'd keep feeding them these names—this was long before computers. Just before I'd return to that town (Indianapolis, Cleveland, Cincinnati, etc), they would send out cards printed with my photo that said, "Coming to town . . . opening at such and such a place . . . please come by and say hello!" When people showed up, they'd always bring a friend.

If you know the concept of "Rusty Warren"—it was always a shared experience. You never sat alone and listened with earphones like people do today in the '90s. I was a "party album" concept—you shared my records with friends at a barbecue or party; in the '60s people were becoming suburbanites.

The next year in 1962, my second album *Knockers Up!* won a national award—I was the Number One female comedy album seller, and was on *Billboard* charts for close to ten years after that. "Bounce Your

Boobies" was used a lot by go-go girls (who were very big at the time) and drag queens who would walk around with balloons in their brassieres and do a red-wig takeoff on Rusty Warren.

♦ **VALE: *So at first you sold your records only at live shows—***

♦ RW: Then Jerry Blaine, the president of Jubilee, made sure that wherever I performed, the record stores had all my records. There was one town in Michigan where the clergy didn't want my records sold or have me come to town ... I wrote all my own material, except for parodies or opening and closing numbers which had to have a sensitive or serious meaning; e.g., "You're Nobody 'Til Somebody Loves You." I got that from BELLE BARTH—she'd used it a lot in performance, and when she died, I started using it more and more.

♦ **AJ: *You must have known everybody—***

♦ RW: There were so few of us in this *risquè* business. I was the one who never said the four-letter word; I used "hell" and "damn" which were pretty heavy at that time for a woman to assume in an on-stage persona. I wasn't crude-looking; I always dressed beautifully and had lovely diamonds and clothes. I titillated rather than projected an aggressive attitude. I'm from Boston and have a more or less New England accent— I didn't have that boisterous, loud, aggressive New York accent that went along with some comediennes. At that time I used to sing, too—I can't do that now; my voice went years ago. I sang "I Wish That I Could Shimmy Like My Sister Kate" and "Rusty's Back In Town"—there were a million songs written by Bill Le Blanc or Marge Kierman or Karen Andrews. A lot of people offered me songs they wrote, and I would buy them from them.

My own talk was written by me; I did a lot of ad-libbing. If I got stuck, I would go into another number, or I did a parody of a song popular at the time. It took quite awhile for my show to evolve into a solid stand-

up comedy routine.

♦ **AJ: *How did you get into this business to begin with?***

♦ RW: I graduated from the New England Conservatory of Music in Boston, in 1952. For awhile I taught, but the teaching profession was dull and quiet; my personality or need for excitement made me want more out of life! There were other students at school who were so much more musically talented than I was, in piano or composition. One of my boyfriends at the time suggested, "Why don't you go play for a summer at a restaurant-lounge in upstate New York?" I said, "How do you *do* that?" Then I found out about the New York agencies that booked this sort of thing. Of course, in my day, there were nothing but lounges—the whole country was *inundated* with lounges! That was *the* venue for entertainment—not like it is today. We could play these lounges for four weeks, eight weeks, a whole season; I played Phoenix from December 'til April.

♦ **AJ: *These lounges served food—***

Rusty Warren, "Mother of the Sexual Revolution"

♦ RW: At the beginning, they did, because I played mostly restaurant-lounges. Then I started playing at more nightclubs that had *stages,* where the audience came in for a dinner-package: dinner and the Rusty Warren Show. As I got bigger I started doing theaters and big convention halls with thousands of people.

♦ **AJ: How did you start doing sexually-implicit material?**

♦ RW: That started in Fort Lauderdale and even before that. I used to sit at the piano and talk to people from the audience, and they would talk back to me. Sometimes it would be titillating—I have no idea why it started, but that's where it ended up. I used to steal songs from recordings by Sophie Tucker or Ruth Wallis or others until I got my own flavor of where I was coming from—it takes a while to develop your *self.* Once I did, it was just part of my natural BS!

♦ **AJ: How did people respond?**

♦ RW: Of course, a few people would walk out: "I didn't come here to be insulted!" But 92% of the people stayed, and they told their friends, and we built ourselves a following. The boss would want you to

come back to town because he did nothing but business. We played a lot of little towns in the Midwest (the Clevelands, the Indianapolises); every town had a cute little dinner bar, and we would be performing in it. We'd become friends with the bosses, and they'd have us back at the same time every year; it was nice. Much different than being a so-called "star" today—being hidden away and *securitized!*

♦ **V: How did the media treat you?**

♦ RW: *Time* magazine did a big article on me and called me the "Barnyard Bellower" because I had all these women in the audience marching with their busts held high. They came in on big buses that were chartered from fifty-sixty miles away, because I had written and told them I was going to be performing nearby, and they would make plans to come in with their friends, stay the weekend—it was party time!

♦ **AJ: But both men and women would see you—**

♦ RW: Mr and Mrs America. I never did the Men's Private Smoker circuit. My material revolved around how the sexes interact, but from the female point of view.

♦ **V: Can you describe the "Knockers Up!" routine—**

♦ RW: I'll tell you how it happened. I was at Mike Longo's Italian restaurant in Toledo, Ohio. I was talking about "Come on, get your knockers up, girls! C'mon—put a big smile on your face! Let's show these guys that we like it"—that sort of thing. Mike got up and started to march around the room with a plate of spaghetti in his hands, and I said, "Ladies, go march after him—show him who's got the knockers!" and began playing a march on the piano. All of a sudden, women in the audience started marching after Mike, and it was hysterical. I worked this up into a routine and kept using it, and it could go on for as long as you wanted—women used to march outside, around buildings and all over the place!

It was silly—I had no idea it would be that hot of an act. Like anything else that happens, it was a fluke—you never know what's going to be a hit. But that hit people. In the '60s, people were starting to show their sexuality. Even men were getting out of their blue (or brown) suits and black shoes, and were wearing Nehru jackets, gold chains and letting their hair grow longer and becoming sexual animals like we see today—they were becoming more of an *attraction.* And women were admitting that they liked sex, and that they liked men looking sexy. They were coming out of their shell of sexual inhibitedness—the way they'd been trained. That's why I was titillating them; they were trained *not* to talk this way, and here I was doing it!

♦ **AJ: You were embracing women's sexuality—**

♦ RW: I did that in the '60s—that's why women today call me "The Legend." I was saying that we liked it long before it was popular to say that we liked it. Back then, people thought women were just supposed to lie there and shut up. But I told the world that we liked sex, and that made men pay more attention. I used to tease them a lot on the records: "You sit there with your beer, watching TV, in your funny t-shirts and shorts on—there's *nothing* sexy about that. We'll have to turn that around." So she comes out in her nightgown, and he's clicking the channels—we dealt with situations that were part of life in these households.

♦ *V: You put out an album,* **Banned in Boston**— *were you really banned there?*

♦ RW: No, we just named it that. We tried, because it would have been fun, but they wouldn't go for it! At the time Belle Barth was coming out with her material—she was older and ahead of me in the business. She was very nice to me; she helped me with agents and said nice words about my act: "You lookin' for a funny act? *Hire* this kid." This was important, because my manager was trying to book me, and a lot of places wouldn't buy my act.

I was saying that women liked sex long before it was popular to say that we liked it. Back then, people thought women were just supposed to lie there and shut up. But I told the world that we liked sex, and that made men pay more attention.

♦ *AJ: Can you think of any incidents that happened on tour?*

♦ RW: There's a lot of 'em. Once in the mid-'60s, I was in Detroit talking about a housewife who has a million things to do. She's taking the kids to a Boy Scout meeting, has a van full of children and the truck breaks down and she has to wait for a tow truck. I happened to mention the brand name "Toyota." Unbeknownst to me, there'd recently been a big protest against the importation of Japanese cars which had just begun. A drunk guy in the audience threw a glass of booze right at me, and my drummer, a big Italian, got up ready to start something and I said to the guy who threw the glass, "Wait a minute—is there something wrong?" (I broke off my act.) The guy snarled, "Yeah, I'm laid off work because of those goddam Toyotas." By that time, the Greeks who owned the restaurant had come up and made sure nobody would get hurt.

Another time, I was at a huge theater-in-the-round in California—this was miserable; you had to keep turning around. In my act I was talking about somebody's wife always "wanting it" and the husband never wanting to give it to her: "How come we can't get more sex, girls? We gotta shout, 'We want more! We want more!'" and some guy in the audience shot a

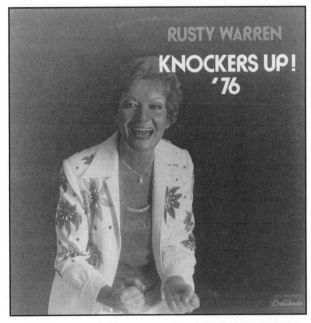

Rusty Warren's *Knockers Up! '76,* © 1975 GNP Crescendo Records. Album cover credits: cover: Jim Britt, makeup-hair stylist: Hugh York, costume designed by: Michael Travis.

gun! Nobody knew where it was coming from; I hit the floor, and the security people subdued the guy. It seems that his wife had left him, and of course it's my fault, right? They hustled him out of there. A circle in the round has no backstage or wall behind you, so we never found the bullet. Sometimes people get nutty . . .

I often autograph records after my shows, but at one show a woman with absolutely enormous breasts said, "Would you sign my boob?" I said, "Well, if you hold it I'll sign it—what can I tell ya?" I had the pen out (and I could have written the Bill of Rights on her boob)

Rusty Warren's *In Orbit,* Jubilee Records. Album cover credits: cover design: S. Haas Studios.

59

Belle Barth's *The Customer Comes First*, Laff Records.
Album cover credits: artist: Howard Goldstein.

and was signing my name and she was saying she was never going to wash it off, and her husband came up— I said, "Don't even ask!" [laughs] Well, that started something—one woman wanted me to sign her leg, I had to sign a guy's bald head . . . But I will never do that again—I did it once, but will never do it again— because even though the crowd was going crazy, I didn't sell one album. We got back to the hotel and were laughing about this, and I said, "Remind me, guys, to never do that again!"

♦ *V: Recently I found two albums autographed by you,* More Knockers Up! *and* Rusty Warren Sings Portrait of Life—

♦ RW: A lot of people have died, and their kids end up with their house full of things to get rid of.

♦ *AJ: Did you ever get any male groupies?*

♦ RW: No. My persona on-stage was never a sexual one; it was androgynous. It was just me talking about us. I wasn't like today's comics who say, "My boy-friend . . ." or "My live-in . . ." or "My mother . . ." or "My father . . ." My comedy was mostly third person: "Remember when your husband did that?" I've gotten a few letters from churches, or notes hoping that god will save me, or against mammary glands, or some-thing like that . . . That was in the early stages. Then I had a marvelous career in Las Vegas for 25-30 years.

♦ *V: Did you live there?*

♦ RW: I had a home there, a home in Phoenix, and I worked in Europe also—mainly England. That's un-usual for a female comedian; female singers are one thing, female comedians are another. My albums were sold in Germany, Japan, and Hong Kong because of the military bases there; they were sold at the stores on the base. We had a pressing plant in Asia that would press the records and distribute them there; we had a press-ing plant and publisher in London that would press

the records and export them to Germany. This was at Jubilee Records, before GNP Crescendo got into the act. I worked for Gene Norman on Sunset Strip in the early '60s; he was one of my first bosses. After Jerry Blaine died, I got my masters back from Jubilee (they belonged to me) and I gave them to Gene Norman to manufacture and distribute—that's what he does now, plus being a wonderful friend.

♦ *V: Do you still perform?*

♦ RW: Very rarely. Once in a while I'll emcee an AIDS benefit or a "cause," but my voice doesn't sustain the tremendous amount of breath energy I need to per-form; I have a bronchial condition now. But I enjoy running around playing tennis and golf—I can do that, but I can't get the stage character going—not for any length of time, that is. Maybe 15 or 20 minutes. But in the 14 records I put out, I think I said all I wanted to say. Seven of them were gold, and this was when you had to sell 500,000 copies to make a "million"—I don't know how they figure that out.

The media today are so vast; unknown people put out an MTV video and before you know it, you're platinum! Back then, I was in a specialized field: sexu-al comedy of a lighter vein than some of my contempo-raries. But partly because of what I did, women comedians today like Elaine Boosler and Paula Pound-stone and Gilda Radner have been able to open their own doors and make their own mark, after I blazed the trail.

♦ *V: So you knew Ruth Wallis—*

♦ RW: She came up in the late '40s; she's very funny. For many years she was very big in Australia as well as the United States. Her husband was the manager, then he passed away. I bumped into her in Vegas, and my manager may have taken over her career for a short period of time. For some reason I think she's still alive,

Sophie Tucker's *Her Latest and Greatest Spicy Songs*, Mercury Records.
Album cover credits: illustrator: Fred Stellen.

because—I'm in my '60s, so she's not *that* old.

♦ *AJ: Did you grow up hearing Ruth Wallis?*

♦ RW: Oh yes, I used to *do* all her material. I'd take it off the albums when I was in college; my mother would sit there and play her records over and over on the phonograph to help me memorize them. I played a little lounge called Steuben's in Boston and she was working in a lounge outside of where Sophie Tucker

I often autograph records after my shows, but at one show a woman with absolutely enormous breasts said, "Would you sign my boob?" I said, "Well, if you hold it I'll sign it—what can I tell ya?" I was signing my name and she was saying she was never going to wash it off, and her husband came up—I said, "Don't even ask!"

was working in a big room. Ruth's husband was in my audience, and I was doing Ruth's famous "dinghy" number and he sent me a note saying it would be nice if I would give his wife credit for writing the song. That's when I went over and met her: "I'm the girl across the street who's doing your material." [laughs] I was a kid, about twenty. There weren't many sources for material back then; Ruth had records out, and Nan Blakstone had a few out, but very few women did risqué comedy then—it wasn't called that until the '60s. They were considered piano bar songs. Parodies were very popular in those days. Ruth was one of the first to write her own songs.

♦ *AJ: What do you think about how the media deals with sexuality today?*

♦ RW: The '60s was a time of extremely open sexuality, as you remember from the Beatles and the Haight-Ashbury. There was a huge influx of multi-sexual partners. In the '90s as we look back we see the mistakes that were made, because sex is very scary to young people who want and need to be sexually active, yet have to be *so* careful. You have to wrap yourself in cellophane in order to say hello to anyone! We never thought of that in those days; we were lucky to get it and we ran and went for it. The only thing we worried about was getting pregnant.

♦ *AJ: But there was The Pill, right?*

♦ RW: Yeah, but women would forget, and some of us bloated up on it. Some people didn't use the pill unless they were terribly active, and the ones who were active didn't care! There was a complete abandonment of health and sexual rules; it was a very strange time,

with all that social commentary on the Vietnam War, etc, going on. The young women in the '90s look back on that and I think we're returning to a more one-on-one relationship situation, because of choice by both sexes. I don't say everyone—I say a lot of the more intelligent ones. Instead of thinking, "On the second date we go to bed," they're waiting a little bit longer before they make a sexual commitment. At least I hope they are.

♦ *AJ: With AIDS, that's a necessity.*

♦ RW: True.

♦ *AJ: By the way, did you ever settle down and get married and have kids?*

♦ RW: No. I have a stepdaughter but I have no children. I was always very busy. I used to say that I had a lot of husbands—but I didn't know whose they were! [laughs]

In the beginning, it wasn't that easy for me because I was going against the grain . . . against the notion of what girl singers were supposed to do. Some women who came after me just didn't make it—I think of SAUCY SYLVIA, who has records out and lives in Rhode Island. She should have made it; she was clever, she was talented, but for some reason she never hit it big. But she always worked. I just happened to hit with "Knockers Up!" but you never know how these things work.

Nobody ever threatened my life; I got some letters from people who were disenchanted—they'd never seen my show, but they'd just heard about my reputation from *Time* and other "confidential" magazines that came out in those days. Actually, I mostly had a delightful career; it wasn't a difficult one and it was fun. We worked very hard; I had various teams working with me that were part of my life for 8-10 years at a time, that helped make the "Rusty Warren Machine"

Rusty Warren's *More Knockers Up!*, Jubilee Records.

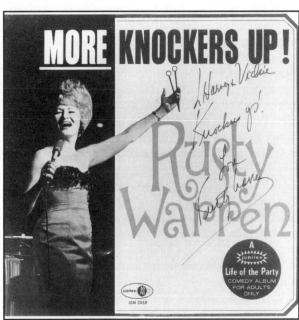

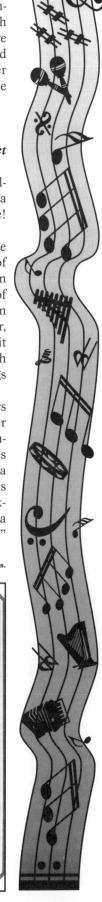

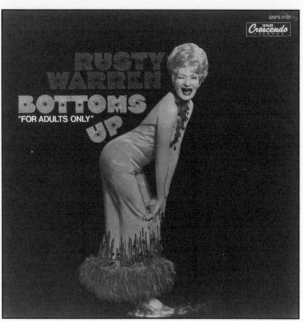

Rusty Warren's *Bottoms Up*, GNP Crescendo Records.
Album cover credits: cover photography: Ed Handler, gown: Ray Aghoyan.

function. My personal manager, Dan Zucker, is in his '80s now. He is a delightful man, and he guided my entire career from the '60s on. It takes a lot of people to do this, plus a public wanting to see it . . . supporting the nightclubs where you came in to work. I used to break records; I used to break my own records . . . at the Aladdin, the Flamingo, and the old International before it became the Hilton. I played for up to 1500 people in audiences, but I never played the vast audiences that today's performers play for—I had more intimate venues. My act was more, "Shhh . . . we're talking about sex now." Everyone felt they were in a living room chit-chatting. People felt they knew me, because they listened to my records in their homes and played them for parties, and when I'd come to their town I'd treat them like a personal friend (at least I tried to): meeting them after the show, shaking their hands, signing autographs, and moving my albums and cassettes and t-shirts—we did that long before these rock groups sold t-shirts. But this wasn't run by a company; it was run by me—we did it ourselves. We didn't have companies coming in and taking over our "visual image" or selling our records and cassettes anonymously. We did it ourselves.

♦ *V: Did you have control over the artwork on your records?*
♦ RW: I was in Europe when *Knockers Up!* came out, so I didn't do that cover. Usually I shot the color transparencies of me in New York or California; I'd send them to Jubilee and their men would make up the covers.

♦ *V: Did you ever write an autobiography?*
♦ RW: I can't get a handle on it; I need help. I'm not a writer, I'm a yakker! I need a collaborator—someone to go through all my memorabilia; there are all kinds of

photos of me with famous people, etc. So I'm waiting, and if someone's interested, please write me! I have everything in storage, including original gowns from the last ten years of performing. There's a story there, but I can't even get it started. I bought a tape-recorder and a computer, but I just sit there and stare at a blank screen, because I'm not a writer. I need someone to ask me questions; someone who's interested in doing the story while I'm still alive, instead of creating one after I'm gone.

♦ *V: How old are you?*
♦ RW: I turned 63 in March. I've never had an age hang-up. Joan Rivers always used to say when I said I played in the over-fifties tennis matches: "Where you gonna find four women who admit they're over fifty?!" Joan always had a problem with that, but I never did.

♦ *AJ: You really are a pioneer; you're a good role model.*
♦ *V: I think a lot of people fall by the wayside because they don't have enough control over their own enterprises, but you seem to have had control right from the very start—*

Most of the female impersonators loved me. They'd put balloons in their sweatshirts and do "Bounce Your Boobies!" and "Knockers Up!" with a red wig on. In my heyday, there was always someone who did Rusty Warren.

♦ RW: Very early in my career I became mentally aware of what can happen. My first check from Jubilee Records was about $25,000 (that was a lot of money in those days) and it went straight to taxes! Then I formed a corporation. I had one manager early who ripped me off for three or four thousand dollars, but I said, "I'm never going to let anyone do that to me again" and exerted complete control from then on. I hired a large firm in California to do my books and payroll and they're still in business; they handle big people like Mary Tyler Moore and Barbra Streisand. For years they were my CPA firm. But I made my own investments, sometimes with them and sometimes without, so that over the years money was made—but not the kind of money people get today.

♦ *AJ: You've always made your own decisions—*
♦ RW: I would discuss things with my managers and people I had respect for. Or I'd have an instinct—back then, Phoenix was growing and if I saw certain areas being developed I'd buy property adjacent. That was my instinct because I lived there; it's good to invest in

things that you *know* about.

♦ *AJ: So many women back then had husband-managers and didn't make their own decisions—*

♦ RW: *No.* If you write your own material and are blazing your own trail in life, you have to fight people's impressions of you, because you're *not* what they say you are. The impression of me at the beginning was: a rough gal, a gal that's "been around," that's "had a lot of men," etc, which of course was a persona that Rusty Warren put forth at the beginning of the '60s, but that wasn't totally true.

♦ *V: Did the media try to vilify you?*

♦ RW: They did, but usually the local towns were pretty nice. The guys who wrote the nightclub reviews were often very, very nice, but some of them *weren't*—that's what a career's all about: some like you, and some don't. But the fans always came, no matter what the critics said. I did very little TV; I never did Johnny Carson because he didn't like me. He knew me from Vegas, but he didn't know what to do with me: "How do you put this on TV? You don't do that." I was interviewed by Merv Griffin and Mike Douglas when they had those daytime talk shows out of Ohio, or by Joe Franklin in New York, but never the major shows, although Dick Cavett did a thing on me once.

Today there are loads of channels, and if I were a young comedian I'd be throwing my material at 'em and they'd be eating it up alive. But . . . what do you do for the next show? You've already shot your wad! Back then, I could take my show on the road for months and go through all the cities and nobody would have heard it. But if you do it on TV, you do it once and that's the *end* of it! Think about it: a lot of comedians today say, "Hey, I got a great show; I'm doing it for cable." It'll be shot in a one-hour special, and when the special's over, there goes the material! You can revamp it in a personal concert and use some of the better bits, but you've gotta stay up-to-date.

♦ *AJ: That's a lot of pressure—*

♦ RW: And my show didn't have any ethnic or political datedness—it was about *sex;* a general subject that fit anybody, not just Mr and Mrs White America.

♦ *V: Did you know female impersonator comedians like T.C. JONES?*

♦ RW: I knew T.C. Jones; we met on Sunset Boulevard when I worked upstairs at the Crescendo. He was still alive then but was very heavily into drugs. But he was talented; he was *brilliant!* And CHARLES PIERCE (who's still alive, I think) and other performers who were impressionists or mimics. There's another heavy-set performer who did fantastic Charles Laughton impressions. There are a lot of performers today who do "reality impressions" of Liza Minnelli or Judy Garland.

Most of the female impersonators loved me. They adored me; they used to do my material. They'd put balloons in their sweatshirts and do "Bounce Your Boobies!" and "Knockers Up!" with a red wig on. In

Rusty Warren's *Bounces Back*, Jubilee Records.
Album cover credits: cover design & photography: Stephen P. Haas Studios.

many towns, we would be invited to see so-and-so do their Rusty Warren impression, so our whole group would come to a club and watch a drag queen do an impression of me—then they'd get me up on-stage with them; it was hysterical. I couldn't ever do lip-synching because I just couldn't; but I'd be listening to them doing my own record and *I* couldn't do it! This happened, especially in bigger cities like Chicago and Detroit that had big drag shows. In my heyday, there was always someone who did Rusty Warren.

♦ *V: You must have come to San Francisco—*

♦ RW: I worked Bimbo's many times, at FACKS (that's a club from the early '60s), and did the Circle Theater in Santa Clara. I was in and out of San Francisco many times in the '60s and '70s; in fact I was playing San Francisco when Kennedy was shot. My mother and my aunt had come up to visit. We didn't do our show as scheduled; the *world* closed down that night.

♦ *V: Was it hard to de-escalate and retire?*

♦ RW: No, the time was right. Times change, audiences change, the lounges changed. Nowadays, there's not that many places to play anymore unless you play in vast venues—and that's not for me. I wasn't a drugger and I didn't get into that kind of situation. I had a good career; I had nice people around me, who supported me. I never lived in Hollywood or New York; I lived on a ranch in Phoenix for 35 years, but last year I wanted to be free of the big home and the ranch and get away and not have to worry about house-sitters and dogs and animals, so I moved to Hawaii. Maybe next fall I'll live in Europe.

♦ *AJ: What did your mother think of your act?*

♦ RW: My mother died recently at the age of 95. She always said, "I know what you're saying, dear . . . but where in god's name did you learn it?!"

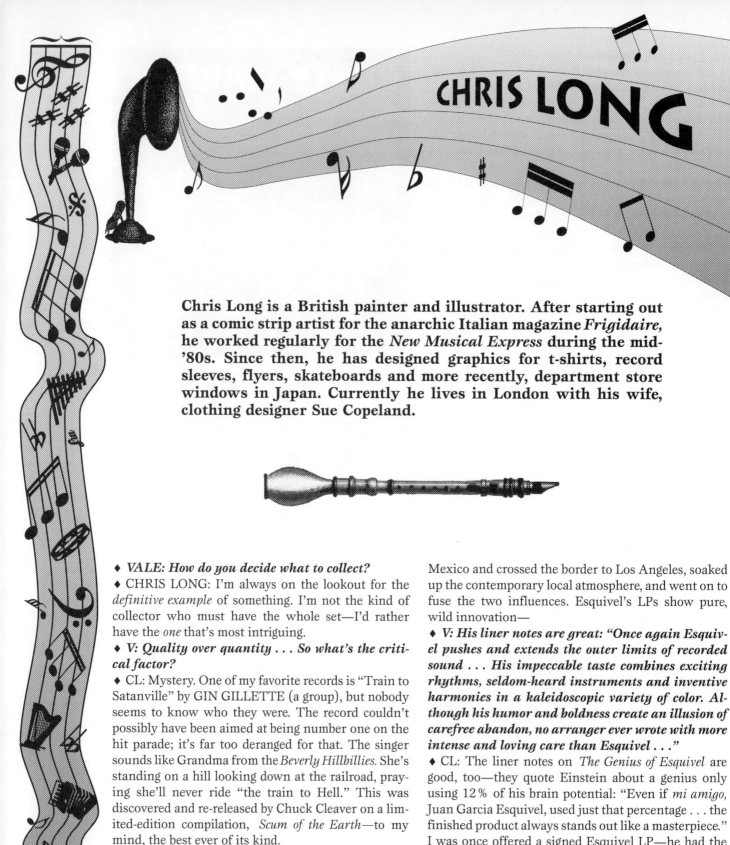

CHRIS LONG

Chris Long is a British painter and illustrator. After starting out as a comic strip artist for the anarchic Italian magazine *Frigidaire*, he worked regularly for the *New Musical Express* during the mid-'80s. Since then, he has designed graphics for t-shirts, record sleeves, flyers, skateboards and more recently, department store windows in Japan. Currently he lives in London with his wife, clothing designer Sue Copeland.

♦ *VALE: How do you decide what to collect?*

♦ CHRIS LONG: I'm always on the lookout for the *definitive example* of something. I'm not the kind of collector who must have the whole set—I'd rather have the *one* that's most intriguing.

♦ *V: Quality over quantity . . . So what's the critical factor?*

♦ CL: Mystery. One of my favorite records is "Train to Satanville" by GIN GILLETTE (a group), but nobody seems to know who they were. The record couldn't possibly have been aimed at being number one on the hit parade; it's far too deranged for that. The singer sounds like Grandma from the *Beverly Hillbillies.* She's standing on a hill looking down at the railroad, praying she'll never ride "the train to Hell." This was discovered and re-released by Chuck Cleaver on a limited-edition compilation, *Scum of the Earth*—to my mind, the best ever of its kind.

Sometimes the cover is enough. I'm sure the music on the soundtrack album *The Thing with Two Heads* has very little to do with the movie—but who cares? You can put it on and study those latex profiles of Ray Milland and Rosie Grier in minute detail while you listen. A few years ago I started investigating records from the '50s and '60s and one of my favorite composers turned out to be JUAN ESQUIVEL. He came from

Mexico and crossed the border to Los Angeles, soaked up the contemporary local atmosphere, and went on to fuse the two influences. Esquivel's LPs show pure, wild innovation—

♦ *V: His liner notes are great: "Once again Esquivel pushes and extends the outer limits of recorded sound . . . His impeccable taste combines exciting rhythms, seldom-heard instruments and inventive harmonies in a kaleidoscopic variety of color. Although his humor and boldness create an illusion of carefree abandon, no arranger ever wrote with more intense and loving care than Esquivel . . ."*

♦ CL: The liner notes on *The Genius of Esquivel* are good, too—they quote Einstein about a genius only using 12% of his brain potential: "Even if *mi amigo,* Juan Garcia Esquivel, used just that percentage . . . the finished product always stands out like a masterpiece." I was once offered a signed Esquivel LP—he had the most florid signature, full of beautiful curlicues. Next to it was Liberace's signature; I think maybe Esquivel opened for him in Vegas. Recently I found *Esquivel '68*—the cover shows a girl with body paint on it.

When they perfect time travel, that'll be my first trip: back to Las Vegas and a front row seat, then off to the nearest record shop to ask, "Do you have the new Esquivel album?" Imagine the in-store display! Recently a Mexican CD (which is basically Esquivel's *Latin-esque*) came out, but except for one track it's all in *mono*. This makes me fear that the spectacular stereo master tapes are lost. And if that's the case, perhaps the RCA recordings of the THREE SUNS and BOB THOMPSON are lost, too.

♦ **V: Tell us about Bob Thompson—**

♦ CL: He was a native San Franciscan who released three albums on RCA. *Mmm Nice!* is my favorite; he also did *On the Rocks* and *Just for Kicks.* It's real bachelor-pad music. He does these vaguely suggestive "naughty" versions of standards, like "Do It Again" or "Hello Young Lovers," or compositions of his own like "Playboy." In fact, the sleeve notes for *Mmm Nice!* were written by a *Playboy* writer. Occasionally at the end of a track, a woman will murmur something provocative like "Mmm Nice!" But musically, he's not nearly as imaginative as Esquivel.

♦ **V: Are there any records by women that appeal to you?**

♦ CL: JULIE LONDON made an album called *Yummy, Yummy, Yummy* singing songs like "The Mighty Quinn," "Louie Louie" (great!), and the Doors' "Light My Fire"—all in the same style as her torch hit, "Cry Me a River." "Yummy Yummy Yummy/I've got love in my tummy" is *so* suggestive. I think this album may have been her last—her parting shot. But did it indicate a spirit of recklessness in her? Of rebellion? What was going through her mind when she thought, " 'Yummy Yummy Yummy' —I've *got* to record that!"?

♦ **V: Part of the appeal stems from the context of her previous career. Perhaps she's trying to make**

Photo: Karen Steffens

the transition into a "new thing"—

♦ CL: Yet with this album she made something which appealed to me much more than anything she'd done before. Around the same time there was another record trying to "get through" to the hippie children of the day: *Silhouette Segments,* a weird spoken-word LP by PASTOR JOHN RHYDGREN. It's reminiscent of Ken Nordine: super-cool, beatnik-style verse spoken with a DJ delivery. "Music To Watch Girls By" provides the musical backing for one poem about the loveliness of women walking along the street. It ends with his syr-

Julie London's *Yummy, Yummy, Yummy*, © Liberty Records, Inc.
Album cover credits: art direction: Woody Woodward, design: Gabor Halmos,
photography: John Engstead.

upy voice saying, "And *God* put them on this planet."
Another poem is urging us not to use guns or fight, etc.

I like poetry-and-jazz albums—there's a good one featuring KENNETH PATCHEN where, at the end of each poem, the engineer turns up the jazz for a mini-crescendo. A great cut, "The Murder of a Man by a Kid Wearing Lemon-Colored Gloves," just repeats two words: "Wait . . . wait . . . *Now!*" [crescendo] In the same vein is an EP put out in England by JEREMY ROBESON called "Blues for the Lonely." He delivers Allen Ginsberg-type poems but in an upper-class British accent like Sir Laurence Olivier: "Can you hear the thunder?/Is the music too high or too soft?" Spoken over a rowdy jazz quartet, it's as if Ronald Firbank had become a beat poet . . .

♦ *V: There's a class incongruity here—*

♦ CL: Yes, *incongruity* is an attractive element in music—as it is in all the arts. It encourages me to search for very odd things.

♦ *V: Why do you like rap music?*

♦ CL: When rap was new it seemed that suddenly you could throw anything into the pot. I remember reading about a block party where 12-year-olds rapped to the intro of "Brown Sugar" played over and over again—to me that was inspirational. Now that rap has been accepted by the mainstream and consequently lawyers have become involved, only the richest (and therefore more conformist) acts can afford to pay for the copyright on samples. Optimists say that'll mean a return to "live" performance. If that happens, I think there will be more emphasis on the actual "rap" itself. And I can think of very few performers who are sufficiently articulate or imaginative enough to withstand any real scrutiny. They should take a leaf out of ye olde school

rappers RAMMELLZEE & K-ROB's classic 12-inch "Beat Bop." Jean-Michel Basquiat produced it for the Profile label before he died.

On the subject of sampling, if you want an example of total appropriation, how about U-ROY, the Jamaican DJ who sampled the first album by THE PARAGONS in its entirety! All he did was dub in a voice-over and re-title it *Version Galore*. Even back then, this sort of thing was not uncommon. But all the same it must have seemed unbelievable for its gall—how could anybody *do* that? The Paragons' album was a hit all over again.

I suppose sampling of some kind will always be a part of recorded music. The general trend seems to be that records incorporating "incredibly strange" sounds are becoming part of the norm. The acceptance of more and more bizarre elements is good, yet . . . the basic criterion for me is that in order for a record to be worth collecting, I have to be able to listen to it more than once. There are records of parrots talking, but is that something you'd return to over and over?

♦ *V: It might be more fun to imagine the parrot record rather than listen to it. Sometimes the liner notes are more interesting than the record, because they'll describe the theory, ideas and intentions of the artist which are not always successfully realized on the recording itself.*

♦ CL: And the parrot record may provide raw material for somebody else to do something with.

"Yummy, Yummy, Yummy/I've got love in my tummy" is *so* suggestive. I think this album may have been her last—her parting shot. But did it indicate a spirit of recklessness in her? Of rebellion? What was going through her mind when she thought, " 'Yummy, Yummy, Yummy'—I've *got* to record that!"?

♦ *V: When did you get interested in American culture?*

♦ CL: I grew up in Blackpool which has a lot of Americana. It's a seaside town with mini-Las Vegas wannabe lights, tacky candy, and all these amusement arcade games imported from America. I remember a DJ named Ian Levine—he went to America, bought loads of soul records and brought them back, and we would listen to them constantly . . . these American soul records from the '60s and '70s.

♦ *V: What's your view on CDs?*

The Three Suns' *On a Magic Carpet . . .*, © RCA Victor.
Album cover credits: Henry Turner/David B. Hecht.

♦ CL: I really only buy the CD of something if the LP is really hard to find, or if (as is often the case nowadays) it hasn't been released on vinyl. People like to have something round and substantial. That's why cassettes are unsatisfactory—besides, they break (the same goes for videocassettes).

♦ *V: Do you think those easy listening records from the past will be reissued?*

♦ CL: Big companies like RCA have all those tapes in their vaults, or maybe they've destroyed the masters—who knows? All those EXOTICA records that came out in the '50s have yet to be re-released; if they were, I'd have them all. I buy compilation LPs of out-of-print obscure rockabilly and early rock'n'roll, but any day the lawyers could close in and shut those labels down. Then those re-releases would become collectible in their own right.

I'm a big fan of reissues. Anything that puts this stuff back on the shelves is OK by me; I wish everyone could get the chance to listen to Esquivel or *Shaft in Africa*. You get the feeling that people are forgetting large chunks of the history of music. If you only listen to commercial radio, your concept of pop history is so narrow. Even in a major city like London there's no radio station that plays old, unusual music—not even pirate radio.

♦ *V: Martin Denny put out 37 LPs, and I doubt that all 37 of them will be re-released on CD. Yet this music is so refreshing to hear, relaxing and soothing to the nerves—*

♦ CL: Exactly, it's like finding something you only dreamed about. When I first heard Esquivel and Martin Denny I couldn't believe it: "Wow, they really *did* make music like this!"

♦ *V: You grew up in the north of England—how did the phenomenon of "Northern Soul" [soul music subculture in the North of England] originate?*

♦ CL: Let's say, for the sake of argument, you were a "mod" in the '60s when everybody was into standard soul music like Otis Redding, Aretha Franklin, and Wilson Pickett. When psychedelia emerged, it seemed that everyone in the south of England accepted it unconditionally, while a faction of northern soul fans remained stubbornly true to what they considered their *roots*. True devotees sewed a patch onto their jackets: "Wigan Casino: Keep the Faith"—that says it all. Things became fractured around the mid-'70s. The Wigan Casino continued to play mainly '60s hardcore soul obscurities, while the Blackpool Mecca began playing '70s soul and more up-to-the-minute stuff. People would travel from all over the UK and maybe do two all-nighters in a row—one night in Blackpool and the next in Wigan.

♦ *V: But what* is *Northern Soul music?*

♦ CL: Underground soul. Obscurities. When you've nothing else but the music, it's too precious to let the uninitiated know about it. So the demand was for rarer and rarer cuts—soul records that would eventually become anthems, like CHUCK WOOD's "Seven Days Is Too Long" or BILLY BUTLER's "On the Right Track." Sometimes DJs would throw in a slice of white bread like LEN BARRY's "1-2-3" or MEL TORME's "Coming Home Baby," or "Afternoon of the Rhino" by THE MIKE POST COALITION (of *Hill Street Blues)* fame, and that was all part of it. Even though the DJs may have been elitist, they weren't purists.

♦ *V: How did the kids dress?*

♦ CL: In "Birmingham Bags"—wide trousers with

Sondi Sodsai's *Sondi,* © Liberty Records.
Album cover credits: color photography: Garrett-Howard.

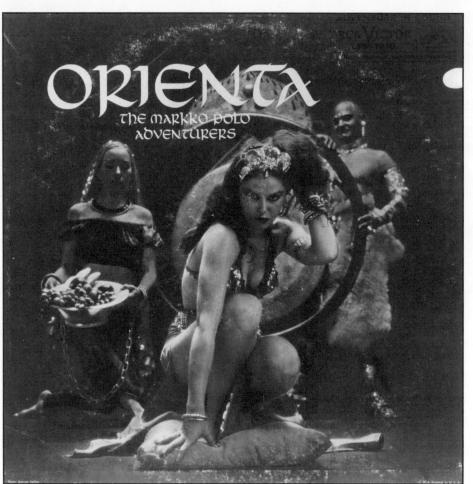

The Markko Polo Adventurers' *Orienta*, RCA Victor. Album cover credits: photo: Murray Laden.

cating feelings about *hardship* and basic themes of *love lost or gained*—there's nothing more universal than that! In the north of England times are tough, so if you find something "special" you hold onto it, because you can gain strength from a song like "A Quitter Never Wins." Songs like that are inspirational; you hear them and feel you can tackle your problems. And the vocals are so good—if you've been weaned on that, it's tough to accept a lower standard of singing ability.

I think you have to be distanced from a culture to properly appreciate it. Whenever I've been scouring record racks in America, I've noticed it's always the British or Japanese or Germans who are buying up all the soul and jazz. Americans don't seem to be bothered. I suppose I feel the same way about British culture; it holds no mystery for me.

patch pockets on the legs and a high four-inch waistband with lots of buttons. Wing-tip brogues. A singlet (undershirt, like the one Stanley Kowalski wore in *A Streetcar Named Desire)* or a cap-sleeve T-shirt which was very much a '70s thing. The girls would dance in exactly the same way as the boys, stomping away in big shoes and big wide '50s skirts. One particular move was to drop back and then pull yourself up on an imaginary rope—I could never do that. It was a marathon. Up in the balconies of Wigan Casino, people would sleep for a couple of hours and then get up and start all over again—or take speed to stay awake.

The scene is still going. Instead of the Casino (now a car park), there are massively popular "Weekenders" which take over holiday camps on the coast. The range of music is much broader now, and they import acts from the 'States who perform live—people like SAM DEES, who has a beautiful voice.

♦ **V: So what drew these working-class white British kids to obscure black American soul music?**

♦ CL: Escapism? I don't know—maybe it was the rawness, the authenticity of the sound. When Northern Soul was at its height in the mid-'70s, everything else must have seemed like so much bubblegum by comparison. Also, a lot of these songs were communi-

Music Inspired by *The Thing with Two Heads*, Pride Records, © 1972 MGM Records, Inc. Album produced by Michael Viner. A Saber Production.

Bob Thompson's *On The Rocks*, © RCA Victor.

That's the bottom line. Obviously America, because of its vastness, has so much more raw material, and the likelihood of finding a decent number of weird things is much greater than if you're stuck on a little island like Britain. And once these records become familiar, you start to imagine the scenarios surrounding the record company's decision-making: how did those "incredibly strange" records get made? Which corporate bigwig at RCA enabled The Three Suns to record so many weird LPs? Maybe one voice still had a final say, rather than a committee.

♦ *V: Now it's the era of the pop video rather than the pop recording—*

♦ CL: I think playing a record should be more like reading a book, where you put a bit of yourself into it, than watching TV—

♦ *V: At the least, be exercising your imagination—*

♦ CL: Video is clearly an inappropriate medium for the interpretation of songs; it closes more doors than it opens.

When I'm at work in my studio I use music as a buffer against the distractions and disturbances of modern life. I couldn't bear to listen to the radio—then I'd have no control. I compile tapes of favorite tracks, and some are thematic where each song will be similar in mood. This helps me focus my attention, and at the least have *some* say in what happens in my environment. The trouble is: I work in the middle of Covent Garden, and there's usually a busker with a nose flute right under my window. But then, no man is an island—unless he's in the bath!

SOME FAVORITE SOUNDS:

ESQUIVEL: "Miniskirt" from *Esquivel '68* (Mexican RCA LP); "Who's Sorry Now?" from *Infinity in Sound,* Vol 2.

PERREY & KINGSLEY: "Cosmic Ballad," from *The Best of Perrey & Kingsley* (available for $20 ppd from Re/Search, 20 Romolo #B, San Francisco CA 94133).

DEAN ELLIOTT: "They Didn't Believe Me" from *Zounds! What Sounds!*

THREE SUNS: "Danny's Inferno" from *Movin' and Groovin'*

MARKKO POLO ADVENTURERS: "The Girlfriend of a Whirling Dervish" from *Orienta*

HUGO MONTENEGRO: "Dizzy" from *Moog Power*

RUDY RAY MOORE: "The Jive Jungle" from *Dolomite* soundtrack

SKULLSNAPS: "I'm Your Pimp" from *Skullsnaps*

LES BAXTER: "Bird of Paradise" from *The Primitive & The Passionate*

ENOCH LIGHT: "Walk On By" from *Spaced Out*

DICK HYMAN: "Give It Up Or Turn It Loose" from *The Age of Electronicus*

ANDRE PREVIN: "Executive Party" from *Rollerball* soundtrack

MYSTIC MOODS ORCHESTRA: "Cosmic Sea" from *Awakenings*

JOHNNY HARRIS: "Footprints On The Moon" from *Movements*

KAIN: "Ain't It Fine" from *The Blue Guerrilla*

BRINKLEY & PARKER: "(Don't Get Fooled By) The Panderman" (7")

THE DEVILS: "The X-Orcist" (7")

PETER TOSH: "Dracula" (7")

U-ROY: "Hot Pop" from *Version Galore*

JOE GIBBS: "Freedom Call" from *African Dub Almighty, Chapter 3*

MERRY MAKER: "Bag-a-Weed" (7")

THE NEW BANGS: "Go-Go Kitty" from *Scum of the Earth*

KING PINS: "Ungaua" from *Forbidden City Dog Food*

RAY COLUMBUS & The Art Collection: "Kick Me" from *Off The Wall*

LUE RENNY: "Your Wiggle Your Giggle" from *Inferno Party*

KENNETH PATCHEN: *Kenneth Patchen Reads With Allyn Ferguson & The Chamber Jazz Sextet*

MELON: *Hardcore Hawaiian* (12")

KEN NORDINE

In 1957 Ken Nordine recorded the first of four pioneering *Word Jazz* albums. In his rich, soothing baritone voice he recited "insane stories" he had improvised over hipster jazz accompaniments by the Fred Katz group (an alias for the Chico Hamilton group), Dick Marx with Johnny Frigo, and Richard Campbell's Northern Jazz Quartet. His imaginative flights of verbal fantasy ("a thought, followed by a thought, followed by a thought, *ad infinitum*—a kind of wonder-wandering") were accompanied by equally adventurous sonic experiments to create moods and suspense, utilizing sound effects and tape modifications.

Additionally, for the past fifty years Ken Nordine has had a successful career in commercial radio and television, having done thousands of advertisements, hundreds of radio shows (over 375 radio shows are available on cassette; see appendix), plus television appearances and public performances—recently with members of the Grateful Dead. Currently he is working on a book titled *Crumple,* in which all the pages are crumpled . . .

♦ *VALE: You moved to Chicago from Iowa, right?*
♦ KEN NORDINE: I was in Iowa for such a short time—the only thing I remember is my mother selling Hoover vacuum cleaners from farm to farm. (*You know,* I lie a lot about what happened to me because it's more interesting that way.) The family moved to Chicago when I was about three and I've been here ever since—although I've been asked to leave many times! Actually, years ago I was invited to Los Angeles to take a bow for a Fred Astaire hour-long spectacular which was broadcasted on prime-time TV. While I was out there, some producers asked me to stay and write material for Jerry Lewis and Dean Martin and George Gobel and the operatic-voiced Helen Traubel; they wanted me to write for *other* people.

I was invited to New York to be on an NBC radio program, *Monitor,* but they only wanted me to read what other writers wrote for *me*—I didn't want to do just that. I suggested that I read the news with a blues background, but they were very *serious* about the whole thing—as people are when a lot of money is invested. That's why the programs then were so *stiff.* The producers have their idea of what should be said, and they don't trust anyone to *ad-lib* . . . and in some instances they probably have good cause because they've been burned: "Wait a minute—did you hear what that guy was saying? He was talking about crocheting a *condom*—well, you can't do that." So I'm not faulting them for their trepidation and their paranoia toward the unharnessed imagination.

♦ *ANDREA JUNO: How did you get started?*
♦ KN: In the business? Years ago I did a primitive TV show called *Faces In The Window:* just one camera on me, late at night. And I read stories by Edgar Allan

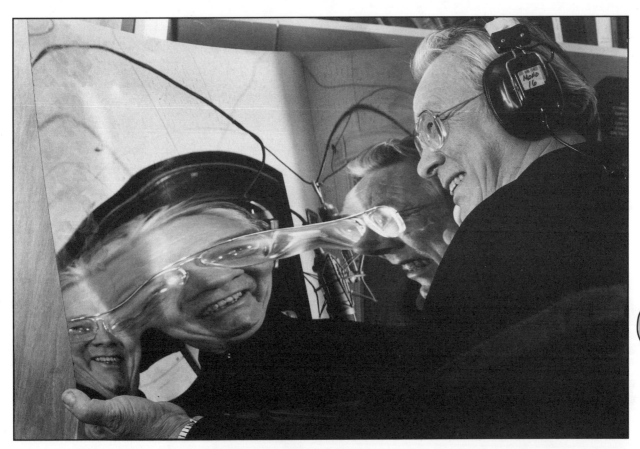

Poe, Balzac, de Maupassant—horror stories by great writers. It was on right after the used car salesmen had quit for the night.

I also did a poetry show. I had a ladder resting against a bookcase filled with books I'd gotten from Houghton-Mifflin, the collected works of major poets (and minor ones, too—some of the best are "minor" poets like A.E. Housman). People would call up and ask, "Would you read . . . ?" I'd look up their requests and read to them, recall a few things I knew about the author, and—

♦ *AJ: What year was this?*

♦ KN: Around 1957. Besides *Faces In The Window* and this poetry show, I was doing my "Word Jazz" show locally in Chicago. Then I did the talking vocals for Billy Vaughn's "Shifting, Whispering Sands"—a most unlikely combination—which became a hit record on the Dot label. From that success I inveigled Dot Record Company to let me record *Word Jazz,* which was an album of little stories I'd made up.

When that came out it caused a little stir. One of the cuts on the album, "My Baby," was based on the idea that the word "baby" was over-used in popular music. Bud Yorkin, who produced Fred Astaire's first TV special, flew me out to Hollywood and I met everybody and went in and out of focus and did all the things you're supposed to do. Fred Astaire was really a marvelous person, as was his choreographer, Hermes Pan. Fred Astaire and Barrie Chase danced to "My Baby," I came out and took a bow, then I returned to Chicago

and did 3 more albums of WORD JAZZ for Dot until they became more enamored of Pat Boone . . .

♦ *AJ: Pat Boone is so conservative—it's ironic that you were on the same label—*

♦ KN: It is an anomaly. People used to say that the son of Randy Woods [president of Dot Records] liked to play my records at the wrong speed—45 instead of 33-1/3. And they said that with a straight face, which worried me. The company didn't really know what I was doing; "Shifting, Whispering Sands" had been such a pop hit that they thought, "Well, we trusted him on that; we'll trust him on this." Actually, it was a wonderful thing to have *Word Jazz* come out on Dot Records, because now all the rights have reverted to me and I can use it any way I want. After that, I went with Phillips [Mercury] and now I have my own company, a very slow-moving label called SNAIL Records.

"Shifting, Whispering Sands" was part of Billy Vaughn's whole rise and fall from fame. This was one of his big hits. It was fun—I'd go into a coffee shop in Chicago and suddenly hear myself on the jukebox! I thought, "Gee, I'll make all kinds of money on this" . . . I didn't, but that's all right. (You know what I made on that? $125 total.)

♦ *V: Did you write that song?*

♦ KN: No, it was written by a Southern Illinois minister about a "sidewinder, a snake running through the shifting, whispering sands." It had a narrative quality that sparked the imagination of people at that time. It was very different from the *Word Jazz* things—it came

time and you couldn't keep repeating yourself. But the beatnik movement happened in San Francisco. I met some of the people when they passed through Chicago, but I never considered myself a beatnik—

♦ **AJ: But you did critique that "Man in the Gray Flannel Suit" mentality—**

♦ KN: Some of it was poking fun at myself, you might say. The "Flibberty Jib On The Bibberty Bop" is a piece I did about a charismatic character—sort of a Billy Graham or Jimmy Swaggart or Jim Bakker—any one of these characters who comes into a social situation and has people going, "Wow, this is *it!*" Maybe today it would be Gorbachev. And it lasts for a certain length of time and falls apart . . . then another guy appears, and the critics tear *him* apart. But I never thought of it as political—

♦ **AJ: —not in a dogmatic, but in a satirical sense. How about your piece "Anytime," with a woman in the background laughing all the way through?**

♦ KN: That was my wife, by the way. Part of the *Word Jazz* thing is: adding audio-writing on top of audio-writing, so that I can amend what is said. I'll write something "straight," then react to it, so that in a sense it becomes a collage of itself with itself.

♦ **AJ: Yes; the conjunction of the two voices changes the whole meaning, adding nuances and complexity—**

♦ KN: But that's what *everyone* does, in a way. What I'm playing with is *time integration* and *mood integration:* the way you used to feel and the way you feel now . . . trying to step in the same river twice! For example, I'm very serious about something when I do it, but then I listen to it again and think, "Wait a minute—isn't that being a little *poseur-y?*" [laughs] It helps to leaven it—to make fun of yourself being serious.

Most of the things we hear we quickly categorize out of existence: "Oh, I know what *that* is."

♦ **V: —Ken, sorry but I'm having technical difficulties recording this—**

from a different part of the brain!

A long time ago when Truman was President, I appeared with Charlton Heston and Cary Grant as part of an Israeli bond drive. Initially, the producer wanted me to play the part of "God." This was on a Thursday, and the show was scheduled for Chicago Stadium on Saturday. But the next day they called me—it seems that Charlton Heston wanted to play God—and they asked, "Ken, would you *mind* changing parts?" I said, "It's a benefit—what do I care?" So in the middle of this big thing I'm the angry Jew and Cary Grant is the gentle Jew . . . suddenly a spotlight hits me in the face—it's a newsreel crew doing a build-up for *The Ten Commandments,* and they're saying to themselves, "Where the hell is Heston?" Now, every time I see Charlton on the tube I think, "There's the guy that aced me out of playing God! And look where he is now!" [laughs]

♦ **V: Were you part of the beatnik movement?**

♦ KN: I was a great memorizer of poems by T.S. Eliot, Omar Khayyam—all kinds of things. I was working in a little joint and ran out of poems I'd memorized so I had to make up new ones. The jazz pianist, bass player (Dick Marx and Johnny Frigo) and I would get up and ad-lib stories because the same people came all the

♦ KN: Maybe it's the C.I.A.! [laughs] No, it's the B.I.A.—the Beautiful Intelligence Agency! This is the kind of story I like: I know a fellow who's very old. And he eats lunch in this very posh arts club. When he comes in alone he has a cane, and walks very slowly and deliberately and sits down, and the waiters are very careful. Except that *now,* the waiters giggle when he appears. Because when he comes in with a young woman, he doesn't have that cane—he walks in as if he's young, healthy and happy! Of course, the waiters and the maître d' think it's very funny—they're the ones who told me about it. I can't tell you who he is because he's famous. He's an Aristotlean philosopher—that's the only hint I'll give you!

♦ AJ: *You do a stream-of-consciousness reflection upon society—*

♦ KN: Right now I'm re-doing an album of mine called *Colors.* The idea came from a series of radio commercials I did for the Fuller Paint Company in San Francisco. They said, "Do whatever you want—just mention our name." So I wrote, "The Fuller Paint Company invites you to stare with your ears at Yellow." And then you'd hear very strange music, and I'd continue, "In the beginning—no, long before *that*—when light was deciding who'd be in—or out—of spectrum, Yellow was in serious trouble. Green didn't want Yellow in—some primal envy, I guess. Things looked very bad for Yellow until Blue came along and said, 'What's the trouble?' and Yellow explained . . . So Blue went to see Green and told him, 'Look—if Yellow and I get together, we can make our own Green. We won't need you.' 'Oh.' So Green saw the light and Yellow got in. It worked out fine: Yellow got lemons and Green got limes." I liked this project so much I thought, "Hey—I'll do these colors as an album."

♦ V: *Literally turning commerce into art—*

♦ KN: And it all began as a commercial—which was great: they *had* to play it on the air. But that caused a problem—people would call up the radio station and say, "Could you play that again?" But because it was a commercial, they couldn't do it—"We don't give these things away for nothing!" It could only be aired when it was scheduled and paid for! Lately I've been working on the idea of "red"—that red means some kind of trouble . . . the red deep in the blush of beginning, inside the nuclear sun. Something like that—

♦ AJ: *I think a lot of people have lost the ability to listen to the oral tradition and appreciate the evocativeness of poetry. We're continually assaulted by a wall of crashing loud monotonous sounds—*

♦ KN: Most radio stations are there to make money; the businessmen who run them think, "What shall we do? Well, we'll grab a certain audience demographically." It's a big industry and their licenses have cost a lot of money. What happens is: people buy what they hear, particularly young people. And if they don't hear anything but the radio playlists, they figure, "That's what we have to buy!" Spending money to them is

proving that they're human beings.

The mainstream would like to think that what I'm doing is so *weird* and so off-the-wall that they don't have to pay any attention to it—"he has a *cult* following." Which in essence is a kind of put-down: "If you're not mainstream, you're not important. If you don't *go platinum,* your work doesn't mean anything."

♦ AJ: *Yet* Word Jazz *and* Son Of Word Jazz *were very successful—*

♦ KN: Oh yes. In fact, people still write me wanting to get copies of everything I've done. I've re-released a lot of those early records myself; I didn't wait for an NEA endowment! After the first edition of A.E. Housman's poems came out, the publisher told him, "You'll have to pay for the second edition yourself!"—which he did. But that's *normal* for poetry.

I'm on public radio in Chicago at 9:30 PM. I've done 300 shows which my son Ken Jr. produced with musical help from my son Chris, and Howard Levy. 77 are called *Word Jazz,* and the others are called *Now Nordine.* They go on satellite each Friday and are heard wherever a station picks up the downlink. I really never know *where,* because they don't tell me.

♦ AJ: *And you still write?*

♦ KN: Oh yeah; I've got *stacks* of stuff. I write short things because my attention span is such that 3-4-5 minutes is as long as I want to stay on a given subject! I've been working on a movie idea about a guy who dreams of making a musical called *Ummm* about two Siamese twins connected by the lips. Of course, it's so crazy and goofy that nobody will invest in it. So this guy wants to put all of his own money into it, and his entire family wants to have him committed because he'll waste their future inheritance!

Billy Vaughn's *The Shifting, Whispering Sands,* Dot Records. Narration by Ken Nordine.

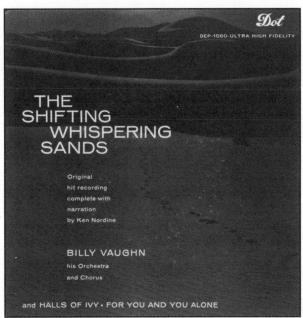

73

Ken Nordine's *Word Jazz* with the Fred Katz Group, Dot Records.

♦ **AJ: Can you talk about some of your influences? Charlie Parker and Freud are mentioned in your liner notes—**

♦ KN: I like jazz for the principle of what jazz is: a flight of musical fantasy within *structure*. The part of jazz I never particularly liked was the opening theme—once we got over that, finally the guy could take off! And Parker was one of many who could do that so brilliantly. I'm trying to do the same thing *verbally*: take off on a theme so you become tangential and transcendent at the same time. If you could just *disorder the order of your thinking*: take a little bit of this and a little bit of that and see how things mix, then—! Like reading Escoffier, for example, on the preparation of some *haute cuisine* rabbit stew, while talking about chipmunks at the same time—

♦ **AJ: Like a Burroughsian cut-up.**

♦ KN: I wish there were a program to do *verbally* what some computers are capable of doing *musically*. There's a program, "M," that I play with: you put in a series of musical patterns and extrapolate all the variables you can think of. If you could program in the lyrics to the "Star Spangled Banner" you might end up with an American *Finnegans Wake*. But I like doing this through the mechanism of *reacting*—that's the glory of over-tracking; it's a *massage to the ephemeral,* if you will.

When I do my radio shows I sit in a room with all kinds of books around me, junk mail, the periodic tables—*anything* as stimuli—and I also play with rhythms verbally. When I re-did "The Days of the Week" as "Seven Ways of the Meek" (a kind of Joycean play on words) I changed the days to Dumb Day, Blues Day, Ends Day, Blurs Day, Cry Day, Shatter Day and Stun Day, figuring that a 7/5 beat would work out perfectly:

"Dumb Day comes and Quick-as-Snap
Fall apart begins
Mr Maybe-Not-So-Smart
Grins His silly grins."

Thus I created a structure that made it not only easier to write, but also easier to remember.

♦ **AJ: This hearkens back to the Japanese haiku structures which squeeze out poetry with philosophy so compactly—**

♦ KN: One of my favorite haiku is a translation of something called "A Net of Fireflies" in that 17-syllable situation they deal with. Dylan Thomas's "In my craft and sullen art" is written to a 7-beat rhythm:

"In my craft and sullen art
exercised in the still night
when only the moon rages . . ."

People don't think of the rhythm; when they hear this, it just "feels right." But—you can't be serious all the time . . . so you can deviate from those strict structures!

One thing I had fun doing on our radio show: we synthesized the sound of a fly. We recorded people who phoned in, and a dishwasher who was a fan of the show called me from the Catskills. I had the engineer add the fly sound, and the caller asked, "Is there a fly on your end of the phone?" "No." "Oh—he's here." "Hey, that's last year's fly." And we began to rap (in the sense of the word but without the incessant drums) about the nature of flies, where they go . . . and when it landed on my nose I stopped the sound-effect and began to get friendly with it: "Oh, you're a *shy* fly?"—that type of thing.

♦ **AJ: Back in the '50s it was pioneering to take sound effects like that and improvise—**

♦ KN: That started out with *musique concrète*. JOHN CAGE was in a different part of the forest from me, but he and MERCE CUNNINGHAM were beginning their relationship, and Cage came into town and listened to what we were doing. HARRY PARTCH also came by—he created special instruments in order to play his concepts, and was a marvelous character. In those days we did things like slow a clock down until it was 8 octaves below its normal sound, creating a strange tick-tock fugue, so we could play with the nature of the sound of time. With something like that going on in the background, you can frighten the hell out of yourself!

♦ **AJ: Who were some other influences in the '50s?**

♦ KN: It's always a special feeling when you read something and think, "Hey, this guy *has* it." I liked James Joyce, Faulkner, Orson Welles when he was starting out in the Mercury Theater, and Terry Southern who wrote *Dr Strangelove*. Nathanael West's *Miss Lonelyhearts* is great, and there's the other Nathaniel [Hawthorne]: *Rappaccini's Daughter*. I used to read all those on the air. I read Pauline Kael's review of a movie with William Burroughs in it, *Drugstore Cowboy,* and she's fantastic—one moment she's saying something *for* and the next minute she's saying something totally *against* it. It's almost as if the connective tissue or structure of the piece got disrupted—maybe by lunch, or something!

Jazz is: a flight of musical fantasy within *structure*. The part of jazz I never particularly liked was the opening theme—once we got over that, finally the guy could take off!

♦ *AJ: Can you talk more about time integration?*

♦ KN: The idea that you go into a room or a bar and think it's the most wonderful place you've ever been in. The second time you think, "What did I ever see in this place?" The place *has* changed, but there's something in yourself that has changed, too. And this overlapping, folding over of time is almost like a convolution of epiphanic moments, if you will. They combine in such a way that you become outside of yourself *inside* of yourself!

For example, I'll be half asleep thinking, "There must be a reason much bigger than *bang*" [inspired by reading, in the tub, a *Scientific American* article on the origins of the universe, like the big bang theory]. Then I think, "What can I rhyme with 'bang'? Hopefully, something outside of yin or yang." There must be a cause that needs no cause! So what you're doing here is eclectically jumping from the human-caused *cause* (which is of course what Saint Francis would harangue about, as well as Aristotle) to the uncaused cause, the unmoved mover. And movement from one time into the other is literary, involving little pieces of your memory. Maybe a series of minor strokes could create a kind of *reverse Alzheimer's,* where you remember flashes of what used to be!

Marcus Aurelius was a great writer about time. He believed there were 3 kinds of time: a time that's past (all your memories); a time that's your future (all your hopes and desires); and the "now" that you're in—and the now contains both the past and the future in a kind of *perpendicular to eternity* . . . a moving line that you can't reverse because time is irreversible.

I did a piece on *Triple Talk* called "noxt," which is an un-word I made up. Something that's noxt just happened a long time ago! "Now" is the fulcrum; noxt sits on one side and next on the other. Noxt is not in the dictionary of words, but it's in the dictionary of thinking . . .

♦ *V: You were one of the first people to critique TV*

when you recorded "The Vidiot" in '57—

♦ KN: [laughs] It would be great if you could do something like *image jazz,* which would keep all the power that the art director in each person's mind has—that radio has—and get asynchronous images that oscillate somewhere between a cloud formation and a fireplace. Actually, what I'd love to see done is a kind of real-time Walt Disney *Fantasia* in which each track of a multi-track would be assigned its own image and rhythm. It would be fantastic: you'd have "on" and "off" signals, squares and rectangles dancing around the rhythm of a speech where little fibrillating lines would dance to the synchronous pulse of the oscilloscope . . . to the bass line, or whatever—crickets, perhaps. As you know, crickets make that noise by rubbing their feet together; it's a way for males and females to get together. A cricket can interpret what another cricket's rubbing-legs-together means.

♦ *AJ: A lot of people don't seem to really think about the inner meanings of things.*

♦ KN: I think they do . . . but they don't verbalize it. I think that everybody does it. That's the nature of dreams—that's why you see a lot of people yawning. I think maybe I'm a frustrated scientist who didn't have the appropriate right- or left-brain intelligence. When I was a kid I used to time fireflies to see how long it took them to turn their little tails on, how long they stayed on, what relation that had to the temperature . . . I even enticed some flies once with some hamburger I put in the crevice of a coral rock so I could take pictures of them close-up (long before *Nova*) for my own little monster movies.

♦ *AJ: Maybe your sound experiments are your personal scientific unravelings of language and human nature—*

Ken Nordine's *Son of Word Jazz* with the Fred Katz Group, Dot Records.

♦ KN: I do an opening for the Chicago International Film Festival each year. This year we took an old alarm clock and my son, Kevin, who's a special effects cinematographer, got an endoscope, a tiny fiber-optics lens that doctors use for operations like taking cartilage out of the knees of wounded football players. Actually, this particular endoscope was invented to examine the movements of the gears in a clock. So, we're inside this clock, and magnified on the screen it looks like some unbelievable machine out of *Metropolis,* with the sound exaggerated, and I talk about how many days and nights there are in 25 years (it was the 25th anniversary of the film festival): how many hours, minutes and seconds in a quarter of a century. So, people were sitting in the dark watching this huge clock going *nine thousand,* etc . . .

Omni magazine put out a record with a piece by me on it, "Think a Thought," along with something by Ray Bradbury. This might be instrumental in showing you *where I've been when I used to be where I was!* I had this idea that a snapshot takes 1/60th of a second. It's a little moment that you take to the drugstore; you get it back and it's a little piece of your life. How many snapshots would you have if you had all the snapshots you could possibly take of your life? And of course 1/60th of a second is a gross slice of time, particularly now when we're dealing with computer nanoseconds. I've never seen a nanosecond, have you?

♦ *AJ: I don't think you can, even though we've lived through billions of 'em.*

♦ KN: Yes, they just slide right by . . . do you think we slide through *them,* or do they slide through *us?* It's probably a two-way street. I don't know if Shirley MacLaine is right on those things, though metempsychosis is a nice idea—

Concert Percussion for Orchestra, Mainstream Records. Album cover credits: album design: Burt Goldblatt.

♦ *AJ: Madame Psychosis?*

♦ KN: Metempsychosis—you know that word? I like unusual words.

♦ *AJ: You're always twisting language to produce revelation—*

♦ KN: Madame Psychosis—poor Shirley, I hope she doesn't take offense.

♦ *V: Reaching into "in"—that's kind of a theme of yours.*

♦ KN: The idea being that the minute you know where you are, you're lost. It's like: the truth is right in front of you when your back is turned. That's the nature of epiphanic moments—you know what it's all about for just a flash, and then you wonder: "Where did the light go?" Probably if it were "on" all the time, you couldn't see it.

My wife once had a party and I thought something was wrong. It took me about two hours to realize that every man she'd invited was named *John.*

♦ *AJ: That's a danger, too—trying to grab hold of it and keep it static.*

♦ KN: You can't. And I don't think you would want to if you could . . .

♦ *V: Have your views on "alienation" changed? I'm thinking about your piece, "Manned Space Capsule," in which the occupant reveals his feelings—*

♦ KN: I became a little angered by the idea that only big officials would have space capsules or time capsules. I liked to think that each person could have their own.

Are you familiar with the tattoo artist I wrote about who used slippery ink? He had a chemist develop an ink that would migrate across the surface of the skin into the nearest opening (there are seven of them) and then disappear inside the person . . . and come back digested, looking like Klee: "Hey—I wanted an *eagle;* what's *this?*" [disgusted] "Where's that tattoo artist? I'll fix him!" Metamorphosis.

♦ *AJ: Do you dream a lot?*

♦ KN: No. If I do, I don't remember them. Of course I'm sort of half-awake most of the time anyway . . .

There's all sorts of ideas out there, but you have to have *marketing* for them. Smoking—I did a whole thing on nicotine suppositories for a *House and Garden* mail order campaign. I can just see some wife exclaiming, "Hey, this would be *just the thing* for John!" That reminds me—my wife once had a party and I thought something was wrong. It took me about two hours to realize that every man she'd invited was named *John*. It was a very silly evening. She's threatening to have a "Mary" party now. She's strange . . .

♦ **V: How did you happen to record with people from the Grateful Dead?**

♦ KN: Several years ago I was invited to come out to the West Coast by Dan Healy, who's responsible for the Grateful Dead's transparent sound. At first I gave the usual excuses: "My wife is afraid to fly," "I can't—I'm being tattooed by a blind tattoo artist," etc. But I finally came out and recorded *Devout Catalyst* with them. It included some things I'd done before (from *Stare With Your Ears)* and some things I ad-libbed. The recording session started around 10:30 and finished at 6 PM—we ended up with 70 minutes of material.

♦ **V: This was mostly one take—**

♦ KN: One take, there were no over-dubs—nothing. Jerry Garcia asked, "Well, what do you want us to do?" and I said, "Well, find a happy groove—*you'll* know when it's happy. I'll jump in, and don't worry about the ending." It *was* improvising, but with a road map—I always like a road map. Actually, I think the best ad-libs are rehearsed!

♦ **V: You have a CD out—**

♦ KN: Rhino released *The Best of Word Jazz,* Vol 1. They leased the masters from MCA. Dot Records was sold to Gulf & Western, then Dot was sold to MCA and MCA was sold to a Japanese corporation who now owns the masters . . . There are charlatans in the recording business, and there were a lot of 'em in the '50s. And they still are there because there's so much money involved—when there's a lot of money, you can get stung by some pretty sharp bees! Back in the late '50s someone decided Dot Records would get my publishing. I got a letter from Opryland [music publisher] telling me, " 'What Time Is It?' is not yours; it was written by Fred Katz."

I called up Fred Katz and a woman answered and said, "Fred Katz's wife died a half hour ago." I said, "Oh . . . I'll call back next week." I heard Fred in the background asking, "Who's calling?" and the woman said, "It's Ken Nordine." He got on the phone, and I said, "I'm sorry; I'll call you back," and he said, "No, no, she was expected to die anyway." I said, "I know that you wrote the *music* for 'What Time Is It?' but I wrote the words." He said, "Yeah, I haven't gotten any money for that either. Write a letter to that lawyer." A bit later the guy at Opryland said, "Yes, you *did* write the words to that after all," and sent me a check for $14! [laughs] Fred Katz and I each got $14, and it cost about $400 to send the legal letter. Intellectual property is going to be the next big legal battleground: "What *is* a thought? What is an *original* thought?"

I write in my sleep—I don't sleep, I kinda half sleep. It's idiotic. And it's very difficult to write without pen and paper. So I'll repeat something over and over until it gets imprinted in my head; for example, last night I

Ken Nordine's *Next!*, Dot Records.

came up with: "A kind of cry I sometimes hear/the like of which is very near/the dark of things that once were bright/so high in hope, so out-of-sight/the fool in me talks in his sleep/of promises I never keep/of vows I make and then forget/allegiances that you would bet/would have to last a lifetime long/they don't . . . the chemistry goes wrong." That's as far as I got—then I thought, "Hey, I better write this down before it fades out!"

I actually get caught up in rhythms of language. What I did there was a four-beat kind of thing; it's very easy. Words in the form of a lyric are much easier to remember. For example, I wrote something that I used for the back of an album: "I've said my say in bits of time/within the strict of simple rhyme/upon a stage of dancing words/as vagrant as the flight of birds/each syllable you hear me say/in zigs and zags is on its way/I'd say up to the highest court/where sits the judge of long and short/who I can tell, that if he's there/just how I feel in trembling air . . ." It's so much easier to remember this because it's musical—I can remember the words because of the lyric quality to them.

One of my favorite writers is Wallace Stevens. He wrote a poem in which the phrase "The Only Emperor is the Emperor of Ice Cream" hit me. I liked it so much I did a theme and variation on that called "The Roller of Big Cigars." People do things like that with jazz; why not with poetry?

♦ **V: You lived through the '50s; do you think things are worse than they were during the McCarthy years?**

♦ KN: Well, you'd think they'd get tired of playing the same political games, the same rhetoric, the same buttons they're pushing. During the last campaign I heard something about "They're more for the Waltons than the Simpsons." [laughs] When you have people like

Ken Nordine's *How Are Things In Your Town?*, Blue Thumb Records, Inc. Album cover credits: album photography & design: Barry Feinstein & Tom Wilkes for Camouflage Productions.

Falwell and Pat Robertson around—*they* should be used to punish people, like, "We'll punish Milken for stealing 500 million dollars by making him live with them for a year while they talk 'family values' to him!" [imitates Milken protesting:] "No no no—don't do *that!*" Right underneath those "family values" is the *violence* that all "righteous" systems depend on: [low, menacing voice] "You're gonna do it *my* way."

♦ **V: Have you written any books?**

♦ KN: I always admire when somebody can use the language, which is so inexact in many ways, and torture it into some beautiful statement, so you can say, "Gee, I wish I'd written that." I've been working on this slowpoke book, a sort of *Image Jazz*, which I'm illustrating. Did I mention psychosomatic microscopy? I made some strange, abstruse doodles on the computer and they turned out to be absolutely beautiful abstractions—through no fault of mine, just through the grace of the computer's ability. They look like cross-sections of something you might see in *Scientific American:* a cancer virus in the brain of a nervous mouse . . . something that might have been caused by a contested tax return! I like psychosomatic illnesses—they are brilliantly imaginary: "My problem is: I got no problem!" The only one that bothers me is coming to terms with death: that's a drag—

♦ **V: Have you?**

♦ KN: If I had had anything to do with creating human beings, I would have left that out. All these people (what Dylan Thomas refers to as "the towering dead") are involved in a reverse mathematical progression: 2,4,8,16,32 . . . in 500 years over a million people are involved as your ancestors. What an inverted pyramid of protoplasm had to go before . . . to create who *you* are!

From outer space, when "they" look down at the earth, all they see is a brilliant blue sky and all the rest that's going on in the water and land masses, but they don't see human beings . . . just as when we walk through the scrub area of a meadow, we don't see the unbelievable insects doing their little jobs—gnats, what we refer to in the North woods as the "no-see-ums": the bugs that bite you that you don't see because they're so tiny.

Today I was thinking of the difference between "ordinary" and "extraordinary.": what an unbelievable leap that is—how *gross*. There should be all sorts of *shades* going from "ordinary" to "extraordinary"; we should somehow divide that up verbally: "This, here, is extra-extra-extraordinary to the power of ten."

♦ *V: Maybe if we were always at a peak of alertness, nothing would be truly "ordinary"—*

♦ KN: I think what creates "ordinary" is, again, the fact that we categorize things out of existence ("Oh, I know what *that* is") and then we don't have to really look at it. If we really were to see everything the way it is, it might be too much input: "Wait a minute; take it *away!*" I think of the computer that remembers dates and times, and how incapable we are of doing that. If I think of "August 12, 1989," I go, "Migod, I don't remember anything about that day." But the *computer* did; and I called it up and realized I had written something that startled me—that leapt out at me: "Did *I* write that? I guess I did."

One of the annoying qualities of "progress" is that you always feel that the latest thing you've done is the best thing you've done—that things get better and better, or: "Oh, that's an *old* newspaper." But if time were more reversible—well, we already went into that Marcus Aurelius business about time past and time future all being part of time now: "Noxt." Of course, if you start playing with the language too much, people say, "Wait a minute!" It's amazing how conservative most people are.

♦ *V: Well, you're certainly trying not to be—*

♦ KN: I tell you something you could do: get yourself a hundred brand-new one-dollar bills. Cut yourself a piece of cardboard the same size. Get some mucilage and then you can create a tablet of one-dollar bills! Then go into your local bar and say, "I'd like to order a beer," and rip off several bills in succession. And the larger the sum—!

♦ *V: They'd probably call the police on you—*

♦ KN: It is strange how comfortably conservative we all are—even the farthest-out people. If you touch the right button, you discover that underneath the apparent eccentricity there beats a very straight heart.

♦ *V: It's important to work against that stereotype that to be creative, you have to be a flaky drug-taker—*

♦ KN: That's true; in fact, the highest form of "high" is asceticism, I'm sure. I get very nervous sometimes when I remember some of my yesterdays: "Ken, you were out of control then; you shouldn't have been there. You didn't know where you were." (This was a long time ago.) I've actually got to the point where I don't eat meat (I have a little fish now and then), I eat a lot of stir-fries; no booze, no smoking, and I actually feel a lot better for it: closer to what's really going on. Now I get high on asceticism.

♦ **V: But you always "tripped out" with your amazing word experiments—**

♦ KN: It's comparable to working on a puzzle where the pieces are constantly changing their shape! Is it any wonder I make mistakes? It's very difficult to get mad at anybody (unless they're zealots, like in Yugoslavia—*they* must have something wrong in their lower brain). I would think that by now, the inventors of pharmacopoeia would have come up with *some* way to protect us from politicians . . . some political sedative, so they wouldn't find it so necessary to say, "I know *exactly* what you should be doing with your life."

The politicians probably want the pharmacists to come up with some pill to put in the water supply: "This will make you want to get up really early and work your ass off! You'll have your nose to the grindstone (sure, it'll be a bloody nose) and then we'll really compete in the world. Globally we'll get bigger and bigger: export, export, export!" ("But the imports cost so much!") "Don't talk about that!" [laughs]

♦ **V: Somebody wrote a book putting forth the idea that instead of being called homo sapiens (or homo faber or homo ludens), humans should be called "homo artisticus"—**

♦ KN: There's no question that there's an art instinct in everyone. My mother, for example, was a very good businesswoman who showed no inclination toward art until she was 55. Then she started to sculpt, and

Life magazine presents the original musical score from *MAG* with Ken Nordine's voice.

the reason she did was: she had hired someone to do a bust of my menopausal younger sister, and when it was finished she said, "That's awful! I could do better than that!" She got some clay and began to poke around at it. My father chided her a bit, but that didn't bother her. She had a little chisel and hammer and was working with marble and started winning all kinds of awards. Now I have these things in my home which are the essence of what my mother was: Moses and the tablets, little peasant women . . .

♦ **V: She was religious—**

♦ KN: She was a still-water Baptist. Every six weeks the minister would have baptisms in this big tank, and he wore thigh-high wading boots—which struck me as totally unfair: the "faithful" who were being baptized were getting totally soaked, while he stayed dry. So I sneaked into his study and cut a little hole in the end of his boot. At the next baptism I watched closely, and could *see* the christian anger arise in his reddening face. He walked out with a big boot full of water and when he got to his study, he released a small flood! He never knew who *got* him. You can see that the church has been a problem for me all along—

♦ **V: As well it should. We're definitely anti-clerical—**

♦ KN: Santayana said, "There is no god, and Mary is his mother." [laughs] A lot of people are religious as an insurance policy, or for high holidays like christmas, easter, weddings and funerals. It's a social thing, really. When you look at somebody like Falwell (or Swaggert's) face, you wonder at . . . not so much their peculiar grotesque bent, if you will, but the *need* of the people who listen to them and dote on what they say. I don't know where this comes from. Maybe people are so scared to death of death that they really can't think

love words

Ken Nordine speaks lyrically of love

Ken Nordine's *Love Words*, with the Fred Katz jazz group, Dot Records.

self white. I called 911 and said, "There's a guy who's painted himself white in my yard," and a couple of unmarked cop cars show up: "Come on, Nordine, are you pulling our leg?" I said, "No, no," and we go to the north side of my house and here's this empty bucket and a big area where he'd washed himself with this white paint—his pants were there, too. They asked, "Where'd he go?" and I said, "I think he went up this alley." So they got on the radio and said, "The guy who painted himself white is heading north, and we've got his pants." [!] Now . . . if I were to *think* of something like that, people would say, "Man, you are really sick." [laughs]

about it; they have to have somebody say, "Oh, you're going to live forever . . . you're going to be okay, don't worry—just send me some money!"

Get people in a huge tent—hundreds, thousands of 'em—and have a huge cash register as the altar, and have Bargain Night. A spotlight picks somebody out of the audience: [booming voice] "You there, we know what you've been up to. But tonight it'll only cost you $39.95 to atone for your misdeeds." A long stick with an offering plate extends in front of the person: "Only $39.95? Okay, okay!" and the spotlight goes off and zaps somebody else . . . How about that Oregon guru with all the Rolls-Royces—somebody had to say, "I think you *should* have lots of Rolls-Royces. Not one— lots of 'em!"

It's pretty hard for me to *write* funny when so many funny things are happening. Our gardener is a 60-year-old Vietnamese man who recently emigrated here, and somehow my wife communicates with him even though he doesn't speak English and she doesn't speak Vietnamese. I was thinking of getting her an English-Vietnamese dictionary so she can translate, "Pick up the papers," or "Get rid of the whisky bottles on the terrace." One morning I was watching him come into the back yard, and from the north side of the house this *apparition* slowly walked by, past the gardener, out of my yard into the alley. I thought it was Marcel Marceau, because this person was totally white: head, face, arms—it was a guy in shorts who'd painted him-

So from the standpoint of a writer, what I write about is not things like that but more about verbal puzzles. I'll be lying in bed thinking, "What am I going to do with this little phrase? Hmm . . ." It's strange how when you're half-awake or half-asleep, it all becomes very *clear,* because there's nothing to interrupt your line of thinking. That's how "I've said my say/in bits of time" came about, or "I never thought in my wildest . . ." (that's the opening line; it's a nice cliche—what can I do to play with that?): "I never thought in my wildest/that I would be king of the hill/high in my strange upper limbo/with nothing but time left to fill/nervous and jerky this king is/uneasily wearing the crown/who can say when you're in solid?/ascendancy can bring you down/I never knew Humpty-Dumpty/the fat guy who fell off the wall . . ." Those are all 8-beat lines. That's how it works: you drift in and out of meditation, or if you will: *fixation.*

If we could take the images out of our heads and have 'em go directly to high-definition digital tape, that could produce some pretty wild visions. Can you visualize eidetically—see people with your eyes closed, or remember how your father looks? Some people can do that, but I can't.

◆ **V: But you work primarily in a word/sound medium, anyway—**

◆ KN: Lines like "Ephemeral, is what it was/I don't know why, don't know who does" perhaps come from too much reading of Edgar Allan Poe, or Fitzgerald's

"The Rubaiyat of Omar Khayyam": "I sometimes think there never grows so red a rose as where some buried Caesar bled"—wonderful lines that just *flow*. With that kind of music in the language . . . when language becomes more musical, it's *forced* to have more meaning. Or at least it *seems* to have more meaning than words in a prosaic style. And music, to me, is the most beautiful thing that man creates—it can tear you apart.

I'll read more: "Each moment came and then it went/My feeling is: the time was spent/The only way it could've been . . ." I'm someone who wakes up in the middle of the night, startled by the fact that he's been dreaming about being lost in the wrong part of town (which is pretty dangerous, if you think about it).

Here's part of "Quatrains Of Thought": "Wonder where I'm going, don't know where I've been/On my way to somewhere, hope they let me in . . ./Just ahead is hind-sight, fill the empty eye/Used to go to Whimsey, every chance I had/Crazy flights of fancy, whimsically went mad/Played with silly notion, made me up new rules/Me the King of Whimsdom, fooling crowds of fools."

◆ **V: Philosophy as entertainment—**

◆ KN: I think there should be *more* to entertainment. The blues arose as a cry of pain. I wrote "Inchoate Blues" which is a little different from "normal" blues: " . . . Tearducts are clogged up, cheeks have gone dry/Eyeballs are hurting, wish I could cry/Crying won't help much, eyelids get red/Tongue keeps on saying stuff that's been said/Story of endless, left us no clues/Only the lonely, inchoate blues/Maybe I've done it, made myself clear/Really don't think so, not even near/Could be the trouble is all in the mind/Imagine a seeker, partially blind/Eight rearview mirrors, seven plus one/My inchoate blues will never be done."

I did an MTV thing called "Charley Bing-Bang" based on a voice-over announcer who jumped off his building. I'd been with him a couple weeks before it happened: "Did he have a heart attack?" "No, he jumped." That's the ultimate form of self-criticism! To get him out of my system, I wrote a blues called "Charley Bing-Bang"—changed his name to protect the widow. I recited this in a rugby shirt using a bullhorn in a local cemetery which has some fancy mausoleums—I wanted to put television antennas on top of them, but you never have enough time to do what you really want to do. Anyway, in front of this rock track I'm reciting, "Charley Bing-Bang near the end/Didn't have a single friend/Couldn't reach him from outside/Died a silly suicide." This is true: "Took his coat off on the ledge/Felt the wind-chill's cutting edge" (this was in January) "Down the dizzy far below/Drifting heavy hills of snow/Arms akimbo, somersault/Criticism was his fault/Hated all his yesterdays/Tried before in different ways/See him do the Fall of Man/Wonder how it all began/Charley Bing Bang near the end/Didn't have a single friend/Couldn't reach him from outside/

Died a silly suicide." And unbeknownst to him, he'd just won the Miller Lite account and the agency was really angry he wasn't around!

◆ **V: It was the darkness just before dawn, only he succumbed to the darkness—**

◆ KN: That's the way it is.

◆ **V: Was there ever a point in your life where you had to "cross the Rubicon" . . . make some moral or ethical decision that—**

◆ KN: Well, I may have chickened out at certain moments of my life. A long time ago back in '58 when "they" wanted me to move to Hollywood, a guy named George Grief (that seems like a strange name for a guy whose first name was George) had a big nightclub there. He wanted to sign me, and the son of the guy who wrote "Sunny Side of the Street" said to me, "You should go straight, Ken." At that time, I didn't know I was crooked! But they felt I should become "legitimate" . . . they felt I was illegitimate, possibly because I'd written things like, "I used to think my right hand was uglier than my left" (was this some kind of masturbating guilt complex?).

◆ **V: And they offered a lot of money—**

◆ KN: Oh yeah, there were all sorts of lures. But I felt that if I did that, I would have destroyed my marriage, my family would have fallen apart—just knowing my own proclivities to get carried away . . . I decided to stay in Chicago, and of course that puzzled a lot of people. I think they *like* the fact that someone like John Belushi (who had a lot of energy and talent) goes out there and destroys himself; they think that's wonderful. I think that's sad.

◆ **V: There are people who seem to need constant approval—**

◆ KN: Maybe they should have a little box with a

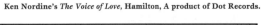
Ken Nordine's *The Voice of Love*, Hamilton, A product of Dot Records.

Teddy Phillips & His Orchestra's *Concert in the Sky*, Decca Records.
Ken Nordine, Narrator with The Jack Halloran Choir.

synthesized applause recording on a chip inside, so if they come up with something like "Never before in the wealth of my days/Did I wake in the middle of time . . ." they can press a button and hear, "Great!'" [applause] "That was brilliant!" . . . Golfers could have a portable version, so whenever they miss an easy hole-in-one they can press a button and hear a groan: "Ohh-hh . . ." But—your reward is the writing of the line itself, not the applause.

♦ **V: One of the problems we always think about is: How do you keep evolving and not stagnating? Because if you achieve success doing something, then people want you to keep on doing that, because they think it'll keep the money coming in—**

♦ KN: They *know* it. My heart goes out to musicians like Neil Diamond who do those tours—it's a lot of work, and it's a big business.

♦ **V: And Neil Diamond has to sing those same songs he wrote twenty years ago—**

♦ KN: That would drive me right up the wall! My idea of a play would be to have three characters on a stage, and then have three people in the audience with wireless mikes telling them what to do. We'd create situations, and they would revolt: "I won't do it!" Then they would go into the audience and force us onstage and tell *us* what to do.

Again, the reason there's so many charlatans in the record business is because there's so much money involved. Like I said, people buy what they buy to prove they're human beings: "Is that what I'm supposed to buy? Okay, I'll buy it. Now I belong." A couple years ago I saw something sad: a girl had "come of age" and was giving away all her teenage records that were so important to her, because now she was into *another* plane of music. It was like giving her yesterday away.

♦ **V: And now MTV has subtracted the role of the visual imagination in pop music—**

♦ KN: If only there could be images which were non-competitive . . . that would aid and abet the imagination each one of us has, like have a real-time *Fantasia* that would not be directing you to see what you're *supposed* to see. TV shows you what an image means. TV commercials show you the product and what it does—they give you lessons on how to drink. There's so much money involved in keeping a society going, that when the consumer confidence level goes down . . . well, we can hardly wait 'til it goes up again: "Look at 'em, they're *running* into the showroom. They're not even kicking the tires; they're just throwing their money at the car salesmen! They're building houses like crazy again; there's going to be a monorail soon—we're going to be so much happier then!" That's what it's all about: if they're not selling something, they're in serious trouble.

♦ **V: Consume, instead of developing creativity or friendships—**

♦ KN: I have a few friends here and there that I can really sit down and wail with. In one sense it's best to become your own best friend . . . then you can even lie to yourself! [laughs] One of the things that bothers me about show business is: I would much rather do what I do very *simply,* without having to be on roller-skates or a teeter-totter—

♦ **V: You mean without gimmickry—**

♦ KN: At one time I *did* have a people-mobile made that would seat four people; it was like a motorized Calder mobile with four seats, and I had it worked out so it would balance itself automatically if you had a 296-pound man on one side and a 96-pound girl on the other. The idea was to film 10-minute events on this, because that was how long a reel of film would last. You could get four sweet octogenarian ladies talking about their earliest memories; then four little girls giggling and having a wonderful time on this people-mobile. Shuffle the deck: maybe have four insurance-adjustors wearing whiplash collars, then a Beethoven string quartet. You could have this mobile in a theater-in-the-round, and maybe have the bartender serving pharmaceutical drinks so everybody could focus in on the conversations.

♦ **V: . . . Going back to the Word Jazz recording sessions, how did you get the freedom to do seemingly anything you wanted to do?**

♦ KN: I was working with Bill Putnam who started Universal Recording here before he went to the West Coast. He was a "with-it" engineer in terms of experimenting with pop sound, and he developed the idea of the echo chamber. He used it for the HARMONICATS in "Peg o' My Heart" . . . he used the elevator shaft in the civic opera building to get that sense of time delay and create an echo effect. Bill and I and Jim Cunningham, an engineer, would spend all kinds of time playing with *musique concrète* . . . manipulating tape to get strange, weird effects. Today that has the high-class name of "sound design."

We were just fooling around, cutting up tape and pasting it back together without worrying about any sequence, just to hear how it would sound—it was serendipitous, totally random selection. By slowing down tapes you could get some strange and weird effects, some of which I used in an ill-fated thing I did with Billy Friedkin: *The Exorcist.* I had to sue them to get my money. That's a movie that should have been a cartoon; what an idea: you get a little Catholic girl just before the time she's starting to menstruate, and turn her into a demon and tie it into the church. So it's got sex and violence and "Great, we'll make a lot of money with this! The nuns will hate it, but . . ." There was a fight between Blatty, who wrote the book, and Friedkin, and all I wanted was the money they owed me. They wanted to do it on the West Coast but I said, "No, I'm doing it here as we agreed." I even bought the equipment: a motion-picture projector that would run the tape recorder synchronously.

♦ *V: You were supposed to do the soundtrack?*

♦ KN: Yeah. In fact, they flew me to Georgetown to train Linda Blair in speaking backwards; "bullshit" backwards is "tea-sloob." I said, "Why don't you just run the film backwards?" But that wouldn't have been as goofy and mind-twisting. I watched the filming in Georgetown: the stuntman jumping out of the window when the devil gets inside, and it's fantastic, the lengths to which they'll go. When Linda Blair does that scene where her head spins around and around, they had an entire room balanced on a bowling ball so they could rock the entire room.

When I saw the movie (just to see how much they'd used of what I'd done), I was surprised that with all

Ken Nordine's *Colors*, Philips, Mercury Record Corp.

the gasps of horror, there were shrieks of delightful laughter! Could it be this was a comedy and I didn't realize it? That was an epiphanal moment; I realized, "I don't think I'll be doing much more of this kind of thing. *Screw* this!" It was a waste of my time.

♦ *V: Back to those* Word Jazz *recording sessions: you could do anything you wanted?*

When you have people like Falwell and Pat Robertson around—*they* should be used to punish people, like, "We'll punish Milken for stealing 500 million dollars by making him live with them for a year while they talk 'family values' to him!" Right underneath those "family values" is the *violence* that all "righteous" systems depend on: "You're gonna do it *my* way."

♦ KN: Most of the time when you're making money with your voice, you're *told* what to do—the script is written: "Talk louder, talk faster, be more persuasive, underline this word." When I started out I did all sorts of things; I'd come off a hangover and be in a recording studio with some cracker from the South, a funeral director with a promotional film titled *New Ways to Embalm.* I'd be watching this awful movie thinking, "Ohmigod—I have to describe what's going on here?" You're asked to do all kinds of things, and you're directed how to do it.

But when it comes to doing something that I wanted to do myself—that was different. I had always loved memorizing poetry—I memorized the entire Omar Khayyam, page after page of T.S. Eliot, all sorts of things out of James Joyce (so much so that I call him "Jimmy" now) . . . After memorizing so much for the love of the sound of the thing, I thought, "I'm going to make some of my own—then I'm not answerable to anybody because I'm doing it for myself."

For example, even the radio shows I put out—most of the NPR radio shows are done with grants. They ask, "Well, what are you going to do?" and you say, "I'm going to do this, that, and the other," and they decide if they're going to give you the money, depending on what it is. So I say, "I'm going to do a show on which I talk to myself about the problem of tying knots—especially knots that I don't know how to tie too well." "Well, what's its social value?" Or, "I'm going to talk about bury-it-yourself time capsules." "*What?*" Right away you can see somebody in Washington, D.C. going, "Well, we don't think this is exact-

ly appropriate . . ." Or if I want to say something like "Here we are inside of *is*/She with hers and he with his," then—! Or maybe I'll tell a silly joke: "A pig was in a poke," and then "pork chops dancing overhead/ ribs are dressed in vivid red/knuckles pickled to your taste." This is a kind of Ode to Terpsichore, goddess of hickory, and you can hear that it isn't quite normal— whatever the hell *that* is. So the best thing to do is to buy the uplink time, put the thing out yourself, and then it's exactly as you would have it be. And you don't have to petition. I'm a poor petitioner.

♦ *V: That's good, because then you're forced to do exactly what you want to do—*

♦ KN: Then when it's finished you say, "Hey—that was fun; I'll do something else now." And you only have to do it as long as it doesn't bore you; you can say, "Hey, that was good for three minutes, but let's not do *that* any longer."

♦ *V: Can you tell me about Fred Katz? I like a lot of his soundtracks—*

♦ KN: You know what he's doing now—he's a professor of anthropology, just outside of Hollywood. He used to be with Chico Hamilton's group playing the cello on tour, and they played a club in Chicago. I met Freddie and he came and wrote all the things for my very first album in my living room here. Some of it was done with Jim Cunningham; on "Hunger Is From" he added a bright, happy, joyous jazz track as I was raiding the refrigerator in the middle of the night. He actually did the music for "Flibberty Jib" which is very strange—that's the thing that Levi's used for "The stranger that comes into town" wearing Levi's, which made a lot of money for the agency, and I made some money, too. Somebody might say that was a subver-

Ken Nordine's *Stare With Your Ears,* Snail Records. Album cover credit: front cover art: Jim Dowlen.

sion, but I don't know . . . the ending was different: everybody was happy at the end.

In another case, I wrote a talking song for my dog, a golden retriever, "Scratch," which is a great name, by the way; it can mean many things. "Scratch, you old devil, I swear you can talk/Go get your necktie, it's time for your walk/Where will you take me? Guess god only knows/Somewhere inside of where yesterday

I was thinking of the difference between "ordinary" and "extraordinary.": what an unbelievable leap that is—how *gross*. There should be all sorts of *shades* going from "ordinary" to "extraordinary."

goes/We're both getting closer, the farther we go/Deep in the shallow of, 'What do we know?' " The agency said, "Hey, take the trademark for a walk." Chris Blum, who was the art director, had these pod-people (like in *Invasion of the Body Snatchers)* floating horizontally in leotards (like in a swimming dream), a miner was mining for gold in the gutter, and I was walking the trademark with a leash through this fantasy . . . What is that saying: "You have to serve god and mammon at the same time"?

I wish you could get streetwalkers—happy hookers—doing the weather forecasts, being obviously flirtatious to the camera like they're working on a john: "Isn't this weather *something*—what would *you* like to do on a night like this?" [laughs]

♦ *V: I love these liner notes where Fred Katz is saying, "I met Ken Nordine . . . a few hours and 37 cups of coffee later, we were still discussing Spinoza, Buddha, Charlie Parker, Freud, and Word Jazz again." This is real life, and any "art" produced is a by-product.*

♦ KN: All that was happening here. Parker was playing on the South Side, and Clifford Brown, Max Roach, and I saw them "live" . . . Lenny Bruce was around, and I got to know him pretty well. He was outrageous. What happened to him: he was working a place called the Liberty Inn where a lot of strippers were, and he was the emcee. Then he became more important than the strippers, and the coppers would follow him around waiting to bust him for something like talking against the Catholic church: "Aw, you can't say that." We appeared together at the Cloister Inn and he did a slide show of just one unbelievably raucous picture after another, showing these strange, wonderfully freakish women he loved so much. He would put strange things together in such a way that it would *have* to violate the "establishment's" sense of propriety. They tried everything; they tried to tempt him with movie contracts to come out to Hollywood and "straighten out"—

♦ *V: Can you describe the slides more explicitly? Were they like photos of people on the toilet—taboo subjects?*

♦ KN: Definitely. He'd have a priest with a topless girl who had a big snake around her neck; he was always looking for strange things to combine in pictures that he knew would be a red flag he could wave in the face of . . . Mort Sahl would get hung up in trying to make fun of all the politicos, but Bruce was making fun of religion, sex—*everything* was fair game for him. He was much sharper and angrier. He could be a lot of fun, but he kinda got carried away and wound up with an overdose.

♦ *V: We need people like that **not** to overdose—*

♦ KN: Well, the only thing they have to do is watch that they don't take themselves too seriously. Or maybe they get to the point where they find it difficult to really talk with other people—they can talk, but only on a "performance" level. That happened to Janis Joplin; it probably happened to Charlie Parker.

Parker had an unbelievable musical intelligence; some of the things he was playing on top of the chord changes—it's impossible to imagine how he came up with them. You'd be in a smoky little room and—

♦ *V: I'll bet there weren't too many white people there—*

♦ KN: Surprisingly, there were quite a few, because it was near the University of Chicago. Although you're right—there were some joints we went to that were . . . I remember hearing Helen Merrill, when her album *What's New* came out. She was in a little joint near 43rd Street that was an out-and-out black jazz joint—great music, but no white people were around except Helen and some of my pals—Dr Zitter and I went there. Zitter has a very quick wit; he's a solid-state physicist at the University of Southern Illinois.

♦ *V: You got to see Clifford Brown? He died at the age of 26—*

♦ KN: Yeah, in an automobile accident. He and Max Roach were doing some beautiful things, way ahead of what was happening. Sonny Stitt used to play here a lot too, and I got to know him pretty well. He would play all sorts of filigrees—never the same.

♦ *V: I saw Sonny Stitt play these really long, complicated sax lines—*

♦ KN: He could get all tangled up, almost like he was forgetting where he was—only he wasn't. He would turn it around in strange, wonderful ways. Another guy who was around Chicago a lot was Lord Buckley, the finger-popping daddy, the hipster's flipster. He hung out at the Gate of Horn, the place that Al Grossman had . . . Bob Dylan played there when he was just starting out.

Let me read an excerpt from "Mr Slick": "Mr Slick as smooth as snake/sliding on a belly-ache/slipping through some awful stuff/never having quite enough/think he'd tire, just get bored/matadors too often gored/see the bull for what it is/catch on quick that that's the biz/but Slick, he never tires/he can pull the damndest wires/what's been done he'll once more try/knowing what the people buy/remake after remake make/causing him his belly-ache/titillations done and done/circles round which runners run/on your mark, get set, let's go/time to do the same old show . . ."

One of the things that happens when I get into writing lyrics is: it becomes a kind of monologue mirror: *this* leads to *that,* and it begins to write itself. It's not automatic writing, but it seems to "make sense" to go the way it's going.

Let me end by reading this: "No way to keep what can't be kept/What little grip you think you had/Now starts to slip just out of reach/Or so you think, you're on the edge/Some awesome brink of what they call/That's it, my friend, you've made it/To the other end . . ./Oblivion, please don't scoff/at those of us who fall apart/Inside this trap we bait with art/The bait is there, make no mistake/As anodyne for you to take/Be one of us, you could become/A different kind of drumming drum/A kind of why for all to hear/With echoes in your inner ear/Like miracles, each come and go . . ./Go do the thing you have to do/Then wake me up, I'd like to, too."

ORDERING INFORMATION

Candi Strecker is the publisher of *Sidney Suppey's Quarterly and Confused Pet Monthly,* an eclectic 'zine about her personal obsessions including obscure music, TV preachers and thrift-store discoveries, and *It's A Wonderful Lifestyle,* a pop-culture history of the 1970s in 'zine form. Candi lives with her husband, Matthew Householder, whose hobby is restoring beautiful '50s portable radios and '70s 8-track players—a few are for sale. For back issues of Candi's publications and inquiries about 8-track players write 590 Lisbon St, San Francisco CA 94112.

♦ *VALE: You have a Panasonic 8-track player—*
♦ CANDI STRECKER: My husband collects and deals in vintage radios and 8-track players. One of my favorites is a Panasonic 8-track player from the '70s shaped like a dynamite detonator—you push down the handle to change the tracks. This has a somewhat negative connotation, like: "I'm a teenager and I hate my life—*boom!*"

We're totally immersed in that flea market and thrift store lifestyle where anthropologically you're sifting through cultural discards. These Panasonic 8-track players came in red, yellow and blue, and there was also a clear plastic model where you could see the innards. Now is a good time to buy 8-track players and tapes—they have *no value* whatsoever. And some very unlikely recordings came out on 8-track—

♦ *V: Like Iggy Pop's* Metallic KO *[with the lyrics, "Butt-fuckers trying to rule my world!"] and Lou Reed's* Metal Machine Music . . . *You're one of the few female record collectors I've met; why aren't there more?*

♦ CS: That's a good question, and one that's baffled me all my life. I've been a comic book collector since the sixth grade, and that's a very "male" hobby. Actually, most of the things I like tend to be things that guys like. I'm fascinated by old cars from the '50s and '60s, though I don't own any—yet. And, I'm much more interested in collecting records than my husband is.

♦ *V: In your publication, you printed an article on Martin Denny—*

♦ CS: But that appeared after *you* wrote about him in the *Industrial Culture Handbook.* How did you discover Martin Denny?

♦ *V: Through Genesis P-Orridge. In the '70s an L.A. correspondence-artist named Skot Armst sent him a pile of Martin Denny albums.*

S: That seems very likely: starting with *one* person, it spread through an international network and returned home.

♦ *V: So how did you start going to thrift stores?*

♦ CS: My folks always poked around in antique shops—maybe I picked it up from them. In the early '70s when I went to college, there was already a consciousness about dressing in Pointer Sisters '40s outfits. I don't collect clothes anymore, but I have cupboards full of vintage dishes—if you ever do *Incredibly Strange Dishes,* give me a call! In the course of looking for dishes, other things started to catch my eye—books, records, paint-by-number paintings, and all sorts of objects that are perfect artifacts of the period when they were made. I guess that's my Primrose Path.

I have a Master's Degree as a librarian, but that line of work never agreed with me. I also have a B.A. in American studies, and I took a lot of anthropology courses which fundamentally altered my way of looking at the world. My husband and I live really cheaply;

we've worked that down to a fine art. We don't have ambitions to own a lot of high-status material things. Instead, we get a million dollars worth of thrills and fascination every weekend from spending a couple bucks on odd things that turn up at flea markets!

♦ *V: Where did you grow up?*

♦ CS: Massillon, Ohio. I went to Kent State during the DEVO years when PERE UBU and other groups were playing there live. I saw Devo before they put out records, and that changed my life! I already liked KRAFTWERK, especially *Autobahn,* recorded in 1974 when they were still hippies. That has the sounds of a car traveling on the autobahn, and we used to play it for acidhead friends when they were tripping. It had car horns and the sound of cars passing by in stereo, and people would fall to the floor to avoid being hit!

♦ *V: So you started collecting records back then—*

♦ CS: I'm still not sure I'm "collecting" now; "accumulating" would be a better term! I moved to San Francisco in the early '80s and after I got bitten by the Martin Denny bug I started buying cheap records *en masse* because the covers had appealing images. Besides, fifty cents is a small investment. Soon they began overflowing the shelves.

I've always had a taste for novelty music; when I was a kid my dad played a lot of Spike Jones records. Recently I started collecting oddball or novelty '70s disco records, like "Disco Lucy," based on the theme from the *I Love Lucy Show,* and disco cover versions of songs like "Baby Face" and Beethoven's Fifth. These weren't obscure songs, either—all three were Top-40 pop hits!

♦ *V: You have a beautiful Emerson TV set from the '50s—*

♦ CS: —that marginally plays. Any vintage electronics appeals to my husband. He's even started collecting antique personal computers—which is pretty scary. I

Photo: Olivier Robert

guess now they're potential "collectibles." [laughs] The early '80s was thousands of years ago in computer time.

♦ *V: How did you get interested in the '70s?*

♦ CS: Back in '86 BAM magazine did an 8-page feature jokingly titled, "Remember the Seventies?" It was written from a musical standpoint, with questions like: "Remember Black Oak Arkansas? Remember Disco? Remember David Cassidy as a teen idol?" I looked at it and thought, "Gee, I could do better than that." So I started keeping a list in my notebook, and every time I thought of something '70s, I'd write it down. At first I thought that if I really padded it out, I'd have enough '70s material for a 16-page issue. Instead, I've filled

Musically Mad, Mis-Led by Bernie Green with the Stereo Mad-Men,
© 1959 RCA Victor.
Album cover credits: portrait of Alfred E. Neuman by Norman Mingo.

two 38-page publications and have enough stuff to easily fill two more.

♦ *V: Your '70s vocabulary list is great; I'd already forgotten that word "unisex"—*

♦ CS: Currently this concept is quite alien; the dominant culture is trying to separate the sexes again—

♦ *V: —attempting to bring back the '50s. However, you still see "Unisex" Hair Boutique signs—*

♦ CS: But they're old signs. [laughs] Early '70s mainstream fashion promoted a lot of extremes: platform shoes, very short or long skirts, extra-wide bellbottoms, bizarre large shirt collars, shiny or glittery fabrics, and all sorts of strange trims and detailings. Probably as a backlash, the "normal" look returned in the late '70s: what I call the "Mindy" look [of *Mork & Mindy*]. Mindy was what Patty Duke was to the early '60s: a nice, well-scrubbed college girl who brushes her teeth a lot. All the extreme-ness in fashion got filtered out by that point.

♦ *V: What is uniquely '80s? Peewee Herman (even though he was remanufactured '50s)?*

♦ CS: He's got a lot of retro in his image. Five years ago the thought of the '70s was very weird and alien, but now it's been revived and subsumed to the point that it's just another "funny" decade in the public mind. To get that same sense of the weird and alien immediate past, I've had to turn from the '70s to a more recent period: the early '80s. And of course, now I keep a list of uniquely '80s things in my notebook, for example, anything relating to Reagan. Do you remember his assistant David Stockman? He was a young guy with glasses who was his budgetary mouthpiece, but then he did something "bad" and vanished from the face of the earth. Or there's Fawn Hall, Oliver North's pretty

secretary, who was briefly in the news.

Another '80s phenomenon was early rap music which was much more lighthearted and adult, like Grandmaster Flash and Kurtis Blow. Early rap was an *adult* voice talking, instead of a teenager trying to prove himself. I liked how low-tech dj "scratching" was, where you had a physical needle hitting a physical record on a physical turntable. And there was the related fad of "breakdancing." Believe it or not, there were at least two videogames based on the concept of breakdancing!

Continuing with the '80s list: remember early video games like PacMan? For about a year all anyone talked about was their biggest score . . . . The movie *Porky's*: a sleazy jiggle-tits jock film that was hugely popular . . . Legwarmers as a "functional" fashion—where did *they* go? . . . The *Flock of Seagulls* hairstyle: the lead singer had this bizarre sculpted haircut with two wings that made him look like a cyberpunk owl. Not many imitators succeeded in achieving this in real life . . . There was a brief moment when professional wrestling was ultra-hip in an ironic way . . . the Australia fad, with Men at Work and the movie *Crocodile Dundee* bringing several Aussie slang words into our vocabulary . . . Rubik's Cube, a multi-colored brainteaser toy . . . Brooke Shields' gigantic eyebrows . . . The *US* Festival which computer nerd Steve Wozniak produced so he could personally be backstage with bands he liked. Around 1983 punk crossed into the mainstream when MTV reached a saturation number of homes, and people who wouldn't be exposed to this music through the radio (due to its very rigid formats at that time) actually *saw* weird-looking punk or new-wave bands for the first time. Logically, punk should have been dead by '83, but instead that was when it exploded, and bands that had been slogging around since 1977 like DEVO and Talking Heads made their big commercial breakthroughs.

♦ *V: You're chronicling fads which sweep in and out of our lives—*

♦ CS: I kept all my old diaries so I can painfully re-live the experience of being in college and hearing a Bruce Springsteen album for the first time. I'm glad I *am* a packrat and have saved old rock'n'roll magazines like *Creem* and *Crawdaddy*. My mom still lives in the same house I grew up in, and has all the stuff I didn't bring to California.

♦ *V: Let's talk about your favorite records—*

♦ CS: My parents were a lot older than most; they were 40 when I was born. Their tastes in music were very smarmy: Lawrence Welk, Percy Faith, Hugo Winterhalter, Nat King Cole, Tom Jones, Floyd Cramer. They kept the radio tuned to the easy listening station and it didn't occur to me to change the station until I was eleven. I was riding in a car to a girl scout outing and one of the girls riding with us piped up, "Mrs Strecker, can we change the station?" She changed it to a rock'n'roll station and I realized, "Wow—there's other music out there!" The first rock tune I remember hearing was the Mamas and the Papas' "Monday Monday." I realized music could be *relevant;* that song expressed something I personally felt: "I hate Mondays." So to use a cliche, "My life was saved by rock'n'roll." For years that's all I listened to.

But when I passed the 30-year mark, I realized that I had effectively stopped listening to contemporary rock music, because it's a lot of work to ferret out what's truly interesting. I have this theory as to why rock'n'roll isn't fun anymore. In 1966, rock'n'roll was really exciting because I had to *work* to hear it. I had to leave my parents' living room where Percy Faith was playing and go into my bedroom and tune in Chicago and Detroit radio stations on a tiny transistor radio; I got a lot of gratification from being barely able to tune in "Satisfaction" by the Rolling Stones. But today, the Rolling Stones' "Satisfaction" is what you've heard every time you walked into the local corner store for the past twenty years. Where's the fun in hearing it now, when it's all you hear, over and over again? It's out of your control, and in fact rock'n'roll *is* the current elevator music; it's the fishtank water we're all swimming in now. Because of this, what *used* to be elevator music is now interesting because you have to *work* to hear MARTIN DENNY; you have to actively seek it out. With rock'n'roll you're just a passive consumer; it's played everywhere you go. But with the old *exotica* music you can again have a sense of discovery, *and* it can still be found fairly cheap—cheaper than the price of a CD, in most cases.

The *context* makes a lot of difference in making music exciting, too. I was listening to the radio recently and heard something that sounded both futuristic and barbaric, and it turned out to be the battle music from *Star Trek:* the music that plays during fight sequences, not the theme—that's why I hadn't recognized it. I never paid particular attention to it all those times I watched *Star Trek* on TV . . . but hearing it abruptly coming out of the radio was just electrifying! PBS has started showing old Lawrence Welk videos, which I would never have watched when I was living with my parents, but now, after 15 years of post-punk, industrial performance plus MTV, watching them almost seems like an avant-garde experience!

♦ **V: What easy listening records are still findable?**
♦ CS: Here's a BURT BACHARACH record, *Make It Easy On Yourself,* which I found in a dumpster. He has a lot of melodic themes plus a wide dynamic range (the music will be playing along, nice and soft; then suddenly he'll blast you). Or he'll have 4/4 time going, and then throw in a 7/4 section—that's a trademark. One of my favorite instrumental tracks is "Pacific Coast Highway" which alternates between a brassy, big-band sound and a little ocarina faintly carrying the melody. The rest of the songs on this album are so-so, but this one is great.

♦ **V: A lot of albums only have one outstanding**

track on them—
♦ CS: Yes. Are you familiar with YMO (Yellow Magic Orchestra) who were Japan's equivalent of Germany's KRAFTWERK and America's DEVO? The first generation of electronic musicians tended to use the Moog or Mellotron as a substitute instrument, making it sound as much like a "real" string section or organ as possible. But DEVO and YMO had a pro-technological viewpoint and made bleeps for bleeps' sake! Ages ago YMO covered Martin Denny's "Firecracker" (from his *Quiet Village* album), so in a way they were ahead of their time.

Another singer I like is AKIKO YANO, who is the wife of YMO's Ryuichi Sakamoto—she's extremely talented in her own right. Japanese female pop musicians tend to use little-girl voices, and she started out with that quality but then went far away from that. She's like the Kate Bush of Japan, and sounds a bit like Flora Purim. She's not quite Diamanda Galas, but goes about as far as you can go and still remain within the boundaries of accessible pop music. She has a classically trained voice and can sound like an operatic soprano or a jazz singer.

From the number of weird records I've found, I've concluded that 1955-1965 was a peak period where the hardware was ahead of the software—in other words, hi-fi stereo equipment was coming out in the marketplace; people would first buy this gear and only then ask, "What do we play on it?" So there was a wide-open, new market for records of all kinds. It seemed like anybody could start a record company, find ten local groups to record and put out ten records— a window of opportunity arose where a lot of performers got access to recording studios. By 1965 that window was shut. The windows of opportunity change with

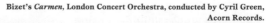

Bizet's *Carmen*, London Concert Orchestra, conducted by Cyril Green, Acorn Records.

the times: in 1966 any four guys with guitars and Beatle haircuts could cut a record, and in 1979 any punk band could get time in a recording studio. But for orchestral novelty records, the time was the late '50s.

Cook XX-3 is a sampler of cuts from ten different albums released on the Cook label—and sure enough, there was a Mr Emory Cook behind the label. He probably had high hopes and plans, but never went anywhere. This record is pressed on blue vinyl and packaged in a high quality plastic sleeve. According to a list on the back cover, the ten recordings include jazz clavichord by "Red Camp," a Mexican marimba band, a Trinidad jazz band, a pipe organ, and a live recording at a burlesque hall with a comedian telling bad jokes— this one was badly recorded; you can tell there was just one microphone at the side of the stage. At the end of the last cut a voice announces, "Ladies and gentlemen: the mystery instrument." The record came with a little coupon on which to write your guess as to the "mystery instrument," mail it in and if you were correct you'd get a free Cook LP of your choice. But if you read the fine print the offer was only good until January 31, 1959! (The mystery instrument turned out to be a jews-harp.) Even though there was quite a proliferation of record labels during '55-'65, only a few survived—just like computer software companies in the early '80s.

Those of us who were raised in the rock'n'roll subculture idealize the singer-songwriter-performer; we think that only a person who "does it all" achieves originality. But in 1960 people had a different outlook: a song was something you took from the already existing culture (one that everyone already knew) and the originality depended on what you *did* with it—how you arranged and interpreted it. One example is MARTIN DENNY's recording of "My Funny Valentine," where the melody is played on a koto—this takes the song into a whole other dimension.

Delirium in Hi-Fi by ELSA POPPING and her Pixieland Band actually was done by an arranger/conductor named Andre Popp. The album first came out in France, but when it was released in America on Columbia as part of the "Adventures in Sound" series, it received a cute title, a cute fake name for the band, and a cartoon cover showing audiophiles listening to speakers. The record is pure avant-garde experimentation with sound. For example, some parts were recorded double-backwards: a singer sang the phonemes backwards so that when the tape itself was played backwards, the words could be understood, yet the attack on each syllable would be reversed—instead of beginning loud and tapering off, the tapering would begin and the sound would grow louder. (It's an unnerving effect which David Lynch used in his dream sequences with the dancing dwarf in *Twin Peaks.*) Also, certain instruments would be speeded up to give a high, faint sound (or conversely, slowed down to give faint sounds in the bass range) . . . a slowed-down flute sounds

quite different from a naturally lower instrument. The effect can be unsettling because there are elements of the familiar plus elements of the completely foreign, and this puts you on shaky emotional ground.

Perhaps my favorite effect on this record is "the fadeout achieved by blowing fuses. These were blown by means of a sunlamp facing directly into the microphone." This really *slays* me—today we have so much recording technology (we can sample and chop the very sound waves themselves into more suitable wave forms; everything's digital and controllable). But the idea of putting a microphone under a sunlamp so that it physically overheats until the tubes blow—just the idea of vacuum tubes is so wonderfully retro. This direct manipulation of the sound is intriguing; I'm in awe of such inventiveness.

◆ *V: What are some of your favorite covers?*

◆ CS: Once in a used-record store I found a group of easy listening records which had been owned by an individual who had a fetish for redecorating the covers—he used squares and rectangles of contact paper to achieve a pseudo-Mondrian effect! Sometimes he'd cross out songs or write little comments, too. These records were like folk art, and it was fun to speculate about the identity of this mystery "artist."

I like commercial/functional records like sound-effects records, and own one example (one's enough!) of a drag-racing record. I've often thought it would be great if those cars and trucks with ultra-powerful speakers which cruise up and down Mission Street playing rap and rock music would blast out selections from these sound-effects records instead, like the sounds of jets taking off or a locomotive pulling into a station . . . Another "commercial/functional" record is this acoustic tile promotional record: *Sound Off Softly* ("from the makers of Gold Bond Ceiling Tile: rich music in hi-fi for your listening pleasure"). It features the usual

Sound Off . . . Softly, Columbia Special Products.

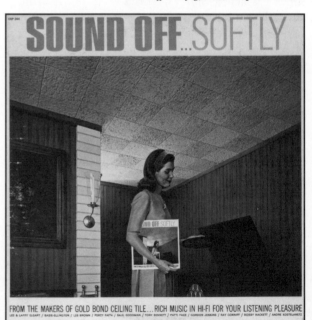

suspects (such as Ray Conniff, Andre Kostelanetz and Percy Faith), but I bought it for the packaging concept. The cover shows a woman putting a record on a turntable; it's photographed from below so that half of the photo is the acoustical tiled ceiling. Also, it's an "infinite recursion" photo: the woman is holding the album cover which shows her holding the album cover, *ad infinitum*. I've never played the record itself—it's worth having for the cover alone.

Here's *Perspectives for the Seventies: The Westinghouse Sixth Future Power Forum, February, 1969*. It's similar to a Broadway cast recording of a musical, except this musical was performed only once. Somebody composed the music, somebody wrote the lyrics, an ensemble of 15 performers sang and danced in costume before an audience at a corporate conference—just *once*. There's actually a minor theatrical industry of people who create these shows for corporate clients' annual sales meetings and such, but they seldom get recorded and preserved this way.

They sing a song called "Power Flower," and there's a photo of the cast members dressed in "hippie" costumes against a Peter Max-imitation background. Remember when the *Beverly Hillbillies* would have hippie characters come on from time to time, and you'd look at them and groan because all the *details* were wrong? These lyrics talk about how "flower power" was big in the '60s, but in the '70s utilities are going to "make the power flower: it's the utilities that have the *opportunities,* man!" There's a Broadway-style overture, a "Blowin' in the Wind"-imitation folk song, and a country-western song called "The Nuclear Kid": "This is the saga of a stranger who came into town one day: Nuclear Power. He was neat, clean and friendly, but the stories of his unruly youth made a lot of townsfolk afraid. Then one day he outgunned the fossil badmen, and became everyone's hero." [laughs]

Here's another kind of functional recording: in 1976, when you took delivery of your 1976 Cadillac, it not only came equipped with an 8-track player but with this tape in the player: *Cadillac Presents the Music Master Enoch Light and the Light Brigade.* Included are "Galveston," "Theme From *M.A.S.H.,*" "You Are the Sunshine of My Life," and other pop songs of the era. The idea was: the instant you took possession of the car, you had a tape on hand you could use to enjoy its stereo system. I have another 8-track titled *Ford Motor Company Presents Stereo for Today.* Apparently, for every car model and every year, somebody would cobble together a different 8-track tape.

I like this album: *Medicine Leads the Way: the Poison and the Antidote,* by Robert Welch who was the head of the John Birch Society in the '50s. It's on Key Records (the Society's label) and is a lecture on the evils of "communist, socialized medicine": "If you aren't a doctor, please see to it that your doctor hears this record. Don't be concerned with whether he's a Republican or a Democrat; the Marxist-Leninist malig-

Robert Welch's *Medicine Leads the Way*, Key Records. Album cover credits: cover photograph: Ellen King.

nancy makes no distinction between the two." It lists other records in their series: *Red Pipeline to Moscow; Inside a Communist Cell; Communist Cancer; Building Balanced Children; The Case Against Fluoridation; the United Nations Hoax; Bipartisan Treason,* and (my favorite) *Cybernetic Warfare.* This came out before '61, because it has a postal code instead of a Zip Code (important dating technique for things I collect; the Zip Code was introduced in 1961. Not everyone adopted it instantly, but it's a very useful dating tool—better than carbon dating.) The cover of this record shows a doctor applying a stethoscope to a globe. The doctor's face has been covered by a black rectangle, as if he were a criminal whose identity has been hidden. Another example of the wonderful world of non-musical recordings (speeches, sermons, self-help, teach-yourself . . .) is *Hear History Begin,* a souvenir recording sold to tourists in Egypt, of the nightly sound-and-light show at the Sphinx.

One of my favorite old albums is *Seduction! For Adults Only,* on the Art Sound label. It's a naughty narrative accompanied by a Hawaiian guitar which provides background music, including sound effects like wolf whistles or "uh-hmm." The narrator tells the story of how he went on vacation and met a girl. They went to dinner; he went to her room; they were necking and petting and suddenly he cums all over her lap! He retreats to his room in shame, but then the girl comes to him and forgives him, and there's a happy ending. This is a '50s adult party record, although it's not as explicit as BLOWFLY or RUDY RAY MOORE.

In the sputnik era (late '50s-early '60s) a slew of records came out which I call Space Exotica. The music was usually orchestral, and the songs had outer space titles like "The Moons of Mars," "Volcanoes of

Mercury," "Cosmic Capers," "Vibrations from Venus," "Jupiter Jumps," "Star Fire," "Outside Atmosphere," "Century 21," and "Mist o' the Moon." They'd include electronic noises and use theremins. Then in the '60s the theremin was replaced by the Moog synthesizer, which inspired a whole genre of "Happy Moog Music"—mostly bright, cheerful mid-'60s tunes re-recorded on the Moog. One of my favorites is *Switched-On Buck: the Songs of Buck Owens Played on the Moog Synthesizer,* performed by Jeff Haskell, then-director of the Tucson Boys Choir. The title is a pun on the best-selling *Switched-on Bach* by Wendy (Walter) Carlos. Haskell included "I've Got a Tiger by the Tail." In the '80s, DEVO released *Devo: Easy Listening Music,* in which they re-recorded all their hits in easy-listening versions—it's funny. Mark Mothersbaugh (of Devo) also recorded two CDs entitled *Music for Insomniacs,* which are in a Muzaky, background, easy-listening style—you can put them on and then go about your business.

Sometimes you pick up records that you think may be great, but they're not, like this mass in polka form: *Father Frank Perkovich Presents More Songs and Hymns from the Polka Mass.* The musicians include Joe Cvek and the Polka Mass-ters Orchestra, celebrated at Resurrection Church, Eveleth, Minnesota, 1976. Unfortunately it's pretty boring; it's basically the same polka played over and over . . . as opposed to this FRANKIE YANKOVICH-Victor Zambrusky album. Frankie Yankovich is number one in the polka field, and this record (which dates back to 1956) still sounds incredible. The sonic quality is marginal—it sounds like the band is playing in your basement, but that makes it all the more beautiful and mysterious.

♦ *V: So you collect religious records—*

♦ CS: A few. One of my favorite Christian recordings is the cassette, *Songs for Souls* by Eve Engelbrite which features "Highway to Destruction," narrated in a *mock-reggae* style: "You're on the highway to destruc*tion* and you're deep in trou*ble.*" It's enunciated very strangely with the accents on the wrong syllables, and there seems to be some metaphor about the need to get on a "better road," but the message doesn't quite get across. The only reason I have this is because the person who sang it works with a friend of mine—I wonder how many recordings like this have been put out?

Christian music is a whole unexplored territory to wade through, with thousands of unknown performers on tiny, essentially self-published record labels. With so many of these records out there, it just stands to reason that some of them are going to be brilliant in some unexpected way. Here's one that I found: *Building On the Rock: Songs and Stories by Jim and Tammy and their Friends.* This was recorded in 1975, long before they had their national TV show. Back then they had a "puppet ministry" featuring a puppet show delivering Christian messages to children. The whole album is Tammy Bakker singing in a high-pitched,

very unpleasant and grating falsetto voice which is supposed to be the voice of a girl puppet: "One-Two-Three/The devil's after me/Four-Five-Six/He's got lots of tricks"—on and on like that. There are wonderful photos on the back showing them wearing '70s clothes with '70s wigs. It's a nice collectible, but you wouldn't want to play it over and over . . .

One of my personal addictions is HANK WILLIAMS, SR. This would have been horrifying to me during my rock'n'roll years, but once you're over 30 you can listen to anything you want! He had a scary vocal quality that's out there on the edge: you could *hear* him dying, incrementally, with each song. "Roly Poly," the first Hank Williams song I ever heard, instantly hooked me: "Roly Poly/Daddy's little fatty/gnawin' on a biscuit." It's a father singing about how happy he is that his son is fat! Today, we associate "fat" with unhealthiness, but this song comes out of the Depression South, where a baby might be skinny because he was starving to death!

♦ *V: What other odd records do you have?*

♦ CS: I have an auctioneer record featuring a real auctioneer spieling off bids as fast as humanly possible. I also have *Double Dutch Bus* by Frankie Smith which is basically pig-latin, except it's done with different syllables: instead of going "ig-pay latin-nay" you'd go "du-dou-vel du-dutch." The song talks about catching your bus and using your "funky bus pass"—it's a weird rap record from the era just *before* the rap style had jelled.

Once in a used-record store I found a group of easy listening records which had been owned by an individual who had a fetish for redecorating the covers—he used squares and rectangles of contact paper to achieve a pseudo-Mondrian effect!

One of my favorite songs is by the NIGHTCRAWLERS: "Little Black Egg." This was a regional hit in 1967 in Ohio. It's very strange and twisted: a guy sings about his "little black egg with the little white specks," and I liked it so much I drew a cartoon about it—a personal homage. Very paranoid lyrics. That would definitely be among my ten strangest records.

♦ *V: What are some of your favorite '70s records?*

♦ CS: In the early '70s GILBERT O'SULLIVAN had a couple of hits including "Alone Again, Naturally" which is a cheerful pop song about suicide! "Get Down" was his third hit, and I have a theory about the "third hit" which helps me wade through '70s music. Any group's first and biggest hit is hard to divorce from all the personal memories you've overlaid on it—in other words it's hard to actually hear what the song sounds like. The same is true of the group's second hit. But by the time they released their third or fourth single, their popularity was beginning to fade—that song only went to #20 or #30 on the Billboard charts. Oldies stations never bother with these lesser-known hits, so they haven't been played to death. The "third hit" has the group's typical sound, but it's possible to hear that sound today in a fresh way. "Get Down" is one of those songs that no radio station plays anymore; it was a bubble-gum tune that used the metaphor of the girl-friend as *dog:* "Told you once before/that I don't want you no more/So get down, get down, get down." Then he changes his mind: "You're a bad dog, baby/but I still want you around." This mixed-message lyric is psy-chotic, yet the tune's so cheerful and saccharine.

Another '70s record I like is by ROGER WATERS (who was in Pink Floyd): *Music from the Body.* The concept was: sound effects that the body makes, so there are belch sounds, chest-hitting sounds and skin-squeaking sounds. It's up there along with Lou Reed's *Metal Machine Music* as one of the more unique con-cepts of the '70s.

Are you familiar with WAZMO NARIZ? For some reason, nobody in the early Chicago punk scene ever went national. Wazmo was weird, even though he looked very normal. On the album he's wearing a polyester salesman's suit and sports a blowdried hair-style, but his gimmick was that he always wore 2 neckties—fat polyester ones at that. On *Things Aren't Right* his voice had operatic qualities (I don't know if he was trained or was imitating the genre). His sound was bizarre and unique.

Some of my favorite cartoon music came from the JAY WARD Studios, who did *Rocky and Bullwinkle* and *Dudley Do Right,* early '60s cartoons where the humor could be enjoyed on different levels by both kids and adults. There was a lot of Cold War humor involving a bad guy Russian No-Goodnik Spy named Boris Badunov. The music was a pastiche of different turn-of-the-century musical styles: tinkly ballads that might have been sung in a Victorian parlor, sentimen-tal love songs, silent-movie piano accompaniment, and Dixieland numbers. On Sunset Boulevard in Los An-geles there's a statue of Bullwinkle outside a store where you can buy the Jay Ward cartoon-music cas-sette—if this was part of your childhood you'll enjoy hearing it again. . . .

Another '80s recording is by PIANOSAURUS, who had a unique conceit: all their instruments were toy instruments—tiny drum sets, mouse guitars, and toy pianos. It makes for a very trebly sound, of course. Their song "At the Thrift Store" had an immediate affinity with me.

♦ V: *I like the idea of home-made recordings and cassette-networking—*

♦ CS: Certainly a lot of home-made recordings have

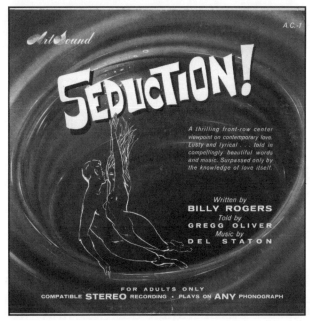

Seduction! For Adults Only, Art Sound.
Written by: Billy Rogers, told by: Gregg Oliver, music by: Del Staton.

been made, and sometimes they get played on the radio, too. When I lived in Chicago in the early '80s the black radio stations were much more open to play-ing home-made tapes and music outside genre bound-aries than commercial rock stations were. This was just before MTV appeared and changed all the playl-ists. One station frequently played a tape some high school kids had recorded and sent to them, which I had the good sense to record off the air. It goes: "We're the class of '83," and then each one takes a verse: "Hi, I'm LaToya, I've been cool; I've been studying and I've got a great future ahead," and then Dwayne comes in and takes a verse, and then the teacher takes a verse about how proud he is of these kids. They stole/sam-pled some bass lines and sang over them, and it's very energetic. I wonder where these kids are today . . .

In the '60s, when the first small cassette recorders appeared on the market, a lot of people turned on their Hammond chord organs and recorded their own songs. The SHAGGS have that sound—they sound like they were recorded on a $40 cassette recorder using the built-in microphone . . . raw yet incredibly emotive. There's a whole world of one-of-a-kind amateur music recordings out there on Radio Shack brand tapes, and I've found a few in thrift stores. This would corre-spond to the current trend in amateur porn videos—

♦ V: *Although most of those videos are not truly amateur—*

♦ CS: They're like hearing a punk rock band on *Co-lumbia* Records; we want "real" amateur productions! Actually, I'm sure people videotape their sexual activi-ties all the time, and it may take 20 years until those tapes actually turn up in thrift stores (when they die and their kids say, "Oh, here's a bunch of old videos; let's just put 'em in the Goodwill box."). I can't wait!

KEN SITZ

Ken Sitz is a San Francisco artist working with "language, diagrammatical texts and extramusical sound." He produces books, photo/text graphics, audio works, films and installations, and with graphic designer Judy Steccone has collaborated with other artists to produce artists' books and catalogs for the San Francisco Art Institute, including Frances Dyson and Douglas Kahn's *Telesthesia,* Carolee Schneemann's *Video Burn,* and Carrie Mae Weems' *And 22 Million.* Ken Sitz can be contacted at PO Box 26562, San Francisco CA 94126.

♦ KEN SITZ: Have you heard of the parrot that sings opera? It was owned by one of the greatest opera singers in Holland, and it learned how to "sing" by involuntarily attending countless practice sessions. This recording of the parrot, with piano accompaniment, dates from the 1950s and was released on "Spiral," a Dutch audio cassette anthology.

♦ *VALE: I'm interested in all such musical "transgressions"—*

♦ KS: Then you've probably heard of *Plunderphonics:* music which was recut (very interestingly) by John Oswald, a Toronto composer who uses a MacIntosh computer. Several years ago he produced a thousand copies of a CD which was suppressed—the cover featured Michael Jackson's head collaged onto a white woman's body. For source material he used everything from Beethoven and Stravinsky to Metallica and the Beatles; one cut begins with "White Christmas" by Bing Crosby and ends with pygmy yodeling. Even though he listed all his sources, the Canadian music industry and Michael Jackson's lawyers came after him for copyright infringement. He made a big point that the CD wasn't actually for sale or being marketed, but he was squashed—the few remaining CDs were confiscated and destroyed. But the rest of them are out there somewhere!

A follow-up to Oswald's outlaw activity: Electra-Asylum Records hired him, in celebration of their 25th anniversary, to digitally "plunder" their stable of '60s artists (like the Doors and the MC5) and produce a promo-only CD. Even though he had access to original master tapes, he chose to digitize from original vinyl discs—I guess he was making the point that anyone could do the same thing; you didn't need privileged access to record vaults. The Doors cut is particularly good, because you can hear all the most interesting parts of their recordings within the space of 3 minutes! In his liner notes, Oswald mentioned other artistic "collaborations" he would love to "facilitate," such as John Coltrane and the Stooges. I'm sure anyone could come up with hundreds more possibilities—I know I immediately thought of pairing Curtis Mayfield with Perez Prado . . .

The MacIntosh has opened up a lot of possibilities: now you can sample and combine all kinds of sounds with non-destructive editing (you can do various edits while still preserving your original sources intact). You don't necessarily have to use copyrighted material; I have a lot of records which are the equivalent of audio "clip art": sound effects records, generic bank ad jingles ("It's great to save/it's great to invest") which leave a space for you to insert your own phrase, like,

"Come to Omaha National Bank at First and Main." These are intended for radio commercial spots when you might need exactly 54 seconds of a sound clip.

One of my favorite plagiarism records is by JAM: The Justified Ancients of Mu Mu. They got their fifteen minutes of fame when ABBA sued them—in "The Queen and I" they used far too much of "Dancing Queen." In "Hey Hey We're Not the Monkeys" they used "Last Train to Clarksville," and they also ripped off the Beatles' "All You Need Is Love." "Don't Take Five" was a take-off on Dave Brubeck's "Take Five," and they also ripped off Whitney Houston in "Whitney Joins the JAMs"—this got recalled immediately. Then they changed their name to KLF, called up Tammy Wynette, and because at the time they had a top ten British hit, persuaded her to fly over and appear in a video playing the Ice Queen and wearing a dress with a huge train. I think they really liked her, so it was one of those postmodern put-ons where it's a put-on but a celebration as well—you know, *multi-leveled*.

♦ **V: *It was a good idea to keep changing their name—***

♦ KS: They owned an American police car which they decorated with a logo of a huge boom box and their name, JAM. In a publicity stunt they took journalists from a big British music mag and drove to the ABBA headquarters in Sweden where they staged a huge ritual record-burning on Abba's front lawn, to show they didn't mean any harm (and please stop the lawsuit)—you know, a kneeling gesture.

808 State, a group from Manchester, England, took

Photo: Olivier Robert

samples of riffs they liked, built up layers on top of them, and then subtracted the original sample. They called this technique "ghosting." What they released was all "original" because the original sample was missing—that's how *they* got around the copyright! That idea appeals to me; an architectural equivalent is the ancient Greek arch built on a huge mound of dirt, which is later removed. For years afterward people wondered, "How did they get that last stone in place?"

The way culture evolves is just like how DNA evolves

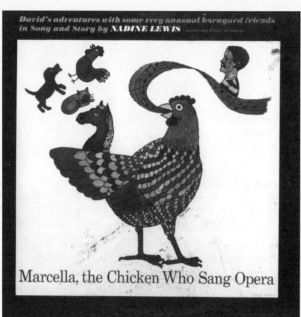

Marcella, the Chicken Who Sang Opera

Marcella, the Chicken Who Sang Opera, Riverside Records.
Song & story: Nadine Lewis, music: Paul Renard.
Album cover credits: artwork: Paul Davis.

or mutates—regardless how quickly it changes, it's based on material that existed before. An accumulation process of small incremental changes can produce sudden "discontinuities" like the collapse of the Eastern Bloc or the Berlin Wall coming down. And sampling at least challenges questions of property rights. John Oswald said, "If creativity is a field, then copyright is a fence."

♦ **ANDREA JUNO: How did sampling originate?**
♦ KS: In the '50s Bill BUCHANAN and Dickie GOODMAN pioneered sampling by incorporating "quotations" from popular songs of the day into their novelty records. They did cut-ins (not *cut-ups*) using a song lyric as a pun to produce the punch line. Sometimes their songs were political or satirical of the Cold War or the paranoia about flying saucers. They got sued, too. I think all their work was in the form of singles (45s), but several volumes' worth are collected on LPs.

♦ **V: Do you have a collecting specialty?**
♦ KS: Anything with steel guitar (Hawaiian, C&W), plus odd items like the LP by Konstantin Raudive. He discovered that on many blank, unrecorded tapes you could actually hear voices of the dead, or from another dimension. Burroughs talks about him in *The Job*. I think one voice was supposed to be Hitler's.

Even though record collecting is generally regarded as passive or receptive, rediscovery can be an active process, with an almost infinite number of editorial possibilities. For example, I love the "Lisa" character in PETER BAGGE's *Hate* comics—she prowls used record stores in order to add to her collection of *Saturday Night Fever* soundtrack LPs—in other words, she just collects multiple copies of the same soundtrack! I

myself collect "horizontally" by song: I'll buy any version of the Alfred Newman standard "Moon Over Manakoora" or Gilbert-Barroso's classic "Bahia." Someday I'll string together all the different versions on a tape to share with friends and fellow "researchers." Two of my collections, "Pidgin Hi Fi" and a "demo" anthology of ESQUIVEL (which I pitched to RCA without success), have been circulating freely. These days a lot of people are making their own "segues" and compilation cassettes, and it's a lot of fun to trade tapes and enjoy other people's discoveries.

The passion for collecting puts us on the terrain of "fan culture," a recently-theorized field of Cultural Studies that owes a lot to British writers like Dick Hebdige, Simon Frith, and Fred and Judy Vermorel, but goes back to the work of Walter Benjamin. Frith's *Art Into Pop* is great reading, just to find out what art school your favorite British punk band came out of! His *On Record: Rock, Pop and the Written Word* is also recommended. Hebdige's *Subculture: The Meaning of Style* is now a classic reading of postwar UK youth, starting with punk and going backward—the only way to go forward!

The Vermorels, early collaborators with Malcolm McLaren's *Sex Pistols* enterprise, compiled a great book called *Starlust*. Basically it allows pop music fans to speak for themselves (through letters and diary excerpts) their secret fantasies, obsessions and ecstasies. The Vermorels treat fandom as a kind of consumer mysticism that transcends devotion to a particular "artist," suggesting that to take publicity *literally* may be more of a critical stance than to actually repudiate it!

The power of nihilism derives from its refusal of the status quo: deliberately *not* going for success or striving to "fit in." You look for all that is *positive* in the refusal of constraints . . .

Related to this is the Constance Penley essay "Brownian Motion: Women, Tactics and Technology" in the anthology, *Technoculture*. This is a study of the "K/S" or slash-zine culture of *Star Trek* fans who construct elaborate stories and videos about the erotic love between Kirk and Spock ("K" and "S"). Any notion that fans are simply passive consumers is blown away by her detailed description of their guerilla erotics, their creation of a hybridized genre, and the feedback effect of all this on *Star Trek* productions and "official" fandom.

♦ **AJ: Tell us about your musical background—**

♦ KS: In junior high school I was in a lip-synch band that was the *Beatles*—I was Ringo, I had the boots and everything, and we "played" two live shows. That was a conceptual high point for me: to be in a band yet not make any sounds. During the '70s punk rock years, I was a deejay in New York City, "Mr Mod Monday"—that's embarrassing.

I grew up in Schenectady, upstate New York, until I was orphaned at age 16. My sister had moved to the Haight-Ashbury around the Summer of Love (1967), and in 1969 I moved to San Francisco and did things like go to old Family Dog concerts at the beach. Then I fell in with the Situationist-inspired *Contradiction* group: Dan Hammer, Ron Rothbart, Isaac Cronin, and Ken Knabb who produced the English translation of the *Situationist* anthology. I was particularly inspired by the *Treatise on Living for the Use of the Younger Generation* and Motherwell's *Dada* book. I also became interested in the postwar neo-avant-garde, the Lettrists and the *Cobra* movement which were precursors to the Situationist International. Asger Jorn, a Cobra and SI founder, had been in the Danish underground resistance movement during World War II and printed a clandestine Communist monthly journal with a printing press hidden inside an ottoman in his flat. Later he established the Institute of Comparative Vandalism, a deliberately playful name for a serious study of prehistoric and middle ages Viking art that was dispersed throughout Europe, and created a book-length study of graffiti on Normandy churches—mysterious embellishments which were literally acts of vandalism!

Having been involved with the "pro-situ's" (a mildly derogatory name for would-be followers of the SI) from '70-'73, I was not too interested in academic semiotics or structuralism. I started taking film classes at City College because I really liked films like JODOROWSKY's *El Topo* and the films of ROBERT ALTMAN. In '72 I became interested in SM and with some friends made a 60-second commercial called *Dominant Manicure* for film class: a guy gets dragged into a dungeon, strapped into a chair, electrodes are attached to his fingers and he gets a "manicure." When making films, it was interesting to see what people bring out in each other: for example, mild-looking people can improvise fierce fight scenes!

♦ **AJ: What do you think was positive about the punk movement?**

♦ KS: The nihilism! The refusal of everything, especially all forms of *cultural authoritarianism.* In '76 I became involved in the New York punk rock scene around CBGBs and became friends with the *Dead Boys,* the Iggy Pop (as opposed to the *Talking Heads)* wing of punk rock. I created a logo for them and roadied for them a few times, but I'm glad that ended—it was dangerous. The lead singer, Stiv Bators, was a real trooper. He was hit by a car in Paris, got up and said, "I'm okay," refused to go to the hospital, went home and died in his sleep from internal hemorrhaging.

♦ **AJ: People who literally couldn't play a note (like the band DNA) could "live out" theories of musical nihilism.**

♦ KS: The power of nihilism derives from its refusal of the status quo: deliberately *not* going for success or striving to "fit in." You look for all that is *positive* in the refusal of constraints—

♦ **AJ: Why would you even bother persisting in a full-fledged refusal of what is, if you didn't intensely believe in and want to make the world better?**

♦ KS: It's like sleight-of-hand: you're negative, but for a *purpose.* My sense of humor is sarcastic but not cynical—I believe in applying negativity for purposes of intelligence or insight. Destruction may be necessary, but in the context of a *plan* or proposal. If you're a rebel performer, you're always walking the line of commercial sell-out; most performers either burn out, self-destruct, or buy in.

What's interesting about all attempts at being avant-garde is the failures: they don't necessarily "show us the way," but a good example is David Cronenberg movies. There's always that dance between the political and the commercial; in New York Jim Fouratt, a Gay Liberation Front founder and Stonewall veteran, also created and ran a nightclub, Danceteria. Bruce Elwell, an artist and American member of the Situationist International, was involved with the band *Made in USA*, which featured guitarist-novelist-screenwriter Howard Rodman, and proclaimed, "Raw power to the workers' council!"—like a heady blend of Iggy Pop and the Situationists.

John Oswald's *Plunderphonics.*

ELVIS PRESLEY IGOR STRAVINSKY COUNT BASIE DOLLY PARTON

Hal Aloma's *Hawaiian Holiday,* ® Columbia Records

I "curated" an experimental, for lack of a better term, series of evenings called "Naive Rhythm Nights" that featured emerging "downtown" bands working within a minimalist rhythm and "dub" approach, including bands like Dog Eat Dog, Y Pants (who played amplified toy instruments and included Glenn Branca's partner Barbara Ess); Konk, and Liquid Liquid, whose vocalist, Sal Principato, refused to sing lyrics and sang in his own "language" of linguistic fragments. I later managed Konk, a seven-piece latinesque-funk band led by Dana Vicek (who had replaced Arto Lindsay in the original line-up of the Lounge Lizards).

I also worked for 99 Records promoting a band called *ESG*—three girls and a male cousin (Puerto-Rican and African-American) from the South Bronx, who played stripped-down, minimal music that bridged punk and what was to become rap—it was an early promise of future cross-cultural synthesis. When I started deejaying it wasn't out of careerism—I wanted to spread *cultural rebellion*. When I managed KONK, just as their record got heavy airplay on the main disco station, I had to quit and go back to a 9-5 job. At work I'd hear the record and think I was literally being tested by god—that had marked the end of any music-business involvement for me. Actually, music is too important and personal for me to want any kind of *career* from it.

Everywhere, music is imposed on us and shoved down our throats—in grocery stores, *everywhere.* If you make a phone call and are put on hold, music comes on. And unfortunately, we don't have eyelids for our ears! Nevertheless, it's still possible to subvert and challenge things by using sound, cut-ups, and tape manipulations.

Before the recording process took over, music used

to be much more of an active part of people's lives. Evan Eisenberg wrote an interesting book, *The Recording Angel,* in which he discusses the experience of music *before* recording and after—the pre-history of recorded sound which includes the music box and musical automata. People used to give their children piano lessons, especially the girls, in order to have music in the home, but the introduction of record players eroded that tradition.

♦ *V: Why do you like Hawaiian music? Is it a response to increasingly more abrasive times?*

♦ KS: Yes. One of the liner notes (that's an art form in itself: the liner note) said, "It induces nostalgia among those who haven't even been there." It's that longing for paradise: the perfect temperature all year 'round, the lapping surf—the vision of a wonderful fantasy-land. The big hit of the 1915 Pan-Pacific Exhibition, held here in San Francisco, was a Hawaiian music troupe, Keoki Awai's Royal Hawaiian Quartette. Many other Hawaiian musicians also appeared during the seven months of the exposition, including the "inventor" of the steel guitar, Joseph Kekuku, plus Frank Ferara, Pale K. Lua and others. More than 17 million people visited the various pavilions and heard Hawaiian music for the first time. That's when Tin Pan Alley discovered Hawaii—within a year the biggest-selling sheet music was Hawaiian, and this continued throughout the Depression. In 1916 there were more Hawaiian records sold than any other type of popular music.

Hawaiian Music and Musicians, edited by George S. Kanahele, documents how countries like Canada and Scandinavia developed their own Hawaiian music scenes! The father of Hawaiian music in Canada, William Miles, was in the navy and he brought back a steel guitar from Hawaii. He started teaching steel guitar

Jerry Byrd's *On The Shores of Waikiki,* Mercury Records.

and ukelele, and even wrote a Hawaiian opera about an octopus, a diver, a mermaid and Davy Jones' Locker that was successfully staged until it turned out that the producer was a German spy (this was during World War I) who was then caught and immediately shot for treason! All of the producer's papers were reportedly seized and burned, including the only copy of this opera, which was never recovered.

♦ *AJ: It's funny to think about people shivering during cold nights in Canada and Scandinavia, dreaming of Hawaii—*

♦ KS: Yes. This book tells how these Hawaiian troupes would tour internationally and lose members in various cities. That's how Ben Hokea wound up in Toronto, performing at night and teaching steel guitar by day—he probably found a Canadian sweetheart. A big department store hired Miles as part of a promotional campaign: "A ukelele, plus four free lessons—only $20." Incredibly, 2500 pupils showed up! [reads] "To teach this huge class, Miles constructed a ten-foot-high ukelele outline with light bulbs at the finger positions. He taught 5 groups of 500 each while he demonstrated chords and techniques on the stage. Surely this is another record for Miles—if not for ukelele teachers everywhere."

All the great steel guitar players in western-swing, early country music, and even bottleneck delta blues, were inspired by Hawaiian music. There were people going door-to-door selling steel guitar lessons for a dollar a week. Even cartoon music was inspired; Carl Stalling's "Merrie Melodies" contains steel guitar. Recently I heard some great music in "Porky in Wackyland," which had Porky Pig searching a Salvador Dali-esque landscape for the last surviving dodo bird.

The steel guitarist Herb Remington reminisced: "I was just one of thousands being enrolled by one of the best organized and largest firms of its kind in the world: the Oahu Publishing Co. I found myself in a weekly class of 15-20 other kids just as enthusiastic as I, making what sounded to me to be the most beautiful music in the world (I'd hate to hear today what we sounded like then)." Since the steel guitar has no frets, even if everyone is "in tune," you're always a little sharp or flat. The best players were allowed to join the "professional club," and occasionally all the professional clubs in Indiana would meet to merge into a band of 225 steel guitarists. Finally, there was a gathering from a five-state area of *1500* steel guitar students! According to Remington, "We tuned the guitars (probably within a few half-tones) and murdered 'Stars and Stripes Forever,' only this time probably a hundred decibels louder. This event took place at Soldiers Field in Chicago in August, 1940—another day that may live in infamy."

♦ *V: Imagine 1500 kids playing steel guitar all at once—*

♦ KS: Yes. And by 1940 there would have been a lot of western-swing music happening, too. When it became

JERRY BYRD HAS NEVER BEEN TO THE SOUTH SEA ISLANDS. BUT HIS LIFE REFLECTS AN OVERWHELMING PASSION FOR POLYNESIAN CULTURE. HE READS EVERYTHING HE CAN FIND ABOUT POLYNESIAN LORE AND HISTORY. HE SERVES POLYNESIAN FOOD IN HIS POLYNESIAN-INSPIRED HOME. HE WRITES POLYNESIAN SONGS. HE IS A PIONEER OF THE HAWAIIAN STEEL GUITAR, WHICH IS WHY WE HAVE NAMED THIS GREAT ALBUM BYRD OF PARADISE

monument

Jerry Byrd's *Byrd of Paradise*, Monument Records.

popular, Hawaiian music was mainly made by non-Hawaiians for non-Hawaiians. Recently I found a record by the ROYAL HAWAIIAN GUITARS which was recorded in Nashville. The liner notes list all the instruments, the technical specifications of the microphones, tape recorders, and the lathe used to cut the master . . . but neglect to mention the *musicians!* It sounds like Jerry Byrd and Chet Atkins.

Jerry Byrd is my favorite steel guitar player; he grew up in the Midwest and took lessons, and on the back of one album he reminisces, misty-eyed, about how if he hadn't gone to one of these traveling tent shows, his whole purpose in life might have been different. He had German parents who were really upset that he was going to go into music; he had to leave home. It wasn't like today when every child aspires to be some kind of "rock star." He played in Nashville and did countless sessions, ultimately retiring to Hawaii where he wound up teaching Hawaiian kids steel guitar! He decorated his house with tikis, got into the food, and adopted the whole Hawaiian lifestyle. He never went over to the pedal steel (which is what we associate with bad country-western: over-expressive, dripping-with-emotion cliches); all the effects he got were with his hands.

I love the liner notes on his LP: "He's never been in the South Sea Islands, but his life reflects an overwhelming passion for it. He reads everything he can find about Polynesian lore and history." Now *there's* a purity of dream and obsession. I thought about doing a book just on liner notes after I got an early Miriam Makeba album where the writer compared her to a *satellite!* The writing, by Hal Halverstadt, was enthusiastic and infectious like a testimonial: "Astronauts and armchair space travelers take note: with this al-

Hawaiian Steel Guitar Classics
Volume 2 (1927-1934)

Hawaiian Steel Guitar Classics Vol. 2 (1927-1934), Polklyric Records. Album cover credits: cover by Wayne Pope. Cover photo: Sol Hoopii leading a group of Hawaiian musicians who all had successful careers in the late 1930s & '40s including the McIntire brothers, Dick, Lani, and Hal. Probably a promotional shot for the National Instrument Company ca. 1930. Photo courtesy Georgia Stiffler (Mrs. Sol Hoopii).

bum, Miss Miriam Zenzi Makeba, the darkly divine enchantress from the South of Africa, has come up with a full bag of songs that will sock one and all into the wild blue yonder faster and higher than any missile ever to cut loose from Canaveral . . . Miss Miriam Makeba. A trip to the moon on bright feathered wings. The sweetest nose cone this side of heaven. And the most exciting space age phenomenon since Telstar."

Sometimes record sleeves show tiny photos of other albums the company has released, and I find these really appealing—they're like those little sex show ads in the newspaper. Maybe they're good because you have to use your imagination to blow up the image in your head.

♦ *AJ [reading liner notes from* **Byrd of Paradise** *LP]: "Multi-millions of the world's population believe in reincarnation. Briefly, this belief sets forth the premise that the soul, in each lifetime inheriting the experience of the previous . . . However, if reincarnation is a truth, Jerry Byrd must have spent at least one happy life as a Hawaiian or some kind of Polynesian, despite the fact that he was born and bred in Ohio and has never stepped foot on a Pacific island."*

♦ KS: Back then it was still expensive to travel to Hawaii. Originally, it was the Spanish who had introduced the guitar to Hawaii—then the Hawaiians had experimented and produced their own styles based on slack key-style open tunings. It's fun to read passionate disputes about the various tunings, some held in strict secrecy, and the confusion that the introduction

of new tunings would cause among students and players. Purists like William Miles even claim the decline of steel guitar music and Hawaiian music began with the introduction of the E7th tunings (he was an original A Major stalwart) in the 1930s. In the '60s guitarists like John Fahey and Robbie Basho produced music that was based on slack key (or tuned down) scales, but that sounded more like instrumental American folk music.

Hawaiian Steel Guitar Classics (Volume 2) is a compilation by Bob Brosman of pieces from original 78 records—it's always interesting when you play a record and hear the surface noise from *another* record on it! In 1977 he was in Jack's Record Cellar in San Francisco and found a copy of an old Hawaiian 78 which changed his life—the music was so beautiful. "Hula Blues" is a melancholy, almost hybrid-blues tune.

I also like HAL ALOMA's LPs, the steel guitar of Keili and Jules Ah See on Webley Edwards' *Hawaii Calls* records, and I enjoy the sacred song stylings of the most famous Christian steel guitarist Bud Tutmarc, who was a friend and follower of Hawaiian great SOL HOOPII, and who wound up being willed Sol's personal instrument. His records are on the Sacred label from Waco, Texas. It's also fascinating to find steel guitar used in other than Hawaiian or country-western styles, such as in Alvino Rey's work. He was the leader and front man of a very popular swing band in the 40s. His *Ping-Pong!* is a near-classic of "ping pong stereo," although the real musical king of ping pong stereo or Stereo Action is undoubtedly Juan Garcia ESQUIVEL. His orchestration includes steel guitar, bass accordion and other unusual instruments and voices—it's staggering. Joe Goldman's *International Steel Guitar Discography* (regularly updated) has complete discographies of steel guitar instrumentals by the major players of all persuasions.

Another thing I like about Hawaiian music is the falsetto singing—the missionaries introduced the Western scale, but the Hawaiians preserved their high falsetto style of singing which is similar to YODELING. Yodeling is another favorite subject—

♦ *V: How do you learn to do that?*

♦ KS: You can attend a yodeling workshop at the annual Cowboy Poetry Festival in Elko, Nevada. It's probably like learning how to swim or dive—you just do it. Once you get it, you've *got* it, but how do you start? I guess you practice alone. Roy Rogers is a pretty good yodeler; recently he recorded a new album—

♦ *V: He's still alive?*

♦ KS: —And Dale is too! Remember that he had his horse, Trigger, stuffed. He got together with some current country stars (there's a category, "New Traditionalists") and recorded an album with some great songs on it, like "Dust" which is really grim, about the Dustbowl.

♦ *V: What other yodeling records do you have?*

♦ KS: There's a great yodeling song, "I Ain't Got Nobody," by Tommy Duncan, the most famous vocalist with BOB WILLS and his TEXAS PLAYBOYS. I have other yodeling records by ELTON BRITT, the "Yodeling Cowboy," who's a famous C&W performer who did yodel duets such as "Quicksilver" with Rosalie Allen. Yodeling always reminds me of those Tibetan monks who can sing several notes at the same time, and who have mastered circular breathing so they're never forced to stop singing. Of course, I also have some Swiss and German yodeling records, plus a yodeling album from *Australia*. Besides yodeling, Australia has its country music, too. *The* Australian yodeler is SLIM DUSTY (could that possibly be a made-up name?) who's the combined Johnny Cash-Roy Rogers of Australia. He's the best-selling Australian recording artist of all time. One of his early songs is "When the Bushland Boogie Came This Way"—

♦ *AJ: Not* Austria, *where yodeling originated?*

♦ KS: No, *Australia*. The songs have regional references, like the "Golden Wattle" (an Australian flower in Queensland) and the "Brumbees" (Australian wild horses). SLIM DUSTY also does recitations, and in one song he does a tribute to King Bundawaal, a legendary aboriginal warrior-king (these cowboys didn't have Indians, they had aborigines). Australia was settled mostly by Irish or English stock (initially, convicts condemned to the Empire's penal colonies) who lived in small cities in the Southeast. Ironically, it used to be the most non-urbanized country in the world, with huge expanses of empty, ominous, deadly landscape, with the vast majority of the population hugging the coast in cities, and this really shaped the Australian character—of the whites, that is. The outback has always been present as a "never-never" land; an undifferentiated expanse that threatens to swallow you up, as it literally did to numerous celebrated explorers and forgotten settlers, and psychologically it's an almost tangible absence that lurks within the Australian identity.

Queensland is the equivalent of our Deep South (but they call it the "Far North"); it has the most conservative, racist population. Australians are embarrassed about this; if you say, "I've been to Queensland," it's like saying, "Yeah, I've been to America—I went to Mississippi." A great history book, *Triumph of the Nomads* by Geoffrey Blainey, tells how the aborigines successfully survived for 30,000 years living in all kinds of harsh climates and terrain. The aboriginals encompass many different racial groups, ranging from light-skinned to dark-skinned. Overall, Australia is a liberal welfare-state—their money displays aboriginal heroes, and they sponsor various ethnic-pride festivals. There are now several commercial aboriginal bands putting out records in various genres including techno-rave. There's even an aboriginal *blues* band.

Country Music in Australia, an historical compilation album, features JUNE HOLM, a virtuoso woman

yodeler—she sings "Sunny Queensland," which sounds a bit like Appalachian music (which also derives from Anglo-Irish folk music). The AUSTRALIAN COUNTRY YODELERS LP features Tex Morton, Buddy Williams, Lily Connors, Gordon Parsons, as well as June Holm and Slim Dusty. Songs include "Music in My Pony's Feet," "Homeward Bound" with yodeled train effects, and "Chime Bells," a yodel standard. A good reference book (available from Roots & Rhythm Mail Order) is *Country Music in Australia*.

♦ *AJ: Have you been there?*

♦ KS: As a kid I saw *On the Beach* and became obsessed with Australia. Finally I visited Queensland in the early '80s. *On the Beach* was a 1959 end-of-the-world movie directed by Stanley Kramer. Gregory Peck is commanding a submarine in the Pacific when the war breaks out and the submariners discover they can't contact anybody in Europe or America; the only survivors seem to be in Australia. They don't know who started the war, but they know a huge radiation cloud is heading south and that the world is ending. The survivors have six months to tie up "loose ends" before they get radiation-sick and die; Ava Gardner, Fred Astaire and Anthony Perkins have some good roles. People have to make moral decisions about "putting to sleep" their domestic animals or farm animals or even their own babies. There's even an in-joke about how rabbits may finally succeed in taking over.

♦ *AJ: In* On the Beach, *doesn't the whole world end?*

♦ KS: Yes, they didn't sell out—apocalypse movies must have that total commitment! I've been renting films like this as part of a "Nostalgia for the Cold War" phase I've been going through.

♦ *AJ: What soundtracks do you like?*

Lani McIntire's *Aloha Hawaii*, Sonora Records. (Four 10-inch albums)

♦ KS: I'm really fond of the "mondo" film soundtracks by Riz Ortolan: *Mondo Cane, Ecco,* and especially Ennio Morricone's *Malamondo.* I'd love to find a soundtrack LP of the Michael Cacoyannis film, *The Day the Fish Came Out,* a garish apocalyptic comedy from 1967 set in the future (1970) where a "broken arrow" incident or nuclear weapons accident on a trendy Greek resort isle causes the "fish to come out"—a real red tide! The film, made in Europe with Tom Courtenay and a sexy SM-tinged Candice Bergen ("Shall I get my whips now?") was probably suppressed here because it explicitly referred to the recent crash in Spain of a nuclear-armed B-52 bomber which contaminated acres of prime tomato-growing topsoil that had to be removed and "dumped." That was a publicity disaster for both the US Armed Forces and Spanish produce-exporters. The costumes and choreography of this pop-hedonist future are great, and the dance music is great Farfisa-organ "rave" music. I don't think it's out on video; I have a copy from late-night TV years ago.

DARIO ARGENTO's *The Bird with the Crystal Plumage* has a great soundtrack: an amplified heartbeat plus a gasping, sexual sound of a woman breathing—it combines both death and sex. Argento is a fan of both opera and heavy metal, and he uses both musical genres to comment on the plot. All of Argento's soundtracks are interesting on some level, and he's one of my favorite filmmakers.

♦ **V: What interesting musical ideas have you come across recently?**

♦ KS: In an article titled "Conceptual Instruments," writer Doug Kahn said, "Everyone's heard of music theory . . . but what about theoretical music (which can only be performed by the 'inner ear')?" Remember that idea of a *Concerto for Factory Whistles,* which originated in the '20s in the Soviet Union? I had an idea for a *Concerto for Abandoned Schools:* flushing cherry bombs down the toilets at intervals to produce a literal *caca*phony. This is an example of something which is theoretically possible to do, but very unlikely. Still, I like the idea of conceptual *anything*: it's easier to propose or describe something in theory than to have to actually make it!

I also had an idea for a publication that prints reviews of art shows or performances that never happened—after all, most people who read about these never actually *see* them. Years ago the artist Lawrence Weiner described classic conceptual strategies: "The artist may construct the work, the work may be fabricated, the work need not be built . . ."

A poet friend of mine, Lisa Manning, and I are working on a film festival catalog that will list films that don't exist. It lists the title, a still photo, a brief collapsed scenario, and is designed to be read by people too busy or isolated to actually attend them—

♦ **V: Therefore each film will "exist" in as many imagined versions as there are readers—**

Noel Boggs Quintet's *Magic Steel Guitar,* Shasta Records.

♦ KS: Right. I read a great quote by Paul Hammond in his book, *Marvellous Melies:* "From Melies we can learn to consider the cinema as a medium animated by marvelous moments owing little allegiance to banal narrative structures that hold them prisoner . . . These images may be thought of as 'shots' in a purely mental film of which we are at best the director or at worst the continuity-girl." A little-known writer, Benjamin Fondane, actually raised a call to "inaugurate the era of the unfilmable scenarios." Again, the economy of all this is really attractive.

There have been a lot of unique musical technologies which have been abandoned (although not necessarily replaced), like the music box or the player piano. There's a micro-genre of vinyl records and CDs that document this "mechanical music," often involving little-known instruments such as Orchestrions, Violano-Virtuosos, Pianolins, "bird organs" and various other "pre-historical" (from a sound-recording point-of-view) inventions. Recently I got a Hawaiian music piano roll, "Way down in a South Seas Island," at a flea market [unrolls it to show the patterns of punched-out slots]. Look how beautiful it is, how precise . . .

♦ **V: This looks like some kind of pre-computer print-out—**

♦ KS: You could get a bunch of piano rolls and splice them together—yet another application of William Burroughs's "cut-up" idea.

♦ **V: It's long enough to use as wallpaper—**

♦ KS: —or as some kind of room divider. And it was published by Sherman Clay, a San Francisco music store that claimed to be the "headquarters for everything in Hawaiian music." The Oahu Company, based in Cleveland, Ohio, was the biggest publisher of Hawaiian music and they also sold electric steel guitars and amplifiers.

♦ **V: Wasn't Hawaiian music also spread by the radio?**

♦ KS: Radio had recently been invented, but was used mainly for ship transmissions or military purposes. It wasn't until the '20s that people started broadcasting sports, music, comedies and dramas, and election results—

♦ **V: FDR was elected primarily because of his radio "fireside chats" featuring his hypnotic, persuasive voice.**

♦ KS: One of my projects is called *The Social History of BANG*: a history of how gunfire has been recorded. With the earliest microphones, sound engineers had so much trouble recording gunshots that they were forced to invent a substitute sound, a simulation. For example, when bullets ricochet (like in Westerns) they really don't emit those characteristic frequencies that trail off into the distance ("ka-pow"). Blanks don't sound authentic, either. In the '50s there was a live television drama starring Humphrey Bogart—this was a big deal because he was a famous movie star appearing on *TV*. In a quest for realism, the director used a real gun with blanks instead of a special-effects gun, and the reviews said that this ruined the drama, because the gun sounded like a cap pistol. So the early recording engineers developed a special-effects gun that sounded like what people *thought* guns should sound like. Nowadays, because we've grown up with the sounds of these special-effects guns, when we hear *real* gunfire it often sounds like firecrackers—thanks to this set of preconceived expectations, this media creation—

♦ **V: The TV simulation sounds more real than the "real thing."**

♦ KS: This is a rich field for theorizing. Rick Altman's anthology, *Sound Theory, Sound Practice,* has a good quote from sound theorist Tom Levin: "That a gunshot seems to sound the same in the different acoustic spaces of the street and the inside of a cinema is a deception . . . familiarity has dulled the capacity to recognize the violence done to sound by recording."

There's a book, *Talking on the Radio: A Practical Guide for Writing and Broadcasting and Speech,* written by the radio editor for the *New York Times* in 1936, Orrin E. Dunlap. All his metaphors are drawn from war. He begins: "There are only 26 letters in the English alphabet. They are the *bullets* of verbal broadcasting . . . The ideal text from which all speakers may learn the tricks of *point-blank* broadcasting is politics." (Here he's probably referring to Roosevelt.) He continues: "The purpose of this book is to reveal to broadcast speakers the knack of gaining the most from their verbal *barrage* . . . how to win a *coup de main* with words . . . In the move from the transcontinental *battlefield* of gab, the tongue's electrified projectiles will not thump as *duds* when the speaker (be he political

warrior or teacher) seeks to capture ears *barricaded* in the *trenches* of home comforts."

I was talking to the president of the Chabot Gun Club and he pointed out the importance of having guns that sound different from your enemy's—so you can recognize who the enemy *is*. Otherwise you don't know if it's your guys coming around the corner, or the bad guys. He also told me about "Hitler's Zipper": a machine gun which fired a thousand rounds a minute—so fast that it sounded like someone zipping up their pants.

Not long ago some minor Australian actor, who was in a minor TV show about models who lead a double life as detectives, played Russian Roulette with a .44 Magnum revolver loaded with blanks. He put it to his head, the gun went off and he went into a coma and died a couple days later. He didn't know that blanks have enough power to kill you at close range.

♦ **V: He needed a little more knowledge about guns . . . Computer editing has made possible flawless sound manipulation. I saw a video of Ronald and Nancy Reagan giving a talk, except that the filmmaker had redubbed their voices so they were saying things like: "Nancy and I use heroin every night." It was amazing—the dialogue was perfectly synched.**

♦ KS: That takes some tedious work, but it's not outside the range of a little dedication. Doug Kahn did a 2-minute piece, "Reagan Speaks for Himself," based on an interview that Bill Moyers did when Reagan wasn't so perfectly controlled by his speechwriting team. Doug took the original (on a reel-to-reel tape) and cut it up and re-spliced it by hand—it took forty hours. When Moyers asks, "Ronald Reagan, you don't understand

Wes Harrison's *You Won't Believe Your Ears*, Philips Records, A Division of Mercury Record Productions, Inc.

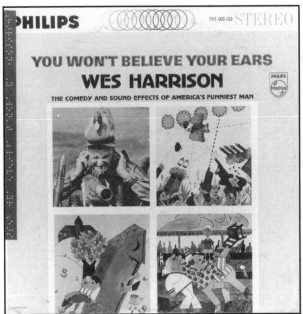

the America of dirty streets and the poor?" Reagan replies, "Uh, sure, poverty—it's *great!*" I asked Doug, "Would the new digital cut-and-paste technology speed things up?" And he said, "Not really, because you still have to do the analytical work to make the bits of speech fit together."

It's interesting how sensitive people's perceptions can be—at 1/20th of a second people can detect discrepancies that indicate you could be lying. I cut up a tape of General Schwarzkopf being interviewed by David Frost and basically re-cast him as John Wayne Gacy, because like Gacy he *did* kill a lot of boys—but they were in the Iraqi army (most of the 300,000 killed in the Gulf war turned out to be teenage kids). Since Schwarzkopf is a colorful speaker, he provided plenty of material to re-cast the war as an enormous magnification of his personal psychosexual conflicts. Like: this was *sexual murder* on a mass scale—legal, too.

♦ *V: Tell us about some more unusual records—*
♦ KS: WES HARRISON's *You Won't Believe Your Ears* has a photo of him holding a microphone shaped like a gun—

♦ *V: I thought it* **was** *a gun!*
♦ KS: No; as Wes says, "I'm the only one with a Shure Brothers 503 microphone that has a six-gun grip." He's a very talented mimic, and makes all the sound effects on the record vocally without the help of tape recorders or other electronic devices. According to the liner notes: "It all began in '41 at the YMCA Boys Camp on Chesapeake Bay. While they were installing a public address system to summon stray campers, he began his first experiment with vocal sound effects. One day the siren failed and Wes was asked, "Can you make like a siren?" He said, "Sure," and from that day on he was the human air raid siren. He didn't mind his

We Came in Peace for All Mankind, **Decca Records.**
© 1969 Doubleday & Co., Inc. Album cover credits: cover design: Edwin H. Kaplin, cover art: Grumman Aircraft Engineering Corp.

job because it afforded him the opportunity to practice his vocal sound effects . . .

"One evening while sitting around playing cards, one of the other players coaxed Wes to make like a siren, not knowing that the outside speakers were on . . . All you could hear for miles was the spine-tingling sound of the air raid siren. The sound was so realistic that the lights were blacked out six miles away at an amusement park, and all the other lights along the Chesapeake Bay. Hundreds of people called the Coast Guard to inquire whether or not there was a real air raid. No one knew, so the lights stayed out. About a week later it was traced back to the Boys Camp."

Wes Harrison made a kind of career out of his gift for mimicry. Even his car had a microphone amplifier with a bullhorn on the roof. As he explains, what he does is basically "old jokes with sound effects"; immediately after making the sound of an explosion he jokes, "There Goes Cuba!" This really dates the album as *before* the Cuban Missile Crisis. We'll probably have another chance to laugh at Cuba soon—I don't know.

One of the more innovative endeavors of the early '60s was the SERIES 2000 MUSIC WITH SOUND series, which produced *Concert Percussion for Orchestra* by JOHN CAGE and Paul Price. Other companion "percussion" albums include: *Percussion Español, Percussion Onstage, Boogie Woogie and Bongos,* and *Gypsy Strings and Percussion.* The Cage album describes itself as "the avant-garde mingled with the living room," and elsewhere proclaims its hope that "people interested in increasing their intellectual and instinctive knowledge toward music and sound respond readily when confronted with new dimensions." What a lofty sales line!

Sidney Poitier's *Journeys Inside the Mind,* Warner Bros.-Seven Arts Records. Album cover credits: cover art: Charles E. White III, art direction: Ed Thrasher.

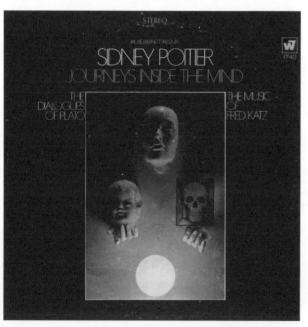

PERCUSSION recording was a big genre in itself during the height of hi-fi and through the birth of stereo. Roland Gelatt's *The Fabulous Phonograph* (1965) provides some background here: "The slogan 'high fidelity' had been bandied about since 1934. It usually meant nothing—except employment for copy-writers. America's leading providers of radio and phonograph sets held strongly to the opinion that most listeners preferred music reproduced at low fidelity (soft, mellow, and flabby) to music reproduced at high fidelity (loud, brilliant, and full-bodied)." He goes on to trace the development of high-fidelity components as beginning in the late '40s, aided by the development of the long-playing 33-1/3 rpm vinyl 12" record by Columbia in 1948. In 1949 the first annual "Audio Fairs" began taking place in larger cities, and thousands of high-fidelity enthusiasts converged to experienced the "state-of-the-art" in equipment and recordings. Gelatt notes that "Bizarre recordings of thunderstorms and screaming railroad trains were concocted for those to whom high-fidelity reproduction was an end in itself and not a means to musical satisfaction . . . [But] the wide and lasting appeal of high-fidelity reproduction went to non-gadgeteers who merely wished the music they heard at home to approximate as closely as possible the sound of live music in the concert hall. In 1954 they spent $140,000,000 in their quest for more realistic sound."

Several companies (notably the COMMAND label) released a line of percussion records. BROADWAY Records released *Pervasive Percussion* without crediting the musicians ("No big deal!") and one song sounds like ERNIE KOVACS' *Nairobi Trio*. TIME Records had as their motto: "For Those Who Dare"! Another percussion series is "Sounds in Motion" on KIMBERLY: *Sounds You See and Hear.*

Most percussion albums are basically big band recordings, like Dick Schory's Percussion Pops Orchestra (twenty musicians playing over 200 brass, woodwind, string and percussion instruments). They did sold-out tours and released LPs like *Politely Percussive, Wild Percussion, Supercussion,* and *Holiday for Percussion*—obviously percussion offered a wide-open field for experimentation, but within a genre identified at the time as hi-fi demonstration and test records. Schory was labeled the "Dynagroove King" after the RCA recording technique, and was credited with helping touch off the percussion craze with his 1958 release *Bang, Baaroom and Harp.* Musically, a lot of these records are pretty standard fare, but it's fun when *quantification* enters the picture, e.g., "William Told": "A takeoff on the classic William Tell Overture with over *fifty-five* different percussion instruments weaving their patterns around the full orchestra." The quantification idea represented a frontier: how many instruments can we record without losing one of them?

♦ **V: *What a job: recording 55 different percussion instruments—***

Norad Tracks Santa, Century Records.
Album cover credits: cover: Bob Haynes.

♦ KS: Another quantification extravaganza is *The Sound of 94 Speakers;* great motion picture themes played by Don Baker on a Rodgers electronic organ in Portland's 14,000 seat Memorial Coliseum. There was also PAUL LAVALLE and the Band of America's 21 Channel Sound LP, recorded with an MGM technique utilizing 21 microphones for ultimate sound separation. The sleeve detailed the microphones used, by instrument and position, and showed photos of the master control consoles.

I also like the Enoch Light Project 3/Total Sound recording of 21 trombones led by Urbie Green. The sleeve lists all 21 trombonists, and rhapsodizes: "The warm, true, unrestricted, vital sound of 21 trombones . . . no overdubbing, no tape tricks, no shortcuts of any kind. *This is unblemished reality!"*

♦ **V: *People were so excited with the potential of recording technology then. And they gave sound a chance, not just music—***

♦ KS: On the back of *Hawaiian Holiday in Hi-Fi* (which was made by a New Yorker, Jack Ladell) it says, "A fantastic four miles of recording tape went into the production of this album." They were hyping the fact that he played all the tracks himself (on 32 different instruments)—that kind of overdubbing had been pioneered by Les Paul. Again, all the technical "specs" are listed; it was recorded in "Spectra-Sonic" sound on the Design Records label. And like a lot of Hawaiian records, if you examine the photo credits you'll see something like "Cover photo courtesy Pan American Airlines." It's like the airlines were in cahoots with the record companies to try to get people to travel to Hawaii. Unfortunately, the record isn't so great—I'm afraid Jack Ladell won't go down in history.

The Piano Artistry of Jonathan Edwards & Darlene Edwards, ® Columbia.
Album cover credits: photo: Leonard Seiken

There are a lot of records I like just for the COV-ERS, like this one: *For Grieving Lovers* (music and narration by Ted Steele). Basically it's insipid romantic orchestral music with Ted's recitations on top. As you can see, part of her problem is: she's smoking too many cigarettes! *A Cure for Loneliness* contains more poems read to music—it shows a woman in a negligee next to a cage holding two lovebirds . . . all the women I know just lounge around the house in negligees! Another favorite is Polly Bergen's *The Party's Over*—I love that faraway, melancholy look in her eyes.

Another nice cover is *Armenian Wedding*—partly because of the woman's expression, and partly because you can't tell if she's wearing any underwear. It was made to capitalize on the belly-dancing craze of the time, and contains Middle-Eastern music which sounds like it was recorded in some club in L.A. The whole genre of belly-dancing records has its appeal—one imagines all these housewives in the suburbs trying to excite their tired husbands after work . . .

♦ **V: Look—on the cover she's holding bags of jewels . . . maybe it's her dowry.**

♦ KS: "Stroke" records are another genre with great covers. What with the current rage for virtual sex recordings such as the *Cybergasm* CD, it's enlightening to examine the early '70s LPs that pioneered this particular hype. *The Sensuous Listener* (Volume One), *The Pleasures of Love,* and *The Sounds of Love A . . . Zzzz (Sensuously Sinthesized)* are just a few examples. Ravel's *Bolero* is a popular "stroke" theme, since it's perfect for the build-up of sexual intensity. You could have an "understanding" (yet authoritative) voice instructing one how to touch oneself, erogenous zone by erogenous zone, climaxing with permission to "let yourself go!" The *Bolero* approach has been used on

other recordings such as LEO DIAMOND's "Never On Sunday" on his *Themes from Great Foreign Films* LP. Speaking of "Never On Sunday," the ORCHES-TRA DEL ORO ("world's largest dance orchestra") did a great version skewing the pop-ethnic sounds of the original, on their LP *Hit Movie Themes Go Latin.* Another LP with a *Greek* approach to pop music hits is NICK DEMETRIUS and the Athenian Forum's *A Touch of Greece.* It includes "Hello Dolly," "Born Free" and "California Dreamin'."

Related to "stroke records" is the genre of instructional "strip" records. ANN ("America's most famous strip-teaser") CORIO's *How to Strip for Your Husband* comes with printed instructions filled with helpful hints, like "Whatever you do, wear high heels! There's nothing like 'em to bring a heel to heel—if you know what I mean! If you don't own a pair of long, black nylons, get 'em and wear 'em right up to the firing line! Remember, the time it takes to roll down a silk stocking can spell the difference between mink and mink-dyed muskrat!" My favorite line is, "Any man will tell you . . . nothing looks better on a woman than anatomy!" Her music is trademark strip-lounge arrangements, heavy on the drums and cymbals.

Speaking of sex and hi-fi, I was reading a 1956 book, *Building Your Record Library,* and the chapter on "Sound, Test and Show-Off Records" noted, "If percussion is the severest test of a sound system, then the Capitol LP *Percussion!* ought to leave any system panting and exhausted!"

The cover of their earlier *The Piano Artistry of Jonathan Edwards* shows two right hands at the keyboard—some people don't notice that.

I also love any "Music For . . ." records, like *Music for Reading, Music for Dreaming, Music to Write Letters By, Music for Painting, Music to Work or Study By, Music to Change Her Mind, Music for Crazy Mixed-Up People*—the list goes on and on. These records promise so much; they're all about *functionality* in the same way that Muzak claimed to employ "music only as the raw material of its service." The liner notes on a Muzak LP claims, "Unlike ordinary music or so-called background music, Muzak is a *non-entertainment medium* employing rhythm, tempo, instrumentation, etc, to *scientifically-determined* specifications . . . making dramatic contributions to the business community through new discoveries in the scientific applications of music . . ." Right—it has nothing to do with music as entertainment!

One of my favorites in the spoken word genre is SIDNEY POITIER's *Journeys Inside the Mind.* He reads selections from Plato's *Republic* (like "The Cave") over light jazz by Fred Katz: "This I know: that I know nothing." Other titles include "Woman's place in society" and "The importance of music in gymnastics." This is great: "Plato's dictum: *Know thyself* is totally pertinent, at a time when every strut supporting our society is being tested."

I also like the covers drawn by cartoonist Jack Davis, who did a lot of work for MAD magazine. He painted a cover for *Sing Along with JONATHAN and DARLENE EDWARDS.* The liner notes say, "We invite you—in fact we challenge you—to sing along with Jonathan and Darlene. If there seem to be a few added beats from time to time, don't be discouraged, and don't blame the record, but rather your lack of imagination." The music sounds like a Mitch Miller singalong except that Darlene is either tone-deaf or incredibly gifted to be able to sing just a little *off;* this record opens up a whole dimension of uncertainty or insecurity. Jonathan's piano playing, described as "confident, yet unpredictable," changes styles all the time; it drifts in and out, and the more you listen, the more the piano playing gets to you. The cover of their earlier *The Piano Artistry of Jonathan Edwards* shows two right hands at the keyboard—some people don't notice that.

Another favorite record is *Norad Tracks Santa,* recorded in 1962 to promote the North American Air Defense Command's Dew Line (Distant Early Warning system). Interspersed with standard Christmas music are reports on Santa Claus—basically, whether or not he's going to be shot down! The underlying message is the threat of accidental nuclear war: "Dear God, let us make it through one more Christmas!" According to the liner notes: "The Norad-tracks-Santa tradition goes back to the late 1950's when a young boy accidentally dialed the unlisted number of the director of combat operations at Norad headquarters in Colorado Springs. The boy was actually trying to phone a department store Santa Claus whose extension was only one digit removed from the phone at the Norad center!"

Like I said, records like these almost make me feel a nostalgia for the Cold War. The Cold War was such a necessary fiction to justify all that extravagant military spending, and it informed so much of that history. But now it's gone, although it leaves behind a rich trail of stories, films and paranoia. As a kid I remember the Cuban Missile Crisis; I remember standing in the schoolyard during the "showdown" (when American destroyers turned back Soviet freighters carrying missiles bound for Cuba) wondering if that would be *it!*

♦ **V: . . . Do you like Crazy Otto?**

♦ KS: He uses a "tipsy wire box" which turns a regular piano into a honky-tonk piano; in effect, what he does is "prepared piano." But he's not that great to listen to, except that many of his titles have the word

If The Bomb Falls, Tops Records.

"crazy" in them—I like that. The liner notes say he was in some bands before '53 (but which ones?) and that he wrote film scores and appeared on TV in Europe and America. Note that "Letters addressed to Crazy Otto, Berlin, Germany will be promptly delivered"—amazing.

♦ *V: What are some of your favorite country music LPs?*

♦ KS: A good LEFTY FRIZZELL album is *Lefty Goes to Nashville,* with a beautiful hand-tinted photo on the cover . . . RAY PRICE is probably my other favorite country-western singer. His songs are simple but effective. I also like Hank Williams, Porter Waggoner and Ernest Tubbs. Recently someone gave me an Air Force recruiting album containing two radio shows. One side was Jim Reeves and the other was Cowboy Copas—both of whom died in plane crashes.

♦ *V: Jim Reeves had a big hit, "He'll Have to Go"—*

♦ KS: And he did! He also did "Four Walls." The funny thing about Reeves is that his death was barely publicized, so for years afterwards he continued to have hits—for example, he was big in South Africa, and fifteen years later was still receiving fan mail. A record company released an LP which mixed together the voices of Jim Reeves and Patsy Cline *after* their deaths ("Now, together for the first time . . .") and that's either a "first" or a new low, depending on your point of view.

I have a crossover record called *Jazz From the Hills*— it's early '50s pre-rock'n'roll or "country-jazz" or "country-boogie," but it's certainly not rockabilly. The cover photo shows Chet Atkins with Homer and Jethro (who were hot players and singers) plus Jerry Byrd. At the time they were working as session musicians backing up other recording artists. Often there would be an

Ted Steele's *For Grieving Lovers*, AAMCO Records, A Division of Alison Enterprises, Inc.

hour or two of leftover recording time available, so these guys would sit around and record tracks for fun (usually standards which everyone knew, like "Stompin' at the Savoy" or "Lady in Red"). This LP was released by Bear Family Records in Germany, who also released a LEFTY FRIZZELL box with 10 LPs and a booklet. Here I should note that Lefty Frizzell is my favorite country singer-songwriter. According to the liner notes, "In October, 1951 he had four songs in the Top Ten"—and this was when Hank Williams had only one in the Top Ten. Lefty's hits include "If You've Got the Money, I've Got the Time," and "Love You A Thousand Ways." He died in 1975 at the age of 47 after influencing artists like Merle Haggard and Dwight Yoakam; he had an incredible voice.

The Country Music Foundation in Nashville maintains a state-of-the-art audio restoration lab and is engaged in lots of music preservation activities. They've released a number of excellent records including Buck Owens' *Live at Carnegie Hall* and a double-LP rockabilly collection from the Capitol Records archives, *Get Hot or Go Home*. Besides their journal, they've also published *Country, The Music and the Musicians,* which has lots of rare photos and chapters by some great writers. I like Doug Green's "Tumbling Tumbleweeds—the Dream of the West," Nick Tosches' "Honky Tonkin'," and Charles Wolf's "Country Radio." Wolf mentions the invention of the Top 40 format in the '50s, a disputed birth claimed by both Gordon Mclendon (who surveyed record retailers and radio stations to determine their top records), and Bill Stewart and Todd Storz who claimed they invented it in 1955 in Omaha, Nebraska, in a bar across from their radio station where they listened to the waitress playing the jukebox and struck upon the idea. Radio

was failing in the '50s because of television; it survived thanks to increased audio fidelity, cheap portables, and new programming. Until the '40s, radio was mainly live talent with local daytime programs and nighttime network programs. Country radio really began to flourish in the '60s, going from 81 full-time stations in 1961 to 606 by 1969. There was a New Orleans station owned by country-broadcasting pioneer-mogul Connie Gay, that featured an all-girl dj staff with the call letters WYFE (wife)! This book also has a nice writeup of Nudie Cohen, the tailor who invented the "Nudie Suit" which is so identified with country music stars.

The Country Music Foundation is also a kind of academic foundation in that it publishes *The Journal of Country Music.* One issue contains an article about JIM BECK who in the late '40s in Dallas recorded Lefty Frizzell and Marty Robbins. Jim Beck had learned electronics during World War II and then built a studio which became *the* happening place—Nashville was not yet a recording center. But while cleaning his equipment with carbon tetrachloride, Beck became overcome by fumes and died! His assistant tried to keep the studio going, but no one could recreate his "sound" and just like that, Dallas as a recording center died! I think of Philip K. Dick's *Man in the High Castle* (an alternative history of World War II, in which the Axis powers win), and imagine Dallas as the present home of country music, not Nashville. And you *know* country music would be quite different today, because Texas is a much more ethnically-mixed state—

Ann Corios's *How to Strip for Your Husband* comes with printed instructions filled with helpful hints, like "Whatever you do, wear high heels! There's nothing like 'em to bring a heel to heel—if you know what I mean! . . . " My favorite line is, "Any man will tell you . . . nothing looks better on a woman than anatomy!"

◆ *V: There would be more Tex-Mex influence—*
◆ KS: More Bohemian (literally Czech and other Eastern European immigrants) influence, plus influence from the Cajuns, the Mexicans, and the Southern Appalachians. In fact the name might even have been different—it might have been called "Western-Country." Beck was a recording genius who invented techniques that were years ahead of his time:

"Beck specialized in recording technology *per se* instead of radio sound technology adapted for recorders. He was first and foremost a sound engineer and would travel to New York twice a year to learn what the latest sound advances were at RCA, get hold of the schematics, come back and build the new systems himself." He died at the age of 39. Elizabeth Beck recalls: "After Jim died I'd liked to never have sold his stuff 'cause nobody knew what it was. He had built it all himself and nobody knew how to run it . . . The studio band gradually broke up."

After Beck died, Owen Bradley established Nashville as the country music recording capital of the world—and he's the guy who brought in strings and that lush sound which many people find *repulsive:* the "Countrypolitan" Sound. Whereas Jim Beck helped define the Honky Tonk Sound.

One of my favorite country-western tragedies involves SPADE COOLEY, a western-swing violinist who became a bandleader—he wound up with his own TV show, leading an all-girl orchestra. He used to host these big dances in the late '40s on the Santa Monica Piers, and incidentally had a great steel guitarist in his group, Joachim Murphy. He got dislodged from early TV by another popular bandleader of the time, Lawrence Welk. [laughs] Later his life took a tragic turn, as recounted by Nick Tosches in his book, *Country.* The chapter is titled, "You're Gonna Watch Me Kill Her," and it told how Spade retired from TV and then tried to build a "Water Wonderland" in the Mojave desert—a doomed enterprise. His wife Ella Mae had been bragging that she was fucking Roy Rogers (Roy will never be quite the same to me again), and this was galling because in some films Cooley had worked as Roy's *stand-in.* On April 3, 1961, Spade came home drunk and tied Ella Mae to a chair. Then he forced his daughter to watch while he burned his wife's breasts with a cigarette and beat her to death. He was sentenced to life without parole in Vacaville, but in 1970 was granted permission to give a concert in Oakland. During an intermission he died of a heart attack. Oddly enough, one of his last recordings had featured a woman, Betsy Gay, singing a song Cooley had written, "You Clobbered Me."

Spade Cooley did mostly WESTERN-SWING music (another genre I like; it's a combination of Country and Big Band), but he also did things like "Oklahoma Stomp" which begins with a swirling orchestral harp (a real harp) and then goes right into this rockin' music. Spade appears in a few Columbia short films. After he went to jail, most of his band joined TEX WILLIAMS' Western Caravan—Tex's big hit was "Smoke, Smoke, Smoke That Cigarette."

Nick Tosches has a raw writing style which I like. He wrote a sordid biography of Dean Martin, *Dino,* which chronicles drug use, alcohol abuse and the reasons behind the break-up with Jerry Lewis. He also wrote *Unsung Heroes of Rock & Roll,* which is mostly about obscure black artists—most people think that it all started with Elvis, but he *ends* with Elvis. When he talks about Wanda ("Fujiyama Mama") Jackson he writes, "She was so hot she could fry eggs on her G-spot." In the second edition this line was deleted.

A lot of people don't know that California pioneered its own country music scene in Bakersfield. WYNN STEWART is the godfather of the "Bakersfield sound"—although the overt, famous father would be BUCK OWENS. Stewart had a few minor hits, but he never did as well as people thought he should have. Among his better songs are "(Here's My Heart) Slightly Used" and "Loversville." He's been re-released on another great BEAR FAMILY production which includes alternate takes of songs.

Another collection I found is *Hillbilly Music, Thank God,* Volume 1, which is a compilation of early Capitol recordings. In '42, Capitol Records was started by Johnny Mercer and Glen Wallace in L.A., partly because ASCAP, *the* music publishers association at the time, was trying to get a royalty rate increase from all the broadcasters, so they threatened a strike: no ASCAP-owned song could be played on the radio until a new contract was signed, and no new recording would be permitted for awhile. Some of the labels didn't want to sign the new deal with ASCAP, so they desperately started recording almost *anything* before the deadline, because they anticipated a year and a half without new product. In this context BMI (Broadcast Music Industries) started up as an alternative music publishing group, and partly because all the "established" musicians had already signed to ASCAP, BMI began signing up a lot of hillbilly performers and songwriters, thus helping hillbilly music become more commercial. This

Polly Bergen's *The Party's Over,* ® Columbia.
Album cover credits: cover photo: Harold Lange.

Spade Cooley, © 1982 CBS Inc.
Album cover credits: art & design: Leslie Carbaga, art direction:
Virginia Team & Bill Johnson, editor: Sally Hinkle, art production: Jeff
Morris. Photographs from the collection of Fred Goodwin.

whole situation created an opening for new labels such as Capitol to emerge.

Hillbilly Music, Thank God includes Buck Owens, Rose Maddox, the Louvin Brothers, Faron Young, Speedy West, Jimmy Bryant, Merle Travis, Red Simpson, and Hank Thompson—all part of an emerging California country music scene. "Mental Cruelty" and "You're For Me" by Buck Owens and Rose Maddox are both good; "Roll Truck Roll" by Red Simpson is an early truck music song about going eighty miles per hour. ELLA MAE MORSE did the great "Hog-Tied Over You" (Betty Page should have been on the cover). HANK THOMPSON is famous for a lot of songs including his classic, "Six Pack To Go." Other western-swing musicians who are great include FLOYD TILLMAN, who did "Driving Nails In My Coffin," "Slipping Around," and "I Love You So Much It Hurts."

I should point out that BUCK OWENS is really important; people mainly associate him with the TV show "Hee Haw," but that's unfortunate because he was a real upstart in country music, and produced a very original sound—he's like Lefty Frizzell in terms of influencing a *lot* of people. His songs are great—they're so simple: "Excuse me, I think I've Got a Heartache . . ." I went to see Flaco Jimenez's band play and they opened with "It's Crying Time Again"—they did three Buck Owens songs in a row because he fits in so well with that Tex-Mex sound. Buck Owens' *Live at Carnegie Hall* from 1966 is a great LP, with his amazing guitar player Don Rich and the excellent steel player, Tom Brumley.

Another great steel guitarist is SPEEDY WEST; I like *Spaceman in Orbit* which was re-released as *Speedy*

West, Steel Guitar From Outer Space. He and JIMMY BRYANT played on each other's albums all the time. I got a Jimmy Bryant reissue on the Stetson label and tried to scrape off a bargain-price sticker on the cover, only to realize it was *in* the cover; the company must have re-photographed it from an old album! On *Jimmy Bryant: Guitar Take-Off,* the engineer simply put a microphone between Speedy West and Jimmy Bryant and they traded riffs back and forth. Apparently Leo Fender developed the Stratocaster guitar just for him: that's where "Stratosphere Boogie" comes from. I think Jimmy Bryant died from lung cancer—he was also a tragic figure: a drinker, etc. And I think Speedy West wound up getting a stroke, so he could no longer play in the same style. For my taste he overdoes the gimmicks somewhat, but he's still great. If you compare him to Jerry Byrd—well, they're quite different.

♦ *V: What's the Louvin Brothers' "A Great Atomic Power" about?*

♦ KS: It's about the atom bomb, of course—back to that Cold War theme. This song is on the *Atomic Cafe* film soundtrack, which brings together '40s and '50s songs dealing with the threat of nuclear war. Recently I started an art project which I named "Misty Echo" (the title of a nuclear test in the '80s). I think of the bureaucratic naming procedure of nuclear tests and military operations as "the poetry of power." I called the Department of Energy in Nevada and requested a listing of all the nuclear tests that have been done—over 700 were performed in Nevada alone. Worldwide, counting the Soviet Union and other places, there have been over 2000 of these useless tests.

♦ *V: Why isn't the earth completely radiated?*

Western Swing, Blues, Boogie and Honky Tonk, Volume 8—The 1940's & '50's,
Arhoolie Records. Album cover credits: cover by Wayne Pope.

♦ KS: A lot of it is—we just aren't continually *reminded* of this on a daily basis. I talked to someone who had toured a nuclear plant in Minnesota, and as a souvenir he'd received a little clip-on radiation exposure gauge. He said that years later the meter was still going up—in other words, the background radiation in general had gotten higher and higher. And he hasn't been to any more nuclear power plants, either. Today, the *symmetry* of the old power balance is gone, but of course, the nuclear threat isn't over by any means . . .

BIBLIOGRAPHY

George S. Kanahele, ed. *Hawaiian Music and Musicians: An Illustrated History,* 1979. Essential!

Robert Kamohalu Kasher & Burl Burlingame, eds. *Da Kine Sound: Conversations with the People Who Create Hawaiian Music,* 1978.

Bill C. Malone. *Country Music U.S.A.,* 1985. Revised; a classic.

Country Music Foundation. *Country: The Music and the Musicians,* 1990. Great pictures and exciting essays by the best writers. *Journal of Country Music* appears 3 times a year.

Thomas B. Holmes. *Electronic and Experimental Music,* 1985. Disappointing but useful guide, with lists of recordings, books, etc.

Joe Goldmark. *International Steel Guitar Discography.* Updated regularly, with complete discographies of steel guitar instrumentals by major players.

Dick Hebdige. *Subculture: The Meaning of Style,* 1979. A classic. *Cut'n'Mix: Culture, Identity and Caribbean Music,* 1987. Hebdige tries his hand, less successfully, on identifying sources of Caribbean music.

Nick Tosches. *Country: Living Legends and Dying Metaphors in America's Biggest Music,* 1985. *Unsung Heroes of Rock'n'Roll in the Dark and Wild Years Before Elvis,* 1984. Scandalous, extensive, essential!

Fred & Judy Vermorel. *Starlust: The Secret Fantasies of Fans,* 1985. Poignant.

Simon Frith & Andrew Goodwin, eds. *On Record: Rock, Pop & the Written Word.* Essays range from sociology through feminist & semiotic readings.

Tania Modeleski, ed. *Studies in Entertainment: Critical Approaches to Mass Culture,* 1986. Excellent essays by Raymond Williams, Margaret Morse, Rick Altman, Kaja Silverman, etc. Bernard Gendron's "Theodor Adorno Meets The Cadillacs" updates Adorno's analysis of popular music by examining the productions of pioneer doo-wop group The Cadillacs.

Douglas Kahn & Gregory Whitehead, eds. *Wireless Imagination: Sound, Radio & the Avant-Garde,* 1992. Groundbreaking; focuses on avant-garde theory & practice of sound.

Rick Altman, ed. *Sound Theory, Sound Practice,* 1992. Excellent critical essays on issues in cinematic sound.

Roy M. Prendergas. *Film Music: A Neglected Art,* 1977. Important.

Dan Lander & Micah Lexier, eds. *Sound By Artists,* 1990. Great braille cover!

Germano Celant. "Record As Artwork," orig. pub. in *Studio International.* Survey of avant-garde use of record medium to explore sound and language. Reproduced in shorter form in *Flash Art, Two Decades of History,* 1990.

Simon Frith & Howard Horne. *Art Into Pop,* 1987. The art school & pop music connection. Fascinating.

Constance Penley & Andrew Ross, eds. *Technoculture,* 1991. Essays on the politics of technology.

Paul Nougé. *Music Is Dangerous,* 1972. Pamphlet by Belgian surrealist, 1929.

Public 4/5. *Sound,* 1990. Contemporary writings on sound issues.

October 55, **1990.** Adorno's writing on phonography, etc.

Plunderphonics, Box 727 Station P, Toronto, Canada M5S 2Z1. Send 4 IRCs for catalog.

Accordion Hits, Gallo Records.

ACCORDION HITS

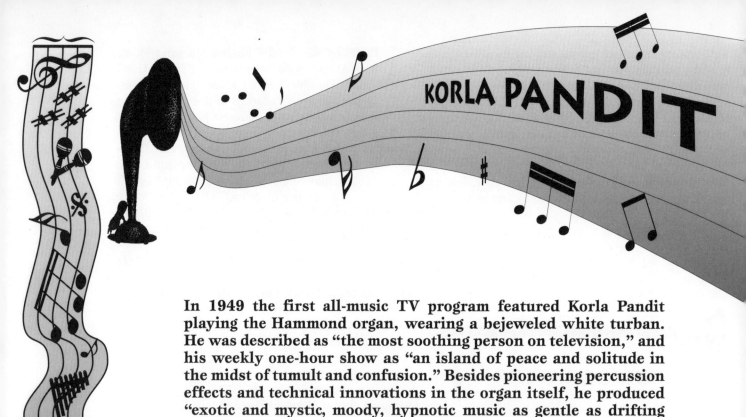

KORLA PANDIT

In 1949 the first all-music TV program featured Korla Pandit playing the Hammond organ, wearing a bejeweled white turban. He was described as "the most soothing person on television," and his weekly one-hour show as "an island of peace and solitude in the midst of tumult and confusion." Besides pioneering percussion effects and technical innovations in the organ itself, he produced "exotic and mystic, moody, hypnotic music as gentle as drifting lotus blossoms, as savage as jungle drums." He captivated millions of (mostly female) viewers the world over, despite the fact that he never spoke. Korla Pandit still performs and lectures; currently he lives in Los Angeles.

♦ KORLA PANDIT: More than 40 years ago I began communicating the idea of the *Universal Language of Music* . . . transcendent sound which transcends all borderlines, expressing universal love. That was always my theme, yet I never *spoke* it in my more than 900 live television shows—it was expressed only through the *music*. Now there's a whole new generation of young people interested in the sounds I originated. Recently I played a recital for the woman who founded the Montessori school, and a teenager came up to me and said, "All the young people I'm around now are talking about you—there's a new interest in your work." A couple years ago the AMOK people put on a concert for me, and I got a big write-up with a photo in the Los Angeles *Times*—which isn't easy.

♦ *VALE: How did you get to be on television in 1949?*

♦ KP: There used to be "telescriptions": short programs on which all the top names recorded (Peggy Lee, Nat King Cole, Count Basie, Woody Herman, Perry Como)—these were the film equivalents of music video today. At first the programs were broadcasted only in the Los Angeles area where they were made, but then they began spreading across the country (includ-

ing my program). Soon I was receiving 700-900 letters a week—more than all the other big names put together! The producers noticed this, and wanted to record me for a regular program. I did two shows for them, but they would never pay me, and when I protested they said, "We'll just go over and record Liberace" (who was playing a club on Sunset Strip). That didn't work out like they hoped, so they came back with a contract.

In the meantime I'd found out that people had sent me all kinds of gifts—cufflinks, rings, diamonds—one lady who said that I "saved her life" sent me a grand piano! But since I never spoke on my program, I wasn't asking for anything—I was only interested in giving love through my music. Soon these programs were broadcasted all over the world. Despite language differences, they didn't have to change *anything* (except for the local narration giving station identification). Because the music already was universal—and I never spoke anyway—every country felt I was playing for *them*. A Japanese girl wrote (and I had to have it translated), "You have fan in Japan." People all over the world had sent me gifts and letters, and the TV people decided to exploit that to the hilt—to promote me bigger than Michael Jackson or Madonna. At that point I said, "I don't mind you cheating *me* (Well, I mind it, but I can accept it), but I'm not going to let you exploit people who think they're supporting me, while you run off with everything!" Their answer was, "You'll never work in this town again," and I've never been on a major network since. That's what happened to my career.

A lot of people still know me, but they know nothing about my work with metaphysics or my work in Canada, or that I've dedicated a Jewish synagogue and played for the dedication of a new Catholic church in Chino, California: with 27 monks there from Montezuma, the priest asked me to play and I had to create an E-minor mass right on the spot! People said, "You captivated everybody."

Korla Pandit's *The Grand Moghul Suite—Part 1*, India Records.

What I'm trying to communicate through music is true love and the divine consciousness (regardless of religious belief—*that* doesn't matter). TV isn't real, it's just light, and in my programs I was expressing love through *sound and light vibrations*—actually, that's what *we* are. We reflect light, and that's what determines what "color" we are.

What I've been concerned with all along is basic truth; what is *real*. And what *is* real? You are, and I am. I'm not preaching, but the only thing that can save the earth now is men and women of good will throughout the world. We know what our differences are, but if someone doesn't speak up for what is basically universal truth, we're lost. We can't get so involved in all this high-tech we're living with now that we forget that we're not robots—we are *people*. And we *are* all one.

I'm aware of what's "happening" in music today—my son's a musician and he knows all about synthesizers and midi—he knows how to set up a concert so we'll be heard properly. But if it's a question of "Bach or Rock?" I ask, "Is it *good* Bach or *good* Rock?" I was asked to play a concert for a "tough" high school. The teachers were afraid the kids might throw things, but I got a standing ovation! It took ten football players to

escort me out—the kids didn't want me to leave.

Even though I regret not being on the air for so many years, what I did on films and tapes can't be taken back. Be it Holland or Russia or many other countries, if I go there, people remember—if I'm in a supermarket, someone will come up and say, "My mother (or my grandmother, or children or grandchildren) all remember watching you on TV." That has kept going, because, like I said, music is a form of love, and there was a purpose to my music: to spread love.

♦ **V: Well, *your records are now being collected more than ever*—**

♦ KP: I put out 14 records on the Fantasy label in San Francisco. They may not have given me a true accounting, but they did get my music all over the world. The same thing with those films—they kept showing them, and they're still showing them. Some young kids in Florida got hold of some of my old broadcasts and released them on two videotapes as "The Hollywood Years." They're not accounting to me [laughs] but they're keeping my name going—it's helping me be seen by people who've never heard of me before. Also, I did a score for Eastman Kodak's recent re-release of *Phantom of the Opera* (starring Lon Chaney; 1925). I did the introduction on a big pipe organ, and my son

and I played keyboards hooked to midi. When people saw the film, they asked, "Where are the strings? Where's the orchestra? Where's the opera singer?" (because I included a human voice). I made the music really "nervous" when the Phantom was about to fall, and the soundtrack is full of subtle effects. That tape has been distributed all over Europe (not here, because *I'm* here!) but again, it's being seen by people who never heard of me before.

♦ **V: You were born with a musical gift—**

♦ KP: Almost anything I hear I can play by ear; I can hear sounds as they really are. When I went to the University of Chicago, they tested me and found I had a 99.9% tonal memory and a 98.9% rhythm memory. So when I started doing orchestral arranging I knew what the range of all the instruments was, and could "hear" what they would all sound like together before putting pen to paper. When I began using a Novochord and a Hammond organ, I succeeded in imitating orchestral instruments through combining tonebars because I *understood* the harmonics. I could evoke tonalities that had never been evoked before.

♦ **V: You expanded the limits of what could be done with the organ—**

♦ KP: When I developed all my left-handed percussion patterns on the Hammond organ, I experimented with the drawbars so that, combined with my foot pedals, I could produce the sound of bongo drums or Indian drums or a whole variety of percussion while maintaining melody and harmony with my right hand. This required intense concentration, clarity of mind, and manual dexterity on such a high level that I don't know if I could ever do it again! I only knew that I had

An Evening with Korla Pandit: A Concert Performance, **Fantasy Records. Album cover credits: photo: Bob Willoughby with technical advice by Christopher Stewart, models: Margo Moore and Nick King.**

to *do* it; I had to summon up the dexterity to make that happen. You can watch those old videos and see that I was really doing it all in real time, and that won't be easy to copy! All my shows were done when TV was still "live" (none of that pre-recorded taping) and they were all done in *one take*. And all my records (with the exception of those on which narrations were over-dubbed) were also done in one take!

TV isn't real, it's just light, and in my programs I was expressing love through sound vibrations and light— actually, that's what *we* are. We reflect light, and that's what determines what "color" we are.

I've played with a lot of people. I was called in to help accompany and arrange for a singer named Fran Warren who sang with the Skip Henderson Orchestra. Most of her songs took about 20 takes to record, but with me she did her number in one take and it was her only hit off the record: "Hindi." I also played with the Sons of the Pioneers, and in honor of our work together they dubbed me "Cactus Pandit." (By the way, they could really sing!)

Over the years I've met a lot of people. As a teenager, before I was old enough to go to bars, I went to these after-hours places where jazz musicians would get together and play after their gigs. The blind pianist ART TATUM, who was not only a very great technician but could play *anything* from jazz to classical, took a liking to me (and he was very particular who he played with; not many people could keep up with him). I played with him several times at after-hours parties; there are no recordings of these sessions, they were just for fun. Whenever I sat down and started playing he knew immediately who I was and came over.

Yogananda, author of the best-selling *Autobiography of a Yogi* (he was very influential in the '40s-'60s) heard me "live" on the radio and invited me to play a concert at his ashram. When I met him, he immediately treated me as an equal and told me how much he appreciated my work. I also met Manly Palmer Hall, who was probably one of the ten most intelligent people on earth (he founded the Philosophical Research Society and wrote *The Secret Teaching of All Ages*). He talked to me as a person who could *understand*. We had several conversations about philosophy and the meaning of life, just talking one-on-one, and he immediately understood my concept of spreading love through music. I have a photo of myself with him. He died recently.

♦ **V: A lot of what you did could be considered music for meditation. The world is so hectic and stressful; now there's a whole new audience for you. Actually, you pioneered New Age Music—**

♦ KP: The planet is becoming poisonous to live on. There's so much corruption and evil in government and big business that people almost seem to have *given up.* They're being brainwashed and controlled by television as never before in history. We need to turn off all that external programming and really go down deep into ourselves to tap our deepest resources—the intuition and knowledge that we were born with and which never leaves us. If we do that, perhaps *there* we can find the *peace* we really need . . . to survive.

♦ **V: Describe your TV show a bit more—**

♦ KP: When I was first on television, I never spoke at all, but my non-verbal message: releasing stress and tension through sound and sound vibrations, was there, and now people are picking up on it again. *What's supposed to happen is going to happen*—all we need to do is turn down the noise and tune into it, I always say.

The idea of "spreading love through music" is very basic. In a sense the whole universe is based on love—it's what holds it all together. If there wasn't that universal thought, nothing would have survived this long. When we were born, there were a million things waiting to "do us in" here on earth, but we must have had antidotes for them because we're still here in spite of AIDS or whatever the scientists in the laboratories are putting out. (I do think AIDS was the result of germ warfare; it's pure biological warfare that was slanted to hit whoever they wanted to put down and it may have gotten out of control, or maybe it *isn't* out of control—maybe it's doing exactly what they wanted it to do. But they must have an antidote or they wouldn't have put it out, because their own families would have been endangered. Or maybe it's like the poison gas in World War I—the wind blew it back on our own troops).

The true basis underlying all of our genuine communication is love, and love is universal. We don't talk to our cats in German or French or Russian or English or Chinese or any of those languages—and the cats don't respond in any of those languages, either—but they know what we're saying and we know what they're feeling. They *do* understand when there's hostility, or when there's respect or love. And all my pets understand—I've had birds, cats, dogs, or what have you—tigers and all.

♦ **V: You've had tigers?**

♦ KP: Well, I didn't "have" a tiger—and it didn't *have* me! We never own our "pets"—we live with them. A few years ago I thought all the trains in America were going to be eliminated (it did almost happen) so I took an Amtrak trip instead of flying back East to do a

Korla Pandit's *Love Letters*, Fantasy Records.

concert. It took me two-and-a-half days. Anyway, I did a concert and stopped off at St Louis to see the famous zoo. It was the last day of school so the zoo was crammed full of children; I hopped on the little train that circled the zoo to the big open-air Siberian tiger enclosure. These tigers are 200 pounds bigger than the Bengal tigers of India. There was a big one lying there, and the man told me I could walk across the track and get a photo of him. I raised my camera to take the picture and the tiger gave me a great big beautiful grin—the zookeeper asked [surprised], "How did you get him to *do* that?!" I said, "Well, he's a friend—I just talked to him and he recognized me."

I don't know how old I am—I think I'm 2028; this year makes it 2029. I never did tell my age; when I was a teenager on TV I said the same thing. I didn't know I was older until I watched a 45th anniversary Paramount TV retrospective—a kinescope of one of my original shows opened the two-and-a-half hour program. The show said, "We're going into the '60s . . . '70s . . . '80s" and I said, "Hold on! I don't know anything about all that; I'm still here in present time. That's all I need to count!"

♦ **V: Tell us more about your early life—**

♦ KP: I was born in New Delhi. My mother was of French descent—a coloratura soprano opera singer, and my father was a Hindi Brahmin high up in the government of India, along with Nehru and others. However, I don't want to get into political and religious situations—as with Gandhi, my goal is to bring love and understanding to all people, and to eliminate all these different systems of castes, countries, and borderlines that are destroying the world. I was guided in this from the very beginning, because my father broke away from some of the precedents and tradi-

tions when he married my mother. My mother was European, and she visited India (as did Caruso, Jenny Lind, and all the famous opera singers of that time). My father was in charge of the promotion and presentation of these visiting singers, and of course, that's how he met my mother.

There were seven in my family; we had a big two-story home in India. When I was two years and four months of age, my parents heard someone downstairs playing the piano, and they thought one of my brothers or sisters had stayed home from school. They came down and discovered I had climbed up on the bench and was picking out melodies on the piano. They left me alone and I played other melodies. By the time I was five, I had quite a repertoire of songs. My parents took me to British teachers, who played some songs which they were going to teach me—and immediately I played them back to them.

Before I even knew what an organ was, I could play a piano in such a way that you wouldn't know if I were playing a guitar or a train whistle—it was all combinations of piano tones. I understood the laws of harmonics, and that was the basis of my "universal language of music and love." All my programs are based on *transcending the differences,* in "A Golden Wedding of East and West," as someone once said. That was the concept I followed in any recording or presentation that I made. I played music from every country, but the secret was: every number I played, I played it in a way that the people of that country would claim it as their own. I didn't do a European's version of a Hindi number, or a Chinese version of a French number, but I tried to capture the true feeling of every song I played so that people would recognize it as their *own* music. This was why I was able to transcend the differences of religion, race, etc, and have an audience that was a cross-section of the world.

♦ V: Where did you travel in Europe?

♦ KP: I didn't travel to very many countries. When I left India, we went to England and I was there for awhile. At age 12-1/2, I came to America. This happened because of a conference in India, whose purpose was to try to keep alive ancient, traditional Hindi music. Indian music was gravitating more toward Muslim or Turkish or belly-dancing music, but the traditional classical music of India (which Ravi Shankar and others brought to America in more recent years; previously his brother Udai [sic] Shankar had brought a star troupe to the U.S. in the '40s or '50s) was in danger of being lost, because it was always taught master-to-pupil; it wasn't something you could put on a recording or video. So people wanted to standardize it somehow, but it wasn't written on the same scale as Western music, so you couldn't learn it that way.

People from all over the world attended this conference. Some British people had asked my father to bring me—they thought it was a publicity stunt that I could do all these alleged "feats."

Korla Pandit In Paris, © 1963 Fantasy Records, Inc.
Album cover credits: cover art: Don Stivers, typesetting: Jim Melvin Typographers, cover design: Balzer-Shopes.

♦ V: What do you mean?

♦ KP: Well, at this conference, a British teacher brought an 11-year-old pianist who had written a song of her own, which nobody else could possibly have known. In front of all these people, she played it on the piano. Then they asked me to play it exactly as she played it. I did, and then my teacher said, "Now Korla, play it right"—she had made a mistake. I played it again and corrected the mistake, and that created quite a sensation and brought me some attention internationally.

My father had always said, "Complete your education—they cannot take that away from you. People in show business and the concert world are heroes today, bums tomorrow!" Promoters and impresarios were notorious for making money from artists but not paying them, and there's no difference today. My father did not want me to get caught up in that, but when an opportunity arose for me to come to America, my mother thought I should do it. My father had an associate from World War I who was a chaplain in the British Army, and this chaplain told him, "If he comes to America, I will be his guardian." My education had been in English, so I didn't have to learn the language. I went to several preparatory schools before I attended the University of Chicago, where they gave me those tests I mentioned earlier. They put me in a room and played the most complex chords to see if they could lose me, but they didn't. That's how they discovered that I had this inborn talent.

This also paved the way for me to play the organ. In high school, I was called upon to play for some program that the pianist hadn't showed up for. I did, and a few weeks later the call came, "Can you play the organ?" I said, "I think so," even though I'd never seen one; I'd only seen the harmoniums in India. At this time I was studying piano with a German teacher at a big music store in Chicago, and he always said [about me], "He plays with a crystal touch . . . don't spoil his ear." Anyway, when they called me out to play this Hammond organ, it was for a big home trade show. I got interested in it because it had these drawbars, and by moving them in or out I could create all these different sounds, ranging from violins to flutes to drums to brass—tones that really weren't in the instrument; most musicians could only produce flute tones.

I started going down to a music store several times a week to play and experiment on the Hammond organ, creating my own sounds, and I had that perfected before I ever came to California. I could create and play drums, bells, brass, violins—people said, "There's no violin on a Hammond," but I could play a violin on it. One organist asked me how I played drums on the Hammond, because when he pulled the first white drawbar out, all he could get was a flute sound. I asked him, "Do you know how to play drums?" He replied, "No," and I said, "That's your first problem—you have to first know what a drum *does.*" No one else had ever done this before, and few people have done it on a Hammond since. Of course, now they have all these synthesizers, but they weren't available when I went on TV.

At school I played string bass with the symphony orchestra. From my vantage point I was able to hear all the instruments and learn their range and limitations, and also know accurately what the *sounds* were. I started out as Number Eight and moved up to Number One because whenever the conductor stopped and wanted to hear a certain passage again, I could remember it and play it. I could hear the orchestra as it really was; nothing can quite replace being right in the middle of the orchestra! This was vital and important; it gave me the scope I had for the orchestral numbers I played when I went on TV.

I did some programs on network radio, and I remember Rudy Vallee telling me, "Korla, no one could believe you're doing all those sounds yourself . . . until they *see* you." When I went on TV, then everyone *could* see that I was actually creating all the sounds they heard. And I would go from the organ to the piano and back again, and play both together, without ever missing a beat.

♦ V: *Did you work with the Hammond Organ Company to develop a new instrument?*

♦ KP: Well, the company invited me out to visit the factory, because no one had ever done what I did before. At the time their instrument was new; it had been invented by a clockmaker who had discovered he could get a definite rhythm going and could create a musical scale by regulating tonal wheels. The company told me that they had difficulty getting permission to call their instrument an "organ." So they arranged for an experiment at the University of Chicago. They mounted big speakers next to the pipes of a pipe organ and did a "blindfold" test on an audience—50% couldn't tell the difference. That was enough to allow them to call it an "organ."

A new keyboard instrument was developed using a tube for every sound, and it could do some of the things that a synthesizer can do now. It had several sounds which were not in the Hammond organ, like a guitar or accordion sound. It was the Novochord (mentioned earlier). It didn't go over as well, because it didn't have a bass you could play, so you had to be playing with somebody else if you wanted that bass accompaniment. As a solo instrument, it was a natural for me. But they couldn't sell as many of those as they could the Hammond.

When I came out to Hollywood, I started appearing on radio programs. Initially I had to make a demonstration recording, because I couldn't explain to anybody what I was doing. If I said, "I play organ," all people could think of were skating rinks or churches or films or weddings, and in those days most jazz groups wouldn't even consider using an organ or even a harmonica—that was the way the music world was. When I first approached agents, they weren't too interested, so I had to have something to show what I do.

I went to four or five places before I found a radio station that had both a Hammond organ and a piano, so I could play what I play. The recording company was several blocks away, and the radio station had to wire the music over to them—I had to go back and forth just to arrange things. Finally, I had it all together. The disc jockey was sitting in the next room. After awhile he came over and asked, "What are you doing?" I replied, "I'm playing the organ and piano to-

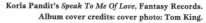

Korla Pandit's *Speak To Me Of Love,* **Fantasy Records. Album cover credits: cover photo: Tom King.**

Korla Pandit's *Music of Mystery and Romance*, Fantasy Records. Album cover credits: cover photo: Nicole Schoening.

gether, simultaneously, creating new and unique orchestral sounds as well as sounds that are familiar." "Yeah? How'd you like to be on my program?" I said, "On one condition. You give away free tickets to events on your program, don't you? I'll play on your program if you hold a contest asking people to guess how many people are playing." "Okay; can you play 'Tico Tico'?" (By the way, Ethel Smith heard me play this. She met me through the Sherman & Clay Music Company and took me to her apartment in Hollywood and fed me cake and ice cream and wanted me to show her how to play the drums. I didn't show her that, so she went and got the Brazilian rhythm section from Carmen Miranda's group [Joe Carioca and others] and made the only hit record she ever had, "Tico Tico.")

So on this radio show I was a "mystery guest." I carefully set up the organ and piano so I could play both of them at the same time, and then began. Listeners were invited to call in and guess the number of people playing—and no one called. I kept playing and still no one called. Somebody in the station remarked, "Well, I guess nobody's listening"—and then the phone rang; it was the *phone company* calling to say that so many people were calling in from all over L.A. that all their lines were jammed! Finally, a few people got through and they all guessed from 3-15; not a single soul guessed that there was only *one* person playing! After that response, I started being invited to play on the radio regularly . . . and that led to my own television show—which began as 15 minutes and built up to an hour-and-a-half, because whenever anyone would call in or write letters, they would say the show was too short, so the station kept extending the length of my program. They put me on the air every afternoon on KMPC. I played behind people like Peggy Lee and

Mel Torme; whoever came there, I had to play for them.

♦ **V: You were on Chandhu the Magician—**

♦ KP: That was before I went on television. I was doing radio work, and one of my jobs was to check the scores of Jack Benny, Bing Crosby and others to make sure there was no copyright infringement, even on their in-between-scenes music. I did radio transcriptions for Capitol. I also performed a night-time program with a girl who used to sing with big bands, and an afternoon pipe-organ program. The two major networks had big pipe organs in their studios, plus a grand piano and the Hammond, and I played my orchestral sounds plus the rhythms (Brazilian and all the others) on the Hammond and the piano, and on the big pipe organ I played what I called "symphonic" music—that was on CBS radio. I did guest shots on programs such as Kay Kyser.

I started doing a night-time program for ABC called "Hollywood Holiday" which was taped at a big club on Vine Street. One night two men from the audience came up and talked to me afterwards—they had been involved with the *Chandhu the Magician* radio program years before. When they saw me, they wanted to revive the show. They played some 16-inch transcription recordings for me, and I liked them and joined the show. It took place all over the Orient, from Europe and the Balkans to Tibet, and no matter where they went, I could play suitable music. If they wanted a gypsy violin, I could play a gypsy violin. If they went to the Tibetan mountains, well—I knew a Tibetan nun and had studied the religion, so . . . This was something no other organist could do. Other organists tried to take my place, but one of the producers was a West Indian who had been on the original program which was so successful, and he said, "I'm sorry, but Mr Pandit is the only one who can do this music—that's it!"

The show always opened with a big gong and the announcement, "Chandhu the Magician!" Then I started my theme (which I also used in my *Grand Moghul Suite*) called "The Trance Dancer." The White King Soap Company had been the sponsor of the original program, and they also sponsored the one we did. This was the last radio program I did for the Mutual network, and we won an Emmy. I have some tapes of those shows, somewhere.

♦ **V: You joined the Musicians Union—**

♦ KP: When I came to town, there was no place for a Hindu musician in the Union. Local 47 didn't know what to do with me. They had a "Latin" division (mostly around Alvaro Street), and across town they had another division for the Blacks, which included Nat King Cole. I didn't fit into any of these; I was still Me, Myself and I, and I said, "Here's what I'll do. I'll play the Latin music." So they gave me a Latin name, and I recorded about 50 Latin songs on 16-inch transcription records. I had learned them earlier, when I first came out to the West Coast. I had been in Orange County for about a year, staying in the big home of a Latin family who owned half of downtown Santa Ana. So I learned all these Latin songs—as soon as I heard them, I could play them.

I did the same thing with Hawaiian drums. There was a man who put out a whole series of records on Decca of Tahitian and jungle drums, and I learned them so well that when I was doing a show on KTLA he called me and said, "You've got it, by George, you've got it!" This man, who had brought together some of the best drummers in the South Seas (as well as Latin and African drummers), came and asked me to do a recording for him because I had captured the spirit so well.

♦ **V: What Latin name did you record under?**

♦ KP: I did those tapes and transcription recordings which radio stations played, and appeared on shows like Bob Hope, under the name "Juan Orlando." When I started doing *Chandhu the Magician,* I began using my own name because—why should I use a different name? Then I started on television, and I've used my own name ever since. But by any other name, "a rose is still a rose"!

♦ **V: It's key to your later music: that you learned Latin and Tahitian rhythms—**

♦ KP: Before I came out to California, I played with opera companies and a symphony orchestra, as I said. One time we traveled to Kansas City, and the head of the symphony heard me play and told me, "I would give up my whole career as a conductor if I had your ability to *project.*" The key to my television programs was: I was able to project this music into the hearts of listeners. I concentrated on playing music of transcen-

dence—that was the whole basis of my programs on TV, recordings and live performances. It didn't matter whether I was playing rock, jazz or classical—I captured the true feeling of what that song was supposed to do. That's why I could even play with a country-and-western group—like I said, I recorded a series of records with the Sons of the Pioneers. I also recorded with ROY ROGERS & DALE EVANS on RCA Victor; I created the thunderstorm on "Stampede": the wind and thunder effects. We were on a lot of programs together. I recorded with Shirley Temple, too.

♦ **V: You've played all types of international music; you've lived your philosophy of universal music—**

♦ KP: After I left Hollywood, I lived in Northern California for awhile and then moved to Canada, playing there in different churches. In Surrey, B.C., there are a lot of first-generation immigrants from Europe; their ancestors hadn't come over 300 years ago. There are first-generation Scotch and English and Dutch and French people there, and there were hardly any of their songs which I didn't have a real feeling for. I wasn't playing somebody's song because it was popular; I actually *experienced* it. That's a basic difference.

♦ **V: Tell us more about the year you spent in Orange County—**

♦ KP: I stayed with that Latin family, then took a trip back east, and when I returned they had left, so I stayed at the YMCA for awhile. The USO and the Air Corps were there, and I played for the USO. The Ecumenical Center wanted me to play for them—all these people from various religions would come in from all over—and I could play all their hymns, too. So when I went on TV, I wasn't creating a "new thing," I was showing people what I already knew. I was on daytime television for two-and-a-half years, and one of the things that happened was: a local Catholic school gave their pupils stars for watching my program—they felt it was *that* beneficial.

♦ **V: On your TV shows, sometimes there's beautiful background footage of clouds, dancing girls, etc. How did that evolve?**

♦ KP: After I had done a whole series of concerts with people like Rudy Vallee and Jose Iturbi, a producer arranged for me to play for a big fur fashion show, which would be televised. I really didn't want to do this, but I did. The producer told me afterward, "You know, you have a very sensitive face—give me a call." Well, you know how *that* is—getting through is almost impossible.

Meanwhile, I went to NBC with a complete program format including projections of clouds and mists at the beginning, settings, backgrounds, and a narration which I wrote myself for all the programs. The opening musical theme was "The Magnetic Theme," which is on some of my records. I used quotations from the poet-laureates of England and various great books on music and philosophy and tied it all together; I had a definite plan. About 2 hours after NBC accept-

ed this, that producer contacted me and said, "If you do the score for this new children's program, I guarantee you'll be on TV for one full year." NBC had said they would carry the show for a few weeks, after which they might drop it—you never knew. So I accepted the producer's offer and played for the children's show—it turned out to be *Time for Beanie,* with Nan Freeberg, Doris Butler, and Captain Huff'n'Puff. It won an Emmy. My own show started out as a half-hour and soon was a full hour on Sunday, after which it became permanent. Then they added another hour, involving guests like Manly P. Hall in the same format as Johnny Carson, years later. On one show the inventor of the theremin played "Moonlight Sonata" while I played piano. I was on a lot of shows on all of the networks, either "live" or on those films or telescriptions I made, and once I was on every TV station in Hollywood on the same day!

♦ **V: But what about the actual backgrounds of your TV programs?**

♦ KP: My wife was an artist and worked in studios before we ever met. She and her father worked on Disney's *Fantasia;* she did the cloud sequences, and because he knew aviation, he did the pterodactyls and creatures that flew. He had invented a device used on ships and airplanes to regulate them, but was also an artist—a very good artist. Some of the backgrounds I wanted, my wife could create; I did some of them myself. When the show got bigger, the producers brought in some big names (like Barry Ashton, who did choreography) and included footage of dancing girls, etc when they compiled a full-length film which they would send all around the world. Cecil B. DeMille's son was the director of my KGLA show at the beginning. My wife would draw black-on-white, and he would work with that and create special effects. For example, if I wanted to enter into a crystal ball, they could arrange that. We developed the CBS "eye" logo which CBS uses to this day; my wife drew that. So most of the whole formula: the background, projections, narration and all, were created by us. Of course, they grabbed it and ran off with it and sometimes they got away from what we had originally done—and it wasn't as effective, either.

We did most of the special effects on the show, and there was one special effect which was sensational. I wrote a tune, "Theme of the Underwater Worshippers," which has to do with a legend: Along the Mediterranean coast of North Africa at nightfall, lonely travelers tell of hearing chants on top of the wind, accompanied by an insistent drumbeat not unlike that of the human heart. This legend has to do with an underground civilization which came to the surface one time and then vanished. We didn't have access to many of the special effects available now, so we put a Dixie cup with a pinhole in it over the camera lens so that all you could see was my face. Then we set up an aquarium with fish swimming in it, put a miniature

Korla Pandit's *Music for Meditation,* Fantasy Records.
Album cover credits: cover: Atwood/Weiss.

temple at the bottom, and it looked like Jacques Cousteau's deep seas. Slowly the camera moved in, and through the temple door my face came into view while the fish were swimming all around. What was unusual was: the fish picked up the tempo of the musical rhythm and were swimming to it! Anyone who saw the show could see, in *action,* my theory of the universal language of music and love—spreading love and understanding around the world through music. If you meditate strongly enough, you can do these things!

♦ **V: You started your own Do-It-Yourself record company—**

♦ KP: It was a necessary thing to do: in order to be recorded, I had to record myself. And I had a following. My first recording was made on India Records, my own label—Korla Pandit Productions. I put together a program of my most popular numbers (classical, popular, and Latin) and released *The Universal Language of Music,* Vol. One. This was based on my ABC TV program. I had a narrator who had written poetry himself, and his narration was so good that I included it on the record. "How Do I Love Thee?" was based on the theme of *Clair de Lune,* and Joan Fontaine liked it so much she included it in one of her TV programs. This album was recorded at my ranch in Santa Cruz. I ran two Ampex tape recorders, dubbing one track on top of another (which was the new thing); I did everything myself while playing the piano and organ. I took the tape to San Francisco and had it mastered in a studio (they were impressed with how professionally it had been recorded), and took it to a pressing plant. Then I recorded other albums, including *The Grand Moghul Suite.* I also had a studio in Palm Springs with a pipe organ, piano and several organs.

♦ **V: How did you sell your albums?**

♦ KP: Through the mail, at live concerts, and at record stores—a lot of the top names made guest appearances at record stores. Then I recorded a series of about 12 albums for Fantasy, but I never got a proper accounting for any of their sales. You can send an accountant out there, but it'll cost you $200-$300 a day just for that, and they can string him along for months. So I retired, more or less, in 1965. However, people still ask me to do concerts, and lectures on music, meditation and healing—I did several for Manly P. Hall at his Philosophical Research Center. I've taught classes in Pacific Palisades, Carmel and in the Bay Area as well.

♦ **V: Have you appeared in any feature films?**

♦ KP: I was in *Something To Live For,* with Ray Milland, Joan Fontaine and Teresa Wright, directed by George Stevens (1952). This came out when I was appearing on television—they had to get special permission from TV so I could be in a movie. I also had a brief part in *Which Way Is Up?* (1977), with Richard Pryor. I played the part of a yogi, because I knew what a yogi would say, and I blessed a baby. Also, I'm in Tim Burton's film on Ed Wood, Jr. I appear in one scene in which I'm playing the organ, as I always did.

♦ **V: You've been through a lot; how have you kept from becoming cynical?**

♦ KP: People are cynical because since World War II, they've been under constant bombardment by those who would control their thinking and their lives. A Christian Scientist said: "If you're doing something you didn't really want to do, maybe it wasn't you doing it!" Perhaps someone implanted a suggestion in you, and you reacted—you weren't acting, you were *reacting . . .* to inflammatory information from the news, advertisements, or whatever. Now they're implanting cues at your brainwave level; after generations of psychological experiments they've learned what *works.* So what's your solution to that? Stay in tune with your true self. Believe in your self, stay sober, and don't be pulled out of your true reality-space by force or suggestion or drugs or alcohol. Don't look to TV to find out what you should be doing.

♦ **V: Media control is subtler and more effective than ever—**

♦ KP: Take the Top 40: did *you* pick them? No. Don't wait for the next Top 40 or Top Anything, because it's not *you* thinking, rather that *they're* going to tell you what "you" selected. But *you* didn't have anything to say about it! You didn't have a vote—you know what I'm saying? I saw an article in the paper saying that there's a U2 concert soon, and scalpers will get as much as $2000 for tickets! In reality, maybe only ten people will even pay over $100. The paper editorializes that this is "wrong," but still, it's been implanted that people are paying that much, with the result that after you read this, *any* price won't seem too much. That's just a sample of how people can be manipulated through suggestion.

All the people in the United States pay an astounding amount of money in taxes—if people really knew how much, there would be a great deal more concern than there's ever been. But nobody realizes the bigger picture. The true data regarding all the people who are out of work, and how much total money is taken in taxes—those figures are astounding. All that will have to be changed.

This economy is the result of a group that came in about 3 or 4 administrations back, beginning with Nixon and steadily stripping off all controls so that the billionaires, powerful companies, etc could do exactly what they wanted to do. Having all manufacturing being done overseas, and not using American labor, meant that sooner or later all these workers have to be laid off. The people in the know cover this up—they don't talk about it, but the people who are being laid off know! People who were once making good salaries are out, too. These men at the top are determined to stay in power, and they'll do *anything* they can to stay there. Change can only come from upheaval!

SOME ALBUMS BY KORLA PANDIT:

Christmas with Korla Pandit
Universal Language of Music, Vols. 1-3
At the Pipe Organ
An Evening with Korla Pandit
The Grand Moghul Suite-Part 1
Hypnotique
In Paris
Latin Holiday
Love Letters
Music for Meditation
Music of the Exotic East
Music of Hollywood
Music of Mystery and Romance
Speak to Me of Love
Tropical Magic
Tropical Paradise
Currently available: *Music For Meditation*—order by mail from GNP Crescendo, 8300 Sunset Blvd, Hollywood CA 90069, (213) 656-2614. For mail-order information about other recordings or videocassettes, send a self-addressed stamped envelope (or 8 international reply coupons) to K.P. Productions, PO Box 3683, Palos Verdes CA 90274-9519.

DEAN SANTOMIERI

Dean Santomieri is a musician, filmmaker and electronic music composer currently associated with the California College of Arts and Crafts, Oakland, California.

♦ *VALE: What's your favorite instructional record?*

♦ DEAN SANTOMIERI: A multimedia box called *Let's Look at Great Paintings: Art Appreciation for Children,* by DORA JANE JANSON (1959). She must be related to the H.W. Janson who wrote *The History of Art* that everyone had to read in school. There's a 10" record, a booklet and 8 color prints; it's part of a series called *Learn for Pleasure*—actually a good title! The booklet starts out with drawings of Mickey Mouse and Japanese rabbits to get the kids interested, but turn the page and *behold:* the "Hell" panel from Hieronymus Bosch's triptych, which Dora Jane describes as a "bad dream." Here she can't resist including a moral injunction; according to her, "Bosch tells us, 'Don't live for pleasure, or it will turn into a nightmare.'" Since Bosch left no writings I'd say that was a pretty liberal interpretation of his painterly intent.

♦ *ANDREA JUNO: What is the narration like?*

♦ DS: Well, according to the liner notes, "The *rich, friendly* voice of Miss Ann Loring makes the paintings about which she talks *come to life.*" The booklet itself, *Let's Look at Great Paintings,* reveals quite a bit about Dora Jane Janson's mentality. She has a pretty narrow view of what art is, although she does include Picasso's *Three Musicians.* She compares learning how to understand paintings to learning how to swim or ice skate—it might be hard at first, but once we learn how, we can have fun for years. When she gets to the problem of abstract art, she says, "[This painter] does not show things, but rather feelings. Yet he has the same fun with paint that Velàzquez had—he likes to feel it *squish* under his brush."

♦ *V: I guess that made kids want to rush out and paint . . . Do you ever collect records just for the cover art?*

♦ DS: Well, when I saw this cover on Berlioz's *Sym-*

Dora Jane Janson's *Let's Look at Great Paintings,* Cabot Records. Prepared under the direction of Harry N. Abrams, Inc. ® 1959 Ottenheimer: Publishers.

phonie Fantastique I had to buy it—the beautiful blonde bride with a hangman's noose in the background?! Plenty of subtext there. And note the label on this old RCA Victor album. These are called "shaded dogs," because of the shading around the image of the dog listening to His Master's Voice on an old-fashioned phonograph horn. Records with these labels—usually classical and opera—are highly collectible because the vinyl is heavier and the sound quality superior. Around 1971 RCA started pressing its records on a much thinner vinyl called "Dynaflex" and on high-tech stereos, during the quiet passages, you could actually hear leakage from the other side of the record!

I love covers in 3-D, like JOHNNY CASH:

Photo: Robert Waldman

The Holy Land. He's dressed in black, of course, but with a white shirt on. There have been a number of 3-D covers that I didn't collect, like the Rolling Stones' *Satanic Majesty Requests,* or the early '70s *Captain Beyond* LP by the first singer from *Deep Purple.* Since the '70s literally thousands of picture discs have been released of various shapes and colors—especially in heavy metal and rock music. I like the ones by the Stranglers, *Cramps,* Divine, and Edith "Edie the Egg Lady" Massey.

♦ *V: What's your favorite record production?*
♦ DS: Probably the most *elaborate* record package I've come across is *Sound Image, A Magazine of Aural and Visual Art* (1975). The box contained a book, a record, and beautiful photographs. The text advised you to let the sounds influence how you look at the images, and vice versa. I've only seen the first issue.

♦ *AJ: You could do that with almost any record/photo combinations. What are the recordings like?*
♦ DS: On one cut, "Freeze Madagascar," the editor was eating at a restaurant and heard "the faint strains of a percussive solo filtering in from the kitchen. The drummer turned out to be the restaurant's refrigerator/freezer motor." He taped this and later discovered that some Madagascar music had the same rhythm—

he was alert for the chance opportunity! There's also an aeolian harp segment.

♦ *AJ: What's an aeolian harp?*
♦ DS: Basically, a frame in which piano strings are stretched. People used to put them in their windows. I have a two-record set called *The Wind Harp* from the early '70s. A guy built one 20 feet tall on a farm or commune in Massachusetts and just left it there. It was recorded during spring, summer, fall, and winter (a season per side), and the wind and weather play it differently each season. The recording engineers observed that argyles made better wind screens for their microphones than white athletic socks!

♦ *V: Let's talk about comedy records; tell us about SPIKE JONES—*
♦ DS: "The man who set music back 10,000 years." I used to watch Spike Jones on TV when I was a kid. His band parodied popular tunes and classical music, incorporating a startling array of sound effects, including car horns, police sirens, gunshots and screams. If John Cage said, "Everything we do is music," Spike could have said, "Everything we play is a musical instrument." On tours they were the Einstürzende Neubauten of their day: scouring the dumps of every city for junk instruments like aluminum bathtubs

(pitched to B flat), pots and pans, and glass to break, as well as props and costumes. There was something incredibly adolescent and truly American about their sense of humor.

Spike's band was amazing: studio musicians who somehow managed to perform physical comedy while playing at breakneck speed. They beat banjos with drumsticks; they sang in foreign accents (their 1942 hit spoofing the Germans, "Der Führer's Face," was Jones's first million-seller). The entire band dressed in drag for "It's Tough to be a Girl Musician"—Spike was in false eyelashes and a tutu for the waltz-time balletic interlude.

One of Spike's stylistic trademarks might be described as the extreme exaggeration of Arnold Schoenberg's *Klangfarbenmelodie* (tone-color-melody). It's a compositional device whereby successive notes of a melody are subtly and gradually shifted among different instruments of a section (violin to cello, for instance), and finally to different orchestral families (strings to woodwinds, etc). Jones took this idea to the ultimate extreme—free of subtlety but hilariously fresh. Tuned car horns, gunshots, mouth sounds—in his hands all carry the melody in "correct" pitch.

Spike started out in radio, and in the '50s moved to TV where he could take advantage of the band's virtuosic visual comedy and his penchant for wearing suits with gigantic plaids. Sometimes Spike would emerge after a commercial wearing a suit whose pattern was the "negative" of the suit previously worn!

Dinner Music for People Who Aren't Very Hungry is his take-off on a hi-fi demonstration record; there's pseudoserious voice-over narration between the sound effects. Note some song titles: "Duet for Violin and Garbage Disposal," "Wyatt Earp Makes Me Burp," and the "Black and Blue Danube Waltz." Among the "instruments" used were the sounds of "barking dogs in hi-fido."

When stereo appeared, a lot of labels put out beautifully recorded, hyper-realistic demonstration albums which would sweep the sound from right to left. You'd hear cars and trains rushing past, or a ping pong game with the ball bouncing back and forth, or rain falling, etc. Another genre was the "travel" album which would present the sights and sounds of, say, Tokyo. They'd give you 30 seconds "inside the airplane," followed by the sound of the plane landing . . . next some Japanese voices, and suddenly you're walking in the middle of a fish market . . . all fantastically recorded, taking advantage of the ability to move the sound in space. A favorite effect was to have someone talk in the right speaker, then you'd hear their footsteps traveling left, and then the voice would come out of the left speaker . . . sensational!

Back then, imaginations weren't as tightly tethered to the cash register. In retrospect, there was more risk-taking: trying something because it seemed interesting, or simply because it hadn't been done. One label, COMMAND RECORDS, produced a series of records featuring nothing but percussion instruments—marimbas, castanets and drums from all over the world. The mambo, calypso, bossa nova and other dance fads lasted much longer than the lambada, and there were numerous hits in foreign languages—how often does a dance craze happen today?

When I was a kid, MARTIN DENNY was "patio music" at suburban family barbecues; some of the fathers were into the audiophile thing and had speakers set up outside playing *Exotica* or train sound-effects records. These guys also had giant hi-fi's in the living room. All this paved the way for ethnic music from all over to become available for people who insisted on "the real thing." Around 1971 I bought a record with YVETTE MIMIEUX reading Baudelaire's *Fleurs du Mal* accompanied by Ali Akbar Khan; it's almost impossible to imagine that being released now.

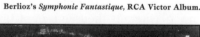

Berlioz's *Symphonie Fantastique*, RCA Victor Album.

Around 1957 the beatnik era was in full swing, and KEN NORDINE brought out his series of WORD JAZZ albums. He was a Chicago deejay with a voice that sounds like aged Scotch; you've probably heard him on Levi's commercials. He would write twisted little stories and recite them with a jazz group in the background, like "What Time Is It?"—an O. Henry-like story in which a guy gets a phone call every night at 2 A.M. from a caller who asks, "What time is it?" This happens over and over, and there's a nice twist at the end. Thirty years later, this material holds up extremely well. Last year the producer Hal Wilner put out a record of songs from Walt Disney movies, and Nordine does two great recitations on it. He also appeared on H.P. Lovecraft's second album.

Here's the famous *Best of Marcel Marceau* record: 19 minutes of silence, 1 minute of applause.

Even MARSHALL McLUHAN, the first influential critic of the effects of mass media, made a record, *The Medium Is the Massage*. Records seem better suited than print to demonstrate his ideas about "technological speedup" and the impact of multiple stimuli, because "the spoken word involves all the senses dramatically"—

♦ V: —*whereas video short-circuits the* visual *imagination.*
♦ DS: This record was McLuhan literally putting his ideas where his mouth was. But I wish he had made more, as this one isn't particularly great. He was about as French as philosophers get in this hemisphere.

The First Man in the Moon! is a pseudodocumentary for kids. This was pre-lunar landing 1960, when people still expected to find large ants or feline women living on the moon. Naturally, the moon men plan to invade earth and colonize it because the resources on the moon are almost depleted. I also have a number of the actual historical moon landing records, including *Man on the Moon,* narrated by Walter Cronkite with an optimistic JFK speech about how "Now is the time for this nation to take a clearly leading role in space achievement, which in many ways may hold the key to our future here on earth." What the hell does that mean—world military domination? Zero gravity Playboy clubs? Now that's Orwellian speech-making: idealistic-sounding but ambivalent enough to mean everything to everyone.

I have about 15 Kennedy records: JFK speeches, post-assassination commemoratives, a two-record set of journalists reminiscing about where they were when he was assassinated—it's amazing how vivid people's recollections were. I have a record of part of Marina Oswald's testimony, plus Oswald's mother reading letters from Lee Harvey. It took me years to find the July '79 issue of *Gallery* magazine which contains a flexi-disc of the Dallas police station recording inadvertently made when one of the motorcycle cops left his radio mike on. We get to hear the sounds of the actual violence: the gunshots reverberating throughout Dealey Plaza.

Any consideration of the genre of "violence recordings" has to include *The Sound of Combat Training* (recorded *live* at the United States Army Training Center, Fort Knox, Kentucky). The cuts include such key experiences as "Inoculation" and "Gas Chamber Exercise"—it's hard to imagine what *they* sound like, but here they are. "This recording creates the effect of placing you in the situation that confronts the trainee. You'll join him as he crawls under live machine gun fire, throws a high-explosive hand grenade . . . The sounds you will hear are a living and dynamic part of his fight for freedom." The record sleeve claims that no studio dubbing was used, so I imagine that in "Mess Hall" you hear the sound of men retching . . .

Here's the famous BEST OF MARCEL MARCEAU record: 19 minutes of silence, 1 minute of applause. Unfortunately it's the same on both sides; I was hoping the times would be different. When I worked at a record store we would put this in the comedy section. Some people got the joke and kept the record, but others definitely didn't and they brought it back—maybe they thought it would be Marceau talking about his art.

Another comedy recording is BENNY GOLSON's psychedelic *Tune In Turn On* (to the hippest commer-

Best of Marcel Marceao, Gone-If Records, MGM Record Corporation. Conceived and Produced by Michael Viener. (Note misspelling of Marceau!)

The Crepitation Contest, Laff Records.
Album cover credits: album design direction: Howard Goldstein,
cover photographer: Dominic Belmonte.

Back Cover of *The Crepitation Contest*.

cials of the '60s). This came out in '67 and instead of doom-and-gloom Big Brother paranoia we got a candy-coated message: "Madison Avenue has been giving us the subliminal musical treatment. They have been cleverly feeding us such irresistibly catchy tunes that we've been swallowing the message while swinging the melody." Then he adds: "Television commercials are now rated by critics as fresher and bolder than the programs that surround them. These days, we head for the icebox *during* the show."

In the late '50s, MAD magazine put out a flexi-disc fart record—I remember my brother and I had to buy a second copy because we wore out the first one. *The Crepitation Contest (The Power of Positive Stinking)* is an entire *album* of just farting, described as "another smash blast-off of fun and fantasy from LAFF RECORDS":

"Crepitate (Latin *crepitare*—to crackle, crack)—To make a crackling sound. *To break wind.* A contest of giants, equal in many ways to the glorious Roman Circus. Hear the mighty trumpet calls to which man has responded since the dawn of time . . . the sounds and aromas of man's grandeur that belches, pops, snorts and blasphemes. If you put your fingers in your ears you can't hold your nose. If you hold your nose you'll have to listen, and laugh!"

Laff Records put out records by black comedians such as RUDY RAY MOORE, RICHARD PRYOR, REDD FOXX—even a black ventriloquist. Rudy Ray Moore could be political: "Put Richard Nixon in the poor folks' line/and fuck him with a banana till he break down cryin'." Jeez! Moore is undergoing a revival; he appears at showings of *The Human Tornado* selling cassettes, ashtrays and other memorabilia in the lobby. I also like BLOWFLY's records; he did an

astrology LP showing a different sexual position for each sign of the zodiac. Come to think of it, you don't see the sexual positions of the zodiac shaped into gold jewelry anymore—small blessing.

Another category of records deals with UFOs. FRANK EDWARDS, who wrote *Stranger Than Science, Strange People, Strange World, Strangest of All,* and *Flying Saucers—Serious Business,* put out a record called *Frank Edwards Presents Flying Saucers—Serious Business* to capitalize not only on his book but his syndicated radio series of the same name. The back of the record shows standard, fake-looking UFO photos: the pie plate, the hat, the hubcap and the grinding wheel. This record keeps company on my shelf with albums like the *Amazing Kreskin, Sleep with Pat Collins: the Hip Hypnotist,* and Louise Huebner's *Seduction Through Witchcraft* (which has a section called "Orgies: a Tool of Witchcraft," and features music by LOUIS & BEBE BARRON, who composed the *Forbidden Planet* soundtrack). Incidentally, the Barrons made hundreds of recordings of raw sound and in a nine-month splicing marathon helped JOHN CAGE edit them into the hurricane of sound known as "the Williams Mix."

In the direction of *inner space* is the original CHARLES MANSON album, *Lie,* which has been reissued several times. The original appeared on ESP RECORDS (short for Esperanto; the owner was trying to push that "universal language"). ESP was an adventurous New York label that put out records by Sun Ra, The Fugs, Patty Waters, the Coach with the Six Insides (Jean Erdman's dance-play based on James Joyce's *Finnegan's Wake),* etc. When I worked at Tower Records in Berkeley, Squeaky Fromme used to come down from Sacramento and pressure us to order *Lie,* some time before she took a shot at Gerald Ford. They would never ship the damn record. The liner notes contain some interesting text: "My philosophy is: Don't think. If you think, you are divided in your mind . . . The truth is in no word form . . . When you look at things in a positive manner, everything can work out perfect . . . And when you tune in with love, you tune in with yourself." When I heard the pop singer Michael Franks, I thought he sounded like a polished version of Manson.

In the late '50s, MAD magazine put out a flexi-disc fart record—I remember my brother and I had to buy a second copy because we wore out the first one. *The Crepitation Contest (The Power of Positive Stinking)* is an entire *album* of just farting . . .

♦ **V: The '60s seemed to open up the floodgates for all kinds of recordings to be made—**

♦ **DS:** Such as Moog records; for awhile there were a ton of those coming out. *Moog Groove* calls itself the first album of electronic music, and it sounds great! The cover has wonderful period details: the Beatles poster on the wall, the empty Chianti bottle with the flowers stuck in it, the Peace poster. The girl on the cover with headphones on is clad in extremely sheer material. The Moog synthesizer with all its patch cords, and the enormous antiquated 8-track tape recorder, look quite impressive, too.

♦ **AJ: Why was the Moog popular?**

♦ **DS:** The Moog could do glissandos and all kinds of electronic timbres other instruments couldn't. Basically, it used patch cords to interface a variety of modules which reshaped the sound wave, each in a different way. The first consumer synthesizers were built by Robert Moog on the East Coast and Don Buchla on the West Coast; they were slow to operate, and complicated, requiring quite a bit of electronics knowledge. They got easier to play (although much more limited) after keyboards were attached. An ad for one of the simpler synthesizers said something like: "If you changed parameters every nine seconds, it would take 167 years to realize all the sound possibilities of this instrument"—and this was a cheesy little unit!

The person who popularized the Moog was WALTER CARLOS, a child prodigy who began composing at age seven and built his own computer at fourteen. Around 1964 Carlos hooked up with Robert Moog to help produce a more expressive instrument. On his first record, *Switched-On Bach,* he contrasted the timbres so you could follow the musical lines more easily, and as a result, hundreds of music appreciation classes used the record. Everyone in America must have heard it, and probably in Europe as well. It was recorded at home for almost nothing and grossed millions for Columbia Records—they were surprised, to say the least.

Carlos opened the way for hundreds of other electronic music recordings to be released. In the '80s the fad died out. Sometimes the sounds on the pop records are more amazing than on the serious academic ones.

♦ **AJ: How did he change from Walter to Wendy?**

♦ **DS:** Apparently he was born with a body more female than male. The only photo I ever saw of him was on a Columbia Records sampler, which shows a young, androgynous-looking man with sideburns that don't appear to grow from his face—they look combed down. In the late '60s he began hormone treatments, and in the mid-'70s surgically transformed himself into Wendy Carlos (described in an amazing, and disturbing, interview in *Playboy,* May 1979).

♦ **V: Carlos was a pioneer in not just one but two areas!**

♦ **DS:** One of the most striking album covers I have is GIL MELLÉ's soundtrack to *The Andromeda Strain* (1971): it's hexagonal and the record is hexagonal as well! Now that record companies are run by cost accountants, this kind of production doesn't happen anymore. Gil Mellé also put out records with a jazz trio plus electronics in a nice blend—it wasn't just pretty melodies played on synthesizer. One is titled *Primitive Modern.* He also did those anxiety-creating soundtracks for Rod Serling's *Night Gallery.*

♦ **AJ: It's a real loss that projects like this are rarely done today.**

The Electronic Concept Orchestra's *Moog Groove,* Mercury Records.

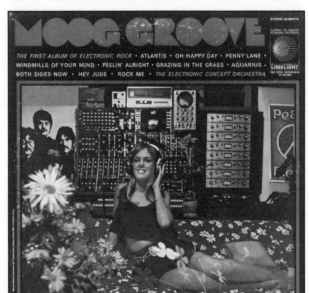

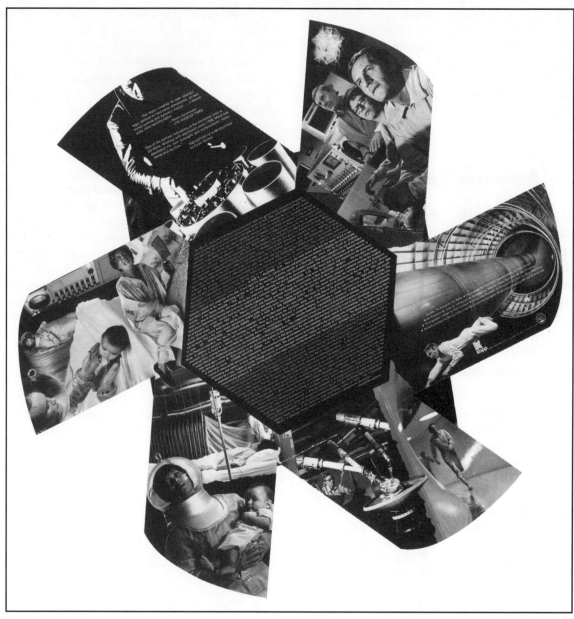

Gil Mellé's *The Andromeda Strain*, Kapp Records, A Division of MCA Inc. 1971.
Album cover credits: art direction: John C. LePrevost, designed by: Virginia Clark, assisted by Joel Shapiro, photography collage: Ruth Corbett.

♦ DS: Gil Mellé composed *Andromeda Strain* inside a special electronic music studio that he built on the Universal lot. He recorded "indigenous sounds of the Jet Propulsion Labs in Southern California, buzz saws, wind, bowling alleys and even the railways," and blended this *musique concrète* into the *Andromeda* score, also using an orchestra and soloists. Oddly enough, he credits the nickelodeon as his antecedent. He considered himself a musical revolutionary. The *Andromeda* liner notes say: "To equip himself with the proper arsenal for *an attack against the musical establishment* [italics ours] Mellé taught himself to be an electronics engineer. Where no instrument exists to provide the sound he wants to create, he invents his own." His studio is described as "a tangled maze of wires, consoles, reels, buttons, charts, lights, levers and other bizarre arrangements . . . "

♦ *V: Tell us some more about Mellé's musical philosophy?*

♦ DS: To continue: "Beneath his reassuring facade beats the heart of a dedicated revolutionary. Not that he's even thinking of tossing a bomb, but he is doing his impressive best to set an academic time-fuse calculated to shatter most of the time-honored patterns of his musical craft." Then he says that he sees no reason to stick to the old 12-note chromatic scale, or only use sounds by existing orchestral instruments or sounds that have previously been heard. "Why not, he openly questions, make use of any sound the human mind can imagine?"

♦ *AJ: What exactly is* **musique concrète?**

♦ DS: The term refers to real sounds manipulated by turntables, tape recorders and electronic circuitry. Pierre Schaeffer and Pierre Henry pretty much started it in Paris in the late '40s. Schaeffer was a sound-effects man who experimented with turntables, changing speeds, making lock-groove records (which allowed a sound to repeat indefinitely, because the needle couldn't escape the groove), and tape recorders. Recorded sounds were slowed down, speeded up, played backwards, superimposed, cut into pieces, appended to pieces of different sounds and run through various electronic devices. Henry's first tape composition, the 2-1/2 minute "Vocalise," was created entirely by manipulation of a single utterance of the syllable "ah."

One of their most famous students was Karlheinz Stockhausen, who augmented the orchestral palette with processed sounds and live electronics. He shared Wagner's preference for working on a grand theatrical scale, as well as Wagner's grand synthesizing intelligence—tempered, however, with a '70s cosmic consciousness cloaked in white guru garb.

In 1971 I discovered the recordings of TOD DOCK-STADER, an American painter/filmmaker who called his version of musique concrète "organized sound"—a term originally attributed to Edgar Varèse. As far as I know, he only made three recordings (Owl label). He adamantly refused to call himself a musician or composer. My favorite piece is "Apocalypse," which has a sound that makes me feel that my visceral organs are suddenly dropping through the floor.

I also like JACQUES LASRY's *The Hypnotic Music of Sculptures that Sound: Chronophagie ("The Time Eaters")* on Columbia. This record actually blew out one of my speakers! The sculptures were made by two brothers, François (a sculptor) and Bernard Baschet (an acoustical engineer). Lasry, the conductor of the Radio Télévision Française, had toured Europe since 1957 with an orchestra of Baschet instruments. They

Jacques Lasry's *The Hypnotic Music of Sculptures that Sound: Chronophagie* ("The Time Eaters"), Columbia Records.
Album cover credits: cover photo: Robin Forbes, sculpture: Baschet.

had a *concept:* "We make shapes and objects with which music can be produced manually—that is, without electricity or electronics. We had to develop metal or plastic surfaces that can be compared to sails . . . The structures also have to be strong—some of them have been played on by more than 150,000 people, including children."

I love their anti-1984 stance: "We feel that in our present-day, computer-card civilization, the public must find new ways of expression. In our performances, whenever it is possible, we invite the public to play. I encountered some people in a Scandinavian museum

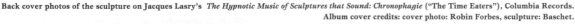

Back cover photos of the sculpture on Jacques Lasry's *The Hypnotic Music of Sculptures that Sound: Chronophagie* ("The Time Eaters"), Columbia Records.
Album cover credits: cover photo: Robin Forbes, sculpture: Baschet.

Photo: Robert Waldman

watching others . . . They said, 'We have never seen so many Scandinavians so happy without being drunk!' "

♦ *V: Tell us more about the instruments themselves—*

♦ DS: François and Bernard classified existing musical instruments into four basic groups: 1) vibrating (e.g. violin strings), 2) energizing (the hair of a violin bow), 3) modulating, and 4) amplifying (e.g., the hollow body of a violin). Then they worked to extend these principles, using new materials such as glass, plastic balloons, and metal cones, foils and rods. I like Lasry's final statement: "Conceptions aren't linear anymore. Not like an onion, where you can peel off one orderly layer after another. Our search is nothing but an attempt to get, through music, what we hear in life." It's hard to imagine a record like this being released today on Columbia Records.

♦ *AJ: But now you hear Philip Glass in TV commercials; his serial music is really pop—*

♦ DS: Ten years ago when we played Philip Glass in the record store, customers would get angry—that *relentlessness* drove them nuts. They couldn't relax and let it just roll over them. There's a local composer, John Adams, who's been accused of plagiarizing Glass. In his defense he said, "Look, don't say I'm ripping Philip Glass off—this is a *style*. It's an arpeggiation— you have a chord here and you're playing each note in the chord, and you're doing it repetitively, gradually changing the voices."

♦ *AJ: What's fascinating is how we've changed. What is this music doing to our nervous systems? Why have we relaxed?*

♦ DS: Repetition! Thousands of people who now buy Philip Glass records never listen to any other classical music; they see him as a branch of popular or even New Age music. He no longer sounds outré.

♦ *AJ: Who are the pioneers now?*

♦ DS: I don't know. In almost anything I hear, I can recognize historical precedents. That's probably why so many people listen to "world music." Interesting music can be found among underground self-produced records and "contemporary classical music," but you've got to wade waist-deep through the mediocre and worse. All the different musical styles that have ever existed are being recycled—nothing even goes out of fashion. What was old hat becomes "nostalgia" or "kitsch"— one never even gets a chance to forget about it.

♦ *AJ: There used to be a big difference between the music kids played, and what their parents listened to.*

♦ DS: I know. Working in a used record store, I see what kids are buying, and occasionally you'll get some ten-year-old oddball who wants Tom Lehrer records. I encourage that—I give them a discount! Recently a 12-year-old was buying a Lenny Bruce record and I asked him, "Are you going to get into trouble with your parents for buying this?" He said, "No, my dad played it for me!" There are a few kids out there searching for more esoteric music; who think that what's on the radio is bullshit or just isn't stimulating, so maybe there's hope.

♦ *V: FM radio used to play much more diverse music—*

Spike Jones' *Dinner Music for People Who Aren't Very Hungry*, Verve Records.

♦ DS: FM radio got off the ground in the '60s, and then gave rise to the hideous behemoth that the record business is today. I remember the first time I heard PATTY WATERS' version of "Black Is the Color of My True Love's Hair." DJs were starting to use 2 and 3 turntables simultaneously; Melanie's "The Boys in the Back Room" was playing and it gradually segued into Patty Waters' caterwauling, more saxophone-than-human voice. That blurred into a Pink Floyd aural tapestry, finally becoming LOTHAR & THE HAND PEOPLE's "Standing on the Moon," which begins with a slow countdown from ten to one, attempting to induce a meditative state. This sort of thing was the soundtrack to my teens . . .

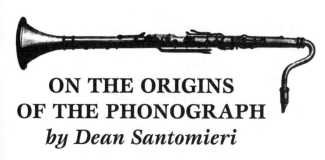

ON THE ORIGINS
OF THE PHONOGRAPH
by Dean Santomieri

The fox terrier and the old-fashioned Phonograph rest atop a highly polished coffin. As the "talking machine" speaks, the dog raises his right ear and cocks his head toward the horn, spellbound by his dead master's voice. Nostrils flaring from the reek of motor oil, he exhibits a rapt, melancholic expression familiar the world over as the trademark of RCA Records.

His Master's Voice, Francis Barraud's painting that originated the trademark, likely commemorates the relationship between Barraud's deceased brother Mark and Mark's dog Nipper. Barraud finished his sentimental portrayal around 1895, and was surprised that it attracted no attention. Finally, a friend suggested that a new brass horn (painted over the black one) would considerably brighten the work. Barraud agreed, and visited the newly-opened London office of the Gramophone Company, Ltd. to request the loan of a brass sound horn. The manager, William Barry Owen, offered to buy the painting—provided that Barraud paint an "Improved Gramophone" (a disc-playing machine that Owen's company manufactured) over the cylinder-playing Edison Phonograph. Barraud agreed, and received a hundred pounds for both the painting and its copyright. Once the trademark became popular, Barraud made a comfortable living reproducing *His Master's Voice* until his death in 1924.

Thomas Edison invented the cylinder phonograph in 1877. After an initial phase of concert hall demonstrations and nickel-a-play arcade use, he abandoned it for ten years to concentrate on developing the electric light. (During this decade Jenny Lind, Franz Liszt, and other artists died, unrecorded.) In 1888 he resumed production of his unglamorous early phonograph which resembled a lathe. To make a recording, a tinfoil-covered cylinder, slightly larger than an empty toilet tissue roll, was placed horizontally on a shaft connected to a hand crank. As the crank was turned, the needle "embossed" whatever sound was communicated to it via the diaphragm. When the recording was complete (two minutes later on early models), the playback needle was engaged, and a raucous entertainment followed.

Speculating about its possible uses in *The North American Review,* Edison gave first priority to "business dictation." "Reproducing music" was number *four*. Number five proposed the audio equivalent of the photo album: a family record, including baby's first words, the nuptial vows, "reminiscences of family members in their own voices," and "the last words of dying persons." It is precisely this moment that Barraud's painting initially portrayed.

During the 1890s, several competitors jumped on Edison's bandwagon and "patent infringement" became a courtroom catch-phrase. Emile Berliner spent the decade refining his flat, round disc which was louder, easier to handle and store, and cheaper to manufacture. The disc also circumvented Edison's patent.

Prior to 1902, the lucrative cylinder market lay in the business sector with its demand for dictaphone machines. However, the popularity of early marching band recordings enabled the Victor Talking Machine Co. to sense a vast consumer potential for pre-recorded music, and it raced to sign classical musicians and opera singers to exclusive contracts. Since the Victor Company was the re-incorporated heir to Berliner's company, they produced discs instead of cylinders. Their large, impressive catalog helped attract consumers to the disc. In 1912, when Edison introduced the "blue amberol," a microgrooved cylinder with a four-minute playing time and fidelity *superior* to the discs, it was too late—the disc had already eclipsed the cylinder.

Now, in the 1990s, it's as if the major record companies were once again revising Francis Barraud's portrait—this time painting a compact disc over the black vinyl LP . . .

SOURCES:

Roland Gelatt, *The Fabulous Phonograph 1877-1977* (NY: Macmillan, 1977).

James R. Smart and Jon W. Newson, *A Wonderful Invention: A Brief History of the Phonograph from Tinfoil to the LP* (Washington, D.C.: Library of Congress, 1977).

Ron Dethelefson, *Edison Disc Artists and Records 1910-1929* ($25 ppd from Dethlefson, 3606 Christmas Tree Lane, Bakersfield CA 93306).

Original Edison recordings are being released on CD by Diamond Cut Productions, PO Box 305, Hibernia NJ 07842.

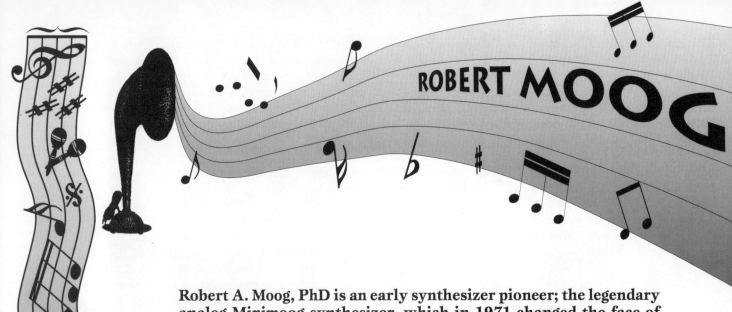

Robert A. Moog, PhD is an early synthesizer pioneer; the legendary analog Minimoog synthesizer, which in 1971 changed the face of rock music, bears his name. He began making electronic musical instruments (including Theremins) in 1954. In 1968 he incorporated as R.A. Moog, Inc, which he remained with (through several corporate buyouts) until 1977. In 1978 he formed another company, Big Briar, Inc, and in 1984 he joined Kurzweil Music Systems until 1989. From 1989-1992 he was a Research Professor with the Music Department of the University of North Carolina at Asheville. Recently Robert Moog (pronunciation: rhymes with "rogue") was prominently featured in a documentary film, *The Electronic Odyssey of Leon Theremin*. He remains president of Big Briar, Inc, which produces Theremins [yes, they're available now] and other electronic music equipment—send a self-addressed stamped envelope to Route 3, Box 115A1, Leicester, NC 28748.

♦ *VALE: You invented one of the first synthesizers. What's your background?*
♦ ROBERT MOOG: I have a PhD in engineering physics. I was making Theremins from 1954 on, and in 1964 I began making synthesizers.

I had piano lessons and also theory and ear training in the pre-college division of the Manhattan School of Music. But my main interest was engineering. When I was a kid (eleven or twelve), sound was a hobby of mine. I started making sound-producing devices, like one-note organs. A popular project of the time was building a THEREMIN—which I did at the age of 14.
♦ *V: You wrote, "The project that really seized my attention was a very simple Theremin that I built in 1949 from a magazine article. For me, that launched a period of active experimentation, where I actually attempted to come up with my own circuit designs. It was also a period where I struggled to play the Theremin, and in doing so I improved my ability to hear intervals and dynamics."*
♦ RM: Yes. At the age of 19 I wrote my *own* "How to

Build a Theremin" article which was published in *Radio and TV News,* January, 1954. The Theremin is an electronic instrument which you play by waving your hands around it; you control the volume and the pitch of the sound by the proximity of your hands to the two antennas on the instrument. You have the same sort of continuous control that you have when you're singing.
♦ *V: It looks so easy—all you have to do is wave your hands! That's like singing with your hands—*
♦ RM: But it's hard, nevertheless. You have to have a good ear and you have to practice. You listen to the sound that's being produced and you adjust it by moving your hands, the same way as when you sing you adjust the sound by moving your vocal chords.
♦ *V: Is it easy to build a Theremin?*
♦ RM: You can build one that's sort of a "hobby" version of a Theremin, but it's harder to build a real musical instrument—it's just like somebody who's an amateur wood-worker building a guitar! You can build something that looks like a guitar and plays a little like

Bob Moog, 1975.

a guitar, but you can't make a *musical* instrument that easily.

♦ **V: So when you started building Theremins, this was before electronic music was generally familiar—**

♦ RM: Not really; there was electronic music all the way back to 1920 or so—that's when the Theremin was invented. By 1930 there were people concertizing on it in the United States—actually giving concerts with major symphony orchestras. In my mind that's how far back electronic music goes. My wife and I produced the only good Theremin record on the market: *The Art of the Theremin* by CLARA ROCKMORE; it's on CD now (Delos #D-CD1014). They did a good job remastering it to CD.

♦ **V: When you were a kid, did you go to a Theremin concert?**

♦ RM: No, but I heard them on the radio once or twice. My knowledge of the Theremin as a kid was primarily as a hobby project. This was before rock'n'roll and the whole '60s thing; Benny Goodman and Ralph Flanagan were still on the radio—it really was a different era. I never watched TV, so any awareness I had of technological advances in pop music was what LES PAUL and MARY FORD were doing—their advances in recording techniques were new and exciting.

In 1961 I wrote another "How to Build a Theremin" article which appeared in *Electronics World* (January, 1961). It was the cover story, and at the end of the

article there was a notice: "If you want to buy a kit, contact me." Over a thousand people did! So over the next 6 months, in the living room of our 3-room apartment, my wife and I had to crank these out.

♦ **V: Did you think you were doing something new and exciting?**

♦ RM: No, the Theremin's very old. It was invented in 1920, and the inventor, Leon Theremin, died in November 1993 at the age of 97. I first met him in 1989 at an experimental music conference in Bourges, France; he was the guest of honor there. The French government paid for it; they *support* the arts there. He could still walk on his own two feet, which was amazing.

♦ **V: So when you made the Theremins, you were fascinated by the tonalities and sounds you could generate—**

♦ RM: And the way of controlling it, too.

♦ **V: It seems like a very populist instrument, in that you don't need any training—**

♦ RM: Oh, you do need training—actually, it's an *elitist* instrument, because if you contrast it to something like a guitar or a ukelele or accordion or piano, there are few people who have the talent to be able to even get a melody out of it. It takes thousands of hours to get *really* good, although if you're a good musician, you can get musical sounds out of it. There's only been *one* really great Theremin player; she's still alive, and that's Clara Rockmore.

♦ **V: When did you start meeting avant-garde mu-**

THE BIG BRIAR SERIES 91 THEREMINS

left: MODEL 91A   *center:* MODEL 91C   *right:* MODEL 91B

BIG BRIAR, Inc.   Rt. 3 Box 115A1   Leicester, NC 28748

sicians like John Cage?

♦ RM: That came in the '60s. As far as I was concerned, the Theremin is a very specialized instrument. We did get orders from all over the world, and a lot of musicians knew of me because of that. Then in 1963 I met Herb Deutsch, who was a composer at Hofstra University, Long Island. I was interested in what he was doing and he was interested in my electronic abilities, and we started brainstorming. Out of spending two or three weeks together, we were able to pin down the basic ideas of the synthesizer.

♦ *V: Can you summarize those ideas?*

♦ RM: First, it would be *modular,* so you can connect the output of one thing into the input of the other, and make up your own systems. The second is: use *voltage control,* which enables you to use one module to change the operating point of another module. You could have electrical signals make changes. This made possible all sorts of interesting patterns and textures in sound that weren't available before that.

♦ *V: So the two of you worked out ways of modifying the voltage control oscillators, amplifiers, and filters, with knobs and sliders—*

♦ RM: Yeah.

♦ *V: Did you sit down and systematically work out all the ways sound could be affected?*

♦ RM: No, we just did one interesting thing after another. I suppose in a vague way we knew we were "on to something," but there was no sense of becoming important to anybody except a few experimental people; we weren't doing it to make money or start a business or anything like that. I'd build something,

Herb would take it and put some music together with a tape recorder, layering. I had a little kit business going and had rented a storefront—that's where we started. It was little more than a hobby. At one point Herb and I got together and took what we had built to the University of Toronto's Electronic Music Studio and showed it to the people there—they were very encouraging. Electronic music had begun at the university level around 1952.

♦ *V: When did the first Moog synthesizer become available?*

♦ RM: We exhibited just the hand-made modules that Herb and I worked on, at the Audio Engineering Society Convention in October, 1964. From that came the first orders. That early history from '64 to the present I have written down in some detail; it's very accurate and complete. I don't like to repeat myself, so I'll send it to you . . .

HISTORICAL & PROPHETIC WRITING
by Robert A. Moog:

"My most extensive and fruitful collaboration outside of our studio was with Wendy Carlos. Carlos was a student of Vladimir Ussachevsky's when I first met her, and took a job as a recording engineer in New York shortly after that. She built up her own composition facility over a period of several years. She would buy a small number of modules from me, then give me a detailed report of her observations and comments. She was, and still is, a perfectionist. Nothing escaped her attention. She would tell us that a knob was not in the right place, or it was too small; that one function was very useful and that another was not; that one module was prone to distortion, but another was clean.

The Theremin is an electronic instrument which you play by waving your hands around it. You have the same sort of control you have when you're singing—the same sort of continuous control.

From Wendy I learned the importance of optimizing every aspect of an instrument—of remembering that in being used by a musician, an electronic instrument becomes an extension of a sensitive *biological* system, and that it is necessary to match the two so that the musician uses the instrument with as much comfort as possible.

"Carlos and her collaborators, Benjamin Folkman and Rachel Elkind, worked for more than a year on developing techniques for using our modular equipment in conjunction with multi-track tape techniques to realize the music of Bach. The result was *Switched-on Bach,* a recording that was released at the end of 1968 and went on to become one of the best-selling classical albums of all time. The success of this record, and the attention that it focused on our instruments, pushed us further away from 'development' mode and more deeply into 'manufacturing' mode. Our little store-front operation expanded threefold, and at our peak, we had 42 employees. For an engineer who enjoys working with musicians, or working alone, our new-found success spelled *big trouble.* After 1967, there was little opportunity for new product development. In 1969 and 1970 we struggled to meet the increased demand for our modular systems, and then, when the market saturated, a recession set in, and competitors came out of the woodwork, we struggled to recover from the sudden dropoff in business. In 1971 I relinquished control of the business . . . More than 12,000 Minimoogs were produced from 1971 to 1981. Since 1981, the commercial electronic keyboard scene has gone digital, and experimental musicians are focusing their attention on the capabilities of computers . . .

"But there are some features of the now-obsolescent analog modular equipment that seem to be absent in today's commercial digital instruments. First is lack of continuity of sound parameter change . . . Second is a lack of visual and tactile accessibility to sound parameters . . . The third is the fact that analog equipment is inherently unstable . . . Does it help a musician if his instrument is always changing in subtle, complex ways? More and more, musicians are telling me that the answer to this question is 'yes.'

"Finally, we ask the question: Can we 'fix' digital systems so they have all the desirable properties of analog? Here I'm optimistic. Lack of continuity of sound parameter change has to do with system resolution. All that we have to do is design digital synthesis equipment that is fast and precise enough so that sound *changes* do not have *audible steps* . . . Lack of visual and tactile access has to do with the user interface. Large, high resolution, touch-sensitive screens, or maybe an actual patch-cord jungle, are possibilities . . . And unpredictable performance, drift, jiggling? How do we get that stuff into a digital system? Well, how about a few 'micro-viruses': little routines that, in effect, travel throughout an operating system, degrading its stability to a very small extent. Is that idea metaphysical? Irrational? Just plain silly? I don't think so."

ELECTRONIC MUSIC: WHAT IS IT?

"My own definition of electronic music is very broad: Electronic Music is music which is made with electronic equipment . . . The question, 'Is electronic music less natural than music played on acoustic instruments?' No music is natural! Music is produced only after people invest strenuous and extended effort to gain intimate control over vibrating systems such as vocal cords, a violin, or a synthesizer. Furthermore, all

Dick Hyman's *The Age of Electronicus,* Command Records. Album cover credits: cover/liner design: Byron Goto/Henry Epstein, photos: Roger Pola, Eric Goto.

musical instruments, except for the human voice, are highly contrived technological artifices. They are differentiated not by their degree of 'naturalness,' but by the technological periods in which they were developed. The string instruments were perfected when woodworking was a flowering technology. Piano designers utilized the processes of a fully industrialized society. And the electronic music medium is being developed now, a time when electronic technology is dominant and the golden age of manufacturing appears to be yielding to what people are calling 'the post-industrial era.' "

ELECTRONIC MUSICAL INSTRUMENTS PRIOR TO 1945

"Through the years, the technologists of the electronic music medium have tended to be frustrated musicians and chronic putterers. Thaddeus Cahill, developer of the TELHARMONIUM, was also endowed with the ability to think big. Although not strictly electronic (it predated the invention of the vacuum tube by about a decade), the Telharmonium embodied many basic principles that have been used in the electronic music medium: the generation of pitched tones from alternating electricity, the addition of harmonies to determine tone color (additive synthesis), and a touch-sensitive keyboard to shape the sounds and control their strengths. Cahill generated his signals with a bank of over *one hundred* alternators, each capable of producing as much as 15 kilowatts of power! The tones were combined in giant mixing transformers, and then sent out over leased telephone lines to subscribers who heard the music on telephone receivers fitted with horns. The musicians performed at the touch-sensitive keyboard console, while listening to their playing over 'monitor speakers' of the same type that subscribers had. Cahill's Telharmonium was built

in Holyoke, Massachusetts, and shipped to New York in 1906 in some *thirty* railroad box-cars. This first polyphonic, touch-sensitive music synthesizer remained in service in New York for only a few years, until the forces of electronic technology (the invention of radio) and crass economics conspired to end telharmonic music as a viable commercial venture. The basic idea was resurrected again in the 1930s in an instrument that was somewhat more of a commercial success: the HAMMOND ORGAN. Instead of monstrous generators, the Hammond Organ used tiny tone wheels to generate individual pitches, and employed electronic amplification to boost the tone wheel signals to drive a loudspeaker. Designed and tooled by a group of master machinists (Hammond manufactured electric clocks before it got into the music business), the Hammond organ offered musicians a few potent musical resources plus that most valuable attribute of all: *reliability.* Hammond remained the largest manufacturer of electronic organs for decades, a tribute to the enduring value of a well-designed musical resource.

"The THEREMIN was one of the very first wholly electronic musical instruments. Developed during the 1920s by a Russian physicist and amateur musician, Leon Theremin (Anglicized adaptation of his Russian name, Lev Sergeivitch Termen], the Theremin is played without being touched. The performer moves his hands in the space surrounding the instrument to vary pitch and loudness of the tone. Theremin licensed RCA to make and sell his instruments in the United States. RCA built Theremins on the same production line as their first superhet receivers, and attempted to sell them through the same dealer network of radio stores. From this venture, RCA learned that introducing a

Richard Hayman's *Genuine Electric Latin Love Machine,* Command Records. Album cover credits: cover art & design: Stephen Maka/Hentry Epstein, cover photographs: Norman Trigg.

Enoch Light presents *Spaced Out,* © 1969 The Total Sound Inc.

new musical instrument into the consumer marketplace requires a combination of delicacy and tenacity. A merchandising approach involving classical promotion and distribution is sure death. This lesson is being relearned even today by musical instrument manufacturers large and small. After a brief time in the musical instrument marketplace during which only a few hundred Theremins were sold, RCA discontinued production and sold the rights back to Theremin, who continued developing the instrument as an experimental venture.

"In Europe, the same pattern emerged with different instruments and inventors. Friedrich Trautwein developed the TRAUTONIUM, an electronic musical instrument controlled by a fingerboard-like rheostat. The rights were sold to none other than Telefunken, which, it is reported, made a grand total of *fifty* instruments before bowing out! Maurice Martenot, a French instrument designer, developed the ONDES MARTENOT, a monophonic (single tone) electronic musical instrument whose control-means included a six-octave keyboard, continuously variable pitch band, and touch-sensitive articulator bar. Unlike Theremin or Trautwein, Martenot not only kept production of his instrument under his own control, but he also established a school for developing and teaching performance techniques. Original compositions for the Martenot are routinely performed in Europe, even today.

"All of these instruments, Theremin, Trautonium, and Martenot, pointed the way to experimentation with new control devices for electronic musical instruments. The SOLOVOX, and similar instruments that were less successfully marketed, were some direct precursors of the whole class of instruments called synthesizers. The Solovox contained a single tone generator and a variety of waveshaping, frequency-dividing, filtering, and envelope-shaping circuits. Each circuit could be switched in by the musician. In other words, the musician *synthesized,* or assembled out of aural components, the sound quality he desired. Manufactured by Hammond, the Solovox was designed to be mounted on a piano right in front of the keyboard. By depressing a specified combination of switches, the player could set up an orchestral-like timbre, which he could then play monophonically with one hand while he played the piano with the other.

"The use of electronic technology to assemble, store, and manipulate sound sequences may be traced back to the COUPLEAUX-GIVELET SYNTHESIZER, which was introduced in 1929 at the Paris Exhibition. The Coupleaux-Givelet system used punched paper tape to pneumatically activate controls that determined the parameters of four independent voices. Programmed mixing and level control was accomplished by varying the coupling between two coils, by moving one of them with a bellows. The HANERT ELECTRICAL ORCHESTRA, developed by John Hanert around 1945, enabled the musician to draw a 'score' (program) for a piece of electronic music on a continuous roll of paper. A carriage containing an elaborate photocell array traveled down the paper, 'reading' the score and 'conducting' the ensemble of sound-producing circuitry. After World War II, the RCA ELECTRONIC SOUND SYNTHESIZER was developed under the direction of Dr Harry F. Olson. Programmed by a paper roll punched with a set of binary codes, the RCA Synthesizer produced four independent lines of sound. Each line was programmed with a degree of detail that allowed the sound parameters to be redefined as often as thirty times a second.

There are few people who have the talent to be able to even get a melody out of the Theremin. It takes thousands of hours to get *really* good. There's only been *one* really great player; she's still alive, and that's Clara Rockmore.

"The availability of the TAPE RECORDER immediately after World War II added a new dimension to electronic music. With tape recording, any sounds, electronic or acoustic, brief or extended, ordinary noises or pure pitches, could be manipulated, assembled, fragmented, combined and stored . . . Music using electronically-generated sounds came to be known as just plain 'electronic music,' and music using recorded 'nat-

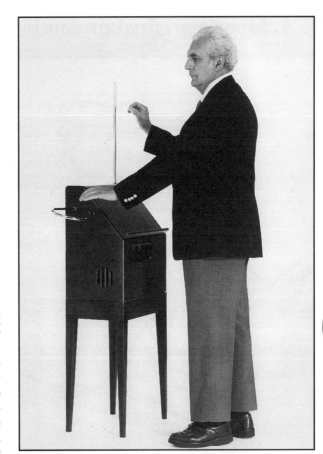

Bob Moog playing the Big Briar Model 91A Theremin, 1993.

ural' sounds came to be known as 'musique concrete' . . . The listening public first became aware of the electronic music medium subliminally, through radio and TV commercials. ERIC SIDAY, RAYMOND SCOTT and other pioneers explored electronic sounds in widely-heard commercials during the 1950s and 1960s, well before electronics infiltrated pop music through the rock'n'roll idiom.

"Developments in the electronic music medium come about when musical needs and emerging technology are combined with a touch of imagination and foresight. Imagination often involves the utilization of ideas that were previously *discarded.* In future decades, the influence of personal computing will be the major technical force shaping electronic music . . . As the complexity of control-means increases even further, the information content of the sounds themselves, as well as the music into which they are assembled, will also increase . . . Finally, the exotic, technological mystique surrounding the electronic music medium will wither away as the whole electronic involvement continues to infiltrate our daily lives."

(*Note:* Much of the information here is taken from Dr Thomas L. Rhea's "The Evolution of Electronic Musical Instruments in the United States," PhD dissertation, George Peabody College, Nashville TN, 1972.)

This is the position the performer assumes when playing the Theremin. Notice that the performer is not in physical contact with any part of the instrument.

"The musical possibilities of the Theremin are infinite."
Sir Henry Wood

In conception as well as in mode of operation, the Theremin is the most modern of musical instruments. Its tones are produced electronically, but are controlled by the movements of the performer's hands in the space surrounding the instrument. There are no buttons or keys that determine the pitch or intensity of the Theremin tone. The Thereminist exercises virtually the same amount of control over the production of the Theremin tone as the singer exercises over his voice.

One of the great advantages of the Theremin is its unusually versatile pitch range. Any pitch within its range may be produced. A continuous glissando, or glide, from one pitch to another may also be readily produced. In determining the pitch, the performer places his right hand in the space surrounding the pitch antenna, a slender rod extending from the top of the instrument. To raise the pitch, he brings his hand closer to the antenna; to lower the pitch he moves his hand away from the antenna. A beautiful full vibrato may be easily produced by moving the right hand back and forth rapidly through a small distance. This produces minute and rapid variations in pitch, corresponding to the effect a violinist produces in moving the wrist of his left hand back and forth rapidly.

The performer uses his left hand to determine the loudness of the tone. To make the note softer, the player brings his left hand nearer to the volume antenna, a slender curved rod extending from the left hand side of the instrument; to make the note louder the performer moves his left hand away from the antenna.

These are the only movements involved in playing the Theremin. As with all musical instruments, some practice is necessary to achieve a proper technique. If the prospective player has had any musical experience, or is musically inclined, the fundamentals of Theremin playing will be quickly mastered. Once the fundamentals have been learned, the player will find it easy to develop techniques and effects to suit his needs.

Originally developed in 1928 by Leon Theremin, the Theremin quickly gained acceptance in musical circles. Because of its ability to impart intense emotional qualities to a melody, it has been used to produce the theme music for Spellbound, the Lost Weekend, and other motion pictures. Performances of orchestral and chamber music on the Theremin were given at frequent intervals between the years 1930 and 1948.

In 1954, the R. A. Moog Co. began to produce Theremins of new design. The existence of these instruments encouraged many Thereminists to once again perform in public. This has initiated a revival of interest in Theremin music. In 1957, the R. A. Moog Co. started an extensive development program, the object of which was to design Theremins which would embody all features which most Thereminists deemed desirable. The instruments described in this brochure are the result of this development program. The Vanguard Model Theremin is a modern adaptation of Leon Theremin's original design. The Professional Model Theremin is a completely transistorized instrument, and in addition offers the musician a choice of four tone colors. Both Theremins are played in the same manner; their difference lies in the mechanism of tone production, and in the variety of tone color which is available.

THE *Vanguard* MODEL THEREMIN

The Vanguard is a completely self-contained electronic musical instrument. The tone is generated by purely electronic means, without the use of motors, strings, or other mechanically moving parts. A specially designed vacuum tube oscillator circuit, whose operation is sensitive to movements of the player's hand, generates an electric wave. When this wave leaves the oscillator, it passes through another circuit which adds the correct degree of overtones to give a pleasing and musical quality to the tone. Without this circuit, the tone would sound dull and mechanical.

Still another circuit enables the loudness of the tone to be controlled by the player's hand. After leaving this circuit, the tone is amplified, and converted into sound waves by a loudspeaker. The entire electronic mechanism, including the loudspeaker, is housed in a single cabinet.

The pitch range of the Vanguard encompasses three and one-half octaves, extending from an octave below middle C to two and one-half octaves above middle C. The loudness range extends from full volume to the softest whisper, and even to complete inaudibility. At full volume, the instrument may be heard by an audience of any size.

The mechanism of the Vanguard is housed in a handsome, hand-rubbed solid mahogany cabinet. The tuning adjustments and two switches are located on a panel which the performer faces while playing the instrument. The cabinet is twenty inches high, seventeen inches wide, and twelve inches deep at the base, and is designed to stand on a table twenty to twenty-two inches high.

Setting up the instrument is extremely easy. The cabinet is set on a suitable table, and the two anodized aluminum antennas are inserted in receptacles. The power cord is then plugged into a convenient power outlet, and the instrument is turned on. After a one minute warmup period, the instrument is tuned, an operation which takes but a few seconds.

The Vanguard Model Theremin.

Aside from the plugging in of the Vanguard, no other connections to the instrument need be made. In addition, the Vanguard will require little maintenance. A periodic service inspection every two or three years will usually suffice, since there are no moving parts to wear out or components to go out of tune. This combined simplicity and reliability of operation which is inherent in the design of the Vanguard Model Theremin is a prime requisite for a true musical instrument.

THE *Professional* MODEL THEREMIN

The Professional Model Theremin differs from the Vanguard Model in two main respects. First, the Professional Model is completely transistorized, and uses no vacuum tubes. Second, a choice of four distinctive timbres is available to the musician.

The introduction of transistors within the last few years has revolutionized the electronics industry. A transistor is a device composed of a specially produced single crystal, and is capable of performing virtually the same functions in electronic equipment as vacuum tubes. Its characteristically small size has permitted the design of electronic instruments with a degree of compactness and lightness that would have been impossible with vacuum tubes. The Professional Model Theremin

is such an instrument. In addition to all the features of the Vanguard, the Professional Model contains the means of providing four different tone colors, and a larger loudspeaker to give voice to these timbres with greater fidelity.

Tone color, or timbre, is that characteristic of a tone through which the listener usually identifies the nature of the tone source. The four tone colors of the Professional Model Theremin are named PRINCIPAL, HORN, WOODWIND, and STRING. These names are not intended to indicate that the Theremin tone will exactly duplicate the effect of another musical instrument, but rather indicate the broad general quality of the Theremin tone. The Principal tone is mellow and ethereal, like a flute, and is the timbre traditionally associated with the Theremin. The Horn tone is sharp and nasal, like that of an oboe. The Woodwind tone is hollow and woody, like a clarinet. The String tone is rich in overtones, like that of any stringed instrument.

These four timbres may be selected by a switch on the front panel of the Professional Model. The choice may be made while the instrument is in operation, to provide contrasting tonal voices within a piece of music. The different tone colors also encompass different pitch ranges. The Principal and Horn tones encompass a pitch range of from one-half octave below middle C to three octaves above middle C. The pitch range of the Woodwind and String tones extends from one and one-half octaves below middle C to two octaves above middle C. Thus, the total pitch range of the Professional Model is four and one-half octaves.

The Professional Model Theremin.

The cabinet is of solid, hand-rubbed mahogany, and is twenty inches high, eighteen inches wide, and ten inches deep at the base. It is designed to stand on a table twenty to twenty-two inches high.

The Professional Model Theremin has been designed to meet every need of the accomplished Thereminist. No effort has been spared to produce an instrument of as high quality as the state of the art of electronic instrument manufacture permits. As such, the Professional Model proudly takes its place in the foreground among modern musical instruments.

ACCESSORIES FOR THE THEREMIN

The Theremin Stand is a table twenty-two inches high, which is designed to support either the Vanguard or Professional Model Theremin. Like the Theremin cabinets, the Theremin Stand is tastefully styled in solid mahogany, and has a hand-rubbed finish.

The Theremin Carrying Case is a hardwood case that is specially fitted to house either the Vanguard or the Professional Model while it is being transported. The interior of the case is padded with rubberized padding, and completely lined with heavy velvet. A cloth cover which is supplied will convert the carrying case into an attractive stand for use at public performances, thus eliminating the necessity of supplying a separate stand at temporary locations.

The Theremin Carrying Case, when covered by its cloth cover, makes an attractive stand.

The Theremin Stand.

The Theremin Carry Case in transit.

This instrument, which is a portable, battery operated Theremin, is representative of the custom Theremins which the R. A. Moog Co. has made in the past.

CUSTOM MADE THEREMINS

The R. A. Moog Co. has had years of experience in designing and constructing Theremins to order. Virtually any special requirement can be met. For instance, Theremin cabinets made from any hardwood can be supplied, or a specially shaped cabinet can be designed.

An example of special Theremin design is a completely transistorized, battery operated, portable Theremin. This entire instrument weighs only eighteen pounds, but has the same range and playing characteristics of the standard models.

Inquiries concerning custom-made Theremins will receive the prompt and careful attention of the R. A. Moog Co., and will be promptly and courteously answered.

GUARANTEE

All R. A. Moog instruments carry a one-year guarantee against failure due to defective components or construction. All instruments are supplied with a service manual, with the help of which a competent electronic technician can correct most troubles that could arise. Any cost of servicing an R. A. Moog instrument by a competent technician will be borne by the R. A. Moog Co. for the first year of the instrument's operation. For those who wish to send the instrument to the R. A. Moog Co. to be serviced, a prompt repair service is offered.

This information is stated more for the customer's assurance than out of practical necessity. Experience has shown that most R. A. Moog instruments perform for five years or more without requiring repair.

R. A. MOOG CO.

REV. WARREN DEBENHAM

One of the foremost collectors of comedy records in the U.S. is The Reverend Warren Debenham, a Bay Area minister with more than 10,000 comedy LPs, 45s, 78s and CDs. Besides corresponding with a worldwide network of comedy collectors and supplying material for comedy radio shows, he is the author of a classic reference book, *Laughter On Record: A Comedy Discography* (1988; $40 from The Scarecrow Press, PO Box 4167, Metuchen, NJ 08840).

♦ **VALE: When did you become interested in comedy?**

♦ THE REVEREND WARREN DEBENHAM: I've always liked comedy. In high school in the late '40s (I was born in 1933), I remember buying these 78 rpm records that were part of the "Top Ten Series," which featured Jack Benny, Eddie Cantor, etc. My parents had RUTH WALLIS and other blue records which they hid from us kids—of course we discovered them and played 'em when they were gone. Years later, I was just out of the seminary and found myself in a Sunnyvale record store looking at a couple rows of comedy albums—that's when a *collecting urge* came over me, where you want one of everything, even if it's terrible. So my actual *collecting*—where you really go for the *throat*—didn't start until the early '60s.

I started going down to Los Angeles once a year to the used record stores, and giving want lists to dealers all over the place. Things just evolved. A friend of mine, Brian Burney (of A-1 Record Finders in L.A.) started saying he was going to do a book listing comedy records, then the two of us talked about doing it together, and then he pooped out because doing this book would be like a busman's holiday. So I ended up compiling LAUGHTER ON RECORD myself.

♦ *V: Well, it's people like you (rather than the* academic establishment) who are preserving popular culture like this. Although, who knows: maybe the Library of Congress has a complete run of MAD magazine—

How To Speak Hip, Mercury Records.

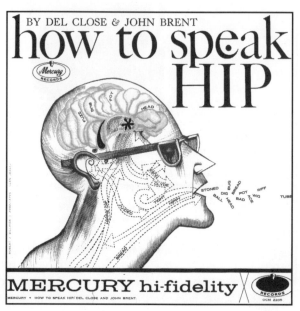

142

Photo: Olivier Robert

♦ WD: They've got quite a record archive, and so does Stanford University—there are about 5 big archives in the country, and those are 2 of them. In my will, the main comedy collection will probably go to Stanford.

♦ **V: So how do you account for the drive behind the collector?**

♦ WD: I have a friend in Palo Alto who collects model trains, and his wife observed, "When 'I would *like* one of those' changes to 'I *need* one of those'—*that's* the operative word!" You become a "collector" when you start trying to get a complete everything by a comedian—even if it's a *terrible* comedian. Actually, the book project helped me to try and be as definitive as possible—I had a goal. If I didn't have a particular record, I would search for it in other people's collections or archives, and if it were too expensive in a store, I'd just write down the information.

♦ **V: When did you start your book?**

♦ WD: I started collecting information around 1970, and it wasn't until 1984 that I felt I had enough to make a worthwhile book. I used 5"x8" cards, and a number of teenage typists helped out—I'd haul a box of records to their house and they'd type up the information. The index in the back lists all the records by subject (e.g., "fat" jokes)—I really needed a computer

to sort all that out, and I finally got one.

♦ **V: Is there any conflict between being an Episco-palian minister and a comedy record collector?**

"When 'I would *like* one of those' changes to 'I *need* one of those'—you become a collector".

♦ WD: You mean in terms of having raunchy or blue material on some of the records? Well, I figure if I'm going to collect comedy I should get *everything* and not limit it—even stuff that I disagree with. But what is most "obscene" to me is material that is *racist,* so I didn't put those categories in the index. I also didn't put in "gay" or "ethnic" (Jewish, Polish) jokes. And I made a deal with myself that if *apartheid* wasn't out of South Africa, I wouldn't include any South African records.

♦ **V: But there's something to be said for preserving "taboo" materials and bringing them to light—not**

143

Rudy Ray Moore's *The Beatnick Scene*, Kent Records.

just burying them and forgetting they ever existed. If you look at LIFE and other magazines from 1942-1944, you'll see some virulently racist cartoons and undiluted racist statements from people who are still revered—

♦ WD: That's something for me to think about. I do know an African-American who collects black caricatures from the '20s and '30s. I was in the third grade when a Japanese classmate of mine went off to the "detention" camps—at the time I knew he was going, but I didn't have any understanding of what was really going on.

As kids we would play the CREPITATION CONTEST record when our parents were gone. It's like a boxing match: they describe the different kinds of farts, and you get points for different ones.

I don't mind swearing on records—that's more of a linguistic than a moral issue. I use jokes in sermons (not the dirty jokes, however) because comedy can help illuminate. One of Jesus's main points was: things aren't always as they seem; God's ways aren't man's ways. And comedy has a way of sneaking up on you; often, what makes you laugh is the *unexpected.*

♦ *V: Comedy has to do with taking advantage of metaphor, simile, ambiguity in language—actual-*

ly, a lot of comedy is a form of poetry. It may not be versified or in rhyme, but it takes advantage of unexpected correspondences in words that surprise and delight. One of the manifestations of fascism is dogmatic language which you cannot challenge— you're not supposed to make fun of the President or the Pope. But to me, 1) the emperor wears no clothes, and 2) there shouldn't even be an emperor. So I'm interested in comedy, especially when it undermines authoritarianism or fascism in any of its forms. And obviously, comedy records have yet to be taken seriously by the Academy—

♦ WD: Before the '50s, comedy wasn't so much of a *public* thing; people would hear it on the radio or own a few records, but it wasn't like now where there are comedy clubs all over the country. Now comedy is taken more "seriously"—one woman is doing her PhD thesis on MOMS MABLEY.

♦ *V: Can you name some blue or sexually explicit comedians?*

♦ WD: You've probably heard the CREPITATION CONTEST record. As kids we would play this when our parents were gone. It's like a boxing match: they describe the different kinds of farts, and you get points for different ones. Often the records credit pseudonyms like "Lord Wyndesmere of Whopping Farthole, England" and "Paul Boomer of Breaking Wind, Australia." There exist maybe 18 different editions of the same material, including bootlegs. The other day I found a 10" version I'd never seen before. This record probably originated as a silly improvised contest, much like a garage band—and it became part of the culture.

♦ *V: This was one of the earliest blue records you ever heard?*

Rudy Ray Moore's *The Cockpit*, A Comedian, Inc. Enterprise. Album cover credits: cover photo: Gladys Allen, cover art: Ralph Pierce.

144

Rudy Ray Moore's *Return of Dolemite*, Kent Records.
Album cover credits: cover photos: Gladys Allen, cover art: Coop.

♦ WD: Yes. People of my generation remember it fondly; it's a part of our growing up . . . RUTH WALLIS was on 78; she sang suggestive lyrics like "He had the cutest little dinghy in the Navy." At that time Lenny Bruce hadn't yet appeared, so these were considered quite risqué although now they're fairly tame. They were just double-entendre, sexual lyrics . . . REDD FOXX started performing in the '40s; he has the most records of anybody in my book—about 90 LPs and a lot of EPs. It seems that every time he did a performance someone put out a record of it; he was very prolific. DOOTSIE WILLIAMS (who owns the Dooto label) is the expert on Redd Foxx. He put out a lot of 45s, EPs and LPs—the promo for the LP might be an EP of 4 cuts especially for the disc jockey.

Before the '60s, you couldn't perform blue material in public unless you were at very "underground" nightclubs. That's where RUDY RAY MOORE got his start.

♦ V: *[looking at discography] He's produced at least 24 albums so far:* **Below the Belt, Close Encounter of the Sex Kind, Eat Out More Often, I Can't Believe I Ate the Whole Thing, This Pussy Belongs to Me**—*great titles! Plus* **The Streaker** *(with Lady Reed)—I'd forgotten about that little fad: streaking.*

♦ WD: Since the '60s he's produced a lot of records, videos and movies—right now he has a movie he really wants to do, that he can't get produced. But on 78rpm, there weren't many risqué comedy records produced. You had other double-entendre comedians like CHARLIE DREW and DWIGHT FISKE. There were maybe 10 different blue labels like STAG, PARTY, PAR-T, PEARL, RISQUÉ, and GOOD HUMOR that specialized in adult comedy, and you'd never know who the

performers were. JIMINY CRICKET (Cliff Edwards) recorded some blue material, sometimes not under his own name. JOHNNY MESNER ("She Had to Lose It at the Astor") did some that were on no label; you'd hear a man and a woman speaking dialogue like:

Woman: "What's going on here?"

Man: "I'm trying to get a drawer into a dresser."

Woman: "Oh dear . . . can't you get it all the way in?" [etc.]

They'd do double-entendre dialogue using games like golf or shooting pool as their metaphors . . . Now there are the COPULATIN' BLUES compilation CD and LP sets out, featuring famous women blues singers like Bessie Smith.

JIM BACKUS released *Dirty Old Man* where instead of a swear word, there would be a sound effect. Then he did *Magoo in Hi-Fi,* but as far as I know *Dirty Old Man* is his only blue record.

In the '50s you had the rise of the BREAK-IN records, which would take phrases from popular songs and insert questions—in other words, the excerpt from the song would be the "answer." DICKY GOODMAN did that famous one on visitors from outer space. He's profiled in the book COMEDY ON RECORD (by Ronald L. Smith (published by Garland Publishing, NY & London). This complements my book by giving the background on the comedians, while mine lists their records: "A pioneer of *collage comedy,* Goodman (born 1932) took pop tunes, scissored them around a narration, and produced a string of hit singles. 'The Flying Saucer' was released on his own *Luniverse* label in 1956. Goodman continued to have hits using the same premise, asking interview questions and letting rock song snippets supply the answer, scoring in '74 and '75 with 'Energy Crisis' and 'Mr Jaws.' "

JIM BACKUS released *Dirty Old Man* where instead of a swear word, there would be a sound effect. Then he did *Magoo in Hi-Fi,* but as far as I know *Dirty Old Man* is his only blue record.

♦ V: *[looking at book] Goodman definitely was a forerunner of sampling in rap music. Here's an example of his technique. [question] "What would you do if you saw a UFO?" [Elvis Presley sings] "Take a walk down Lonely Street."*

♦ WD: One person who gathered a lot of these records together, and released compilations, was DR DEMEN-

TO, who's been on the radio since 1970 playing unusual records.

♦ *V: So there weren't that many blue records that came out in the '50s?*

♦ WD: Well, just on the DOOTO label alone there were several hundred. There was the notorious "Big Ten-Inch" record [Bullmoose Jackson]. The TRASH label had the comedian Sad Sack (not to be confused with the cartoon personality, a soldier) who was pretty raunchy.

LOBO and RIOT labels would put out the same record in different jackets to get you to buy it twice.

MORT SAHL did some taboo-breaking on the establishment and political comedy. LENNY BRUCE was more on sex, prejudice (or racism) and drugs—an Episcopal priest called him "an honest man—sometimes a shockingly honest man." There's a 1962 10" record of his San Francisco obscenity trial that's very rare; he made it to use as evidence (I've only heard of five copies in existence). And there's nothing unique on the record, it's just his night club act—he wanted to show that it wasn't obscene. Periodically, undercover police would attend his show and get "evidence" against him. After being thrown in jail several times, he finally died of an overdose. Near the end he was trying to defend himself and go through his legal nightmare in front of the audience, and he would sometimes be hazy

The Groove World of Trustin Howard, Horoscope Records

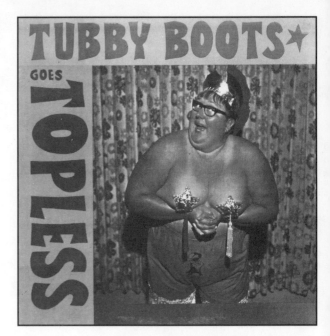

Tubby Boots Goes Topless, Sound Arts Inc.
Album cover credits: photos: Dick Le Page.

and go off on weird tangents that people had a hard time following—it was sad. I guess it was "real life" up there on the stage, but it wasn't too funny!

♦ *V: Any more women comedians braving taboos?*

♦ WD: PEARL WILLIAMS and BELLE BARTH were fairly raunchy. Belle Barth did *The Customer Comes First;* she was on the LOBO and RIOT labels. Those companies would put out the same record in different jackets to get you to buy it twice. Besides LOBO there was BOLO records as well—same company. Belle Barth is also on these labels: ENTERTAINMENT PRODUCTIONS; LAUGH TIME; SURPRISE; and AFTER HOURS—

♦ *V: [reading discography] —with nice titles like I Don't Mean to be Vulgar—But It's Profitable; If I Embarrassed You—Forget It!; and My Next Story Is a Little Risqué.*

♦ WD: RUSTY WARREN released an album called *Banned in Boston.* She's still performing and is very amenable to talking; she sent me a photo for my book.

♦ *V: Banned in Boston was on the JUBILEE label—*

♦ WD: Jubilee put out some mildly suggestive records—they did those BLOOPER LPs, but they weren't as blue as some of the others. KERMIT SCHAEFFER put out a lot of records on his own label, where he had complete control over everything. His humor involved bloopers, where somebody makes a mistake in public and says, "The breast in bed" instead of "the best in bread." "Hoobert Heever" was another famous blooper.

♦ *V: RUTH WALLIS did a lot of LPs:* **French Postcards; Here's Looking Up Your Hatch; He Wants a Little Pizza; The Spice Is Right; Marry-Go-Round—**

146

♦ WD: She had her own label as well: Wallis Originals.

♦ *V: Here's a woman, MARSHA WARFIELD, and her album's titled* **I'm a Virgin**—

♦ WD: She's contemporary—in fact she's on the TV show *Night Court*. She was a stand-up comedian with some fairly raunchy or blunt lines. Another somewhat blue woman comedian is Nancy Steele who did *Playgirl*.

Other contemporaries of Lenny Bruce, like Mike Nichols and Elaine May, were more straight . . . SANDY BARRON did some stuff that was more emotional/psychological—

♦ *V: Like* **How I Found God, Zen, Yoga, EST, Arica, Sufi, Scientology, TM—and My Life Still Sucks!** *Plus he did* **God Save the Queens**—

♦ WD: He would also do material that went straight for the throat. There are still people taking up the political mantle of Mort Sahl: *Saturday Night Live!*, the *National Lampoon,* etc. What "good" comedy does is: *it puts down the people in power,* whereas "bad" comedy puts down the guy who's powerless. For that reason I really don't like Andrew Dice Clay; he puts down women and gays. Do you know about CHARLES PIERCE, the famous female impersonator? He gets dressed up as Judy Garland or Lucille Ball and does a lot of gay double-entendres. He's been around since the beatnik days.

♦ *V: I like beatnik comedy records, like JOHN BRENT and DEL CLOSE's* **How to Speak Hip**—

♦ WD: That's a great record. They did another one entitled *Do It Yourself Psychoanalysis,* but it wasn't as good . . . Other comedians in the "beatnik" vein include LORD BUCKLEY (he was before them but he was an influence), BROTHER THEODORE, STEVE ALLEN, and AL "JAZZBO" COLLINS.

The Group Therapists' *Sick Aong With Us,* Strand Records.

♦ *V: Beatnik comedy's successors include THE COMMITTEE, THE CONGRESS OF WONDERS*—

♦ WD: JEAN FARMER did comedy involving drugs. The ultimate drinking story involved Sam Kinison who used to do a routine *defending* drinking while driving. In his routine he would say, "After you get drunk, what are you going to do—*walk* home? Of course you're going to drive home!" In real life he got killed by a drunk driver. Another comedian who went from the seminary into comedy is David Steinway, who did *The Incredible Shrinking God.*

♦ *V: Do you know much about hillbilly or "white trash" comedy records?*

♦ WD: Those are usually singles rather than LPs. I'd never want to compile a discography of comedy singles—there are so many small labels. In my book I figure I got between 80-90%—but I'm always finding out about more records, so I have to lower that estimate! On 45s I wouldn't even come close.

What "good" comedy does is: *it puts down the people in power,* whereas "bad" comedy puts down the guy who's powerless. For that reason I really don't like Andrew Dice Clay; he puts down women and gays.

♦ *V: In your book, you do include in the index "race," "bigots," and the "Klan."*

♦ WD: But that's putting down bigots and the Klan, it's not "pro." Did you know that Frank Sinatra and Shirley MacLaine did a song referring to the "Japs"? It's on a soundtrack for a movie. There are a lot of "Southern" comedians, like Brother Dave Gardner who makes jokes referring to rednecks; Lewis Gizzard; James Gregory; Jerry Clower; and others who do Cajun comedy.

♦ *V: Burt Henry did a record,* **At the Hungry Thigh.** *Is that a send-up of the "Hungry i" in San Francisco?*

♦ WD: He was a blue comedian on several different labels; he would put out the same record "straight" *and* with a well-developed topless woman on the cover. He did the famous "finger" cover where he's flipping you the bird—that was fairly unusual in those times. He was on FAX—another blue label.

WILD MAN STEVE was another blue comedian on the RAW label; he put out quite a few raunchy records like *Dealer's Choice* which was on DICK-ER Records, and *The Six Thousand Dollar Nigger.* BLOWFLY takes white contemporary songs and parodies the lyrics into blue material. I didn't include him in my book because

I considered him more "novelty"—he does songs rather than jokes.

Even Jonathan Winters did an album of blue material. He was sitting around a table with some friends and they got him to improvise while a tape recorder was turned on. This was put out as a bootleg; it was never officially released. In my book I listed it under "J.W.: Hee hee hee-larious."

The ultimate drinking story involved Sam Kinison who used to do a routine *defending* drinking while driving. In his routine he would say, "After you get drunk, what are you going to do—*walk* home? Of course you're going to drive home!" In real life he got killed by a drunk driver.

♦ **V: What's the FRIARS club?**

♦ WD: That's a men's club for show business personalities; there's one in New York and one in L.A. At certain meetings they'll select a guest of honor to be "roasted," where six or seven people will get up and tell put-down jokes about him. Sometimes someone will release privately-pressed recordings of the "roasts" of the persons in attendance. One record actually had

Redd Foxx's *You Gotta Wash Your Ass*, Atlantic Recording Corporation, © 1975 EF-OH-EX-EX Productions.
Album cover credits: cover concept: Redd Foxx, photography: David Alexander.

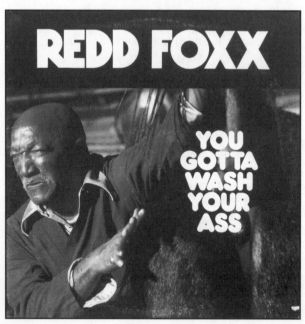

Adam Stag Party Record 5, © 1962 Fax Record Co.

Art Linkletter swearing—it's listed under "Harry Joe Brown" in my book. Art said later that he hoped people wouldn't get to hear it.

Another bootleg recording I've heard is by Elvis. He's singing "Are You Lonesome Tonight?" live when suddenly he starts laughing and can't stop—he laughs till the end of the song. I heard a story that whenever he screwed up the lyrics for a song he would never do that song again—I don't know if that's true. But on this record he tries to start the song again and again, but keeps laughing and finally just gives up.

One of my favorite comedians that I've seen live is Professor Irwin Corey, who calls himself "The World's Foremost Authority" (he didn't say on *what*). He gets up and rambles on and on about any topic that comes to mind, all the time rattling off clever puns and jokes and absurd statements like "I feel more like I do now than I did before." He's the ultimate put-down of authority.

♦ **V: When did you start collecting MAD magazines?**

♦ WD: In the mid-'60s. My kids started reading them, so I gave all 3 of them a subscription. Then my son and I started collecting back issues, and now I have a fairly complete collection, back to Number One. I've got HELP (which was similar to MAD); the complete PANIC, as well as the reissue hardback sets of MAD and PANIC which mostly consist of the earliest issues from the '50s. The MAD WORLD OF WILLIAM M. GAINES is pretty hard to find; I've only seen one copy. I visited the offices on *MAD*ison Avenue in New York— they were very relaxed and gave me a tour of the place.

Whenever I have a chance to meet a comedian in person, I ask them to sign a copy of my book—I have one copy which is starting to get filled with signatures. Recently in San Francisco I saw EMO PHILLIPS. In one skit he told how when he was growing up, there was one door in the house that was always kept locked, but one day he managed to open it and saw sky, trees, grass—he'd been locked in the basement all his life! He also told how his parents had given him a big metal pole to carry "to protect him from lightning." I went backstage and while he was signing the book he asked, "How many comedians are listed here?" I said, "Four thousand." "And how many signatures do you have?" "Oh—thirty." Then he said, "Well, now you've got 3,969 to go!"

♦ **V: Did you know that a lot of the historical articles for the 1889 Encyclopedia Britannica (the great Ninth Edition) were written by country clergymen?**

♦ WD: A lot of clergymen have been fairly healthy about having some kind of semi-consuming hobby that gets them away from the ministry. I know another minister whose hobby is photographing wildflowers, and he'll fiddle for hours just getting the right light and focus. He said, "That's how I get that urge to manipulate out of my system—so I don't manipulate *people.*"

REFERENCE:

ARTISTS WHO USED BLUE MATERIALS:

Patsy Abbott; Frank Alesia and Timothy Blake; Billy Allyn; Judy Andraws; Angelina; Mike Anthony and Bert Roberts; Alice Arthur; Roy Awbrey; Bill Ballance; Belle Barth; Bea Bea Benson; Rex Benson; Don Bexley; Nan Blakstone; Baroness Bobo; Davey Bold; Tubby Boots; Rae Bourbon; Oscar Brand; Tommy Brown; Lenny Bruce; The Bucknell Sisters; Butterfly; Chester Calhoun; Mr. Lynn Carter; Doug Clark; Lenny Clark; Kate Clinton; Billy Connoly; Peter Cooke and Dudley Moore (as Derek and Clive); Joel Cowan; Leroy "Sloppy" Daniels; Miss Dee; Richie De Marco and Tommy Day; Billy Devroe; Tina Dixon; Allan Drew; Charlie Drew; Uncle Dirty; Dynamite; Jeb and Cousin Easy; Cliff Ferre; Tottie Fields; Dwight Fiske; Vicki Ford; Bill "The Fox" Foster; Redd Foxx; Some Friars; Marty Gale; Weela Gallez; Marjorie Garretson; Rozelle Gayle; Gene and Freddy; Big George (George Henry Kerr, Jr); Silent George; Stu Gilliam; Booty Green; Buzzy Greene; Hap Happy; Baron Harris; Eddie Harris; Sonny Hachett; Jimmy Heap; Bert Henry; Cha-Cha Hogan; Hap Hogan; Roscoe Holland; Brenda Hollis; Hurricane;

Autry Iman; Kenny Karol; Prince Kelly; Dave Ketchum; Sam Kinison; La Wanda (La Wanda Page); Rickie Layne (ventriloquist); Mr. Billy Lee; Stella Lester; Colleen Lovett; Don Lucas; Jimmy Lynch; John Mabbott; McLean and McLean (Blair McLean and Gary McLean); Barbara Markay; Kay Martin; Jackie Martling; Chuck Mason; Hal Masters; Billie McAllister; Michelle; Richard Milner; Minka; Rudy Ray Moore; Eddie Murphy; Mantan Moreland; Sam Nichols; Hattie Noel; Terry "Cupcake" O'Mason; Omo the Hobo; The Original Dirty Old Man; La Wanda (La Wanda Page); Jak Parti; Richard Pryor; Lady Reed (Nancy Reed); Reynaldo Rey; Richard and Willie (Richard Sanfield and ventriloquist dummy, Willie); Faye Richmond; Lynn Robinson; Timmie Rogers; Betty Ross; Joe E. Ross; Sad Sack (the comedian); Tony Savone; Ray Scott; Baby Seale; Skillet Mayhand and Leroy "Sloppy" Daniels; Lynn Snyder; Society's Hotnuts; Sonny and Pepper; Al Sparks; Dave Starr; Nancy Steele; Howard Stern; Wild Man Steve (Steve Gallon); Sylvia Stoun; Bub Thomas; Jimmy Thompson; Betty Thorton; Ting-a-Ling (Terry Powell); Gene Tracy; Dave Turner; Gregory Tutt; Clay Tyson; Larry Vincent; Ruth Wallis; Marsha Warfield; Rusty Warren; Jim Watson; Claudia Wheeler; Ava Williams; Pearl Williams; Mr. X.

LP LABELS THAT USED BLUE MATERIALS:

After Hours; Beacon; Bolo; Borderline; Comedian; Davis; Dealer's Choice; De Luxe; Dick-er; Dingo; Dooto; Fame; Fax; Gala; Generation; Gross; Ha Ha; Hilarious; Hot Box; Hudson; Jubilee; Kent; King; Koala; Laff; Laugh Time; La Val; Lobo; Norman; Off Hour Rockers; MF Records; No Holds Barred; Par T; Partee; Party Time; Pel-Nor; Record Productions; Riot; Schlock; Spicy; Surprise; Tampa; T and L Records; Trash; Twilite; UTC Records; Wallis Original.

78 RPM LABELS THAT USED BLUE MATERIALS:

Blu Records; Blue; Bourbon; Burlesque; Burley-Q; Davis; De Luxe; Dooto; Fiske; Friskana; Fun; Gala; Good Humor; Hi Lite; Hi-Society; High Society; Hollywood Hot Shots; Hush-Hush; Imperial; Joe Davis; Jubilee; KEM; Hicks; Laff; Let's Have Fun; Liberty Music (some); LD Records; Miltone; MJ Records; MR Records; National Hollywood; Novelty; Party; Party Noveltys; Party Platters; Party Time; Pearl; Risk-K-Fun; Risque; Stag; Star Garter; Tampa; Top Hat (some); Wallis Original; Western Record Co.

MAIL ORDER:

- Ronald L. Smith's *Comedy On Record* (counterpart to my book, *Laughter on Record),* available from Garland Publishing, New York City.
- *Laugh* magazine. Peter Tatchell, 40 Bambra Road, Caulfield, Victoria, Australia 3161. $5 U.S. cash.

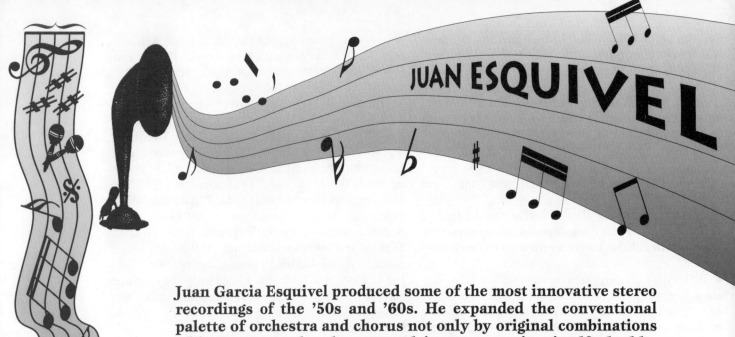

Juan Garcia Esquivel produced some of the most innovative stereo recordings of the '50s and '60s. He expanded the conventional palette of orchestra and chorus not only by original combinations of instruments, but by unusual instrumentation itself: double-neck steel guitar, harpsichord, theremin, whistling (by Muzzy Marcellino), and exotic percussion (including a real jawbone, with rattling teeth). As *Variety* said, "Esquivel is to pop music approximately what Aaron Copland is to serious music, or what a John Coltrane is to jazz. He achieves a strange new sound by dissonance, unusual juxtapositions of instrumental or vocal sounds, and rapid switches in tempi, volume and mood." Throughout a 50-year career, Esquivel also produced music for numerous radio and TV shows (including Ernie Kovacs), live shows (with six musicians and four female singers), as well as films, both in North and Central America. Currently he is staying at the home of his brother Sergio, near Mexico City. Our thanks to Ken Sitz for his research on Esquivel.

♦ VALE: *I read that you won the Mexican National Lottery—*

♦ ESQUIVEL: —not once, but *twice!* That's practically unheard of. The first time was in the '50s; I won $400,000, which I split with my band. The second time was in 1964; I won $240,000. This time I kept it all for myself—and my wife, of course.

♦ V: *Do you consider yourself lucky?*

♦ E: Oh, yes; I have been extremely fortunate. I definitely believe in luck.

♦ V: *Let's start from the beginning: you were born in Tampico, Tamaulipas, Mexico—*

♦ E: —January 20, 1918. At the time Tampico was well-known, because at the beginning of the century it had plenty of oil, and a lot of American people went there. My father was a customs administrator, and he traveled a lot. Our family stayed in Tampico for awhile and then moved to Guadalajara in the state of Jalisco.

♦ V: *I read that at the age of 12 you had a 15-minute radio show, at 14 a full band, and a 30-piece orchestra with singers at 17—*

♦ E: That's more or less true. I think it was my destiny to be a musician, because at the age of 10 I used to go regularly to places that had a piano and play it—my family had to go out looking for me. I was playing just for the pleasure of it; I didn't receive any money. Then my family moved to Mexico City, where XEW, a local radio station, was very popular. I started playing piano on their radio programs, and won several contests (later, in 1946, I won an award for "Best Piano Player in Mexico City"). The radio station was the founder of *Televisa,* the most important chain of TV stations in Central America.

After playing piano at XEW for awhile, I decided to form a small group. However, making the arrangements was difficult because I couldn't read or write

music very well. So at the age of 14, I took three years off and started learning on my own, studying harmony, composing and arranging. (I never attended music school until I went to Julliard, but that was years later.) It was my desire to create a different sound; I was trying to do what now is done with synthesizers—but with normal instruments. It took *years* to finally find a style.

It would take too long to summarize my whole career, but . . . I was brought to the United States by RCA with a 3-year contract which was extended year by year. In New York I was on The Pat Boone Show and in Hollywood I was on The Danny Kaye Show and on Johnny Carson. I formed a 10-piece orchestra and performed at the Stardust Hotel in Las Vegas under contract for 26 weeks a year. We played there for 12 years until I returned to Mexico to write the music for *Burbujas,* a children's show on *Televisa.*

I've been active all my life. I belong to BMI, and I've written music for many TV series. While living in Beverly Hills, back in 1961, I was playing with my wife, lifting her in my arms on a highly polished wood floor. I slipped on a small rug and fell with her on top of me. She wasn't hurt. I didn't pay any attention to that accident, but it broke a vertebrae in my spine, which resulted in a deviation of my lumbar column.

Thirty years later I had another fall [July, 1993] and broke my hip, and because of the previous spinal injury, I now have to be in a wheelchair.

♦ *V: Is your wife still alive?*

♦ E: Which one—I've had four wives! What I did wrong was: I didn't pay attention to my back problem right away. At the time I would stay awake working 32 hours at a time playing the piano and writing at my desk, then I would sleep 8 hours, then work 32 hours . . . the barber would come to my studio and do his job while I was practicing. I practiced constantly to improve my agility; I've been awarded several trophies for my piano playing which was very agile and very clear.

I've tried all my life to be *clear.* When I write arrangements I try to not be confusing, while using instruments in non-traditional ways. Again, I was trying to get sounds that now you can easily get with synthesizers—they would have saved me a lot of problems!

♦ *V: You first studied engineering, but then gave it up for piano—*

♦ E: When I was quite young I took two or three courses in electronic engineering, but it was *music* that really attracted me. At age 12 I started going to XEW, waiting for the chance to play the piano on the radio.

The Latin Sound of Henry Mancini, © 1965 RCA Victor.

Finally I met Mr Azcarraga, the man who founded the station. The most important artists of the day had all gotten their start playing "live" there, like Agustin Lara who wrote "Granada" and "You Belong To My Heart" (in Spanish, "Solamente Una Vez"), and Armando Manzanero, who wrote a song which Perry Como introduced to the US, "It's Impossible." Anyway, that's how I started: I quit engineering. My first radio program was 15 minutes every day, and I got paid two pesos. Right now a US dollar is worth 3,000 pesos, but 65 years ago, for two pesos you could buy a sandwich and take a taxi home. So I considered myself quite privileged to be earning that much money.

♦ **V: Did you actually take piano lessons?**

♦ E: When I was very young, about 6 or 7 years old, I had a lady teacher who taught me how to read elementary piano music. My parents had a pianola or player piano. You could put in a piano roll, push the pedals and the keyboard would start playing—at the time these were very popular. I asked my father if it would be okay to convert it to just a regular piano. I did that, and it wasn't so satisfactory to my parents because I would practice day and night! But when we are very young we don't think of considerations like that. My parents never questioned or stopped me, because it was obvious I loved the instrument and they thought it was good for me to practice.

At that time I didn't have the remotest idea that I would write music. My teacher taught me and my younger sister simple pieces by Beethoven and others for about a year. Then I built a crystal set and started listening to XEW, learning the most popular songs of the day. I became curious and wondered, "How could I write popular songs?" I bought music paper and started writing melodies.

♦ **V: Describe this process—**

♦ E: I learned songs by ear and tried to play them on the keyboard, finding out that some keys were easier. At first I played only in the keys of C or G, or D or F. Then I became curious about the other tonalities, and not soon, but finally, I was able to practice in other keys like F-sharp, B Major and B Minor, E Major and E Minor, and A Major and A Minor.

♦ **V: How did you develop the ability to write your own tunes, not just play other people's songs?**

♦ E: Let's just say that I started taking popular tunes of Mexico and converting them into something strange! My music couldn't be danced to; I was experimenting with different rhythms. My first small group consisted of a viola, an accordion, and myself on piano, plus a rhythm section. Little by little, as my radio program grew in popularity, I started thinking in terms of an orchestra, and then started using two trumpets and four saxophones. Of course, my early arrangements were very tentative because I didn't know how to combine the instruments.

♦ **V: What was your first big break?**

♦ E: A very popular radio comedian, who had a program at 8 o'clock at night, asked me, "Do you think you could use an orchestra?" Of course I said, "Yes!"— I never said no to any proposal! He asked me to supply little pieces of music as a background for his comedy skits.

♦ **V: Your music had to be funny or witty—**

♦ E: Yes. Back then it was very expensive to use musicians for rehearsal, but fortunately our program was sponsored by the Colgate-Palmolive Company. They asked me to write advertising jingles to promote their detergents or toothpaste, which I did. They had a big radio program at night with a live audience, and it became so popular that we always had crowds. Of course, after midnight, it was a different type of audience: taxi-drivers and night-shift workers—people who could attend in the wee hours. XEW was the first radio station to broadcast all day and all night.

Each day I had to write new background music. The entire orchestra would arrive at ten o'clock in the morning, the comedian would give me the script for the day, and the boy who set up the music stands would give each musician a pencil, an eraser, and blank music paper. Since I got a new script each morning, I couldn't write for the musicians in advance, so I did it on the spot. In this way I learned the limitations and possibilities of each instrument; for example, a "C" on the piano is written as a D for the trumpet. I would ask the trombonist, "Can you make a 'shake' from A down to C?" "I can't." "How about a glissando?" "I can't, because I would have to change the slide to opposite positions, and that's not possible." I would ask the tenor and alto sax players, "What's your best sound range? Can you do this trill?"

The comedian was very pleased with the musical backgrounds I invented. He might say, "I want background music for a Frenchman walking in Russia." [laughs] I would think, "How can I describe *that?*" This is how my imagination started developing. Fortunately, I had all these instruments to experiment with: five trumpets, four trombones, five saxes and the rhythm section, plus violins, violas, cellos and a harp. The radio station became interested because I was the only one doing this—other musical directors weren't interested in experimenting or in being imaginative. They would buy "stock music": orchestral arrangements printed in the United States, and all the orchestras sounded the same because no one would write original arrangements.

Besides the musical backgrounds for the comedian's sketches, I started writing my own arrangements, with me at the piano conducting at the same time. The radio station and sponsors gave me a free hand—there were no budgetary problems. Sometimes I used an orchestra of 54 musicians in live programs, which at the time was unheard of—usually orchestras had 18 musicians in them. All the time I was trying to change the system; trying to change the sounds.

♦ **V: You mentioned you went to Julliard—**
♦ E: This was after I had already worked with a big 24-piece orchestra. At Julliard I was auditioned by a professor of music from France, and he asked me to play something on the piano, which I did. Then, after listening to my Mexican recordings and examining my musical scores, he told me, "Listen, Mr Esquivel, I don't think it's a wise idea for you to change your systems. We would teach you certain things that you are doing very badly, but these things you are doing very badly are also very commercial—you are creating something of your *own.* I'm afraid you would lose your style if you followed our instructions." I took his advice; I had just wanted to learn about certain little details, but I certainly didn't follow the conventional ways of composing, arranging and conducting. This was my brief encounter with a traditional music school. At times I wondered if I did wrong, because I felt I should have studied for at least six months. But he had told me, "When you write, you break certain musical rules—but don't fight success!"

♦ **V: It was great that this teacher didn't try to control you—**
♦ E: Yes, instead of forbidding me to do certain things, he said, "Go ahead and just do whatever you want to do." I followed his advice.

Coming to the United States I didn't know what I was going to face, but I found some very fine musicians, composers, and arrangers. I met Stanley Wilson of Universal Studios and he introduced me to Henry Mancini. When we shook hands, Hank (that's what we called him) said, "I admire your work, Juan." My English was even worse than now, so I answered, "Me, too!" He must have thought I was very egotistical, but I meant that I admired *his* work and his ideas. Stanley Wilson straightened it out by saying, "He's trying to

say that he admires you very much." I was lucky to have also met Quincy Jones. We weren't intimate friends because we didn't have the time, but we met on several occasions and—had I known that I had to compete with such talents, I probably would have quit! But I was glad that I was accepted by them.

♦ **V: On the back of one album, it says, "Juan Garcia Esquivel was a big music man in Mexico before the Yankee disc jockeys discovered some of his RCA Victor singles on the 'for export only' label"—**
♦ E: One of the songs was "Lamento Borincano," a famous song written by Rafael Hernandez, a prolific Puerto Rican composer and songwriter. I can't recall the other songs on those singles. There were only three or four of them, chosen from the best recordings I had made in Mexico.

♦ **V: Your first LP to appear in the USA was To Love Again—**
♦ E: Right. That was recorded in Mexico City around 1957. The musical director for RCA Mexico, Mariano Rivera-Conde, was kind enough to send a copy of the tape to RCA in New York, and they became interested enough in my work to re-release that LP in the U.S. They asked Mariano, "Do you have Esquivel under contract?" Mariano said, "Sure, I have him for years."

♦ **V: Was To Love Again your very first album?**
♦ E: No. Before that, I had recorded an album titled *Las Tandas de Garcia Esquivel.* Our orchestra would play prom dances for graduating engineers, architects, and medical students. From 10 PM to 3 AM we played dance sets called "tandas," and each contained six or seven numbers. These weren't very special; they were pre-"Sonorama" (a term I used for my style of unusual arranging), so they were more like conventional dance

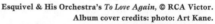

Esquivel & His Orchestra's *To Love Again,* © RCA Victor.
Album cover credits: photo: Art Kane.

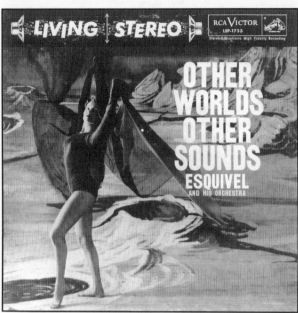

Esquivel & His Orchestra's *Other Worlds, Other Sounds,* © RCA Victor.

music. I wasn't very proud of this record; musically, it wasn't worth much. It was recorded only in monaural.

♦ **V: On To Love Again,** *it says you "had a special electric guitar designed and began to work out various uses for it"—*

♦ **E:** Perhaps you will recall ALVINO REY and his steel guitar. I liked his style, and wanted to get that same sound. I discovered that he used a Hawaiian guitar. After some searching, I found a more-or-less similar instrument which had two bridges. I started training a Mexican player, but it took awhile for him to get used to the tuning; also, he had to learn how to use a metal bar to make the glissandos. He was a very fine musician, but in rehearsals he would sweat very nervously because previously he hadn't known anything about the instrument. I started experimenting with arrangements, trying to make it easier for him. But as soon as he got to the studio he would start sweating. Finally he asked me to write out the parts so he could study them at home.

Anyway, RCA New York asked Mariano, "How soon can Esquivel have another LP's worth of arrangements?" Mariano told me, "Juan, they want you to make another album, this time using your 'Sonorama' style, but in stereo. How soon can you have it ready?" I said, "Frankly, it takes me about one month to prepare and rehearse one arrangement." The problem was: my 5 singers (a girl and 4 male voices) didn't read music, so it took them hours of rehearsal to memorize every sound. And sometimes I would write music that would have more than 5 voices, plus the duplication of the melody an octave lower. My singers were used to singing ballads and Mexican music that weren't as complicated as my arrangements. So I told Mariano, "If they want an album of 12 numbers, it will take 12

months." "What?!" "Just consider that I require all this rehearsal time." And in those days it was standard for an LP to have 12 numbers, not 10.

Of course, the United States had excellent musicians. RCA New York made a fast decision, "If Juan can't record because he needs singers who know how to read music, and more versatility from the musicians (e.g., oboe, bass-flute, English horn, etc) then instead of recording in Mexico, let's bring him to the States. Juan can choose whatever musicians he needs; all he has to do is ask the musical contractor." By mail I replied, "Well, for my first recording I will need such-and-such players."

So in January, 1958 I drove from Mexico City to Hollywood to make the recording of *Other Worlds, Other Sounds.* I think RCA wanted to "test" me to see how fast I could finish an album, so they allowed me only *five* hours to record twelve numbers. I was lucky enough to finish the job in three-hours-and-a-half! You see, I had rehearsed with my Mexican orchestra to make sure everything in my scores "worked"; every note had been tested and proven. Then Johnnie Camacho, the producer, told me, "We still have an hour-and-a-half; what do you think you could do?" I said, "Well, I could dismiss the orchestra, sit down at the piano and need just a rhythm section and a flute." He asked, "What about the repertoire?" I said, "I have an idea: let me choose numbers from different countries, and we could call the album *Four Corners of the World.*" He said, "Excellent—how long would it take?" Previously I had been used to producing music almost instantly, so I replied, "Practically no time."

> **I think RCA wanted to "test" me to see how fast I could finish an album, so they allowed me only *five* hours to record twelve numbers. I was lucky enough to finish the job in three-hours-and-a-half!**

I used a rhythm section (which included a guitar) plus a flute, and started improvising. The musicians were very capable; they included a great bongo player, JOE LOCO. He was very agile in following my instructions, and I was very impressed by his crisp sound. The flute player was agile, too. We didn't have a general rehearsal, we just rehearsed each number and then recorded it. Really, it was a cinch—the musicians adapted very quickly to my requirements. We started with "Dark Eyes" and ended up with "Cielito Lindo." Johnnie Camacho was very satisfied. But I had made a mistake: having recorded an album with a big orches-

Esquivel & His Piano & Group's *4 Corners of the World*, © RCA Victor.
Album cover credits: photo: Irv Bahrt.

tra and dazzling stereo effects, the audience didn't expect the next album to be with a small combo. *Other Worlds, Other Sounds* got a wonderful reception; at Music City on Hollywood and Vine it was Number One for 12 weeks. But *Four Corners of the World* didn't get that acceptance.

♦ V: **Wasn't Alvino Rey on** Other Worlds, Other Sounds?

♦ E: Even though he was very busy, Alvino Rey was nice enough to attend three of my recording sessions (*Other Worlds, Other Sounds;* and *Infinity in Sound,* Vols. One and Two). At the time he was very popular, and some of my arrangements used a guitar in his style. I was afraid he would say that I was following his particular sound, but he didn't. He was married to one of the King Sisters.

By the way, the company had wanted to call my first album *Beguine For Beginners*. I didn't agree with that title, but I went along with the idea of recording an album in the "Beguine" tempo. I wrote all the arrangements but didn't use the numbers they wanted me to record, because I wasn't happy with them. Instead, I thought of taking well-known tunes like "That Old Black Magic" and "Nature Boy" and giving them a unique style.

♦ V: *How did you get to record what you* **wanted** *to record?*

♦ E: When I met Johnnie Camacho, I had to invent a little white lie. The first thing he asked me was, "Did you finish your arrangements?" I said, "You know what happened, Johnnie? My copyist was robbed— they thought he was carrying a lot of money instead of the arrangements. So I didn't bring what you asked for." He said, "Juan—that's terrible. The material is very important; what do you intend to record?" I said,

" 'Granada'—I play piano on it, and I think you will like the recording." He said, " 'Granada'—*ohmigod.* That's been recorded so many times; I don't think it will work." I said, "I can also record 'Begin the Beguine' and 'Night and Day' and 'Poinciana.' " I started conducting the numbers, and when Johnnie heard my arrangements he changed completely. He said, "Juan, this is *far* better than we expected."

When the tapes got to New York, RCA said, "This title *Beguine for Beginners* doesn't have anything to do with what's on the album." They decided it was music from other worlds, so they changed the title to *Other Worlds, Other Sounds.* And it was a hit nationwide. Again, looking back I can see that my mistake was recording the big sound of the orchestra in full stereo, then making my next album with just a piano group. I wasn't happy with my piano playing because it was improvised; it was done in a hurry; and I wasn't happy with my interpretations. But the album was a last-minute thought, and I learned a lesson: that I should stick with my sound, my arrangements and especially stick to big bands. Because when the public bought my next album they bought it thinking it was the Esquivel sound, and instead they were disappointed.

♦ V: **The** Four Corners of the World **doesn't have the Esquivel orchestral stereo impact, but it still has some great playing on it. For example, "In a Persian Market" sounds quite original—**

♦ E: Well, I had a lot of practice, thanks to the musical sketches I had to do for that comedian; he gave me all the experience in the world! I had to provide musical backgrounds for all kinds of different jokes and situations, and I had the opportunity of having 24 musicians 8 hours a day, all of us making notes of the

Alvino Rey's *My Reverie*, Decca Records.
Album cover credits: cover photo: Burt Owen.

results of my experiments with new chords and sounds. I learned dynamics and the difference between chords used for saxophone players and trumpet players (what was good; what wasn't). This was a very important part of developing my career. I was experimenting without having to pay for it, and this was fabulous for me!

♦ *V: What happened to all that sheet music?*
♦ E: When I left Mexico, the boy who passed out the blank music paper kept all the pages the musicians had written on. But it turned out that they were not legible—no one else could decipher them! The musicians had the good will to make notes, but usually they wouldn't record the names of the sketches or the dates or even their own names or instruments. They would jot down what they would soon be playing while it was still "fresh."

When I left for the States, Panseco (the name of the comedian) tried to duplicate his radio success on television, but he didn't count on the fact that on the radio, the audience has to use their imagination. He had a certain group of actors and created many types of comics, and the public would imagine what they looked like. When television arrived, incautiously he prepared some TV programs, but the audience discovered that Panseco (may he rest in peace; he died a few years ago) was a fat man, although not ugly. They wouldn't accept him, and he faded from view. Nevertheless, he was my school, my theory and my practice—you can have all the theory in the world just in your head, but as for me, I was practicing my theory and having almost instantaneous results. I didn't have to *imagine* for very long how a group of brass might sound; I could try it out almost immediately.

♦ *V: On* **Other Worlds, Other Sounds,** *you certainly got a good recording—*
♦ E: I was very happy with the engineer, Val Valentin. We both had the same ideas, and he recorded the sounds of the individual instruments very well. Sometimes a bad recording engineer can ruin a good arrangement, and sometimes a good recording engineer can greatly help a mediocre arranger. Also, the studio itself is important. Due to the design and construction, or the conditions of the weather (if it's moist or warm), the studios contribute greatly to the sound. In Mexico City there were some excellent studios; four or five times engineers from RCA New York visited them just to examine the way they were built. Also, the human factor is important. I had people who were very bright, very intelligent, and who worked *together* with me. To work with people, you need to share a special sense of understanding.

♦ *V: Can you recall any other musicians you worked with in Hollywood?*
♦ E: The guitarist Laurindo Almeida; Stan Getz; Ted Nash (a sax player who had his own group); the organist Buddy Cole (I heard he died); and Bob Anderson, who was an excellent trombonist.

♦ *V: How did you decide which tunes to include on your later albums?*
♦ E: Sometimes the producer or record company had a particular interest in having me record a song; then I would create an arrangement based on my taste. Occasionally a publishing company would offer me a percentage of the royalties if I chose a particular tune, but I never did that. I just followed my liking as to which songs were most suitable for me to make something out of. Often I deliberately chose songs that were well-known so the audience could appreciate the *arrangements,* because my thinking was, "If you record an unknown tune, people can't tell if something is the idea of the composer or the arranger."

Once, a San Francisco radio station had a contest giving a little award to whoever could correctly identify the tempo of my version of "Bye Bye Blues" (*Infinity in Sound,* Vol. Two)—the tempo and arrangement were unusual. At the time I was living in Beverly Hills, and the disc jockey asked me if I would autograph some albums to be given away. Finally, somebody won. The melody wasn't distorted; all the time you could identify what tune it was, except that the background was very rhythmic, with unusual accents. I liked that recording a lot.

♦ *V: On your next album,* **Exploring New Sounds,** *you used a theremin—*
♦ E: That was on "Spellbound," the theme for the motion picture directed by Alfred Hitchcock. That instrument was very hard to play. Sometimes I recorded it with a musical saw played by a small hammer or a violin bow. I also used a German harpsichord, and on "My Blue Heaven" I used boo-bams. On "'Whatchamacallit" I included an ondioline, and on "Lazy Bones" I used a buzzimba. That album was recorded in New York, and while there I was asked to work on *The Merriest of Christmas Pops.* I arranged and recorded six Christmas songs with four male voices and one girl lead singer. [The rest of the LP tracks are by Mimi Hines with Ray Martin's orchestra.]

♦ *V: How did you get from Hollywood to New York?*
♦ E: I drove from the west coast to the east coast with Dorothy Vance, a woman who became my agent. She knew a lot of people at radio stations all over America, and was experienced in promotion. A musical director was being transferred from New York to another part of the country, and she got me his apartment. The building was on East End Avenue by the Hudson River, near the governor's mansion, and had a uniformed doorman, a garage and an elevator. I moved in with a Wurlitzer electric piano and signed a 3-year lease; the rent was $217 a month.

While I was in New York, RCA tried to experiment with my arranging abilities. They asked me to write for somebody completely opposite to my style: the country singer Eddy Arnold. But right from the beginning, things went wrong. Dorothy Vance told me to be at the studio at 7 PM, but the appointment was actually for 6. We arrived one hour late and all the musicians were waiting for me—I was quite embarrassed. She explained the mistake to Herman Diaz, a gentlemen from Cuba who was in charge of international music at RCA, and we proceeded with the arrangements. But after two numbers (one of which Mr Diaz thought had an interesting combination of sounds at the beginning, and might be a novelty hit), Eddy Arnold became very uncomfortable. He was used to more conventional music behind him, and he didn't adapt very well to my style. I don't know if these recordings were ever released.

♦ **V: This is an aside, but do you remember Martin Denny?**

♦ E: Yes—he recorded

Esquivel's *Exploring New Sounds,* © RCA Victor.

with ambient sounds, like crickets or frogs. He caused quite a sensation with his style.

♦ **V: Your next album was** **Strings Aflame**—

♦ E: That was recorded in 1959 in New York with strings and my piano—sometimes I would play the harpsichord. After recording *Strings Aflame,* I went to Hollywood to appear at a nightclub on Beverly Hills Boulevard where there were lines down the street waiting to see me. I had a small combo (guitar, drums, bass); my contract was for four weeks but I stayed eight weeks!

♦ **V: Tell us about your next album,** **Infinity In Sound, Vols. One and Two**—

♦ E: Each album was recorded on a separate occasion in Hollywood, 1960. I like them both, but I prefer Vol. Two because Vol. One didn't have the sound I wanted. As a matter of fact, I had to *insist* that certain numbers be re-recorded, because I wasn't happy. Mr Neely Plumb, the producer, worked with the re-recording and I think he improved the sound very much, especially on a song called "Frenesi." He finally got interesting stereo effects: the left side answered the right side like a ping-pong effect.

At a certain point in the mix, Mr Plumb asked me, "How do you like the album?" I answered, "Quite good." He almost threw a tantrum: "*Quite* good? Mi-

god, Juan—when will you be satisfied? This is *excellent!*" I said, "Well, I still think it's 'quite good.' " Perhaps I was too demanding. Of course, it's very difficult to be completely happy with something—one will always think, "This could have been more clear," or "I don't like this effect . . . or this sound. If I could do this again, I could improve it." One is full of little complexes! But this is part of one's mind: to never be happy with the results.

By the way, did you know that RCA in New York asked me to record an album with The AMES BROTHERS: *Hello Amigos* (1960). They managed to pronounce Spanish very well except for one word, "señal" (this word doesn't exist in English; it refers to a sign made when Catholics cross their fingers to give a blessing)—only someone who knows Spanish really well could have detected the mispronunciation. I was amazed that this album was never released in Mexico; it's a very good recording with a Mexican and Cuban sound.

♦ **V: What was your next LP?**

♦ E: A Los Angeles disc jockey named Bill Stewart had become very enthusiastic about my music—he used to announce me as "Juan Garcia Esquivel, mi amigo." He invited me to his home, and there I met the actress Brenda Joyce (who played Jane, opposite Johnny Weissmuller in *Tarzan),* and William Holden, who

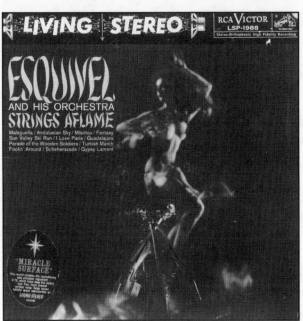

Esquivel & His Orchestra's *Strings Aflame*, © RCA Victor.
Album cover credits: photo: David Hecht.

was nicknamed "The Golden Boy"—he won an Oscar for his performance in *Stalag 17*. I played some piano pieces for them. When I quit RCA in 1961, Bill Stewart proposed to my manager that I make a new album for Reprise, a company owned by Frank Sinatra. This LP was called *More of Other Worlds, Other Sounds*. It was all right, but it didn't have enough promotion. But it had some very interesting arrangements. I presented well-known American songs with a 28-piece big band, plus 5 voices.

By the way, Mr Sinatra used to go quite frequently to the Stardust Hotel in Las Vegas to watch my show, when I was appearing with 6 musicians and 4 girl singers. I would know when he was there because he would send me a note that said, " 'Bye Bye Blues,' Juan—*please*. Frank." He liked my arrangement of that a lot. Whenever Frank was there, he would always introduce me to whoever he was with; through him I got to meet other artists like Yul Brynner, Bob Hope and Sarah Vaughan. Once after a performance I came downstairs to have dinner and he said, pointing to me, "He's our boy."

♦ *V: What were your most imaginative sound experiments on* **More of Other Worlds, Other Sounds?**
♦ E: Bill Stewart gave me the authority to do whatever I wanted, so I included the sound of a marimba. My brother bought it in Mexico and sent it to me by UPS. I didn't want to use its sound too much because I didn't want to be classified as "Mexican"; I wanted to be international—no nationality. So it was used just as a background instrument in places where I felt it was needed.

The studio rented a Bosendorfer piano for me, which has 5 extra-low keys, and I took a very popular American classic, "I Get A Kick Out Of You" and played it.

On another tune, "Canadian Sunset," I changed the tempo from 4/4 to a combination of 6/8 and 12/8, and when you first hear it you might think something was wrong, but it was *planned* to give you that impression. We also included "Dancing in the Dark," another classic from the American repertoire. I wrote several originals: "Chant of the Night," "Travelin'," and "La Mantilla"—that's a kind of shawl used in Spain. "Primavera" was composed by my American wife, Joyce McCullough. I took her melody and wrote a middle part because it was unfinished; originally it just had the main theme. That was a nice tune. On the LP, these 4 original tunes were all credited to my wife and I don't remember why—for some reason I gave the credit to her, as I had to give her many other things at the divorce! "Primavera" *was* her tune, but the music of the other 3 was mine.

I remember that at the time I was working on this album, I was living in Beverly Hills on the top of a mountain. From my desk I could enjoy quite a view: to my left, on days when the smog was not so heavy, I could see the Los Angeles Civic Center, and on my right I could see the Catalina Islands—most beautiful.

The only thing I didn't like about this album was the cover—it was like a Picasso painting of a girl's face, but it means nothing.

♦ *V: Then you recorded* **Latin-esque** *in 1962—*
♦ E: *Latin-esque* was written for a campaign: RCA would give away an LP (as part of their "Stereo Action" series: "The Sound Your Eyes Can Follow") with each new stereo record player. The album was presented very nicely, in a hard cardboard cover with a cut-out exposing an op-art design on the glossy inner sleeve. I was very happy with this project. It wasn't done with a big orchestra; sometimes I would use just the essential parts (sax and trumpets and rhythm). Some arrangements had voices. RCA was still trying to discover how much I could make of a given situation. They would tell me, "Juan, let's try to use fewer musicians," and then, "Juan, use as many musicians as you like!" So I didn't have a steady number of musicians available.

In their attempt to get the best quality stereo sound, RCA had to specially wire 2 or 3 studios together! I think this was at Hollywood and Vine. The musicians could see me on closed-circuit television, and they could hear me with earphones. The goal was to obtain "optimal" separation and eliminate unwanted sounds. If I wanted to isolate the brass from the rhythm section, I would put the rhythm section in one studio and the brass in another, and if I used piano or strings they were in another studio. If I wanted to get a "dead" sound, I would enclose the brass section in a studio with rugs hanging from the walls, or if I wanted them to sound more brilliant, I would have them play in a room with a wood floor and walls. I think this took a lot of time and imagination from everyone, but it was worth it. Despite the fact that recording in 4 channels was a new process, sometimes we could get the effect of having 16 or 20 channels. Recently I visited a studio in Mexico City that was built by the Mexican Association of Composers, and it was capable of recording 160 tracks. But 40 years ago, that would have just been a dream.

♦ **V: What was it like to work with MUZZY MAR-CELLINO (whistler) on Latin-esque?**

♦ E: I thought it would be interesting to combine whistling with a background of voices that were not singing with the open mouth, but were humming. In addition, I used 24 tuned bongoes called boo-bams; they spanned two octaves tuned chromatically from F to F, and were played with the fingers. I used them for short passages, and their sound was interesting. I was always trying to produce amazing sounds, different sounds—sounds that would attract the attention.

♦ **V: Was Muzzy Marcellino easy to work with?**

♦ E: I was surprised by his ear, because he had very precise pitch, especially when he had to whistle in front of a background of voices by the Randy Van Horne vocal group. The voices were excellent, humming the backgrounds; it's difficult to be exact in the intervals. I listened to the song "Adios, Mariquita Linda" years later and thought, "I should have used this effect much more." The combinations are very agreeable, and you can hear the melody clearly.

Previously, I didn't know Muzzy Marcellino; I listened to the information the musical contractor gave me and then contacted him. I wasn't familiar with the *variety* of musicians available in America, having only heard records that had found their way into Mexico. I knew the work of Stan Kenton, and I was very happy when I got invited to meet PETE RUGOLO at his

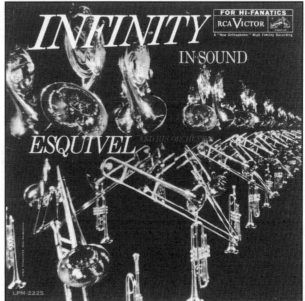

Esquivel & His Orchestra's *Infinity In Sound,* © RCA Victor. Album cover credits: photo: Dan McCormack.

home—I never thought I would even get to shake hands with him! Ray Coniff impressed me too—especially the sound he created with *voices and trombones;* it's quite imaginative. Also, I liked Billy May—he used saxophones to bend sounds with glissandos.

♦ **V: On "La Paloma," you used a real jawbone, with rattling teeth—**

♦ E: Originally that was a typical Mexican song played by trios (three guitars, three male voices). I played it in a very different tempo—things happen when you have to create what you feel! I imagine it's like a poet when he has to write: he gets inspired by circumstances or his feelings, and on "La Paloma" [hums tune] well— the most satisfactory thing is when you write something and then have the chance to listen to your creation. Sometimes I was happy with an experiment, but most of the time I would say, "No, that could have been better." But I was a harsh critic of my work—I think this is true of most artists.

I was at times criticized very much, because a lot of people (this happens in all fields) didn't want to accept anything out of the norm, outside of their way of thinking. On "It Had To Be You," I had the singers hum "ra ra ra ra reee" instead of "da da" or "ta ta." My producer accepted this, but RCA executives didn't like it. When criticism is well-based, you take it very seriously, but when you believe you have to get out of the norm, the important thing is not to quit.

♦ **V: What are your favorite tracks on Latin-esque?**

♦ E: Stereo-wise, "La Raspa." It starts with the sound of a "scratcher" [a gourd with grooves cut in it] jumping from the left to the right. To me it was an interesting challenge to record a "conversation" between a scratcher and a trumpet—the scratcher would make scratching sounds, and on the other channel the trum-

Esquivel & His Orchestra's *Infinity In Sound, Volume 2,* © RCA Victor. Album cover credits: photo: Garrett-Howard, Inc.

pet would answer. By the way, the trumpet player, Louis Valizan, was excellent. He could reach incredible, unbelievably high notes, but I'm sorry to say he used to drink a lot, and he lost his ability.

Do you remember an early electric piano called the Fender-Rhodes? A man got in touch with me and said, "Mr Esquivel, I'm an admirer of yours. My name is Rhodes, and I'm associated with Fender-Rhodes. I was driving in my car when I heard your music, and I was so impressed that I had to pull over and stop the car and listen to you. The disc jockey played 3 or 4 of your arrangements, and I was impressed by the quality of the guitar sound. We manufacture all kinds of guitars and keyboard instruments." At the time, I was looking for a steel guitarist, so I asked Mr Rhodes, "Do you know someone who could replace Mr Alvino Rey when he is not available?" He replied, "Yes, I know a fellow. And as a matter of fact, you can count on any kind of Fender guitars, amplifiers, or keyboard instruments from us." He also said, "We are building a new keyboard instrument which we will call the Esquivel model, and we'll send one to you." He drove from Los Angeles to Las Vegas with a U-Haul trailer and delivered the piano to me personally—I remember it was late at night. He saw my show, and when he saw my guitar player, Perry Lopez, he was ready to give him as many guitars as he wanted if he would allow Fender-Rhodes to use his name in an endorsement. I can't remember if they completed the deal, because my guitarist was playing another brand of guitar!

♦ V: *Tell us about your next album,* **The Genius of Esquivel**—

♦ E: I think it was recorded around 1967 with my Las Vegas group. I don't particularly like the album because it didn't have a full orchestral sound or many stereo effects. The only interesting piece is "Malagueña Salerosa," which is a traditional Mexican ranchero number. I had one of our girl singers do *yodeling* on it, and this wasn't accepted by the Mexican audience. But times change.

Actually, another number I like a lot is "La Bikina" (The Bikini), which was written by Ruben Fuentes, a Mexican composer who is also an influential mariachi arranger—he experimented with adding flutes, oboe and bassoon, trying to update the music and help it evolve. This tune, which was unknown at the time, was sent to me by the musical director of RCA Mexico; he wanted to see what I could do with it. It was written in a 3/4 waltz tempo—too slow, so I sped up the rhythm to 6/8, recorded it, and it was appreciated by all the trios and country/ranchero singers. Now, every popular Mexican group performs it, and I'm happy, because they all follow *my* tempo. I played it on the electric piano which Mr Rhodes built for me.

I wrote the tune "Question Mark." "Surfboard" was written by Antonio Carlos Jobim, who wrote "The Girl From Ipanema." He was at one of my shows at Lake Tahoe, and I introduced him to the audience. I

LSA-2418 STEREO ACTION

LATIN - ESQUE

ESQUIVEL
AND HIS ORCHESTRA

La Raspa · Adios, Mariquita Linda · Jesusita en Chihuahua · Cachito (Pedacito) · Latin-esque · La Paloma · Estrellita
Cachita · Jungle Drums (Canu Kwalali) · Mucha Muchacha · You Belong to My Heart (Solamente una Vez) · Cariaca

Esquivel & His Orchestra's *Latin-esque,* © RCA Victor.

had a nice lakeside home nearby and invited him and the musical director of *The Andy Williams Show,* Dave Grusin, over and we built a fire. Jobim played "Surfboard" for me on the guitar, and told me he was going to introduce it on his next recording. Then he said, "No—*you* do it first!" That's why that song is on my album. However, I should have made my arrangement last longer—the song could have been explored more.

♦ V: *Your next album,* **Esquivel 1968,** *was also released in Brazil under the title,* **O Piano, As Vozes E O Som de Esquivel!!** *It contains a song you wrote titled "Yeyo"*—

♦ E: That's just a nonsense word. I wrote that song for a dance scene in a Mexican movie in two minutes just to fill up the film—it's of no importance whatever. This album was recorded with the small group I had for 12 years. It has my compositions "Mini Skirt" and "Guanacoa," plus songs like "Melancholy Baby" and "El Cable." The recording was done in a rush—we had to make the trip to Hollywood and return to Las Vegas in time to perform at the Stardust. It was in the style of my live show, "Esquivel!," and actually, I don't think there's anything worthwhile on it—nothing comparable to my better stereo recordings. It was done to satisfy some contractual obligation. Unfortunately, I lost my collection of albums (I had a complete collection of albums still sealed in cellophane in a valise which got stolen), but I used to have that one.

♦ V: *Tell us more about your "live" show*—

♦ E: Without wishing to appear immodest, I will say that I had a good group then, with a very powerful trumpet player and guitarist. The show was programmed for 50 minutes, but it almost always lasted for an hour and 20 minutes because the audience was so enthused that they wouldn't let us go. I wish you could have seen the four girls. Each was of a different nationality. One was Japanese; one was Swiss; one was French (and a very fine dancer) and one was Italian. They were the singers for the group, and the surprise was: each girl was better than the previous one.

I was very happy with that group, which stayed together for 12 years from 1962-1974. Our first show was at The Wagon Wheel in Las Vegas. The critics would say, "Esquivel conducts his group with an iron hand," because no one—especially the girls—would look at anyone but me. I would conduct from the piano, and at just a small signal from me they would perform different movements. Or if I smiled at them, they would smile in response. It was musically disciplined, and at the same time they would flirt with me—that is, with what I suggested at the keyboard. It was a very interesting dynamic.

Also, the girls weren't allowed to mingle with the public after the shows. And according to the rules and by-laws of the Esquivel Organization, there could be no fraternizing *within* the group, because if I had problems with one of the girls or boys, automatically I would have to confront *two* of them! So this was an example of what one could do—it was a small group, but sometimes we got the sound of 25 musicians with just 10.

♦ **V: Who booked your group's shows?**
♦ E: Frank and Rocky Sennes produced and presented their *Lido de Paris* show at the Stardust Hotel for many years—it was very successful. My business manager, Samuel Singer, worked with them to send my group on tour to Puerto Rico, the Bahamas (at the King's Inn) and almost all the islands on the Caribbean side; we played a lot of casinos there. We also played places like Hot Springs, Arkansas; North Carolina; and Mexico City.

In Chicago I was a success at Scotch Mist, which was a rock'n'roll/jazz club—the owner took a chance and hired me. Before I arrived, a newspaper critic wrote, " 'Esquivel!' is coming to town. We wonder: why does he use an exclamation point after his name?" After he saw my show, he wrote, "Esquivel is so good he deserve *two* exclamation points!" Another critic wrote, "The crowd ranged from blue jeans to mink stoles." I played two shows a night and there were lines for both; the first audience had to leave to make way for the second. Popularity-wise, this was very good for me, because the news got back to Las Vegas, and a nightclub called The Desert Inn tried to steal me away from the Stardust Hotel. The owner of the Stardust got annoyed and said, "No, Esquivel belongs at the Stardust and that's where he'll stay."

The job at the Stardust was difficult, because I was performing in a lounge near the poker, blackjack and roulette tables. The main room housed the *Lido de Paris* show, and we had to be interesting enough to attract the crowd that was leaving, but quiet enough to not distract the poker players! Even though we couldn't play loud, we had to attract the attention of the people: "Hey—here we are!" It was a challenge. The *Lido de Paris* was crowded every night, and we would start our show at the time the crowd was leaving the main room, to try and get them to watch *us*.

By the way, our show was titled "The Sights and Sounds of Esquivel!" because I had my own lighting system that would accentuate or emphasize my musical sound effects, like: "Pow! Pow! Pow!" with lights. I had a good light man who knew all my arrangements. I used to end my shows in the dark, and once someone criticized me, saying, "At the end, you have to have on full lights." But I found it was more effective to end in darkness. I wasn't trying to milk applause out of the audience, but they were waiting for something to happen, and usually they still wanted *more*. We had a rotating stage, too.

♦ **V: Did your 4 girl singers also dance?**
♦ E: Not dance, but move according to the tempo of the arrangement. We had a lot of variety in the show. The French girl, Yvonne De Bourbon, would present herself in an elegant gown, but in the middle of a song she would suddenly tear off her skirt (her costume was tear-away, with velcro) and her beautiful legs would be exposed. Then she would start dancing all these dances of the time: the Twist, the Philly, the Swim and the Bully-Bully, plus the Tango and the Cha-Cha-Cha. I had an American girl with a high soprano voice, Della Lee, and she would sing classics from musicals like the ones Julie Andrews performed in. But after finishing a ballad, she would suddenly start *yodeling* very powerfully, and this was so different that people would burst into applause—she'd have to per-

Esquivel & His Orchestra's *More of Other Worlds, Other Sounds*, Reprise. Album cover credits: cover: Norman Gollin, art direction: Merle Shore.

form an encore. She was a *show-stopper!* . . . After the girl from Italy had sung, I would say, "Now, I present to you Nana Sumi, who is very special. She was 'Made In Japan' "—that line would always get a laugh. Miss Sumi, who was 5'3" and very delicate and fragile, would then sing a ballad like "Cry Me a River" in a voice lower than a male bass voice—it was surprising.

♦ **V: *How did you discover that Della Lee could yodel?***

♦ E: When she auditioned, she was this fresh-faced 18-year-old American girl. It took awhile to discover she could yodel, but when I found out, I changed her nationality to "Swiss." Part of my presentation was to have each girl be of a different nationality. The girls would all dress in the same material, but each gown would be in the style of her "country of origin." The girl from Greece, Jashmira, would put a jewel in the middle of her forehead.

♦ **V: *What kind of music did you play?***

♦ E: I would play some jazz, some ballads, some Latin music, and feature the girls. We played Puerto Rico 3 times and played a lot of the music of Rafael Hernandez; his "Lamento Borincano" was almost the national anthem there. We did a lot of unexpected musical transitions; in the middle of a ballad our arrangement might turn into jazz—that would surprise people. One of my "firsts" was: having the girls sing in unison with the orchestra, then spotlighting them one by one, each in a different style. And each was an exceptional singer.

♦ **V: *I read that you led your group "with simple finger movements, pointing here and there as the instruments bounce in and out during the performance." Wasn't it difficult to keep 10 performers together for 12 years?***

♦ E: Sometimes girls would leave the show because of things they shouldn't do—like get married! When I had to replace a girl, her replacement had to see the show for 60 days in order to learn the dance steps and the songs. I had to constantly make all kinds of efforts to keep the same musicians and the same girls, because it was invaluable having highly-disciplined, skilled performers. While I was performing a piano solo with the orchestra, the girls would help the next girl change (one would change the top of the costume, another the bottom); a girl would only be absent from public view for 40 seconds before she reappeared dressed in a completely different way. This act was developed through years of discipline. I would fine the girls if they didn't keep their weight down, because if they gained too much weight, I would have to spend a lot of money re-doing the gowns. We played 3 shows a night, with 4 gowns for each show, and we had 18 gowns for each girl—a total of 72. And each gown cost as much as $400-$500! This was quite an investment. My manager used to yell at me, "Juan, what's this bill for $2,000? What are you *doing* with this money?"

Our group also went twice to Hawaii, and we found

the people there to be very conservative. On one tour our regular dancer, Yvonne De Bourbon, had to have an appendix operation, so I replaced her with a very beautiful and talented girl, Jacqueline Douget, who was causing a sensation in Vegas by dancing ballet in the *nude:* absolutely no clothes. I knew I couldn't get away with that in Hawaii, so I made her wear some tiny veils. We opened at the Royal Hawaiian Hotel, and the next morning an article appeared in the local paper: "The Royal Hawaiian Is A Royal Bust!" Our show had caused a scandal; she *was* wearing some veils, but they were transparent. She was tall, with a very nice body, beautiful legs and big breasts, and she worked with a very strong male companion dressed in tights and no shirt. In some numbers he would hold her up with one hand (balancing her on her back) while he walked among the tables of the audience. This caused a small uproar; the audience was mostly retired people and they weren't used to that—they didn't know *what* to do.

I would fine the girls if they didn't keep their weight down, because if they gained too much weight, I would have to spend a lot of money re-doing the gowns.

The chaplain for the Marine Corps wrote a letter to the manager of the Royal Hawaiian, telling him that it wasn't suitable for Marines to attend our show. We thought, "Migod, we're scandalizing the *Marine Corps?*" The hotel manager came to see us, saying, "Juan, what can we do to cover up this girl more?" But my road manager stood firm: "We will perform for the Marines just as we are used to doing." I agreed, "You're right. We will perform; the Marines won't be scandalized." That night, Jacqueline Douget was so well received that for an encore, she performed her act again—but this time *totally* in the nude! The following day I got a letter from the chaplain which said, "I had been warned about your show, but I want to tell you that we truly appreciate your artistry. We were delighted, and intend to see your show again."

♦ **V: *Didn't you play Lake Tahoe?***

♦ E: At Lake Tahoe I performed at Harvey's, across the street from Harrah's where Lawrence Welk was playing. I attended his show, and in front of the audience he said to his orchestra [pointing to me], "I'm going to take all of you to see what this guy does with six musicians and four girls"—*he* had an orchestra of 24 players.

Once, when I knew Henry Mancini was performing at The Sahara, I sent him a magnum of champagne as a way of saying, "Welcome to Lake Tahoe." Then he invited me to his show. He was conducting an orchestra, his back to the audience, and in front of him on a big screen, scenes from a movie made in Africa were being projected [*Hatari!*, 1962]. He explained how he would follow the mood of each situation or scene. I was very impressed with the music he wrote for an elephant: instead of choosing a bassoon (which any arranger would have used for elephant-walking), he used a piccolo! [hums theme] Hank was explaining how he used different sounds, and then he said, "Speaking of this topic, we have in the audience tonight a guy who probably knows as much about sounds as any of us. Where are you, Juan?" The audience gave me a hand; I felt honored that Henry had paid me such a tribute. To me he is an extraordinarily talented composer and orchestra conductor; he's a genius.

I also admire enormously John Williams—he's quite the talent; and I also admire many of the fellows who write for Universal and other film companies. However, while trying to learn, I have been very careful not to follow in their style. If you talk with a fellow, you learn two things: what you should say if you're talking to a smart fellow; and what you shouldn't say if you are talking with a moron. So you have two choices: what you should say, and what you shouldn't. Always, I admired enormously those fellows, and respected their talent, but I tried not to follow their steps.

♦ *V: You also wrote for TV shows—*

♦ E: Soon after I met Stanley Wilson, the musical director for Universal Studios, he asked me, "Are you familiar with writing for motion pictures?" I said, "Yes; I know how to do it." We signed a contract, and at the first recording session he started out at the podium conducting my scores. Several times he said, "Oh, this is a *very* nice sound." Then he handed me the baton, saying, "Now it's your turn, *Maestro.*" He was very surprised at my arrangements and my ability to conduct. I went on to arrange and conduct for Bob Cummings, and for Barry Sullivan who was in a Western series, *The Tall Man.* I also wrote music for several other TV series including *Markham* (with Ray Milland), *Kojak, Charlie's Angels, Simon & Simon, Magnum P.I.* with Tom Selleck—plus about 18 other well-known shows whose names I can't recall!

When I started doing the music for *The Bob Cummings Show*, I flew to Palm Springs to meet him. We walked out to the parking lot and got into his little two-seat car and he said, "I'm going to take you for a little ride." Then he drove to another part of the airport, where a couple of mechanics came out and attached wings, a tail and a propeller! The next thing I knew we were up in the air high above the ground, looking down. I was scared, but the flight was very smooth and we landed safely. Whenever I tell this story, nobody believes me; they ask, "How come I

The Ernie Kovacs Album, Columbia Records, © 1976 CBS Inc.
Album cover credits: cover art: Richard Mantle.

never heard of this invention? Why hasn't this thing been marketed?" But it really happened. When I was around him, he was eating vitamins day and night; his pockets were full of bags of 'em. I think he was very interested in futuristic ideas, like taking vitamins to ward off aging, and this automobile-airplane. At the time he was very good-looking and looked quite young; I think he was about forty.

♦ *V: **Popular Science** had an article on this invention . . . Your music was used on an ERNIE KOVACS TV special, aired May 28, 1961—*

♦ E: Ernie Kovacs called me while I was living in Beverly Hills (he got my number from RCA Victor) and told me he had dramatized my recording of "Jealousy" [from *Infinity In Sound*, Vol. Two]. He had made an animation of furniture and items from the kitchen (including a dancing plucked chicken!) and the living room, trying to follow all the accents and moods of my music. He was very nice. He invited me to his home for a party, and introduced me personally to all the guests: the late Edward G. Robinson, Ricardo Montalban (I sent an album to him), Shirley MacLaine, Kim Novak—in person she was exactly like she is in the movies. Peter O'Toole, who was in *Lawrence of Arabia*, was there, as well as Jack Lemmon. I was very flattered by the courtesy shown to me by every one of the guests; it was gratifying to be so recognized.

Throughout his home, he had placed many TV sets so the guests could see his latest show which featured my music, and they all gave me a hand, even though I hadn't done anything but the arrangement—all the merit was actually due to Ernie Kovacs. He had managed to accentuate every one of the sounds in my recording by having a piece of furniture or an appli-

ance move. He was very imaginative; very interesting. At the time, Ernie was living in Coldwater Canyon close to my home. Unfortunately, he died in an accident in his Corvair a few months after this, at the age of 42. This was tragic; he was at the peak of his career. At the time he was married to the singer Edie Adams.

♦ **V: Do you enjoy conducting music?**

♦ E: If I were to be asked, "What's your forte?" I would reply, "To conduct and to write, in combination with playing piano." Thanks to working with that comedian, I gained experience in the art of conducting: from slow to intermediate to fast—among *other* things! Many of my scores were marked in places, "Follow the baton!" This ability could only be obtained with practice; you can't get it just with *theory*. As I said, I had the beautiful chance to learn-with-practice at the same time.

Many musicians and people I met in the recording studios would compliment me on my precise conducting of the orchestra—sometimes they would ask, "May I see your scores?" "Yes," I would reply, "I'd be very happy for you to take them home." I interpret situations in a *descriptive* way—playfully. Actually, "Playfully" [on *Other Worlds, Other Sounds]* is an arrangement I wrote because RCA was asking arrangers to donate a song-arrangement royalty to the widow of a musician who had died suddenly. But to me "playfully" doesn't mean without discipline; I tried to preserve discipline everywhere; I'm kind of a perfectionist. When recording, without having to overwork my orchestra, I would repeat as many takes as necessary to be satisfied by the results. I was a bit demanding.

♦ **V: In an article, you said, "I even demand that the group has a good time!" . . . Did you ever make any mistakes in your career?**

♦ E: The owner of The Melody Room on Sunset Strip in Hollywood invited me to play his club for 8 weeks—I stayed for 12. While there, a friend advised me to sign a new management contract with Lutz and Loeb, who used to manage Lawrence Welk. This was a complete mistake; they didn't do *anything* for me. In fact, they suggested I leave RCA, claiming they would get me a better record contract (which they didn't do), and claiming they would enhance my career. But the fine print in their contract didn't state that they would provide *jobs* for me. So for 8 months I had no income; I had canceled my contract with RCA, and my earnings stopped. Luckily, at that time, following Stanley Wilson's advice, I signed with BMI and started receiving royalties from them. At the time BMI was seeking fresh talent, and I signed a contract for $100,000 just for the rights to research payment of royalties anywhere in the world. They charged a fee of 3% of my earnings, and that has been very good for me. Since 1961 I have received royalties (proving them to be an excellent company), not only from the United States but world-wide: Japan, Germany, South Africa, etc. Some royalties are from the music I wrote for Univer-

Juan Garcia Esquivel's *Y Su Piano Cristalino*, RCA Victor.

sal TV shows; they would dub the dialogue to different languages but the music would remain the same.

♦ **V: So after your group ended in 1974, you went to Mexico—**

♦ E: Yes, but after a couple years I returned to the States because a friend of mine sent me several offers by telegram to re-form my group. But it wasn't the same. I would do one-night shows in places like Bakersfield or North Dakota. I think this was from '76-'78.

♦ **V: What did you do in Mexico City for Televisa?**

♦ E: Among other assignments (including writing music for some Mexican B-movies, the names of which I can't recall), I wrote the music for a children's show which sold more than a million albums (*Burbujas*, 1978, and the 1979 follow-up, *Odyssey Burbujas*, on the America label, owned by *Televisa*). The lyrics were written by Silvia Roche, who became president of the creative department there after the success of *Burbujas*. She presented a series of short spots. One gave children advice, like, "Don't go with strangers!" Another one told fathers not to beat their children, but to count to ten first and then act without needing to beat them. Silvia told me to write children's music for "characters" like an elephant or a mouse or a frog, and I would record melodies at home and send a cassette to her. She's very imaginative; it's not easy to write words to fit music.

After the success of *Burbujas*, the son of the man who had originally hired me at XEW, Mr Azcarraga Jr, made me a very generous offer. Many years before, he had visited me in Beverly Hills, right after I had received 7 nominations to the National Academy of Recording Arts and Sciences, and had been amazed: "Juan, how did you manage to do this?" Now, after *Burbujas*, he asked me to join *Televisa:* "Money doesn't matter; how much do you want?" But my back problems had begun, and I knew I could no longer work long hours. Regretfully, I had to refuse.

♦ **V: What did you do after** Burbujas?

♦ E: I wrote a musical which never got produced because one of the principal singers got sick. We had to suspend production, because her physician said she would be okay in a couple of months. But instead she got worse, and the project was abandoned. I can't say I lost money, because I got an advance of half of what I was promised. After that, my back really became so bad that I had to stop. I still exercise my fingers by practicing at a small keyboard, because the piano is a very jealous mistress. I would hate to sit down at the piano and have it suddenly appear totally unfamiliar—like a typewriter keyboard or something!

♦ **V: What was the name of the musical?**

♦ E: At first it had something to do with the Aztecs, but as the project continued, the producers thought it was so good that they didn't want to restrict its appeal to Mexico—they thought it could open in Los Angeles or New York. The project was abandoned before they decided upon a name. I kept the music, but my mind still keeps working, revising what I have done. You get new ideas, new combinations—and now with synthesizers, something good can be done if you know how to use them. I know how to create something different, and I'm waiting to be able to walk or at least sit at a desk again. I'm doing rehabilitation therapy. Back in '86 I had two intraocular lens implants, and I can see very clearly now. I no longer wear those thick glasses you saw on the back of my album covers!

♦ **V: There is an intriguing sentence on the back of** **To Love Again:** *"As for Esquivel's romantic life, fortune has amply blessed this good-looking young Latin American—there has been a long and uninterrupted succession of names of beautiful and famous women mentioned in connection with him, and it does not seem very likely that the end is in sight."*

♦ E: I know; that was one side of my life. I loved music, cars (my last one was a red Cadillac El Dorado) and women—not necessarily in that order! That was one of my weak points. I don't think it would be right to mention names if they are still alive and active. I can say that some of those relationships cost me money and gave me experience—both. There's a famous opera, Mozart's *Don Giovanni,* and my friends used to call me by the name of the hero, "Don Juan Tenorio." I was very lucky, not for my facial features necessarily, but because I was young and played piano. At first I was involved with one or two ladies, very famous and very successful, and that gave me a kind of "halo." Curiously enough, this would attract the attention of other beautiful ladies who would be *very* nice when I approached them . . . Let's just say that I had many relationships with beautiful and very well-known names, but I don't dare to name them!

♦ **V: But you can tell us the names of your 4 wives—**

♦ E: In 1941 I married a dancer and professional model, Blanca Servin, and we had a son, Mario. Then, around 1950 I married Virginia Llaca, a singer, in Mexico City. We worked together for awhile. After her singing career ended, she started doing oil-paintings, and now she's a sculptor. My third wife was Joyce McCullough—she was the co-owner of The Melody Room on Sunset Boulevard, where I played. We got married before I formed the group, "The Sights and Sounds of Esquivel!"

♦ **V: She must have been a musician; she wrote** **"Primavera"—**

♦ E: She whistled and hummed the tune to me. She had an uncanny ability to put words to melody, although I didn't publish those. She was very smart—but very jealous! She was a great companion, and so were all the other women in my life. I couldn't say anything bad about any of them, and in any case I was the one who, in some sense, spoiled the marriages.

My fourth wife was Yvonne De Bourbon, who we introduced in our act as "The French Girl"; she was born in France. I met her during my time off at the Stardust. I saw her dancing with another act, and I happened to have a vacant spot in my group. One of the rules and regulations of the Esquivel Organization was: if I wanted to dismiss one of the girls or musicians, I had to give 3 months' advance notice (and vice versa). Fortunately, only rarely did anyone quit; we had a very tight affiliation. Yvonne wanted to belong to our group, so I told her, "You have to watch our show *every night* for 3 months, in order to learn the movements and the musical interpretations." She thoroughly learned our "book," and was an extra attraction for us because she could dance so well and was so beautiful.

Pete Rugolo's *Percussion at Work,* Mercury Records.

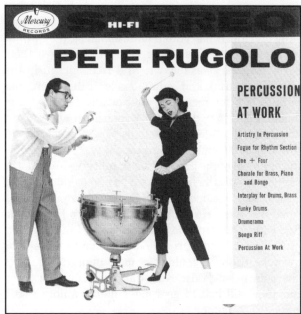

The Best of Esquivel, © 1966 RCA Victor.

After our divorce, Yvonne went to work for Howard Hughes's corporation, as she had a rare capacity for understanding electronics and computers. I think this interest was sparked because in Vegas we started using wireless microphones. The transmitter was next to the organist. At the Palmer House in Chicago, in the middle of one of the songs, we suddenly heard a voice: "Car 44, proceed to the corner of State Street and . . ." Whenever this happened, Yvonne would quickly disappear from the stage and adjust the transmitter, much like you would adjust a radio dial. So she already had an interest in electronics.

I think that anyone who worked with the Esquivel group improved their artistry and talents quite fast. The girls in the show were competing with each other a bit, because if they noticed that the girl who had sung previously had gotten more applause, they would try to get even! This encouraged them to improve their performances. I was lucky to find excellent musicians who didn't drink and didn't smoke. If they were one minute late for rehearsal, they would be fined one dollar, up to ten dollars. If a musician showed up drunk, he was fined fifty dollars. The second time the fine was $100, and the third time it was submitted to the approval of the group if we should give him another chance—*plus* he had to pay a hundred dollars. I had an excellent trumpet player, Louis Valizan, who was fined just once. He apologized and paid a fifty-dollar fine (it was the first time) and remained in the group until the very end. A couple of musicians were stolen by orchestras who could offer more money; I couldn't give a musician a raise every time he got another offer. But they still had to give me 3 months' notice so I could train another.

♦ *V: Isn't your brother in the music business as well?*

♦ E: My brother, Sergio, worked for XEW for the past 40 years; now he's retired. When television came to Mexico, it was still experimental (just a test) and XEW's earnings supported television while it got off the ground. My brother was my recording engineer on those radio programs I told you about.

♦ *V: You played Bimbo's in San Francisco in 1964—*

♦ E: Yes, twice. The second time wasn't very successful because it was during Lent; the first time was very good. I'm sorry we missed you!

♦ *V: You've had a long and fairly uncompromised career—*

♦ E: My arrangement with RCA Victor was: nobody could put their hands on my recordings, and everything would have to be supervised by me before and after the final pressings. If I wasn't satisfied with the sound, I would mix and re-record certain passages or work with the engineer. For example, *Infinity In Sound* was recorded by John Norman, and we got 7 Grammy nominations: for the best arrangement, best performance by an orchestra, best engineered recording, etc. By the way, I think American musicians are superb: very imaginative, highly disciplined, and with an extraordinary sense of humor in their performances, because sometimes when we had to ad-lib a show—I remember I was very happy with a trumpet player named PETE CANDOLI; he was just fantastic. He could easily hit a "high C" with no effort.

For the recording of "It Had To Be You," I had written on the sheet music "cantabile" [in a singing fashion; flowing and clear]. I had wanted the solo to be more melodic, but the trumpet soloist, Shorty Sherack, played it with a very humoristic interpretation; like "*Aha!* It had to be you!"—that was *his* idea. Often I was very surprised by the musicians of the United States. I was very grateful that they would accept my ideas, and at some recording sessions I had the honor of being applauded by the orchestra as an acknowledgement of my arrangements. Again, in general I tried to write lines that were easy to play—that is, to not overwork the musicians, yet give the impression that these were things that were very difficult to play (although actually they were easy, because they were written within the capabilities of each musician). I tried never to force or strain the capacities of the players; I tried to obtain the results with a minimum of effort. I think every musician was aware of that, and they were happy to play with me.

If the recordings were good, it was due to excellent studios, excellent engineers, and excellent musicians who were well-trained, had very good sounds, and an understanding of everything I wrote. I wish I could have the chance to work again, but things are very difficult now because of my back. But I'm quite satisfied that I've left behind a work that luckily, may be recognized again. I wish I had the opportunity to re-present my recordings with a modern sound, because I don't think the arrangements are old. Listeners can tell they are agile and transparent. Those recordings were made 30-35 years ago, starting in 1958, and if we could use the modern technology available now, then . . .

SOME OF ESQUIVEL'S RECORDINGS

45s on the RCA "For Export Only" label (Mexico City, '50s)

Las Tandas de Garcia Esquivel (Mexico City, n.d.)

To Love Again (Mexico City, 1957)

Other Worlds, Other Sounds (Hollywood, Jan 1958)

Four Corners of the World (Hollywood, Jan 1958)

Exploring New Sounds (NYC, Nov-Dec, 1958)

The Merriest of Christmas Pops (NYC, 1959; six tracks)

Strings Aflame (NYC, Jan-Feb, 1959)

Infinity In Sound, Vols. One & Two (Hollywood, 1960)

More of Other Worlds, Other Sounds (Hollywood, 1961)

Latin-esque (Hollywood, 1962)

Genius of Esquivel (Hollywood & Las Vegas, n.d.)

Esquivel 1968 AKA *O Piano, As Vozes E O Som De Esquivel!!*

Burbujas (Mexico City, 1978)

Odyssey Burbujas (Mexico City, 1979)

La Bamba, La Raspa (CD reissue of material from *Latin-esque* on BMG label, 1986. "Carioca" is missing, replaced by "La Bamba" from *Infinity In Sound,* Vol. Two. Unfortunately, all tracks are in mono except for "La Bamba" which is in stereo).

Note: A new 14-track Esquivel compilation CD has been released! Write Bar/None Reissues, PO Box 6258, Hoboken NJ 07030.

Additional Note: It is difficult to determine all the musicians and singers ESQUIVEL has worked with in his live show, but *Variety* provides some clues. According to *Variety, 7-8-1959,* Esquivel's group at the Melody Room on Sunset Blvd in L.A. included Tony Reyes (bass), Augie Alvaraz (flute and bongos), and John Clauder (drums) . . . From *Variety, 7-29-1964:* "The Sights & Sounds of Esquivel" appeared at Bimbo's in San Francisco ("this same group also recorded the *Esquivel 1968* LP"—Esquivel), and includes Adolfo Calderon (mini-bass), Roberto Casanova (congas and bongos), Tommy Vig (drums), Dick Sparks (organ), Perry Lopez (guitar), Louis Valizan (trumpet), and vocalists Maria Caruso ("the 'Italian girl' in the act who sang Broadway tunes;

she died a couple years ago in Las Vegas from terminal cancer"—Esquivel), Nana Sumi, Della Lee and Carolyn Day ("very good; almost the same style as Penny Pryor. But she had a manager, Bob Day [unrelated], who was a pain, so we didn't work together long."—Esquivel) . . . *Variety, 6-23-1965:* at Harvey's, Lake Tahoe, Esquivel worked with the previously mentioned group, plus a new singer, Jashmira ("the Greek girl who wore a jewel on her forehead; she replaced Nana Sumi."—Esquivel) . . . *Variety, 2-15-1967:* Sheraton Hotel, San Juan, Puerto Rico: New singers are American blonde Penny Pryor ("a great ballad singer; she was excellent"—Esquivel) and the diminutive Philippine beauty Monette. The other personnel are not listed in this review.

SOME OF ESQUIVEL'S TV/FILM MUSIC:

Wrote theme and/or background music for *Markham* (detective; 1959-60), *The Tall Man* (western; 1960-62), an Ernie Kovacs special (1962), The Bob Cummings Show ('50s sitcom), *plus '70s TV shows Kojak, Charlie's Angels, Simon & Simon, Magnum P.I.,* etc. Also appeared on Johnny Carson, The Pat Boone Show, and The Danny Kaye Show, and created music for [unknown] Mexican B-movies.

O Piano, As Vozes E O Som De Esquivel!!, RCA Victor.

167

YMA SUMAC

The legendary five-octave vocalist Yma Sumac has been named as an influence by Diamanda Galas, Nina Hagan, Kate Pierson, and many others. Promoted in the '50s as an Inca princess directly descended from Atahualpa, the last emperor of the Inca empire, Yma Sumac enjoyed international fame from the '50s through the '60s. Her first Capitol album, *Voice of the Xtabay* (1950), is the only LP in history never to have gone out of print! The back cover text read: "The Xtabay is the most elusive of all women. You seek her in your flight of desire and think of her as beautiful as the morning sun, touching the highest mountain peak. Her voice calls to you in every whisper of the wind. The lure of her unknown love becomes ever stronger ... you follow the call of the Xtabay, though you walk alone through all your days." In the '70s she retired to Spain, then Peru, although she never ceased working; to date she has created over 2,000 compositions. In 1984 Alan Eichler brought her to Los Angeles, and since then she has given concerts all over the world. Yma Sumac's words supplied by Alan Eichler, her manager (1524 La Baig Ave, Hollywood, CA 90028).

♦ YMA SUMAC: Since I was a very little girl, I was singing, and each year my voice developed more. I was born with a high voice, but I worked to make it better. When I was 14 or 15, my voice changed and became lower, and I took advantage of this, going from sub-contralto to high soprano. I constantly studied how to project my voice better. I also studied opera and sang arias; I have very good technique.

When I came to America, I was first living in New York. Then I did university concerts all over the U.S. I returned to New York and was working in a very small club, *The Blue Angel,* where a lot of great stars who later became famous were working. I was with my ex-husband [Moises Vivanco] and cousin as the Inca Taqui Trio, dressed in beautiful Peruvian costumes. One night a man named Walter Rivers came to our dressing room and said: "I'm from Capitol Records, Los Ange-

les." He was there to talk business with another talented male singer, but when he saw *me*, he became very impressed with my performance. He said, "You will hear from us in a few days." He and my ex-husband exchanged letters, and in a few months Capitol brought me to Los Angeles to prepare the first album.

We had the greatest musicians and arrangers including Billy May; also, my ex-husband. We worked for 3 months to prepare the right way to present in the United States the first Yma Sumac album. First we studied the psychology and mentality of the American people: how they think, and what kind of music they like.

After my album came out, people were very intrigued—they had never heard this kind of singing before. They didn't know how to classify it; whether it was classical or mumbo-jumbo! We chose the title, *The*

Voice of the Xtabay, and let people judge for themselves whether the record was classical, semi-classical or contemporary. When I say "classical," I don't mean opera by Puccini or Verdi or Wagner; I mean classical Incan music.

I constantly tried to be better, to please the public. I gave people the most outstanding performance of this kind of music. At that time, in the '50s, there were some very cultured critics who gave me marvelous praise, such as Glenn Dillard Gunn; he's dead now. In the Washington, D.C. *Times-Herald* he wrote, "There is no voice like it in the world today. It has a greater range than any female voice of concert or opera. It soars into the acoustic stratosphere, or it plumbs sub-contralto depths of pitch with equal ease. Such voices happen only once in a generation." Then Yma was in tremendous demand from different countries; I went traveling all over the world.

For a long time many people thought Yma Sumac was dead or had retired. I used to live in California in a beautiful home, but at the end of the '60s I left the United States. Then I traveled in Europe and Japan

Show business today isn't like it was in the '50s and '60s. Even when I was performing in small nightclubs, I played with big orchestras. I can't sing with just two musicians!

and Israel. I had traveled so much in the '60s, doing concerts for the socialist countries and the rest of Europe, and one day I became very sick. My doctor said I should stop singing; I had lost so much weight and looked very skinny. I went to Spain to rest, because I have a home there, and I stayed six months. I felt very tired and sick, and thought, "This is the time I should go to the Andes, to be with all of my family: my mother, my father, my sisters"—I'm the youngest. I sent a wire to my parents that I was coming home. When I arrived in Peru, my mother and father were crying, and I said, "Mama, I'm going to stay here as much as possible." They said, "What—are you giving up your career?" I said, "No, but I want to rest." They asked, "How long are you going to be here?" Well, I stayed close to 14 years!

Meanwhile I was preparing my own compositions for the future, thinking that someday I would perform again. I was happy to be with my family, seeing my friends from my childhood, and I thought my show business was completed. But in the beginning of 1984 I received a letter from the United States [from Alan Eichler] saying, "Please, Miss Sumac, come back to the United States." At the beginning I said, "No, perhaps next year." But he continued sending more letters

Yma Sumac's *Fugeo del Ande,* Capitol Records.

thought that people remembered Yma Sumac, because after 14 years—if people don't see your face for *two weeks,* they forget everything! That's show business. But for every night there was a line for five blocks. They built a special platform so people could see me, because the club was so crowded. I performed for two weeks, and from 1984-86 I performed. At the end of '86 the Roosevelt Hotel in Hollywood called me, and from '86-89 I played there.

In 1987 I went to New York City, where I had performed at Carnegie Hall and big hotels. I played The Ballroom, and it was so crowded. I was interviewed by CBS, NBC and ABC . . . press from all over the United States came to New York to do an interview with Yma Sumac. The international press came to New York, too, because they had thought Yma Sumac was dead! One lady asked me, "Tell me, Miss Sumac, what's the secret of your success now? Usually, when an artist doesn't perform for a week or two, people forget their face." I answered, "I think there's no secret. In the '50s and '60s I performed often in New York. When people who saw me back then saw my name in the newspaper again, they were surprised: "Ohmigod, she's *alive.* Let's see how she looks today. And let's see if she can still sing those high notes!"

When I was in the Andes, my parents had a very powerful short-wave radio. When I first arrived in the United States, I heard this melody: "To Each His Own," and when I heard that again, back home, I started crying. My sister asked, "Why are you crying?" I said, "Because I remember my friends and I miss my home." She started crying, and when my mother found out why we were crying, she started crying too! I had come to the United States when I was very young—that's where I grew up and became a woman.

Today, the music I sing is my own compositions, which have the flavor of the Peruvian Andes mountains. But it's blended with contemporary musical arrangements, to make it easier for the new generation. I've met young rock'n'rollers who tell me, "I have all your records—you are my inspiration. I've learned so much from your records, but to see you in person is *another world.*"

A lot of famous rock'n'roll people—I never remember their names—have come to see Yma Sumac. These young people gave me tremendous support to continue singing for them, and I'm very grateful to them for their love.

until he convinced me. I said, "All right, I'll come to Los Angeles if you prepare everything."

Show business today isn't like it was in the '50s and '60s. Even when I was performing in small nightclubs, I played with big orchestras. I can't sing with just two musicians! At the beginning I was not happy, but I started thinking; and understanding the situation of today. My music is very exotic, and I need musicians . . . a lot of instrumentation. They prepared my opening at a very small nightclub in Los Angeles, the Vine Street Bar & Grill. There was a big line for five blocks, and I was very nervous. Previously, I don't think they

Yma Sumac's *Inca Taqui* with Moises Vivanco, Capitol Records.

BRIEF BIOGRAPHY & DISCOGRAPHY

Born Zoila Augusta Emperatriz Chivarri del Castillo. Yma's stage name derives from her mother's name, Imma Sumack Emilia Atahualpa Chivarri.

Birthdate unknown; may be Sept 10, 1927, in Ichocan, Peru (North Lima; pop. 250), or possibly 1923 (according to a 1950 *Time* article).

Married Moises Vivanco and with a cousin, Cholita Rivera, formed the Inca Taqui Trio. In the late '40s: made several recordings in Argentina, later released on Coral label as *Presenting Yma Sumac* (10"; and boxed set of 45s). Son Charles born 1949.

1950 on the Capitol label: *The Voice of the Xtabay* released as 10" record. Second release: *Inca Taqui,* on 10". The 12" LP & CD combine *both* of these 10" recordings. Yma's favorite tracks are "Chuncho" and "Hymn to the Sun."

1950s: Recorded Capitol LPs *Legend of the Sun Virgin, Legend of the Jivaro, Mambo!* and *Fuego Del Ande.* Also sang on the *Flahooley* (a musical) LP. Appeared in two movies, *Secret of the Incas* (1954) and *Omar Khayyam* (1957). Unfortunately, she didn't appear in the movie version of W.H. Hudson's *Green Mansions.*

1960s: Played USSR several times; sang for Soviet Premier Khrushchev, and met Shostakovich and Khachaturian. Also, she toured Europe many times, and played Albert Hall in London.

1972: recorded *Miracles* for London Records, produced by Robert Covais, Jim Branciforte and Bob Kreppel (on the LP, Les Baxter is credited as producer).

1975: meets manager Alan Eichler at a Town Hall concert in New York.

1984: Alan Eichler brings Yma Sumac from Peru to Los Angeles.

1988: Hal Wilner produces *Stay Awake* (various artists), on which Yma Sumac sings one track: "I Wonder."

October, 1993: Yma Sumac lectured and performed at Miami-Dade Community College, Florida.

REFERENCE: Nick Limansky has written a biography, *Yma Sumac: The Art Behind The Legend.* Gunter Czernetsky has done a documentary on Yma Sumac for Rubican Film in Munich. Gino Falzarano's article and discography, "The Legend of Yma Sumac," appeared in *Discoveries,* Feb 1990. Matt Groening's article, "Yma Sumac: Return of the Legendary Sun Virgin," appeared in the Los Angeles *Reader,* March 30, 1984.

CURRENT DISCOGRAPHY: (Order from Tower Records, 1-800-648-4844):

The Spell of Yma Sumac (16 Capitol tracks); Pair PCD-1172

Voice of Xtabay/Mambo Pt 1, EMI France 796641-2 Vol. 1

Mambo Pt 2/Legend of the Jivaro, EMI France 796642-2 Vol. 2

Stay Awake (1 track), A&M CD 3918

Russian Tour (live 1962 concert), Electra 2116

Enchantress, cassette-only, Capitol 4XL 57080; only

Yma Sumac's *Legend of the Jivaro*, Capitol Records.

album to contain "Babalu"

1991 CD Dance Single: "Mambo Confusion" (Deutsche Schallplatten DSB 3025-5; write Vertrieb Deutschland-Ideal, Vertrieb, Wichmannstr. 4, 2000 Hamburg, Germany, tel 011-49-40-890-85-100).

The following deleted CDS & cassettes may be found in used stores:

Voice of the Xtabay (16-track version) Capitol CDP 791217-2

Legend of the Sun Virgin, Capitol CDP 791250-2

Yma Sumac's Voice of the Xtabay, © Capitol Records.
Album cover credits: photography: Tom Kelley.

O. Rodger Harris has been collecting and selling records for the past two decades, and notes regretfully that "Most of the great vinyl records left America by the late '70s, snatched up by overseas collectors." Send $1 (or 8 International Reply Coupons) for his next mail order catalog to O.R.H., 2001 West Orange St, Winchester IN 47394.

♦ *VALE: How do you find records?*
♦ O. RODGER HARRIS: I *don't* go to thrift stores, because there's always a local collector who knows when they put out the new records (like at 9 AM Thursdays) and is there. Periodically I go on buying

* Eddie Baxter's *Temptation*, Rendezvous Records.
Album cover credits: cover photography: Phil Howard.

trips—I go out in my van and don't return until it's full, and sometimes that takes me ten days or a month. I'll figure out a territory and hit every record store on the route; I'll go in and ask, "What do you have that isn't moving?" Someone who specializes in rock may have a couple thousand soundtracks that have sat there for years, and a jazz store may have a pile of easy listening. I don't go through every record, I just buy the lot and when I get home I'll go through them and figure out what I got. Right away I put the "dogs" in the trash, otherwise I'd be inundated. I've got a five-bedroom house with a basement and garage, plus I rent a small warehouse; at any given time I may have a few hundred thousand LPs plus 50,000 45s. The reason I can sell records cheaper is: my rent is so low. I don't begrudge the prices those dealers in New York City get—they're paying ten times as much rent as me, plus they have to man a store and deal with all that overhead. That's why I like selling by mail. The only thing I don't like is the buying trips—it's hard to find decent food.

The selling is the easy part—I've got far more customers than I have records. I like selling LPs; it takes three times as long to process an order for the same number of 45s than for albums. And 45s usually don't have beautiful covers. Recently I started to get all these orders from Japan which at first puzzled me—then I realized that the one thing they had in common was: they all had gorgeous women in seductive poses on the covers. I consider it a great day when I get an order for a dozen Ray Coniff or Mantovani or Bert Kaempfert or Andre Kostelanetz albums—I assume they're being bought for the covers.

♦ **V: You still see those records in thrift stores—**

♦ ORH: I always know when I've priced an album too low, like for ten dollars, because immediately I'll get ten or twenty fax orders from New Jersey or New York. Periodically a dealer will come visit me; Craig Moerer from Portland was here a couple months ago and he spent a whole day picking out 2,500 albums. Whenever I send out catalogs, the jazz albums are the first ones to go. I don't type, so I have a guy who types out each catalog for me.

♦ **V: Why don't you use a computer?**

O. Rodger Harris

A Moment of Desire, Orchestra conducted by Gerard Blené, Jubilee Records.

♦ ORH: When I get an order, I just draw a line through the record in my catalog—that's quicker than any computer, because it takes so long to delete something! Basically, I keep track of people's orders in my head—*that's* the computer.

♦ **V: You must have had met some strange people on your buying trips—**

♦ ORH: I visited one dealer who was super-paranoid and secretive—his collection was on the top floor of a warehouse, and each level required a key; if there'd been a fire we would have been trapped and burned to death. He had over a million records, though, and I bought quite a few. On another trip I went to New Orleans and found myself in a really bad neighborhood—if I wanted something to drink, I had to peep out the door, look up and down the street checking for people with machetes, and then run for my life across the street, buy what I wanted, and dash back. But I got some good blues and jazz records, though.

The most spectacular sale I went to was outside Detroit. This collector had started out buying records in the early '60s and had bought every record he could find. But he had never played them (so they were all mint)—he always said, "*Someday* I'll get around to

George Cates' *Exciting*, Coral Records.
Album cover credits: cover photo: Garrett-Howard.

playing them." He always talked about wanting to alphabetize all his records and make up some kind of discography, but was so busy buying them that he never got around to it—then he died at the age of 63. His son was out in California and didn't want to deal with the estate, so he hired someone to dispose of everything. I got there a month late (whenever something like this happens, I'm *never* there first) but I still got about 10,000 really good records.

I have one customer who's in his fifties and still lives with his mom. He's got records everywhere—in the garage, under his bed and in every room, but he still buys regularly from me. Whenever he places an order he calls and says, "You have to tell me *exactly* when they're going to arrive, because if I don't stay home and wait for the mailman, my mom'll refuse the package and order it sent back!"

♦ **V: What's your most spectacular record "find"?**
♦ ORH: A soundtrack record price guide claimed that the rarest soundtrack in the world was *The Caine Mutiny*—only one copy was known to exist. My sister-in-law was at a garage sale and she found a copy for a quarter, except she immediately thought, "This *can't* be it; this *has* to be a counterfeit." So she passed on it. However, she got to thinking about it, and in the meantime bought a little vase for 75 cents. The woman holding the sale said, "Here—I'll throw in that record you were looking at," and my sister-in-law took it home, put it up on a shelf and forgot about it. Several months later, she happened to mention this to me, and I said, "Do me a favor—bring me that record." It took awhile (she lives out-of-town) but finally she brought it to me and I looked at it and said, "Listen, this is the real thing. We'll go into partnership on this; I'll put it

up for auction, and we'll split the profits." She asked, "How much do you think we'll get—fifty dollars?" I said, "I think we'll get more than that." I put an ad in *Goldmine* listing the condition of the record as "VG + " and the first bid came in at $2700, the next at $4000, the next at $6100, and the final bid (from a producer of the Jay Leno show) came in at $10,000.

This producer was so excited that when I telephoned him that he had the winning bid, he immediately hopped on a plane and in a matter of hours was knocking at my door. For about fifteen minutes he looked at the record, examining it closely, and then to my surprise said, "I can't take it—it's not mint." I said, "But I listed it in the ad as VG + ." He said, "I know, but I was hoping it was *mint.* I just can't take it." I said, "You mean to tell me you flew all the way out here, and now you decide you don't want it?" He said, "I'm afraid so." So I ended up selling it for $6100.

That'll never happen again! There are records that are valued even higher than this, but as far as I know this is the highest price ever paid for a *soundtrack* album—it's a candidate for the *Guinness Book of Records.* The reason it's so rare is: immediately after this record was pressed it was destroyed because of threat of lawsuit. Maybe a few copies survived because some worker at the pressing plant took them home.

♦ **V: Do you think you've seen almost every record there ever was?**
♦ ORH: One thing about records: no matter how long you collect, there's always more. I knew a guy who set out to compile a discography of every 45 that had ever come out, and he was a heavy-duty collector himself so he had a huge collection. It took him nine years to

A Love Affair with The Golden Leaves, Challenge Records.
Album cover credits: front cover: one of 113 photographs from MIRROR OF VENUS, a love story by Wingate Paine.

Michael Strange's *Something Strange*, RKO Unique Records.
Album cover credits: Burt Goldblatt.

compile a pair of books that resemble telephone directories. One volume was alphabetical by artist, and the other by title, so if you wanted to know who had recorded "Blue Moon" you could look it up and see that there were fifty different versions; they were cross-referenced. He published these himself, and they listed *250,000* 45s, but it cost so much to have them printed he had to charge $160 per set, and nobody bought them. I bought a thousand sets from him cheap. The thing is, he included a notice, "If any reader knows of a record that isn't included here, please send me all the information on the label and I'll include it in the next edition." He started getting letters from all over the world, and very quickly discovered that someone like Eddy Arnold, who had forty titles listed, had probably put out 4000! *That's* why I don't think there'll ever be an end to records . . .

♦ *V: Plus, there were so many regionally-produced records that were only distributed locally . . . Did you ever have any problems selling records?*

♦ ORH: I got sued by Time-Life-Warner Brothers once. Years ago on TV, Time-Life had marketed a box set of albums with beautiful artwork on the cover, like a drive-in with a girl on skates or a guy with sideburns on a motorcycle. It was advertised "Only $19.95—not available in stores!" These were compilations of greatest hits from the '50s-'60s. Then they had discontinued the campaign, and the pressing plant still had 500 of them sitting around (which Time-Life hadn't paid for, as they paid the plant only for records that were actually sold). I met an employee at the plant, and he told me they were thinking of dumping them in the trash. I bought 'em all up and placed a tiny ad in *Goldmine,* offering them for $10 postpaid. Almost im-

mediately I received this huge, two-inch-thick envelope in the mail from some law firm in New York, telling me that I had possession of stolen property, that I had infringed on their copyrights, that I had violated fair-trade practice by underselling their product (in all, there were about a hundred charges), and ordering me to ship everything back to them and pay them a million dollars—plus they wanted the names and addresses of everybody I had sold a set to. I guess they figured, "Here's this redneck in Indiana—let's squash him like a bug!" And I guess I was just supposed to flush myself down the commode . . . send them a big apology. However, these records had never *been* their property—the factory hadn't been paid and were getting ready to dump them in the trash. I wrote 'em back saying that I wouldn't offer them for sale in *Goldmine* anymore, and that if they sued me I'd declare bankruptcy and the only way they'd get their money would be for me to come and work for them! I never heard from them again.

♦ *V: What does the future hold?*

♦ ORH: A lot of people want a bargain, and that don't happen anymore. The days of finding a $2,000 record for a quarter at a garage sale are over. Records are definitely getting harder and harder to find, so I plan to retire in a couple years. I still get excited by a "find" though—recently I found this record on the FAX label which was recorded in the fifties by some guy out in San Francisco who was really concerned about prostitution—he interviews maybe a dozen prostitutes about why they got into the business: "I was beaten as a child," "I never got enough attention from my father," etc. The cover features a gorgeous naked woman, and is printed in those great '50s colors—to me that's more beautiful than the *Mona Lisa* . . .

Sex Is My Business, Fax Records.

Introducing "Elisabeth Waldo and Her 'Music of the Spirit' ": recording Pre-Columbian instruments for the very first time in the late '50s, musical archaeologist Elisabeth Waldo and her orchestra produced their first LP, *Rites of the Pagan*. Tracks such as "Chant to the Sun" and "Ritual of the Human Sacrifice" evoked visions of exotic jungle villages and high mountain peaks. As an orchestrator who spent many years studying the aboriginal music of the Americas, her goal was "to combine primitive and modern instruments in the perfect setting." Besides numerous tours of South America and the U.S., and appearances on radio and television, she has produced albums such as *Maracatú* (featuring Afro-Brazilian, Mayan, and Panamanian themes), *Realm of the Incas,* and *Viva California,* blending American Indian and Spanish/ Mexican instruments. She also created several TV documentary scores and is now producing a series of four videos; the first is titled *Song For The New World Peoples,* dedicated to the Indigenous Americans. For mail order information and a complete listing of cassettes, CDs, videos, narrative booklets, and music scores write The Multicultural Music & Art Foundation of Northridge (MCMAFN), PO Box 101, Northridge CA 91328, or phone (818) 349-3431; fax (818) 349-0716.

♦ *VALE: How did you start creating your own music?*

♦ ELISABETH WALDO: I was comfortably ensconced in the first violin section of the Los Angeles Philharmonic Orchestra when I realized I *had* to get out of exclusively Western-oriented music, where I was playing Brahms and Tchaikovsky year in and year out. As wonderful as that is, it didn't adequately express the feelings of the world that I feel are out there for both musicians and audience. I decided to try to be creative and original from scratch, and hopefully I could make a contribution along that thorny path when you don't follow the prescribed road. You're always subject to *time*...the time it takes to see your dreams unfold and your sound produced the way you want it. But I do feel rewarded; I don't regret at all that it has taken this long for the public "to catch up."

There are a few people in the world who love to listen to new ideas, although in the past most people were quite closed to anything innovative. I grew up being in tune with a "sonic" approach to music—when I was five I lived on a ranch near a Yakima Indian reservation in Eastern Washington. It wasn't exactly the thing for a tiny girl to do: to sit and watch the Indians fish and listen to them chant, but through the 8th grade that was what was most intriguing to me.

Then my family insisted that I have classical music training, for which I am grateful—I would recommend this to anybody wishing to pursue a unique path because I still think the "basics" can be of great help. A lot of young kids want to start at the top in rock music: "I want to make a lot of money!" yet they can't read a note of music, and they can't count or keep a beat unless they have a *boom-boom-boom* in their ears.

After graduating from high school in Seattle I attended the Curtis Institute of Music in Philadelphia on a scholarship. I had a lot of wonderful experiences playing classical music—at the time no ethnic music was permitted. Violin was my first love—even before I was 5 years old I had the smallest violin available. I also had some piano training, which is useful—plus I have absolute pitch.

In Philadelphia I was fortunate to be chosen by Leopold Stokowski. He was traveling all over the United States looking for young talent to take to South America. His personality and genius influenced my musical thinking and even my personality because he was interested in people who would dare to take a different path . . . who had ideas other than the norm. He was genuinely interested in youth and was a great inspiration. For three years I was involved in his training; then I joined the Los Angeles Philharmonic. But after that experience with Stokowski, I just couldn't stay put—all these ideas began to combust! Even in movie studios the recording orchestras are very static—if you have any ideas of your own, that's *not* the place to be, either. So I just took off and barnstormed all over Latin America.

From three resource areas (Indian, Hispanic and African) you get a totally different sonic picture (let's call it a *soundscape)* than if you're listening to a string quartet. When I studied ethnic music at a girls' school in Panama, I heard drums going all night long. Right away your vision of doing a conservative *opus* just goes right out the window! You hear this cacophony of sound and become very excited. From there I voyaged into other Indian influences, especially from the Andes. I still think that area produces some of the greatest music in the world—as long as they don't get "electrified"; as long as nobody convinces them to add a rock bass to their music. I hope that won't happen.

♦ **ANDREA JUNO: Their music is created in the context of a religion or spirituality—**

♦ EW: Absolutely. Over a period of time I've collected a great library which emphasizes working with "ori-

work—I don't want to leave it unfinished, or in such a state that somebody else couldn't continue this work in the future. I still go to remote Indian villages because I'm motivated to develop Indian violins for string playing which you can be sure does not sound like Bach, Beethoven, or Brahms. It features glissandos and portamento and odd keys (the equivalent of five or six sharps in our Western notation system). I wrote a violin concerto called "Concerto Indo-Americano" which I performed in China in 1987. They were so thrilled they published a program.

Each Christmas our artists create Pageants at the Gene Autrey Museum and our own Mission Theater based on religious ceremonies dating back to the miracle plays of St. Francis of Assisi. These plays have a lot of humor involving devils and angels, and they're quite wonderful.

♦ **AJ: *You spent a lot of time with villagers in Latin America—***

♦ **EW:** Yes, all my music is inspired by those experiences. My experiences in the rain forest are a *source* that remains intact in my psyche. Around 1980 I developed an interest in Asian music, and made several trips to China. I debuted an orchestral suite at the Pacific-Asian Museum called *Tales of the Golden Mountain,* using exotic instruments from China combined with Western instruments.

Sometimes the pre-Columbian or Chinese tones can be part of our scale, but sometimes they cannot. They might be higher, or use a lot more harmonics. For example, if I'm using a wind instrument to hit an "A" (in our scale) it might simultaneously be overblowing in a two-octave range above that note.

When I studied ethnic music at a girls' school in Panama, I heard drums going all night long. Right away your vision of doing a conservative *opus* just goes right out the window!

♦ **V: *One of your reviews said: "The effect was slightly devastating; the external world was suddenly thrown out of gear, and I found myself sitting in the middle of an upper-Amazon harvest festival, a veritable riot of tonal color and aboriginal emotion."***

♦ **EW:** We try to have a good setting for our live performances so we can elicit a response of beauty from our audience. I never want to commercialize what I believe in—for instance, I wouldn't dream of playing "La Bamba" on a show. It's never been my goal to be a pop artist—I would accomplish nothing reaching for a rung up on that ladder!

gins" rather than just performing music. I always wondered: "What was the first music of the Americas?" The pre-Hispanic, pre-Cortez, pre-Columbus people had no musical notation whatsoever, so I had to start from scratch imagining what it might be. I was free to collect instruments, study them and familiarize myself with their micro-tones or quarter-tones which are totally different from our "normal" scale. I have a large collection of instruments (including pre-Columbian instruments) in my music/art/dance center in Northridge, near California State University, Northridge.

When I returned to California, I started blending pre-Columbian instruments and scales with Western music ideas. From that, I developed a Mayan and Incan idiom which I still periodically return to, in order to create some specific theme. For example, I composed Ballet music based on the book of the *Popol Vuh,* the ancient creation myth of the Quiche Maya. For years I've had what I call my *Musical Bank*—I've been working on various projects and recording as much as possible on paper so they won't be too hard to recall when I get the right opportunity to record them. Some of my experimentations are also recorded on "practice" tapes.

I also have a studio and a non-profit organization to further develop performing ensembles. This is *lifetime*

♦ **AJ: What is your goal?**

♦ **EW:** To create original material. To create music that nobody else would go through the pain and suffering to create! A lot of people might think, "This doesn't make sense—I'm not getting paid for this, so why should I do it?" But I don't have that feeling. I'm not only interested in working with instruments from other countries and eras, but in extending the possibilities of the western flute or cello, for instance, because they can do "far out" things—only nobody asks them to! (Maybe John Cage did, but that's another extreme.) I spent at least a year researching old Cantonese music for *Tales of the Golden Mountain,* and was able to incorporate some ancient chants. Now I'm working with a fabulous core of musicians who play both traditional and ethnic instruments. It's exciting to combine a Chinese *pi-pa* (similar to a mandolin) with a violin, for instance.

When people hear my soundscapes, they say that they feel transported into another world and are sorry when it ends, because they feel something is missing in this world.

♦ **AJ: Are you reclaiming sounds from an era that wasn't so alienated and materialistic?**

♦ **EW:** Yes, and if I don't write them down, they might disappear again. I feel I am a serious composer. I haven't made a lot of effort to gain recognition as a composer, but I have done TV music—I wrote the theme and all the pre-Columbian sequences for a 48-part series on the history of Mexico, plus other documentaries. *Realm of the Incas* seems to be a "standard" all over the world—it's been used as background music for films on Peru. There are panpipes on it.

To do "Catalina: Treasure of the Past" and "Viva California" I went to the Channel Islands, where there are petroglyphs, and worked with the Chumash. My center is California, and a lot of what I do stems from the California heritage which includes Indian, Hispanic and Chinese influences. When people hear my soundscapes, sometimes they say that they feel transported into another world and are sorry when it ends, because they feel something is missing in this world.

In written Western classical music, openings and closings are very strict. Yet I feel that music primarily involves a mood, and if the musicians have created a mood they should just retain that until the sound falls off or declines by itself.

Currently, I am now re-editing my early works originally conceived for ethnic instruments into performable scores for traditional musicians, symphony and

Elisabeth Waldo's *Realm of the Incas,* GNP Records.

chamber orchestras, and choruses.

♦ **AJ: You feel that music should involve more spontaneity—**

♦ **EW:** Right. And if the mood hasn't been achieved, it shouldn't be artificially cut off.

♦ **AJ: What was it like to be a woman in your field?**

♦ **EW:** When I was a student, you had to be *better* than a man or you were out! But today women are quite accepted; maybe half of an orchestra is women and nobody pays any attention. I wonder if they try as hard as I did—it seems that girls in my age group had to have far greater discipline. Believe me, you had to be a *Heifetz* or you were just not in!

Elisabeth Waldo's *Rites of the Pagan,* GNP Crescendo Records. Album cover credits: cover illustration is of an Aztec priest dressed in the likeness of one of their Pagan Gods for a sacred Ceremonial.

179

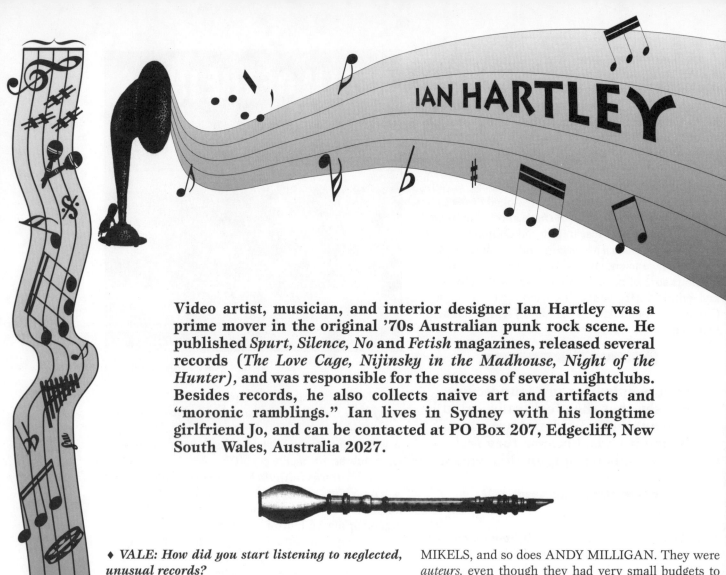

IAN HARTLEY

Video artist, musician, and interior designer Ian Hartley was a prime mover in the original '70s Australian punk rock scene. He published *Spurt, Silence, No* and *Fetish* magazines, released several records (*The Love Cage, Nijinsky in the Madhouse, Night of the Hunter*), and was responsible for the success of several nightclubs. Besides records, he also collects naive art and artifacts and "moronic ramblings." Ian lives in Sydney with his longtime girlfriend Jo, and can be contacted at PO Box 207, Edgecliff, New South Wales, Australia 2027.

♦ *VALE: How did you start listening to neglected, unusual records?*

♦ IAN HARTLEY: For me, the catalyst was hearing YMA SUMAC, MARTIN DENNY, LES BAXTER, and Hawaiian music in general—Hawaii opened the door. And the person who turned me on to all this was a drag queen named Jacqueline Hyde. She would also take me and my friends to these little nightclubs where you'd hear an unknown Italian accordionist playing his heart out. Usually there'd be one outstanding vocalist—the kind who gets down on one knee and cries. Or she'd take us to see a little Latin group playing Perez Prado hits while a woman in a tight dress danced and sang sexy torch songs. Some of my favorite music that I've heard was live, not on record. These unknown musicians can be fabulously entertaining—poignant and funny at the same time . . . incredibly intelligent, yet out of date!

♦ *V: Why did you turn away from contemporary music?*

♦ IH: For the same reasons I ignore most modern movies. In B-movies of the '40s through the '70s, the filmmakers were free to experiment within the genres of soft-core sex or violence or film noir. It was just a 90-minute product, but each director had a distinctive style that was translated onto film. RAY DENNIS STECKLER has a definite style; so does TED V. MIKELS, and so does ANDY MILLIGAN. They were *auteurs,* even though they had very small budgets to work with. Whereas today, individual style is not to be found—not in movies, not in music, and not in life.

All these "artists" of today are just *taking* from different avant-garde and experimental and historical and ethnic areas, then using the rip-offs within a popular cultural mode. All the music that's ever *been* is now being sampled and incorporated into dance music, or put on tape loops or whatever.

Recently, I collaborated with a friend on my first commercial music video; for reference, we watched hundreds of MTV videos. It was amazing to see how every facet of film experimentation and technique has been stolen. This new parasitic medium, the promotional music video short, has inundated everybody with classic images from the history of film. You've got Cocteau music videos and Brakhage videos and Fellini and Bunuel and Nicholas Ray ones—every conceivable directorial style has been appropriated. These video makers have butchered cinema! If you look at a film today, you don't know whether the director has a knowledge of cinema, or just a knowledge of music videos. Because a few days of looking at MTV would teach you the history of film, even though you might not realize it.

♦ *V: Well, you'd get a massive inundation of imag-*

es and styles from this past century, without any of the original meaning and intent. People only know the classics through excerpts—

♦ IH: And it's the same with contemporary music: you can listen to a dance record and hear Erik Satie come through for a couple of seconds. Art is in a crazed state now; artists are like insane plastic surgeons patching together these Frankensteins. Except in science or technology, it seems there are no new ideas in the world. So if you're a thinking animal who feels the need to discover something for *yourself* (it's the only way you can keep your brain ticking), then you get into something like incredibly strange films for experience you didn't know

Ian Hartley being a D.J.

existed . . . that you hadn't been told about.

♦ **V: Watching MTV can certainly scramble and taint your recall of classic films—**

♦ IH: Just as I got into tracking down little-known films, I began doing the same kind of search for music. And once you get involved it's so fantastic, so rewarding! Some of the records I've found at garage sales and in secondhand record shops—there's no documentation on them anywhere in the world. Maybe you've got the only copy in existence, and you don't know where it came from or what it means.

♦ **V: In your search, do you follow any pattern?**

♦ IH: First I went through a spaghetti western movie soundtrack period. I found this record from Italy with the generic title, SPAGHETTI WESTERNS, written in spaghetti on the cover! It's a compilation of tracks by *sub*-Morricone imitators and minor musicians. I have a lot of strange records, but this is one of the best. One of my favorite songs is "Uno Dopo L'Altro" (1968, "Maybe One, Maybe Nine") by FRED BONGUSTO on RCA Italia. Actually, I think it's Richard Harris singing, as he starred in the movie. The lyrics go: "He wants to kill a man . . ." [voice starts ascending] "Maybe one, maybe two, maybe four, maybe five, maybe seven, maybe ten—he wants to kill ten men . . ." And it's got this twangy guitar *Grand Canyon Suite*-type background. The singer can't pronounce English prop-

erly, so it sounds like, "He wants to keel a mahn . . ." Then he leaps from ten men to "seventeen . . . twenty-one . . ." You hear gunshots ricochet [*ka-pow!*]. I also like "Da Uomo A Uomo" (1967) sung by RAOUL, with music by ENNIO MORRICONE.

♦ **V: Cover versions can sometimes be more interesting than the original. Here, this singer is struggling to pronounce these near-psychotic lyrics in thick, Italian-accented English—**

♦ IH: I also have a Taiwanese spaghetti western album; the hole in the record is off-center. There are gunshots all through it, and the sound of horses' hooves, but all of the music wavers up and down in pitch.

In fact, many of my favorite strange records come from film soundtracks or are featured in films. I particularly focus on the ones from low-budget movies. A very eerie soundtrack was composed and played by the great HERSCHELL GORDON LEWIS: *Blood Feast.* I prefer it to the flip side of the album, *2000 Maniacs,* which is straight hillbilly music. Another notable LP is the soundtrack from *On Her Bed of Roses,* an original score by JOE GREENE. Supposedly it's based on Krafft-Ebing's *Psychopathia Sexualis,* and *sounds* like it with titles like "Walk to Hell," "Destruction Part 2" and the imaginatively titled "Melissa Pensive" and "Melissa Glad."

I've always liked *mondo* records. They're so gener-

ic—on them you can find a cross-section of every style of music that was popular in the world at the time of the record's release, except that the music is somehow demented. The interpretations of ethnic music on these LPs are always warped and off-center. Some of the *mondo* records I have include *Go, Go, Go World!* by NINO OLIVIERO & BRUNO NICOLAI, RIZ ORTO-LANI's *Women Of The World* and *Ecco (An Incredible Orgy of Sights and Sounds),* PIERO PICCIONI's *IL Mondo Di Notte, Mondo Cane* by Riz Ortolani & Nino Oliviero, *Mondo Cane #2* by Nino Oliviero, *Malamondo* by ENNIO MORRICONE, and *Amore in 4 Dimensioni* by FRANCO MANNINO.

I also collect soundtracks from Japanese monster movies. On one record a girl is actually singing a love song to Godzilla; it's credited to the STAR SISTERS. Normally these soundtracks alone are strange enough; they're all electronic and ethereal in content, with lots of noises and atmospheric effects.

I've found a number of MEDICAL or PSEUDO-MEDICAL RECORDS. One of my favorites is this 45 where you hear a psychiatrist asking, "Why did you kill your girlfriend?" Apparently the killer can only speak in rhyme, because all his replies are in sing-song: "Mad mad/she made me mad mad/and I was glad glad/she made me mad mad." Then the psychiatrist asks, "Now tell me how it happened?" and he goes, "Sad sad/she made me sad sad/and then I kill kill!"—the record goes on like that. I have another album which was just sold to members of the medical profession. It's one long interview with an English psychopath who tells why he kills and what goes on in his mind. This is the only album of its type I've seen, but the back lists fifty others. I also like the KINSEY REPORT, read by Dr Murray Banks, which is basically

Ennio Morricone's *I Western*, Peters International.

a guy raving about sexual deviations.

♦ *V: How do you decide what to buy?*

♦ IH: What attracts me is the unknown. I'll buy a record if I like the cover, or the song titles or back cover blurbs sound promising. Usually records like these don't cost much, because if *you* don't know what it is, chances are nobody else does either, so they can't sell it for a lot of money. It's a cheap form of *art collecting*—one you can afford to get involved in.

When you listen to records like these, *your* heart has to be in the right place because it's too easy to acquire a misplaced arrogance and feel *superior* to the people whose records you collect.

I also like the genre of SELF-IMPROVEMENT RECORDS. One of my favorites is *You Can Better Your Best* by GLENN W. TURNER, an American harelip who (according to the liner notes) "now owns more than 30 corporations worth over 100 million dollars." He has a terrible speech impediment, and tells you how he made it through life despite this. But since *he's* the one doing the talking, you can't understand a thing! [laughs] I've played this record for friends and they can't figure out what he's saying either—nobody has *ever* found out how to "Better Your Best!" I love records like these, because obviously they're done by people with no conscious intention of being strange. There has to be some naivete to it.

I also collect records by people who evolved through music hall or vaudeville and who have a gimmick: they can whistle with their mouth open, or they're like "Edward, the man who sings with four voices at once!"—he's a vocalist who's like a circus freak. I have a few records on which people play saws and glasses filled with water. In Australia, I saw Ronnie Ronell whistle a concert's worth of beautiful bird-like trills to an audience of little old ladies with blue hair.

I also have a soft spot for old people who play organs and pianos badly. They'll play something like "The Black Hills of Dakota" with a halting, geriatric interpretation that becomes high art through its inanity. They usually do standards like "Greensleeves" or "Tie a Yellow Ribbon." A lot of the songs have Texas in the title, like "The Yellow Rose of Texas" or "The Eyes of Texas Are Upon Me." Many LPs like this have CRISWELL-ian liner notes, like, "We all want a better world, because this is where we're going to spend the rest of our life." Then you play the record and it has *nothing* to do with that; you just know that their heart was in the right place. When you listen to records like these, *your* heart has to be in the right place, too, because it's too easy to acquire a misplaced arrogance and feel *superior* to the people whose records you collect.

There are so many areas to go further into. You can start collecting film footage of people who can't dance, or all those women who did "interpretive" dancing in the '50s. Or strippers who, for lack of training, developed their own style—*incredibly strange dancers.* Basically, we're talking about *any* non-trained people who have a need to express themselves.

There are people who almost invent their own genre, like KEN NORDINE, who did what he called *Word Jazz,* backed by Fred Katz, who composed the soundtracks to Roger Corman films like *Little Shop of Horrors.* He'd do little narratives: [walking string bass intro] "Ever wake up in the middle of the night and feel hungry? Happened to me the other night. I felt like a [snaps fingers] cheese sandwich. First I put on the mayonnaise . . . then I decided to have *cucumber* on it, too." He told you every detail of these *nothing* events in life!

There are so many records that fit into the area we're discussing. Tom Jones did a hit song, "Delilah," right? Well, we found a Chinese version where instead of "Why, why, why, Delilah?" it went "Lie, lie, lie, Delilah!" In this song a guy goes nuts, breaks down the door to his girlfriend's apartment and kills her: "I've come to break down the door/forgive me Delilah, I couldn't take it any more." But the Chinese version is sung by a woman; they didn't bother to change the gender of the lyrics, so now it could be interpreted as a

Rod McKuen's *Beatsville,* High Fidelity Recordings, Inc.
Album cover credits: cover photo: Rick Strauss.

lesbian song. If this had been done *intentionally* it wouldn't have been nearly as good . . . There's also a Chinese version of "Blue Velvet" where the pronunciation is unintentionally hilarious.

Have you heard any of those singing dog records, featuring dog barks spliced together to form rock 'n' roll songs? I heard a canine version of "A Hard Day's Night." Actually, things like that are too consciously cute to really appeal to me. For the same reason I don't like the *Chipmunks*—they're too cute and fake. But Sheb Woolley's "Purple People Eater" or David Seville's "Witch Doctor" are *not* fake. They were recorded by people who basically had one hit and then vanished into obscurity . . .

Did you ever hear SLIM GALLIARD? He's well-known in the jazz world, but he is quite strange. He put out an album of fairly ordinary jazz on which every track has the word "avocado" in the title. It's funny—when you're looking for strange music you can get involved with things that are really quite *square.* For example, there's a song by ROY ROGERS called "I Like to Eat." He goes, "I like to eat/I like to eat/Give me chicken 'n greens/biscuits and beans." Like the title says, he's just telling you what he likes to eat— that's all the song is!

♦ **V: Are there any unusual rock records you like?**
♦ **IH:** Almost anything by JACK HAMMER. I saw a record of his in New York but it was fifty dollars. He was a friend of Jimi Hendrix, so record dealers price it high and write "Friend of Jimi Hendrix" on the cover. Yet it's got nothing to do with Hendrix! "When a Girl Loves a Girl" is a truly poignant song about two girls who are in love. "Switchblade Operator" sounds like the "Pink Panther" theme, and the recurring hook is the sound of two flick blades opening up. The song is

Glenn W. Turner *Speaks Out: "You Can Better Your Best,"* Souncot Records.

Book cover of *I, Paid My Dues* by Babs Gonzales.

about a guy who's hung-up and living at home. His mother tells him, "Look, you're headed straight for trouble—you're going to turn out just like your father." Then he gets into a knife fight with a guy; you actually hear the fight and all these "flick flick" sound effects. He kills the person, comes home and finds out that he killed his father! It's really tragic, almost like Shakespeare, and the singer bursts into operatic bits in the song as well. The pop group *Soft Cell* covered one of Jack Hammer's songs, "Down in the Subway," but nobody ever seems to talk about him . . .

Have you ever heard "West of The Wall" by Toni Fisher? She sounds like she's singing in a wind tunnel: "West of The Wall/I'll wait for you . . ." It's a Cold War type of song—

♦ **V: But now that the Berlin Wall is gone, doesn't that song have a perverted nostalgia—as though one missed being in a state of war? Don't you think all patriotic songs are inherently absurd?**

♦ IH: Well, when John Wayne's "Why I Love America" came out, it sounded psychotic and close to the bone.

♦ **V: You play it for people now and it elicits groans. Like "The Ballad of the Green Berets"—**

♦ IH: Although—I know people who actually like "The Ballad of the Green Berets" because they think, "It doesn't matter how stupid the sentiment is if it comes from the *heart.*" There's one scene in John Waters' *Hairspray* that's worth the price of admission. You see a singer onstage in front of a huge crowd of people in a black dance hall. Then the scene cuts to kids outside, kissing in an alley, and a guy ambles up with a whiskey bottle in hand who sings the song better than the singer inside.

♦ **V: Every city has people on the street who sound as good as people on records—**

♦ IH: Yes. If some old guy who can't really sing or play a guitar nevertheless tries his best and is genuinely sincere, that can be beautiful. When I listen to that Spaghetti Western ballad, I really feel the honesty and poignancy in the guy's voice. Because even though he's singing something almost insane, he really believes it: "This is my big break; I've rehearsed six months to sing this song." It's that kind of spirit that moves you. And you don't have to be a seasoned performer like James Brown to be able to move someone.

Actually, James Brown did an amazing song, "King Heroin," which is a monologue in the "This is the city: the Naked City" vein. The song has lines like "I get a world-famous model, and I take away her looks/I get a famous musician, and take away his hooks." Then it goes, "He can be black or white, Polish or Mex/it doesn't matter to me, I'll take away everything he gets." You catch a vision of this plague of heroin sweeping across the land—it's really chilling, almost like high art. It reminds me of *Macbeth,* and it has a great beat.

♦ **V: I was reading Chuck Berry's autobiography which is written in an incredibly florid, almost high art style. But he doesn't get the $2 words exactly right.**

♦ IH: I love that BABS GONZALES [black jazz singer] book *I, Paid My Dues.* Whenever he refers to a person or city or anything complex, it's in quotation marks. So it always wakes you up to encounter "Sammy Davis Jr." or "Bird" or even "Copenhagen." You know, in the field of jazz, people are *expected* to be "way out." I suppose one qualification for "strangeness" could be: transcending a genre, or combining several genres. BABS GONZALES also made some good records; I like "Lullaby of the Doomed." Recently a CD of his recordings came out.

♦ **V: Those quotation marks Babs uses serve to continually remind you that you don't really know who "Sammy Davis Jr" was, or what "Copenhagen" is. He's the only writer to have employed such a simple distancing device. It's like the writer is constantly nudging you and giving you a wink.**

♦ IH: ISAAC HAYES is also brilliant; his *Black Moses* record is written in the style of the King James Bible.

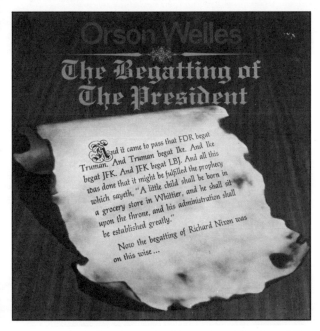

Orson Welles' *The Begatting of the President*, Mediarts Records, Inc.

The black exploitation movies of the '70s often had great soundtracks, like *Cleopatra Jones,* or *Hell Up In Harlem*—that's a good film by Larry Cohen. Another favorite genre is the BLACK MESSAGE SONG, which includes SHIRLEY BROWN's "Woman To Woman" and MARGIE JOSEPH's monologue in her version of "Stop In The Name Of Love"—I usually turn it off when the music begins. In the jazz category, there was a wild bass player named SLAM STEWART who played bass with a bow instead of plucking it, and hummed along with the notes as well. I like listening to him.

It's always strange to watch an Elvis imitator; it brings out mixed emotions. Elvis's most interesting period was at the end of his life when he was extremely paranoid, almost a psychopath, and really fat—in *full bloat.* There's a live recording of "Love Me Tender" where after singing, "Oh, my darling, I love you, and I always will," he forgets the words and does this rambling soliloquy: "We're standing here/and I haven't got a beer/And I'm nowhere/I'm losing my hair." Then he breaks up laughing. In his later years he would occasionally try to express the turmoil that he was feeling about the world. So he'd write songs like "In the Ghetto," "Suspicious Minds," or "On the Edge of Reality."

The psychedelic period produced its share of songs which bring up the question of "bad" taste, like "Moulty" by the BARBARIANS which tells how the drummer lost one of his hands. And while I could never like IRON BUTTERFLY's "In-a-gadda-da-vida," obviously, the band is trying to say something that's really close to their hearts. Maybe in the year 2000 that will be an incredibly strange record, but at the moment I couldn't bear to listen to it.

♦ *V: What other soundtracks do you like?*

♦ IH: The original VALLEY OF THE DOLLS—not *Beyond the Valley of the Dolls* (although that's great, too)—with lines like "You have to climb Mount Everest to reach the Valley of the Dolls . . . to get to the other side." After listening to that record, I started buying more soap opera soundtracks like "Days of Our Lives" and "The Young and the Restless," which is mostly harp music. If I had known 5 years ago I'd be listening to music like this, I would have thought I'd gone totally insane! But if you forget you're listening to "The Young and the Restless" and imagine you're a person sitting in a small hotel room in Hollywood writing a song for this show you hate—then the record immediately *transcends* its original context.

I also think HARPO MARX records are fabulous: *any* record on which Harpo plays the harp. The sound is ethereal and fantastic . . .

♦ *V: Oscar Levant recorded a few classical records that could drive you nuts. His timing was so drug-damaged (or something); it was incredibly jagged and neurotic—*

♦ IH: I like him, especially his frantic version of "An American in Paris" where it goes "ding ding ding ding ding ding" and then becomes syncopated; he shatters the rhythm. He was a great comedian as well—his book, *Memoirs of an Amnesiac,* is worth it for the title alone.

Actually, my favorite composer of all time is CARL STALLING who did the music and sounds for the Warner Brothers cartoons. He's fantastic. If you tape a lot of cartoons, subtract all the "Ehhh—what's up, doc?" interjections, and join the music together, you get the most amazing stream-of-consciousness cut-ups. He's like the William Burroughs of cartoon music. I could listen to him for hours.

Valley of the Dolls soundtrack, Design Records.

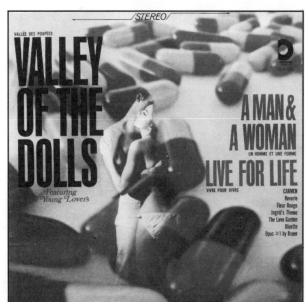

In the category of records by less-than-superstars, Telly Savalas did several albums that are quite strange. Then there's the category of "pop philosophy message records" like Les Crane's *Desiderata*. ORSON WELLES cut a record just before he died: "You don't know what it's like to be old, but I know what it's like to be young . . ." That was the last thing he did; and it fits right in the category of: famous people doing embarrassing things.

Some strange flexi-discs have been given away in magazines. "It's a Gas," which was included in a MAD magazine, is just a guy who repeats "It's a gas!" and then burps. Sometimes medical journals will include a record of a heart beating—or rather, an irregular heartbeat that telegraphs an impending heart attack. And sometimes hotrod magazines would include a free record, or you could send away for an LP that was "recorded live at Daytona Beach!" The *transportation record* is a genre in itself; there's a big cult of people who collect and listen to recordings of trains and who can identify all the different locomotives.

♦ **V: *Some of the records by minor TV or movie stars are so unlikely—***

♦ IH: —when you hear it, you can't believe that anybody could even *think* of that combination, or that it was actually released, and on a major label as well. And obviously the company spent all this money on a full-color cover. The WAVY GRAVY compilation contains a recording by Senator Everett Dirksen singing "Wild Thing" ("W-w-w-wild thing, I-I-I think I love you")—that *must* be a put-on. But the record of LAURENCE HARVEY doing a pseudo-beatnik reading, backed by Herbie Mann, is serious; on it he's reciting all this crazy off-the-wall poetry—

Dirk Bogarde's *Lyrics for Lovers*, London Records.

Laurence Harvey's *This Is My Beloved*, © 1962 Atlantic Recording Corporation.

♦ **V: *The "artist" side of him came out—***

♦ IH: Yeah . . . it's all verses like, "Your hair, your hair . . . your hair goes all the way down your back, and I feel—oh, your high heels." It's a fetishist S&M record, really, although I doubt that was the intention. He's reading from a book by Walter Benton called *This Is My Beloved*. Then there's DIRK BOGARDE reading *Lyrics For Lovers*—it's unbelievable kitsch, high dimension dross. All his songs are about romance: "Night And Day," "You're The One," and "The Way You Look Tonight." He sings "Paris . . . Ah, I was a stranger in the city/full of self-pity/What to do? What to do?" with the London Symphony Orchestra in the background. These are all songs, but he just *speaks* them in hushed tones. I also like to hear BORIS KARLOFF reading horror stories, and I love CHARLES LAUGHTON reading *Night Of The Hunter*.

Memory can play funny tricks on you. I like soundtracks to television shows which elicit some kind of weird nostalgia, even though when you were growing up they represented the most hideous nightmare ever. I don't mean shows like *Mister Ed,* but things like *Family Feud*—that somehow become transformed into *something else* by the passage of time.

♦ **V: *The idea of lovingly cherishing painful memories—***

♦ IH: Another notable genre is TEEN EXPLOITATION SONGS that seem to be done in home studios for no reasonable purpose other than to preach some kind of psycho message about custom car culture, obsessive love, or some home-spun religious philosophy. I'll list a few: "SELWYN COX's "His Name Is Jesus," PORTER WAGGONER's "The Rubber Room," HASIL ADKINS' "We Got A Date," EDDIE NOACK's

"Psycho," and the ZIRKONS' "Congawa"—psycho racist rock. A favorite is HARRIOTT AND EVENS' "Psycho" b/w "How Did She Look?" with its lyrics, "You think I'm psycho, don't you, mama/because I killed someone tonight/You think I'm psycho, don't you, mama . . . you know that girl next door, mama?/ she's not around anymore." It's this guy confessing to his mom that he's killed half the street! When "Leader Of The Pack" came out, a lot of people started recording songs like the one where a guy's girlfriend dies on the back of his motorcycle in a crash—he wants to join her in death so he climbs into the coffin with her. Then there's MOSES LONGPIECE's "Slide Her Under The Door." A guy's taking a shower singing about his girlfriend, and then comes a knock on the door. The visitor yells, "Your girlfriend's just been run over!" "Run over?" "Yes—by a *steamroller.*" And then the guy in the shower says, "Just slide her under the door." There are many more like these . . .

In America, people get all these fantasies going. They become convinced they can be a *star,* so they save up their money and put out a record. Maybe they're not "good enough" for Hollywood, but they're good enough for Peoria—they live in their small town and try to create a career in the entertainment business. In Australia this guy, ROY MUSTACA, emigrated from Greece without a penny to his name. But soon he managed to open his own hamburger joint, and in a few years made all this money. So to say "Thank you!" to Australia, he put out an album: *Yes, I Love You Australia* (RGM Records). And his singing has an operatic yodeling quality that's really unique—he's not just another Frank Sinatra impersonator.

A friend of mine has become obsessed by early '60s Italian twist music; it's hard to find. A favorite song has these lyrics: "Come on, everybody/this is one thing you gotta know/everybody's gotta do this now/it's one thing you gotta do for sure: everybody must chunga, chunga, chunga twist/chunga, chunga, chunga twist!" It's sung with undeniable sincerity and enthusiasm, and in the most oddly accented English as well. Obviously the singer is totally dedicated. The trouble is, you're not exactly sure what the chunga twist *is.*

I also love Hawaiian slide guitar records from the '20s up until now. Those have replaced Martin Denny and Nino Rota's *Juliet of the Spirits* on my turntable— I'm afraid I over-listened to *them.* Beware: if you play a record too much, you may never be able to listen to it again!

♦ *V: I once knew a Leslie Gore fan who put away one album to play ten years in the future.*

♦ IH: You have to be careful about bleeding something dry . . . I also like promotional records that were given away with products. I bought a box of Wheaties that contained a recording of Willie Wheatie singing "Be Bop a Lula," but with a goofy cartoon voice. What's great about *all* this kind of music is that it goes on forever—there's always another area to investigate.

There are so many odd regionally produced recordings that were only sold in the town they were made in. If there were a Top Ten Strange Records, it would have to be redefined every 3 or 4 months because somebody would always come up with one better. And I'm sure there are great records in Mexico that nobody knows about—

♦ *V: That's what we said in the introduction to* **Incredibly Strange Films:** *that we didn't cover all the great films from Mexico, Spain, the Philippines, Hong Kong, etc. I found all these film magazines in Spain with mind-boggling stills from unknown, yet-to-be-translated films. I also heard some beautiful, poignant '60s female pop music, but it was on a home-made compilation tape and the cafe owner didn't know who the artists were.*

♦ IH: I bought a compilation record called *Retribution,* which contains just songs about retribution. Usually those kinds of things are dreadful, but this one contained a classic: "There's a hole in daddy's arm where all the money goes." And the singer sang it like a middle-of-the-road Burt Bacharach tune, instead of the way it was intended, which was Country-Western.

My girlfriend, Jo, has collected quite a few strange singles. I like WALLY COX's "What a Crazy Guy" b/w "Taverne in the Town." which to me is a psychomoronic record recorded by one of Marlon Brando's best friends. There are two delightful 45s recorded by a pair of ex-prostitutes. MANDY RICE DAVIES sang "A Good Man Is Hard to Find," and CHRISTINE KEELER (of the Profumo sex scandal that rocked Britain in the early '60s) recorded "Sex" and "Christine"—*hot stuff!*

Roy Mustaca's *Yes, I Love You Australia,* RGM Records.

AL ENNIS

Al Ennis has been collecting records for the past 25 years, but has followed rock'n'roll since its very beginning. For the past 8 years he has been the rock'n'roll reviewer for Down Home Music/Roots & Rhythm Mail Order (6921 Stockton Ave, El Cerrito CA 94530; 510-525-1494; fax 510-525-2904—a good source for many of the reissues and publications mentioned in this interview). Co-author of *The Roots & Rhythm Guide To Rock,* Al is currently writing a history of rockabilly. He lives in the Bay Area with his wife Christina and their 2-year-old daughter, Cailen.

♦ *VALE: How did you accumulate all these records?*
♦ AL ENNIS: Mostly from record stores and mail order. When I started to collect seriously in the mid-'70s, the original records were already expensive, but fortunately many European labels had begun putting together incredible reissues. I found I could get more bang-for-the-buck by grabbing all the reissues I could find, because if you could find even *one* of the original 45s, it would cost hundreds. Now, many of these *reissues* are out of print and very expensive! At this date I have *thousands* of these reissues, covering mostly rockabilly, rock'n'roll, rhythm'n'blues, blues and '60s punk.
♦ *V: Do you still find records at garage sales and flea markets?*
♦ AE: Sure; just last week I got a call from a company liquidating an estate. When I checked it out I almost fell over—the guy was a pack-rat who had collected *everything,* not just thousands of records. You couldn't even *walk* through the place; he had 50 bedboards, 25 bikes, 40 stereos—a lot of total junk. But I went away with 400 LPs at a dollar each.
♦ *V: What was your best find?*
♦ AE: *An Evening with Jayne,* which doesn't even have her singing, but *does* have an incredibly sexy photo of her on the cover. The music is just generic easy-listening. She *did* sing on several LPs: *Jayne Mansfield Busts Up Last Vegas* and *Shakespeare, Tchaikovsky and Me.*

She does a couple songs on the *Va-Va-Voom!* collection on RHINO, and there's also a 45 on the London label, "As Clouds Drift By"—the B-side allegedly features Jimi Hendrix!

Kurt Jensen's *An Evening with Jayne,* Hollywood Records.
Album cover credits: cover photo: J. Julius Fanta.

188

♦ **V: You have quite a few sexy records here—**

♦ AE: Well, if you collect blues records you'll wind up with plenty of double- (and *single-*) entendre tunes. There's a long history of "dirty blues." Since these records were for the "race" market, the record companies could get away with anything! Of course, they weren't played on the radio.

When white people first started playing their black-influenced early rock'n'roll, record companies started "cleaning up" the songs so as not to offend the white teenage market. Nevertheless, a lot of raunchy songs got recorded—to be sold "under the counter." JOHNNY OTIS recorded a legendary LP under the name SNATCH & The POONTANGS. The music was great, and the lyrics sometimes bordered on the surreal, such as "Two Time Slim": "I bolted down lightning and captured thunder/I done some shit that made the whole world wonder/During the war the army laid down their guns and I won the fight/I've been known to eat a wild gorilla from asshole to appetite."

That number was based on the "dozens": a traditional rhyming game of put-downs, curses, bragging, and what have you. One of the great gospel pioneers, Thomas Dorsey, started out in the '20s doing risque material under the name "Georgia Tom." He teamed up with blues guitarist Tampa Red, and under the pseudonym "The Hokum Boys" they released a series of popular dirty blues. Their *first* record, "Tight Like That," was a huge, influential best-seller. Subsequent-

ly, there was a whole"hokum" movement that spawned hundreds of so-called "dirty" records.

♦ **V: Name some others—**

♦ AE: It seems like *everyone* did at least a few. Blues and jazz historians looked down on these "dirty" records for many years, and some still do. It was only after the so-called sexual revolution of the '60s that critics realized it was okay to express sexual feelings, and started documenting such recordings in their surveys and biographies.

PAPA CHARLIE JACKSON was an early "hokum" performer who in 1925 recorded "Shave 'Em Dry" which many other artists re-recorded. BLIND BOY FULLER sang a classic, "What's That, Smells Like Fish?" and BO CARTER made a living recording dirty songs: "Banana In Your Fruit Basket," "Pig Meat Is What I Crave," "Pussy Cat Blues," "Ram Rod Daddy," "Pin In Your Cushion," "Let Me Roll Your Lemon," and others which leave little to the imagination! In describing the sex act I wouldn't exactly say he was "poetic," but at the least he was *inventive:* "If you don't want my peaches/Then please don't shake my tree/ And if you don't want me to have your potatoes/Then please don't mash my digger so deep." Great stuff!

Women blues singers were just as raunchy. MEMPHIS MINNIE, ETHEL WATERS, MA RAINEY, CLARA SMITH, LUCILLE BOGAN—almost all of the "greats" recorded dirty material. In 1935 Lucille Bogan did an incredible version of "Shave 'Em Dry":

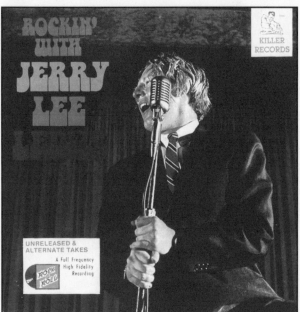

Front cover of *Rockin' with Jerry Lee Lewis*, Killer Records.

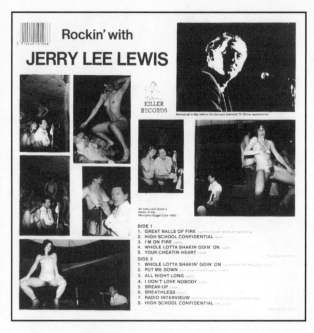

Back cover of *Rockin' with Jerry Lee Lewis*.
All colored photos taken at the Memphis Gigge Club, 1982.

"Now your nuts hang down like a damn bell clapper/ And your dick stands up like a steeple/Your goddamn asshole stands open like a church door/And the crabs walk in like people." She really cracks up trying to sing this verse—it sounds like she was having a lot of fun. I can imagine the chagrin "serious" blues scholars felt when, in their crusade to portray the blues as an "art form," they first heard this. It's art, all right, but on its own terms.

"Hot Nuts—Get 'Em From The Peanut Man" is an early dirty classic by GEORGIA WHITE. In the '60s, DOUG CLARK & The HOT NUTS used this as their theme song. In their performances they were famous for doing epic versions of this, inventing rhyme after rhyme: "You know that man called Mr Clean/He got his nuts caught in the washing machine." They were very popular on the Southern frat-house circuit, and released quite a few records which they sold at their live shows. On *Nuts To You* on the Gross Records label, their version of "Hot Nuts" lasts over 12 minutes. Other filthy chestnuts include "Ding-A-Ling" and "Two Old Maids."

♦ V: Were blues artists the only ones to get away with this?
♦ AE: They were the most prolific, but other musicians got into the act, too. In the '30s, a British orchestra named HARRY ROY & HIS BAT CLUB BOYS recorded "Pussy" in a straightforward, proper English style of delivery—yet obviously it's *not* about his girlfriend's pet. "Pussy, Pussy, Pussy" by the LIGHT CRUST DOUGHBOYS, a white country band from the '30s, is not only lewd but a hot tune to boot!

A lot of top '20s and '30s jazz musicians dabbled in dirty tunes—mostly as back-up accompanists to female singers. One of the best is Shirley Clay's "It's Too

Big, Papa"—the back-up band was CLAUDE HOPKINS' band ... Another party classic was BULLMOOSE JACKSON's "Big Ten Inch"—he's singing about his 10" 78rpm record, of course ... Another R&B classic of raunch was *Stoop Down Baby,* by CHICK WILLIS (not to be confused with Chuck Willis). In the Doug Clark tradition he sings plenty of dirty songs, and on the "Stoop Down" song he makes some nasty rhymes about the women in the audience. It's a live recording, and you can hear people screaming every

Jerry Lee Lewis was one of the wildest—he loved the old dirty blues and covered quite a few of them. In his live shows he could get really low-down and raunchy—check out the photos on this European LP. There are girls stripping on top of his piano while he plays! Records like these are a lot more fun to collect than stamps or door knobs.

time he does it—sounds like they're having much more fun than your average symphony audience. This was popular with the Southern beach crowd. Another recent hit was CLARENCE CARTER's "Strokin' "— about just what you think it's about. And in the reggae genre, LLOYDIE & The LOWBITES put out an incredibly filthy LP, *Censored!,* which includes songs like

"Free Grind Ticket," "Pussy To Kill You," "Bang Bang Lulu," etc.

♦ **V: These days people seem to be able to get away with anything—but it doesn't seem as much fun.**

♦ AE: I agree. Now so many bands are trying to out-gross and out-explicit each other, but there's very little wit. Back then, you had to be *clever* to get away with things, like JOHNNY BUCKET's rockin' rockabilly version of "Let Me Play With Your Poodle." This was a blues number; Tampa Red recorded the original in 1943, and years later LIGHTNIN' HOPKINS re-recorded it a couple times. It has lyrics like "Now your little poodle look kinda good to me/I wonder what it do with some home-fried meat." This was about the most suggestive rockabilly tune I know—even though rockabilly was often wild, it was mostly about getting on the radio and being the next Elvis . . . JERRY LEE LEWIS was one of the wildest—he loved the old dirty blues and covered quite a few of them. In his live shows he could get really low-down and raunchy—check out the photos on this European LP. There are girls stripping on top of his piano while he plays! Records like these are a lot more fun to collect than stamps or door knobs, I think.

♦ **V: What about drug references in music? What was going on before the psychedelic era?**

♦ AE: Back in '30s jazz, there were a lot of drug references. The crackdown on marijuana didn't come until the early '40s, so throughout the '30s almost every jazz hipster sang about getting high. In those days "jive" wasn't just a line of patter, it was a drug reference. CAB CALLOWAY sang "Are You Hep To The Jive," ANDY KIRK & His CLOUDS OF JOY did "All The Jive Is Gone," STUFF SMITH & His ONYX CLUB BOYS did "Here Comes The Man With The

If It Ain't A Hit, I'll Eat My . . ., Zu-Zazz Records. Album cover credits: jacket design: Clive Blewchamp.

Jive"—just to name a few. Another hip term was "viper": someone who smoked "tea" or pot. Along with the HARLEM HAMFATS, ROSETTA HOWARD did a great one: "If You're A Viper." Stuff Smith sang "You'se A Viper" and SIDNEY BECHET did "Viper Mad." Besides the entertainment value of the somewhat taboo subject matter, these are musically superb, too. In the '70s, STASH Records reissued a lot of LPs of songs dealing with sex and drugs (these are hard to find now), and hopefully all will be re-released on CD. In the '80s, the JASS label also put out a series of records like these.

♦ **V: There were also songs about hard drugs like heroin and cocaine—**

♦ AE: Sure, although not as many as the pot songs. Heroin didn't come into vogue with jazz musicians until the '40s. Probably the most famous drug tune of the '30s was done by Cab Calloway, who's still alive: "Kickin' The Gong Around": "It was down in China-town/All the cokies laid around . . . He was sweatin' cold and pale/He was looking for his frail/He was broke and all his junk ran out." Back in 1927 VICTORIA SPIVEY sang "Dope Head Blues": "Just give me one mo' sniffle/Another sniffle of that dope." Even before that, HAZEL MEYERS did a song (backed by Fletcher Henderson) called "Pipe Dream Blues," with amazing lyrics about a night in Chinatown: "Had a golden hop pipe in my hand/Owned a million dollars down in poppy-land." "Jerry The Junker" was a tune from 1934, done by CLARENCE WILLIAMS & His Orchestra—they tried to copy the druggy Cab Calloway style and did a pretty good job, too. Piano player CHAMPION JACK DUPREE did one of the most famous blues-and-drugs songs, "Junker's Blues." He had a strange singing style because he'd lost most of

New Jersey Burners, © 1987 Interstate Music Ltd. Album cover credits: sleeve design: Nigel Goodall/Artsleeves.

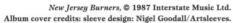

The Premiers' *Songs We Sang At San Quentin*, Calvary Records.

his teeth—it was hard to understand him. The funniest drug song was HARRY "The Hipster" GIBSON's "Who Put The Benzedrine In Mrs Murphy's Ovaltine?" (He also asks the musical question, "Who put the Nembutals in Mr Murphy's overalls?")

Like life, drugs are both fun and tragic, and often, one leads to the other. It's a great loss that talents like Charlie Parker, Art Pepper, Chet Baker, etc, burnt out so fast. For an account of the *lighter* side of drug use in jazz, read Mezz Mezzrow's *Really The Blues*.

♦ **V: You have a lot of '50s records; what are some of your strangest?**

Gustav Holst's *The Planets*, conducted by Sir Adrian Boult, Westminster Gold Series. Album cover credits: art direction: Peter Whorf, photography: Fred Poore, design: Keith Longino/See Hear! & How!

♦ AE: A lot of rockabilly records feature "hiccupping" vocals, and even though we take this for granted now, that's actually a very strange and recent innovation (when you survey the whole history of music). A guy named JOE WALLACE (looks like a regular Joe!) did an amazing song, "Leopard Man": "Oh, the old chief he was a real hep cat/On his head he wore a little red hat/Came up to me and I said, 'Wow/Get away from me, you dirty Mau Mau' "—not exactly PC, but what a delivery! Another incredible vocal performance is "Hot Lips Baby" by HERBIE DUNCAN, who was one of the best hiccuppers of all time, along with CHARLIE FEATHERS.

♦ **V: What are some good Charlie Feathers tunes?**

♦ AE: Classics include "One Hand Loose," "Stutterin' Cindy" and "Bottle To The Baby"—there are so many! It's hard to say who actually *invented* the hiccupping vocal style. Elvis was probably the first such vocalist to go "national," and probably other rockabilly cats heard it and thought, "If Elvis was successful with one hiccup, just imagine what six or seven would do!"

Another wild record fairly bursting with oinky sound effects is "Wild Hog Hop" by BENNY HESS—I guess I'm a sucker for sound effects, period. I'm sure that's an impersonation; they didn't go to the trouble of recording an authentic singing hog. Other great sound effects records include the various versions of "Chew Tobacco Rag," and of course, the legendary "Transfusion" by NERVOUS NORVUS . . . An example of over-the-top passion captured on vinyl is "Dateless Night" by ALLEN PAGE—he's a great singer, and his guitar really kicks into gear . . . There's blazing guitars mixed really hot on JOE CLAY's recordings, especially "Duck Tail"—Mickey "Guitar" Baker plays on some of those tracks. Recently some European rockabilly enthusiasts located Joe Clay; he was driving a school bus in Louisiana. They dusted him off and now he's playing regularly all over Europe, enjoying a second career.

There were a lot of red-hot instrumentals in rockabilly, and some are almost out of control, like "Ghost Train" by The SWANKS. It doesn't get much better than this . . . Here's a one-of-a-kind favorite, "Big Beat" by HOLLIS CHAMPION. He's hilarious; over a musical background he just laughs and shouts like the village idiot. I wouldn't call this "singing," but it's still outstanding. This is what was so great about the '50s: radio wasn't so tightly formatted and regulated like today. Back then, you could take your 45 around to almost any local station, give the deejay a fifth of liquor and he'd play your tune. A lot of these deejays were real characters—check out this reissue of a transcription recording by DEWEY PHILLIPS. When Elvis was just getting started, Dewey was the big-shot deejay in Memphis, and he talks so fast it's unbelievable, doing all these crazy voices . . . just total stream-of-consciousness. He *had* to have been on speed. I read somewhere that he turned Elvis on to "whites" that he

192

got from truck-drivers.

♦ **V: There's so many great little-known records; it's hard to know where to even begin—**

♦ AE: Unfortunately, a lot of European compilation reissues are spotty: a couple of great rockers, some good ones, and a few dogs. But I try to get them all anyway, because I would hate to miss even *one* great song! Fortunately, some of the U.S. labels are trying to release just the cream of the crop. I'd say, get all of the DESPERATE ROCK'N'ROLL series, the SIN ALLEY set, the STRUMIN' MENTAL series for hot instrumentals, and the STOMPIN' and DANGEROUS DOO WOPS reissues for great black rockers. Also, the SAVAGE KICK LPs—there's about 7 volumes out so far. These are starting to come out on CD now, so the youngsters can hear what *real* rockin' was like. Actually, the CHIEF label from Europe has released very good rockabilly CDs. Unlike the BEAR FAMILY label (Germany), they didn't exactly care about making an orderly historical presentation—they just threw together all the best rockers: 30 tracks per disc! A lot of these are available from Midnight Records in New York City, a good source.

The funniest drug song was Harry "The Hipster" Gibson's "Who Put The Benzedrine In Mrs Murphy's Ovaltine?" He also asks the musical question, "Who put the Nembutals in Mr Murphy's overalls?"

A lot of the best rockabilly magazines are *British*—they're really into doing thorough research behind the artists and labels of the '50s. *New Kommotion, Now Dig This,* and *Rock Street Journal* all cover rock'n'roll and rockabilly in much more depth than any American magazine. They can be a bit dry, especially if you're used to Billy Miller and Miriam Linna's *KICKS* (which *is* great), but they're a good source of information. England has some of the best magazines in other fields, too, like *Hillbilly Researcher,* which covers Western Swing, boppin' hillbilly and boogie; *Rhythm And Blues And The Gospel Truth* which covers R&B and gospel; and *Juke Blues,* which covers Blues and R&B. There used to be a lot of good blues magazines (like *Blues Unlimited)* over there, too, but they aren't around much anymore. For '60s garage punk, you have to keep your eyes peeled; there are a lot of interesting U.S. 'zines but they disappear fast, like *Creampuff War* (2 issues). Tom Tourville has been doing a series of amazing discographies on Midwest garage sounds.

In all of these styles of music, you can make your

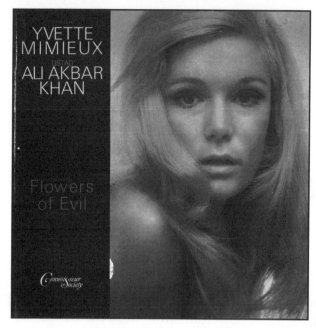

Baudelaire's *Flowers of Evil,* narrated by Yvette Mimieux, original music composed and performed by Ali Akbar Khan, Connoisseur Society.

own incredible discoveries. Some hillbilly walks into a small studio, cuts an amazing rockabilly record, then disappears off the face of the earth—the same is true of a '60s punk band, or an R&B singer. I hate music critics who seem incapable of considering anybody but the biggest names in the genre—I like Elvis and Little Richard too, but they were all beaten at their own game more than once. When you read these pathetic rock'n'roll "histories" that come out every year, they just perpetuate the idea that rockabilly or '60s punk or *whatever* was just worth a chapter. As you can see and hear, they're dead wrong!

Wanda Jackson's *Right or Wrong,* Capitol Records.

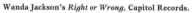

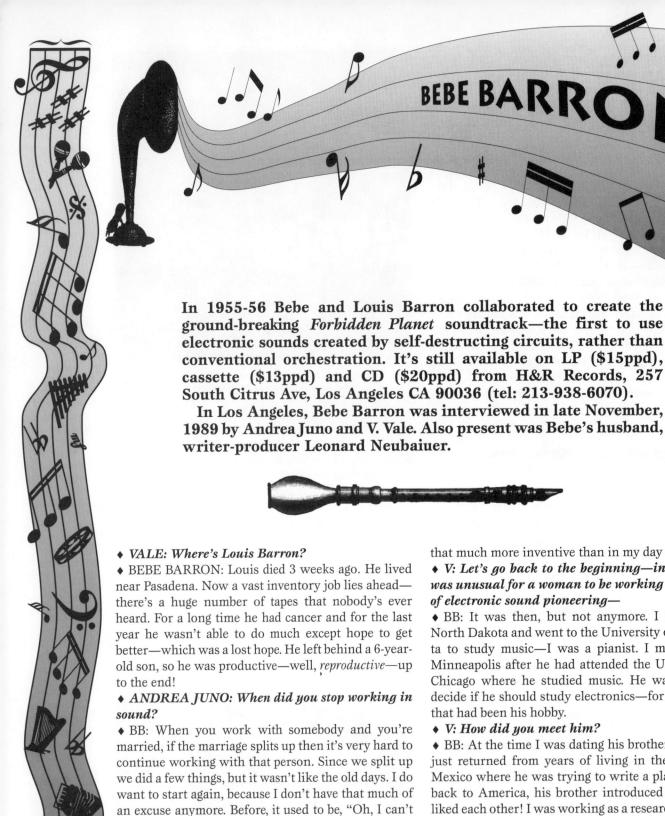

BEBE BARRON

In 1955-56 Bebe and Louis Barron collaborated to create the ground-breaking *Forbidden Planet* soundtrack—the first to use electronic sounds created by self-destructing circuits, rather than conventional orchestration. It's still available on LP ($15ppd), cassette ($13ppd) and CD ($20ppd) from H&R Records, 257 South Citrus Ave, Los Angeles CA 90036 (tel: 213-938-6070).

In Los Angeles, Bebe Barron was interviewed in late November, 1989 by Andrea Juno and V. Vale. Also present was Bebe's husband, writer-producer Leonard Neubaiuer.

♦ *VALE: Where's Louis Barron?*

♦ BEBE BARRON: Louis died 3 weeks ago. He lived near Pasadena. Now a vast inventory job lies ahead—there's a huge number of tapes that nobody's ever heard. For a long time he had cancer and for the last year he wasn't able to do much except hope to get better—which was a lost hope. He left behind a 6-year-old son, so he was productive—well, *reproductive*—up to the end!

♦ *ANDREA JUNO: When did you stop working in sound?*

♦ BB: When you work with somebody and you're married, if the marriage splits up then it's very hard to continue working with that person. Since we split up we did a few things, but it wasn't like the old days. I do want to start again, because I don't have that much of an excuse anymore. Before, it used to be, "Oh, I can't get Louis to work on *anything*," but now that excuse is gone! So I'm starting to fool around with some of the new technology. In a way I'm still back in the '50s.

♦ *V: Some of the new technology makes things easier—*

♦ BB: Those emulators are so wonderful. But . . . have you heard anything that really excites you? That's what bothers me—people just seem to be interested in the *equipment* and what you can do with the technology. But somehow the *end product* doesn't seem to be

that much more inventive than in my day . . .

♦ *V: Let's go back to the beginning—in the '50s it was unusual for a woman to be working in the field of electronic sound pioneering—*

♦ BB: It was then, but not anymore. I grew up in North Dakota and went to the University of Minnesota to study music—I was a pianist. I met Louis in Minneapolis after he had attended the University of Chicago where he studied music. He was trying to decide if he should study electronics—for a long time that had been his hobby.

♦ *V: How did you meet him?*

♦ BB: At the time I was dating his brother. Louis had just returned from years of living in the jungles of Mexico where he was trying to write a play. He came back to America, his brother introduced us, and we liked each other! I was working as a researcher for *Life* magazine, and in 1948 I quit my job, we got married and moved to Monterey, California. For a wedding present a German friend gave us one of the first tape recorders imported into this country. It was the same model Hitler had used to record his speeches, so that if something happened to him people might think he was still alive.

Immediately we became aware of the possibilities. We did the usual experiments: slowing the tapes down, running them backwards, and adding echo. Louis start-

Bebe & Louis Barron, c. 1955

ed building circuits to make sound—ohmigod, every move took forever, but it was *so* exciting!

Then around 1950 we moved to Greenwich Village, New York. The scene there was amazing; all the artists would meet and discuss what they were doing and encourage one another—that was the most wonderful era which a friend of mine, John Gruen, has documented in his book, *The Party's Over Now*. We used to go to what was called the "Artists' Club." Every type of artist went—all the visual artists of the time like Pollock; filmmakers; architects; musicians like Ned Rorem; and that's where we met JOHN CAGE. Soon afterward Cage called us and said he'd just gotten a big grant to investigate the relationship of music and sound, and would we like to work with David Tudor and him? Of course we said yes, and for the next year we worked with him making recordings and doing editing—we also worked on our own projects. That was the most magical year.

♦ *V: People were rebelling against all the old musical forms and theories—*

♦ BB: That's right. The only musicians who were working along the same lines as us were the *musique concrète* people from France who recorded natural sounds and processed them. We were concentrating on generating purely electronic sounds; we used *only* electronics to create the music. Whereas they would use *existing* sounds which they would then process, splice

together, and compose.

At that time things were quite different than now. Louis was always a frustrated engineer—he loved electronics—so he would build circuits that were influenced by the cybernetic theories of Norbert Weiner. Nobody had thought of employing these circuits to create music or sounds. Cybernetic theory held that the identical laws applied to humans, other life forms, and even some types of machines. Louis took some of these circuits and adapted them to produce sound, and out would come funny patterns of sounds which we would amplify and record. It was strange—they would seem to have a beginning of their own, and then we would change them by giving them more or less wattage—we used very primitive ways to bring about change. The sounds would seem to get wildly excited on their own, and then die down. And you could never revive them again! It was like watching a primitive life form come into existence and then fade away—we really started thinking of them that way.

We were also very involved with Cinema 16, founded by Amos and Marsha Vogel, and we began doing the scores for a lot of avant-garde or underground films. Maya Deren formed a foundation for experimental films, and Louie and I, Clement Greenberg and Joseph Campbell were on the board. We have a tape from a party we gave that Joe Campbell came to—he brought his banjo and sang all these songs from his high school

and college days. That tape is priceless, because people think of him as a somber man—but he was really fun. At dinner he was very witty.

♦ *V: What films did you work on?*

♦ BB: We did two films with Anaïs Nin and her husband, Ian Hugo—later she was to became a famous novelist and diarist. The films were *The Bells of Atlantis* and *Jazz of Lights*. We did a film called *Miramagic* with Walter Lewisohn (of the family that owned Lewisohn stadium), and we did a film with Maya Deren. Maya was a good friend of mine, and I was also good friends with Teiji Ito, her husband who died in Haiti under very mysterious circumstances. Nobody knows what exactly happened, but he went swimming in a heavily voodoo-dominated area and then came out and died. He was only 47 years old.

Now there are several biographies on Maya Deren, and reading them I realize that her life really was divided up into periods. In the first period (until she was 22) she was very political—I didn't even know this. She was an anarchist, a Communist—she became involved in all those movements. In the next period she immersed herself in the arts, expressing herself primarily through poetry and writing. Back in the "classical" days of psychoanalysis, her father was a well-known psychoanalyst and these theories, which at the time were fresh, definitely inspired her work. Then she began making underground films, and finally became heavily involved in the investigation of voodoo.

I knew Maya Deren years ago. In 1959 I was pregnant with my son, Adam, and she gave me the most unbelievable baby shower (the shower to end all showers). The guest list read like a real *Who's Who* of the avant-garde artistic world. Cecile Star, the film critic for the *Nation,* was there. So was Hella Hammond (a famous photographer and filmmaker who was married to the filmmaker Sasha Hammond)—she was also one of Maya's lovers. The whole circle was quite sophisticated sexually. Also in attendance was the filmmaker Shirley Clarke, who at the time lived in New York at the Chelsea Hotel—we did sound for an experimental film by her titled *Bridges.* There were all these primitive masks, drums and ritual objects everywhere, and led by Maya, everyone was swaying and doing this Haitian voodoo chanting, and I started giving birth right on the spot, early! The birth turned out to be a complicated breech birth, so I had to be rushed to the hospital where they gave me a Caesarean. Anaïs Nin wrote about this in one of her diaries. I loved Maya, but I was also a bit scared of her; she was an overpowering woman. I guess I didn't want to disappoint her—so I obliged her.

♦ *AJ: Do you think the voodoo incantations hastened the birth?*

♦ BB: I think so. Maya served us this weird drink she had brought back from Haiti—it was some kind of liqueur with tree branches in it. For years it had been ripening or fermenting. Right away it made me feel very good—and very strange. I firmly believe that had something to do with it, and also the chanting—there was such an intense collective energy emanating from the group. I believe in that sort of thing.

There's a book called *Anaïs* by Noël Riley Fitch that's just full of fascinating little anecdotes, including this birth.

♦ *V: I read that Anaïs Nin wasn't really like her diaries—*

♦ BB: Oh yes she was. One of her husbands, Rupert Pole, is still alive and lives in Los Angeles—I see him from time to time.

♦ *V: Can you tell us more about JOHN CAGE?*

♦ BB: Those memories are the foggiest of all. The one thing I do remember about that year with John Cage is: it turned into a kind of cooking contest! We would work all day and whoever was the host-of-the-day would come up with some unbelievable gourmet treat. We all tried to outdo everybody else.

♦ *V: That's great—rather than just working on a music or sound project—*

♦ BB: Well, that was typical of John—he included the whole world in his realm of art. He was so great to work with; he really was. He had us make all these sound recordings (which today would be called samples) and categorize them eight ways: natural sounds, country sounds, city sounds, electronic sounds, voices, small sounds (like striking a match), etc. Then, of course, we spent immeasurable amounts of time cutting them up into little, tiny, tiny pieces of different shapes, like triangles. I doubt if anybody ever "heard" all that went into the work, but *John* knew it was there.

♦ *V: About working with Cage, Louis is quoted as saying [article by Ted Greenwald in* **Keyboard,** *Feb '86], "You realize you don't have to be restricted by the traditions or the so-called 'laws' of music. So we began exploring, and I began developing those circuits."*

♦ BB: That, of course, is what John was so wonderful for: he really gave everybody the freedom to do what they wanted . . . to drop all the conventions and rules and do their "own thing." Well—to a *point* that was true. But then he got annoyed because we took off on our own! [laughs]

♦ *V: Yes, you always have to break away from your teachers. So John Cage paid part of your rent while you were working with him—*

♦ BB: For a year. And this enabled us to really start our *own* work. Cage would bring all these fabulous composers from Europe into our studio: Pierre Boulez, Stockhausen, plus lots of American composers like Lou Harrison. EDGAR VARESE spent a lot of time at our place; we were the only ones who had a real studio for doing this sort of thing. We never met Pierre Schaeffer or Pierre Henry, but we wrote a lot of letters back and forth to Paris. We were all wildly enthusiastic about what we were doing, and at that point none of these people were famous.

At this time Vladimir Ussachevsky and Otto Luening were teaching at Columbia; they worked together and separately on electronic pieces. After he broke off working with Luening, Ussachevsky went on to do a lot. Luening was pretty old when electronics came into the picture, so I don't think he got a chance to do a whole lot more. But they were both very important.

♦ **V: Did you do any other film soundtracks between 1948-1953?**

♦ BB: There was a Maya Deren film, *The Very Eye of Night.* There was a film on Greek art, whose title I have forgotten, by Lewis Jacobs, who was very big in the documentary film scene. Then we did a film with Ed Emshwiller that was really beautiful; it had dance, flashing strobe effects and a rose, and was just gorgeous. We did the soundtrack for a film called *Crystals* (about the growing of crystals) which one of the huge corporations commissioned. We also did a soundtrack for IBM when they first introduced their line of computers.

♦ **V: Did you make a lot of commercials?**

♦ BB: No, we turned down all kinds of commercials—like fools. I don't know why we did; the money was so marvelous. Louie had this theory that "We shouldn't do commercials; it would demean the music." We just did one commercial for the Ford Fairlane.

♦ **V: Back in 1954, how did you get the opportunity to do the soundtrack for Forbidden Planet?**

♦ BB: It was so weird—the way that happened sounds like something you'd read in a fan magazine of the day. We read in the paper that Dore Schary (whose films we liked a lot—at the time he was the head of MGM) was coming to town, and his wife was going to host an art exhibit at a gallery in New York. We decided to crash the opening and introduce ourselves to him—and we did! We didn't know what he looked like or anything, but Louis said, "Look for the least pretentious-looking guy in the whole bunch—I'll bet you anything that'll be Dore Schary."

Metro-Goldwyn-Mayer's *Forbidden Planet* soundtrack, electronic music by Louis & Bebe Barron, © 1956 MGM Inc. Album cover credits: cover painting & art direction: Renate Druks.

There was this man standing in back of everybody—very simply-dressed, all by himself, very unassuming—and we went up and asked if he were Dore Schary. He said, "Yes." Right then and there we started telling him, "We're doing electronic music," and he asked, "What's that?" We told him that it was music that comes out of electronic circuits, that there were no conventional instruments involved, and that we had done a few experimental film soundtracks, and that we'd love to give him a demonstration. Meeting him, it all seemed too easy! (Later on I read his autobiography and discovered that at the time we met him, he'd just initiated an "Open Door" policy at MGM to try to discover new talent.) Anyway, he said, "Sure—anytime you come to Los Angeles, give me a call. I'll be waiting for you." So two weeks later we *shot* down to Los Angeles (my parents lived there), called his number and got right through to him! He asked, "Would you like to come over this afternoon to MGM?" It was unbelievable—a lot of people had been trying to get to him for years and he wouldn't see them. But now he was trying to show the world that he really encouraged new talent. Our timing was absolutely perfect—that's all I can say.

When we went to see him, we brought with us all

Bebe & Louis Barron, c. 1955

the films we'd scored, but he didn't want to see any of them—he just wanted to hear our *music* and form his own mental associations. So we played the soundtrack to *Bells of Atlantis* and we played something we'd done for a pantomime group, the American Mime Theater. He asked, "Do you have any commitments?" and we said, "No," and he said, "Would you like to work on a film?" It all happened just like *that*. (Again, I've heard of people trying for years just to get their music heard.) Immediately he signed us to a contract, sent us down to meet the head of the music department, Johnny Green, who had a "music run" with us just as if what we were doing was conventional music. And that was very helpful, because we were able to understand the feeling he was trying to evoke with each scene; the feeling behind the music. We wanted to add an *additional dimension . . .*

We were given the assignment to score twenty minutes of film, but we didn't know how we were going to do this, as our studio was in New York and the film was in Los Angeles. Of course they wanted us to work in L.A., but we didn't think that was possible, so they ended up giving us a workprint of the film. We took it back to New York and periodically returned to Hollywood to show them what we were coming up with. They liked it so much that they gave us an hour and ten minutes of scoring to do.

At first they were going to use Harry Partch, whom I thought was a great composer. He divided up the scale into (I believe) 48 notes—the tiniest little tones; you could barely distinguish between them, but they formed some fascinating harmonies. Also, he invented a host of wonderful instruments to play his music; his whole musical universe was just beautiful. I think his music has become even more important since he died.

Anyway, MGM had a hard time making up their minds whether it would be Harry Partch doing the film, or us, or conventional music with conventional sound effects—it was a real mess. We were capable of doing (and did) things that could have been considered conventional sound effects; we did scoring; we did "source music" (if you're watching a movie and see somebody put the needle down on a record, what you hear next is called source music); we did all these things . . . but for *Forbidden Planet* we just tossed convention aside, forgot about all that, and just did what we wanted to do. And it *worked*. To some people the movie was confusing, and to tell you the truth it was confusing to me, too. But now it's considered a classic—a lot of people love it. But you know, they pulled the most interesting content out of the film because they felt their audience wouldn't understand it!

♦ **V: They "dumbed it down"?**

♦ BB: It was very Freudian, and that's where they got into trouble—they started "simplifying" it. They removed all the details that made sense about the id (monsters from the id), and what they ended up with was oversimplified and confusing. I still have a 16mm workprint of the film which has all the *original* material. In the future I think we'll donate it to a film archive.

♦ **V: How did they oversimplify the story?**

♦ BB: It was based on the idea that there are real monsters or demons inside us that we aren't aware of, that under the right circumstances can surge to the surface and make us do the most horrific, destructive things. On the planet which the astronauts discover, Alta's power over the animals was based on the unicorn legend—that only a virgin can tame one, and this myth is mentioned in the original script. It was even given a "scientific" explanation: that the brain sends out electronic impulses that are monitored by the glandular system, and conceivably it could send out resonances which would soothe the reflex patterns of a wild animal. But lines like these were eliminated out of fear that the audience couldn't "understand," or that they slowed down the action.

We were supposed to be doing monster music, and we did come up with some horrible, terrible-sounding stuff—the worst sounds we could coax out of our circuits to show how horrible this monster was. Later when we created the monster's footsteps, we did something totally different. The first monster was sound effects; the second monster was a combination sound effects and underscoring. Unofficially, we were combining the jobs of the sound department, the special effects department, and the music department—although we weren't allowed to call what we did "music"; the musicians' union which was very powerful in those days. So instead of the credits reading "electronic music" [by the Barrons], they read "electronic *tonalities.*" That way the musicians union wouldn't sue.

♦ **AJ: How did people respond?**

♦ BB: The critics raved about it—they really loved it. What we did worked very well with the film. People would come up after screenings and say, "It sounds like my wildest dreams!" If Johnny Green said, "I want this scene to have sweet love music with strings," well, we certainly couldn't do *that,* but we brought him what *we* thought was love music, and that's what it sounded like to other people, too. I thought what we achieved was remarkable, considering the technology of the day. The musical themes we came up with seemed to have a sort of universal appeal; they sounded "right" to people. Those circuits really could express a full range of emotions, and we treated each little theme like a *character* rather than a musical theme, because that was how we liked to work. It was more fun to build a circuit, activate it, and *personify* it (we had a pretty good idea of whether the sound would be ugly or beautiful-sounding; whether it would sound jagged or smooth and quite pretty. Although . . . in those days it was hard to do pretty things; it was

much easier to do ugly things.

After we got everything set up, we would tape all the sounds that poured out of those little circuits. Then we would start processing them, and *that* was where our most creative efforts were called for. We would work night and day taking these sounds and transforming them. Laboriously we were composing and producing large-scale overall patterns of sounds, and by the time we'd gotten through with something, we'd look back and realize we'd been working for *months* . . .

♦ **AJ: What is sound "processing"?**

♦ BB: In those days, the technology was so elementary. For example, the original sound that produced the monster's footsteps was slowed down 100 times. And to do this we had to take a 15-inch-per-second tape and run it at 7-1/2 ips, re-record it, and keep on doing this. And by the time we finished, the noise level had become really high . . . but that was the only way we could do it. Sometimes to change the tape speed we would build up the size of the capstan. The technology was pathetically simple, but we did get some remarkable sounds—I still am not sure *how!* I developed a pretty good ear; I could listen to sound that seemed like pure gibberish and *know* that if we worked on it long enough, something musical would emerge. If you could hear the *original* stuff that came out of our monster circuit, you would just be amazed—it sounded like computer noise with no form whatsoever, just lots of little tinkling sounds. Yet . . . as you slowed it down, you began to hear lots of little harmonies in it, rhythmic patterns and even melodies. The sounds that the circuits themselves produced were infinitely more interesting than anything we tried to "compose." Even if we deliberately began with a preconceived musical theme, it would never seem to be as interesting as what the circuits themselves generated.

♦ **AJ: The machine seemed to have a creative soul—**

♦ BB: Exactly. We explored the idea that we didn't want to control the circuits. Whereas everyone nowadays is obsessed with control—just the opposite of our approach. I'm trying to think of who I really love in contemporary electronic music—it's hard to think of *anybody* who really thrills me.

♦ **AJ: You worked with the concept of giving up the control and letting that spontaneity emerge—**

♦ BB: It's like we were the directors, but the circuits were the actors. It was much more complex than merely composing note-by-note. I mean, we *can* do it that way, but we didn't want to. And I think that's why some of the sounds on *Forbidden Planet* are so different and unusual. Nevertheless, John Cage declared that we were "disgustingly orchestral and musical" in our approach—which was amazing because actually we had *less* control; we didn't want the control and in fact had rejected the control—yet it came out sounding "musical." And I never could understand how that happened, yet it did sound quite musical in many

ways—much more so than John Cage's music!

♦ **V:** *A* **strange** **collaboration** *between man and machine—*

♦ BB: I often thought that it might be wonderful if we could combine the technology we had in those days with the new technology—combine the best of both. Although—I don't know if the circuits would ever come to life again, and unfortunately when Louis died, he took the "key" to the circuits with him. I just don't know that much about electronics; I wish I did.

Norbert Wiener's *The Human Use of Human Beings* was published in 1951. Mimicking those experiments done to animals to put them into a state of stress, we would do basically the same things to these circuits, and you could hear them *literally* shrieking! It was like they were alive, and with a lifespan of their own. What we did was pretty elementary: we would attach resistors and capacitors to activate these circuits (obviously, we were changing the resistance) and negative and positive feedback was involved—Wiener talks about all that. The same conditions that would produce breakdowns and malfunctions in machines, made for some wonderful music. The circuits would have a "nervous breakdown," and afterwards they would be very relaxed, and it all came through in the sounds they generated.

♦ *AJ:* *A friend who worked in a record store told us that in the '70s he would play Philip Glass and people would become hostile—even angry. They weren't used to the sounds; the music was too discordant to them. Whereas now, that same music is used for Bank of America commercials. It's like: our brains have been modified; nobody considers this jarring anymore.*

♦ BB: Philip Glass to me sounds like pop music. Steve Reich, that whole gang, in a way sound very simplistic to me—

♦ *V:* *They ripped off gamelan music principles and substituted electronic instrument voicings—*

♦ BB: Exactly. I first heard Philip Glass at the Roxy Theater on Sunset Boulevard, and I feel that's where it belongs! It doesn't really *belong* in a concert hall; I've heard it there and it sounds ridiculously out of place—like light classical music. Oh well—it's fun and people love it.

♦ *V:* *Your music has a much wider, more complex range of emotion—*

♦ BB: That's what we wanted. But that's not what Philip Glass is after. Maybe it's not fair to judge him.

♦ *V:* *In* **Forbidden Planet,** *it's interesting that on this microcosm, this miniature planet, the father's unconscious (or id) which involves his unresolved lust toward his own daughter, triggers the cataclysms that threaten to destroy everything—*

♦ BB: The film originally had a lot of really brilliant content; it was based on Shakespeare's *The Tempest.* What happened when the daughter lost her innocence?—all hell broke loose on the planet. The mad,

ego-driven scientist who is unconscious of his own destructive, twisted sexuality—this psychological content was very powerful. But unfortunately they really did mess it all up.

♦ *V:* *By the way,* **Time** *magazine did an obituary on the Russian inventor of the theremin who died in 1993. Mistakenly, they credited him with doing the soundtrack for* **Forbidden Planet!** *. . . Did you ever put out any records?*

Have you heard anything new that really excites you? That's what bothers me—people just seem to be interested in the *equipment* and what you can do with the technology. But somehow the *end product* doesn't seem to be that much more inventive than in my day . . .

♦ BB: Beginning in 1949, Louis and I recorded a series of records of authors reading their own work, and the first person we approached was Anaïs Nin, because we loved her writing. We made the records look almost like books; they were bound very simply and printed in gold. The records were pressed on beautiful red vinyl—gorgeous!

♦ *V:* *Where did this happen?*

♦ BB: When we were first married, Louie and I moved to Monterey, California (before we moved to San Francisco, and then New York), and that's where we met Anais Nin. We read in the newspaper that she was giving a lecture, so we called her on the telephone and asked, "Can we record it?" She was very nice, very generous, and said, "Sure! Be here at such-and-such a time." Hers was the first to be released on our *Sound Portraits* label, and the records became instant collector's items. They were fabulous records. But we were a little ahead of our time; neither the bookshops nor the record shops would carry them; there was no real market yet. Gotham Bookmart carried them—but unfortunately they never paid us. We simply weren't able to continue.

♦ *V:* *You anticipated the talking book market. What was on the Anais Nin record—this lecture?*

♦ BB: No; we ended up recording her at her home in San Francisco. She read selections from *Under a Glass Bell* and *House of Incest,* and she recorded with Josephine Premice (who was a singer, drummer, and dancer) playing voodoo drums. Anais's husband did a beautiful engraving for the cover.

♦ *V:* *What did you do when you moved to San*

Francisco from Monterey?

♦ BB: I had a job as head of the office for *Coronet* magazine. I finally got fed up with this—I would go off to work at some ungodly hour while Louie would sleep. He was totally a night person; he never went to bed until four in the morning. We were very, very poor, so we didn't do a lot of things because we just plain didn't have the money. We didn't know many people, but we were involved with a woman named Ruth Witt-Diamant and her poetry scene.

Then we recorded Henry Miller. I think Anais made an introduction for us, and we asked if we could record him. We recorded him at Nepenthe in Big Sur. He read from his works and also spoke extemporaneously; he was very good. After recording him, we had dinner and he regaled us with tales of living in Paris—the life of the artist.

♦ *V: I hope somebody re-releases these someday—*

♦ BB: Lots of people have asked, but it's a big problem coping with the legality. Everybody's dead now, and you have to deal with the estates and heirs—it may not be worth it.

♦ *V: How did you happen to record Aldous Huxley?*

♦ BB: We had moved to 9 West 8th Street in New York. His kids were very good friends of ours—that's how we made contact, and he was very nice about reading for us. I can't remember if he spoke extemporaneously, but he was lovely. We recorded him when we made a trip to Los Angeles from New York.

♦ *V: How did you record Tennessee Williams?*

♦ BB: James Herlihy, who wrote a lot of good plays and novels including *Midnight Cowboy* and *Blue Denim*, was a close friend of Anais, and he was also a close friend of Tennessee Williams. He introduced us to Tennessee, and we recorded him when he came up from Florida to New York. That was our fourth and last record; after that we went bust.

♦ *V: How do you support yourself now?*

♦ BB: I had a counseling job at UCLA, but I quit and am again devoting time to music. Recently I broke down and purchased some equipment: a Tascam 388 Studio 8 mixer and a Roland JD-800 synthesizer keyboard—I got it because it's both digital and analog; it's really for people who hate digital. So far I don't find myself coming up with any brilliant thoughts; I think I sound just like everybody else—which to me is the anathema of all time! But I have begun to experiment toward the goal of putting out a new record incorporating our sound with new technology. I always go to new music concerts; I have to keep my ear to the ground.

♦ *V: What does your husband do for a living?*

♦ BB: My husband, Leonard Neubaiuer, is a writer, and it's really kinda sad that one can't write what one wants to.

♦ LEONARD NEUBAIUER: The power structure can't see that its own self-interest lies in maintaining the purchasing power of the beaten-down. As work becomes less and less important in the scheme of things, they're still trying to maintain a system where if you don't work, you don't *get*—you die. They can't face the fact that soon, they're basically going to have to *give* the stuff away. I think there *is* plenty of work to be done in this world—plenty that's not being done, and that we think we can't afford to do (for example, educating our children and taking care of our old people) but we have an incredible waste going on: giving purchasing power to lawyers, stockbrokers and other people who really don't *accomplish* anything. The system's top-heavy and the greed is so overpowering—the waste is overwhelming. And the Eastern Bloc people who have been beaten down by very much the same type of special privilege existing here (of the top-dogs)—they're going to find out that capitalism is not going to give them much of a lift.

♦ *AJ: Yes; all this gives "revolution" a bad name. They've become voracious, materialistic people—*

♦ LN: And they're voracious for things that aren't particularly of value to them: television, VCRs, jeans—it's all image rather than reality, for a world tied into symbols rather than reality. Whenever anyone burns the American flag, conservatives raise a big stink—meanwhile the U.S. is crapping up the landscape—the whole world.

♦ *V: Tell us about your background—*

♦ LN: I'm probably one of the oldest continuously-working people in the film business. I started at Warners in the '30s as a messenger boy, then I did publicity—I did the publicity for Bette Davis in *Dangerous*. I did trailers for all those wonderful Warners pictures and musicals; then I was at Metro. I also wrote a couple of "B" pictures (one was called *Fugitive from Justice*). Ronald Reagan used to do the narrations for me. I did "B" and "A" movies, did a lot of Cagneys—there were so many tremendous pictures made in the '30s. Later on I did the trailers for a lot of Howard Hawks' movies. During the fabulous '50s I worked for Paramount on films like *Sunset Boulevard* and *Lost Weekend* with people like DeMille, Crosby, Hope, etc. I also worked for a company called National Screen Service which did a lot of these trailers; I did the trailer for the first *Fly*, all the Lippard pictures . . .

♦ *V: Trailers are an art form in themselves; in fact, there are video-compilations available through mail order. A lot of them are more exciting than the original films—*

♦ LN: You can compress a lot into a trailer. Recently, in two months I made 16 trailers for European art films that appeal to a homosexual audience—some very good homoerotic pictures that never saw the light of day here. The best was *Hidden Pleasures*, by an Italian director, E. Iglesias.

I've made literally thousands of trailers; I did all the Allied Artists pictures; I wrote the script for a Russ Meyer picture called *Blacksnake*, and scripted another cult film titled *New Year's Evil*. I wrote a documentary

Louise Huebner's *Seduction Through Witchcraft,* Warner Bros.-Seven Arts Records, Inc. Cybernetic music by Louis and Bebe Barron. Album cover credits: cover photo: Jerry White, art direction: Ed Thrasher.

on Marc Chagall that won the Academy Award. I've written a number of scripts, and I've got one now that's on the theme of taking the profit out of drugs: *Money To Burn.* Another script being produced now is *Bob's Ticket To Hell.* It's about a guy who tries to fight a parking ticket and winds up in jail.

♦ BB: He's trying to do the same thing you are: *sneak* his philosophy into a commercial script! And that's very hard to do . . . and keep on doing. But we all have to keep going; we can't give up. Not yet.

Money is to Burn.

PARTIAL RESUME: LOUIS & BEBE BARRON

Collaborated with John Cage in a foundation-sponsored project to investigate further the relationship of Music and Sound.

Composed first all-electronic motion-picture score for the experimental film, *Bells of Atlantis,* produced by Ian Hugo.

Composed "For an Electronic Nervous System, No. 1" for the Illinois Festival of Contemporary Arts.

Score for experimental film, *Miramagic,* produced by Walter Lewisohn.

Score for "Legend," produced by American Mime Theatre.

Aaron Copland presented Barrons' Electronic Music at first concert of B. de Rothschild Foundation for the Arts and Sciences.

Composed full-length electronic sound-score for MGM film, *Forbidden Planet,* the first time a Hollywood feature was scored entirely in the electronic medium. Received nomination for Academy Award.

Score for experimental film, *Jazz of Lights,* produced by Ian Hugo.

Composed electronic themes for George Axelrod's Broadway production of Gore Vidal's comedy, "Visit to a Small Planet."

Composed electronic sound-score for *Ballet* in the Standard Oil TV spectacular produced by Paul Feigay.

Score for experimental film, *Bridges,* produced by Shirley Clarke for presentation at Brussel's Worlds Fair.

Commissioned by General Dynamics Corp. to compose "Music of Tomorrow" to activate system of colored lights.

Invited to participate in Festival de la Recherche presented by Radiodiffusion Television in Paris.

Composed electronic themes for Broadway musical, "The Happiest Girl In the World," directed by Cyril Ritchard.

Composed cybernetic score for Louise Huebner's *Seduction Through Witchcraft* album.

Composed electronic tonalities for John Houseman's production of "The Chinese Wall" directed by Norman Corwin.

Scored Ford Fairlane commercial for J. Walter Thompson.

Guest lectures at New School for Social Research, United Nations, Brooklyn Art Museum, University of Minnesota, Los Angeles City College, Cal Arts, and UCLA.

QUOTATIONS

The following quotations are excerpted from liner notes.

♪♪♪♪♪

Daniel Wildman's "Bees on Horseback" act: it is difficult to visualize the act in detail, but his face was a crawling mask of bees while he performed horseback feats and fired pistols, starting orders which orchestrated the movements of other bees. Pause and brood over the possibilities and audience risks. Blue, plastered and disillusioned, Wildman evaporates into the haze.—**Charles Harris, "Islington"**

♪♪♪♪♪

A woman's passions . . . violent, anguished, poignant, ecstatic . . . are eternally fascinating. Here Les Baxter expresses them in richly orchestrated music, using as an instrument the remarkably sensitive voice of Bas Sheva—a voice whose vivid colorations range from the guttural snarl of savagery to a delicate and lyric beauty.—**liner notes, Les Baxter's** *The Passions* **featuring Bas Sheva**

♪♪♪♪♪

After much research and experimentation, Jim Fassett and Mortimer Goldberg developed means whereby actual symphonic orchestration could be achieved by utilizing the fabulous range of varied bird calls . . . Through a very long and tedious process of editing thousands of feet of tape and then re-recording selected passages, they succeeded, finally, in selecting the basic "orchestra." They found that by re-recording a few notes of a bird call over and over at various speeds (thus raising or lowering the tone) and then superimposing this range of sounds upon itself, they could achieve effects similar to a choir of woodwinds, strings, or brass instruments playing together.—**liner notes, Jim Fassett's** *Symphony of the Birds* **(early '50s)**

♪♪♪♪♪

The voices of ten birds and six frogs are heard on this record at their natural speed; then some are slowed down as much as eight times. Some of the melodies that result have an unearthly beauty; others are weird and strange. But their fascination is unique; everyone agrees that here are the sounds of nature as they have never been heard before.—**liner notes, James H. Fassett's** *Music and Bird Songs*

♪♪♪♪♪

This album is an emotional experience. It creates vision for the inner eye as well as music to the ear. We have taken the Pavlovian concept of reflexes a step further and applied it to the inner eye. This then becomes a matter of stimulated visual imagination. Music and effects will stimulate your emotions. The emotions will stimulate reflexes upon your imagination, which in turn will create the visual picture in your mind's eye . . . Make up your own storylines to the music and effects—just as your emotional reflexes dictate to your inner eye. Create your own mind-picture and play your own novel way of Charades. Try your friends. Test them and see how their mind-picture varies from your—or ours, for that matter. You may be amazed at your own visionary versatility.—**liner notes, Ray Martin's** *The Sound of Sight*

♪♪♪♪♪

Not satisfied with the world they have been born into, teenagers are no longer content to sit by and wait for things to happen. Unafraid, they group together into clubs, political parties and even mobs, and make themselves heard. From London to Tokyo, from Berkeley to Rome, the teenager carries his banners in defiance. *Ban the bomb! Make love not war! Freedom for four-letter words!* Fighting for big changes or little changes, the teenager is revolting against society . . . protest is the symbol of the "now" generation . . . for many, their badge of honor . . . Many try to pretend that teenage pregnancy, narcotic addiction, LSD, homosexuality, and prostitution do not affect young people. However, these subjects are common knowledge to teenagers.—**liner notes, Mike Curb's** *Teenage Rebellion* **(c.1967)**

♪♪♪♪♪

The *East Village Other* guides you through the inner sanctum of facts to a new level of consciousness. Evil?

Hardly. Disturbing? Yes. If your stomach is tied up in *symbolic knots* or your mind buried in the *materialistic mud* of utter confusion, then don't take this trip. But if you have a mind or even half a mind, then Turn On! Tune In! and delve into the depths of a culture's corrosion. Watch carefully, listen intently, for the movement is not a sleight-of-hand but the palsy of prophecy.—**liner notes by Allan Katzman,** *The East Village Other, Electric Newspaper* **(1966)**

♪♪♪♪♪

Finally we take off, our orbit fixed to Venus. We are welcomed to a new world, we sense a strangeness, an unknown mystery which can neither be defined nor spoken. It is like looking in a mirror and seeing, not ourselves, but an endless succession of other mirrors in which nothing is reflected but thin air and hazy dreams. Here we stand on the brink of timelessness, here we feel that we cannot possibly grow old—only younger and more adventuresome. For here we have found one new world and there are countless others which lay just beyond our grasp . . . Now we near the earth once again, and from being giants of space and time, we return to the infinitesimal smallness of our real natures, we realize for the first time since we left that we are but a speck of dust in a sea of nothingness. The earth looks small but friendly; we circle down inside gravity and come nearer to what is green and warm and welcome. It is, perhaps, but one stop in an infinite space parade, but it is *our* stop and we happily disembark.—**liner notes, Walter Schumann's** *Exploring The Unknown*

♪♪♪♪♪

A collection of seemingly unmusical implements from the hardware shelf, such as trowels, putty knives, and crowbar, are blended with more usual orchestral sounds in twelve fun-filled original compositions . . . The story of this album's making can best be told by this scene and situation: A surplus store . . . two rather vague customers, furtively tap-tap-tapping plastic helmet-liners, rattling messkits, plinging matched drill sets with a cold chisel. The clerk approaches and asks, "Can I help you gentlemen?" And the reply, "No thanks. Just listening."—**liner notes, Jack Fascinato's** *Music From A Surplus Store*

♪♪♪♪♪

When this girl sings she takes off into an area where most singers are lost, that area bounded by the libido to the east, the stream of consciousness to the west, the rivers of Lethe to the south, and to the north by the Great Unknowable. To Leda the human voice—her human voice—is a kind of psychosomatic probe, capable of delving into feelings and emotions that are half-admitted or altogether inadmissible in sane, daylight hours. It has no shame. It touches the untouchable and sings the songs that Solomon left out. She uses no

words and they are not missed. She uses the human body—her human body—as a vocal instrument. A singer's body must be open, to sing at all. To be open is to feel emotions as they come, not censored. To feel that way, and to dare to sing that way, is to make yourself available to every kind of dark fear, every passion, every momentary qualm, every sinister seed of horror to which humankind is prone.—**liner notes, Leda Annest & Phil Moore's** *Portrait of Leda*

♪♪♪♪♪

It's very frustrating to have the knowledge that you are living a game, trapped in a diabolical mistake . . . I believe that once people hear my record, everything else will make sense. It will help to wake everyone up to the truth. Oh, they all will still hate each other; they'll still fight and kill and destroy and hate and hate and hate . . . In time they'll come to know that somewhere past this worldly illusion, out there beyond this frozen balloon of nightmares, is a place that isn't held together by telephone pole crutches, a place that can only be called "home."—**liner notes, Kali Bahlu's** *Cosmic Remembrance* **(c.1968)**

♪♪♪♪♪

Modern technology has shrunk distances between continents to such a great extent that isolationism is now a thing of the past. The world of music has reacted with its own characteristic dynamism experimenting with new forms, new techniques and new sounds, thus resulting in several new creations. In the West, today, the most sensational sound in music is the sound of Sitar, the gourded lute of India. When an instrument, designed essentially to present the Indian Ragas, in which melody and rhythm are predominant, ventures into the realm of harmony and counterpoint, the result is bound to be unusual, and in this case, refreshing as well.—**liner notes, Balsara & His Singing Sitars'** *Great International Hits*

♪♪♪♪♪

In the person of Sandra Warner you will find a versatile and unusual combination of beauty and talent. She has graced the covers of all my Liberty albums as the *Exotica Girl.* In fact, it was a standing gag among most dj's that they were unaware there was a record in the album-liner until some time later. Sandra is a lot of woman and to top that has a warm and gracious personality. Her background in show business is most impressive. Not only has she appeared in several top motion picture productions, but she is considered one of our top models and is also a talented dancer. For some time she toured the nightclub circuit extensively with her *twin sister,* Sonia. The girls toured with such notables as Danny Kaye, plus many other famous TV and Picture personalities. When I was asked if I would write these notes for her album I thought it was a fitting switch. In this album, Miss "Exotica" herself

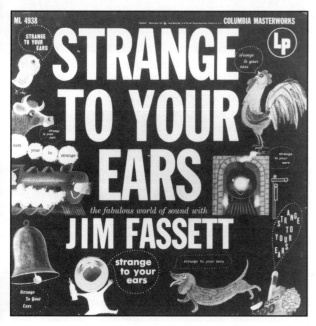

Jim Fassett's *Strange To Your Ears*, Columbia Masterworks.

emerges as a talented performer whose voice and personality merit the attention her lovely face has attracted heretofore. Settle back, relax and listen to the "Exotic" Sandy Warner.—**liner notes by Martin Denny, Sandy Warner's** *Fair & Warner*

♪♪♪♪♪

The *awakening of the ear* has been brought about by electronic and acoustical developments in the last twenty years, which have quite literally broadened our aural perception . . . *Strange to Your Ears* is built around the recognition-factors which make familiar sounds familiar—and illustrating what happens when these recognition-factors are taken away or changed . . . Take the canary sequence. At least a couple of hours of canary-song had to be recorded first . . . Then began a grueling stretch of tape-copying, cutting, splicing and re-copying, in which one false move always could send the experimenters back to the beginning. Fassett and Goldberg cannot remember how long it took them to produce this 30-second passage of triple-trio banshee-wailing, unearthly in its ghostly timbre, but my limited experience would suggest an 18-hour minimum . . .—**liner notes by John M. Conly, Jim Fassett's** *Strange To Your Ears*

♪♪♪♪♪

When word and sound are heard, imagination begins to operate, and imagination is one of the great faculties. This may seem a somewhat portentous note upon which to introduce Jim Fassett and his spoken-and-sonic travelogues. Mr Fassett is an unassuming though brilliant practitioner of a craft much underrated, or at least *unrecognized*. This is the art of arousing immediately, through words and illustrative sounds, some

millions of imaginations, so that they go into *creative activity.*—**liner notes by J. Conly, Jim Fassett's** *Scandinavia: A Portrayal In Sound*

♪♪♪♪♪

For as long as man has beheld the ocean's splendor, inspiration has come with the tides and stayed to work its magic on his imagination. To a composer the sea offers wondrous motion, a shimmering surface of flowing beauty, liquid depths of romance, enchantment and mystery. Composer-arranger-conductor Les Baxter has gratefully accepted these things, and distilled them into exotic miniatures of dream-like orchestral beauty—sparkling, opalescent gems.—**liner notes, Les Baxter's** *Jewels of the Sea*

♪♪♪♪♪

Beethoven had really only one great musical aptitude: he knew unfailingly which note to put after the one ahead of it, making people want to keep on listening.—**Leonard Bernstein**

♪♪♪♪♪

There are some who are feverishly contemporary because if they didn't know where it's at from month to month and year to year, they wouldn't know where *they* were at. There are others, however, who are always tuned in to what's happening because out of a *strong center of self-knowledge* comes a constant curiosity about the time in which they live, the rhythms of that time, the problems of that time, and the satisfactions of that time.—**liner notes by Nat Hentoff, Steve Allen's** *Songs For Gentle People*

♪♪♪♪♪

Like the sea, today's popular music keeps changing, shifting, bringing in new elements from other seas far away. There's never been a time like this in popular music, and the swirling variety of its components keeps opening up new ways of listening. And new ways of *being . . .*—***Ibid***

♪♪♪♪♪

Our educational processes are devoted almost entirely to teaching us *what* to think and rarely give us formal instruction in *how* to think . . . So formidable is the problem, in my view, that nothing short of adding formal instruction in How-To-Think, beginning with our kindergarten-level processes of education, will fill the bill. It has been by no means established that even doing that much will civilize us in time to check man's self-destructive tendencies, but we have a moral obligation to go as far as possible in making the experimental attempt . . . Subsequently, I hope to write another album called "How To Feel."—**liner notes by Steve Allen, Steve Allen's** *How To Think*

♪♪♪♪♪

American boys have always a fondness for the harmonica, also known as the "mouth organ." It remained for Larry Adler to raise the musical toy of boyhood to a concert instrument. He was the first person ever to appear as soloist playing the harmonica in concerts with great symphony orchestras ... Adler's London success was a turning point in his life. He played for royalty; he had an entire revue written around him. Fan clubs totaling a half million Adler devotees sprouted all over England; harmonica sales increased 2000 % after his arrival ... There have been many concertos written especially for the harmonica, all of them specifically for Adler. Darius Milhaud, Jean Berger, Frank Fields are among the noted composers who have written for the harmonica.**—liner notes,** ***Larry Adler & His Harmonica*** **(10" LP, 1949)**

♪♪♪♪♪

"Sensational" is the word for Roy Awbrey, and "unique" is the word for his accordion. Roy plays a $3,000 unit which includes his amplified accordion, an echo unit, an organ unit, and plays through five speakers. Roy gets sounds from his accordion like a violin, bassoon, piccolo, clarinet, bagpipes, bells, and even duplicates the sound of a steam engine chugging along and then letting off steam when coming to a stop ... Between wowing his customers with his musicianship, Roy has a fast line of patter on the style of Bob Hope. Roy has over 1,500 jokes, mostly one-liners, which he keeps firing out into his audience, machine-gun style ... Just when you decide that this hard-working entertainer has plenty on the ball, he sets down his accordion and proceeds to put on various wigs, hats, and many other unusual costumes which he uses during some of the most wild pantomime routines in the world ... it is really three acts all condensed into one: Wizard of the Accordion, Tops in Gags, and King of Pantomime.**—liner notes,** ***Laugh It Up! with Roy Awbrey***

♪♪♪♪♪

It has been said that the property of genius is the capacity for *effecting changes in set ideas.* If this is true, Les Baxter is certainly one of the musical geniuses of the 20th Century ... Les Baxter first began to change the musical face and taste of America in 1950 with an album titled *Music Out of the Moon.* The album signaled two firsts: it was the first time a long-playing record cover had been printed in full color, and it was the first modern expression of all the exotic music to follow. At this time also, Les introduced the ethereal sound and feel of outer space with an electronic musical instrument called a *theremin.* Actually, the Exotic Movement in music can be traced back to Ravel and *Bolero*—this composition had Parisian audiences in a frenzy in the year 1928. But "Exotica" was not heard in a popular sense until Les Baxter embellished the basic classical ideas with his own innovations ... He

spends considerable time in Mexico and South America seeking out century-old manuscripts and storing them away for future use ... Travel—an adventurous search for new sounds, new music—has become a part of Les' life.**—liner notes,** ***Les Baxter: The Sounds of Adventure***

♪♪♪♪♪

My human body holds me its lifetime prisoner. I escape through the tongue, splashing into smiles, tears, yells and screams ... Materialistically the world expects me to communicate on its own terms ... *Straight people are crazy.***—liner notes, Kim Fowley's** ***Born To Be Wild*** **(c.1968)**

♪♪♪♪♪

This album is more than just music. It takes your record player and turns it into an almost movable object. You will experience the movement as the speakers seem to spread out ... or lift from the floor ... or approach you ... or recede in the distance ... Words could not possibly describe even *one* of the tracks in this fantastically unusual and exciting album.**—liner notes, Mel Henke's** ***Dynamic Adventures In Sound*** **(1962)**

♪♪♪♪♪

The voyage lasted 8 days, 3 hours, 18 minutes. It took 952,700 miles. 8 years of rehearsal. And centuries of dreaming. It took 300,000 technicians and scientists 8,000,000 working parts in the space vehicle. Thousands of different flight plans. And over 20,000 companies to accomplish it. The time was 20 seconds after 10:56 PM, Sunday, July 20, 1969. And now we look

Dick Schory's New Percussion Ensembel, *Music for Bang, Baaroom & Harp,* © 1958 RCA Victor. Album cover credits: photo: Warren K. Swanson.

beyond to Mars and Venus and Jupiter. Anything is possible now. Even on earth.—liner notes, *One Small Step: The Voyage of Apollo 11* (narrated by Dr Wernher von Braun & Chet Huntley)

♪♪♪♪♪

The *Space Suite* is a fascinating musical configuration of man's growing absorption with outer space. The musical material is excitingly original and so varied in literally thousands of tonal and rhythmic ideas that it suggests a myriad number of visual images and motions man is wont to associate with present-day information about outer space . . . For example, the music actually seems to suggest words like *apogee* (ceiling in the orbit of a satellite) and *perigee* (point nearest the earth in a satellite orbit), air resistance, acceleration, cosmic wind, circular motion, jet thrust, luminescent coatings, magnetic field, momentum, orbital contraction, gravitational field, re-entry velocity, multi-directional factors, stellar radiation, weightlessness, rotation and scores of others . . .—liner notes, Bobby Christian's *Strings For A Space Age*

Bobby Christian & His Orchestra's *Strings for a Space Age*, © 1962 Audio Fidelity Inc.

♪♪♪♪♪

Basically, this is a record of what happens when a dozen virtuoso percussionists are turned loose on two truckloads of instruments of bang . . . It really did take two moving vans to arm us with instruments . . . a vast stage was a jam-packed jigsaw puzzle of xylophones, marimbas, chimes, tambourines, tom-toms and tam-tams. Two guitars, harp and bass were the only plucked hybrids. Two large banquet tables were crammed with the little gadgets: blocks, horns, slapsticks, whistles, poppers, tuned automobile brake drums [and] a manifold from a 1946 Chevrolet . . .—liner notes, Dick Schory's *Music For Bang, baa-r-oom and Harp*

♪♪♪♪♪

There are many fine percussion albums available, but where else can you find one with: a real live moving tap dancer . . . 13 assorted cymbals simulating moving waves . . . a 50-yard run for a bass drum . . . 7 percussion virtuosos who would just as soon hit an instrument as look at it (121 separate instruments, to be exact). A brass corps playing stereo hide-and-seek in the vast corners of Chicago's Orchestral Hall . . . A phony musical traffic jam (automobile horns courtesy of a dozen South Rampart Street used car lots) . . . Music, too. In spite of all this sound stuff, this is music you can dance, read, drink, relax or eat to.—liner notes, Dick Schory's *Wild Percussion And Horns A'Plenty*

♪♪♪♪♪

One live musician is still the most complex, sophisticated, beautiful musical instrument that will ever exist. Equipped with a computer which allows him to hear music inside himself and dream up sounds which do not yet even exist, the living music-maker in connection with a science-savvy sideman can extend his dreams to incredible depths . . . Violin, guitar and synthesizer can all be extensions of singing, yelling and crying vocal chords; of fingers and lips; of dancing feet, beating hearts, and most of all, minds imagining—just as Edgar Varèse was talking about synthesized music and hearing it in his head twenty or thirty years before RCA-Princeton ever created a synthesizer.—liner notes, Electro Harmonix Work Band: *State-of-the-Art Electronic Devices*

♪♪♪♪♪

In every life there are times when things seem to go exactly right; when business and health, life and love, dovetail into a pleasant pattern that results in "peace of mind." Our troubled and complex world today offers all too few periods when we can relax in this happy mood. At best, perhaps, we have memories of such moments . . . the quiet of a country hillside . . . the glow of achievement that comes with business success . . . the throbbing joy of first love . . . Here, for the first time, Dr Hoffman has recorded the Theremin three times—achieving a trio effect, in perfect harmony, all played by the same artist! . . . This is music that has a message to give, if you will open your mind and heart to receive it. Turn down the lights, relax in an easy chair, and listen. Then, for a few stolen hours, perhaps you will warm to happy memories and blissful hopes: Yours, for as long as you may hold it, will be peace of mind.—liner notes, *Music For Peace of Mind*

♪♪♪♪♪

Catalog

♦ ♦ ♦ N E W   T I T L E ♦ ♦ ♦

RE/Search #15: Incredibly Strange Music, Volume II

Featuring:

♦ *Jello Biafra*
♦ *Rusty Warren*
♦ *Korla Pandit*
♦ *Ken Nordine*
♦ *Yma Sumac*
♦ *Juan Esquivel*
♦ *Bebe Barron*
(Forbidden Planet)
♦ *Elisabeth Waldo*
♦ *and others . . .*

Categories:

♦ *outer space*
♦ *exotica-ploitation* ♦ *Brazilian psychedelic* ♦ *yodeling*
♦ *singing truck-drivers* ♦ *abstract female vocals* ♦ *moog*
♦ *religious ventriloquism* ♦ *sitar-rock* ♦ *theremin*
♦ *and more . . .*

Incredibly Strange Music, Vol. II—a comprehensive guide to little-known yet amazing vinyl recordings—picks up where *Vol. I* left off.

$17.99

RE/Search People Series, Vol. 1: Bob Flanagan, Super-Masochist

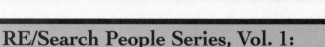

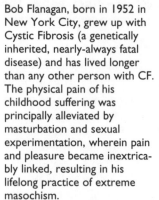

Bob Flanagan, born in 1952 in New York City, grew up with Cystic Fibrosis (a genetically inherited, nearly-always fatal disease) and has lived longer than any other person with CF. The physical pain of his childhood suffering was principally alleviated by masturbation and sexual experimentation, wherein pain and pleasure became inextricably linked, resulting in his lifelong practice of extreme masochism.

In deeply confessional interviews, Bob details his sexual practices and his extraordinary relationship with long-term partner and Mistress, photographer Sheree Rose. He tells how frequent near-death encounters modified his concepts of gratification and abstinence, reward and punishment, and intensified his masochistic drive. Through his insider's perspective on the Sado-Masochistic community, we learn firsthand about branding, piercing, whipping, bondage and endurance trials. Surprisingly, the most extreme narratives are infused with humor, honesty, and self-reflective irony. Bob's sharp intelligence and lack of pretense belie a deep commitment to deciphering philosophical issues regarding the body, power, sex, life and death.

Includes photographs by L.A. artist Sheree Rose.
8½ x 11", 128 pp, 125 photos & illustrations.

$14.99

RE/Search #14: Incredibly Strange Music, Volume I

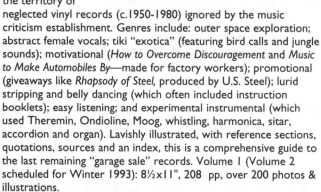

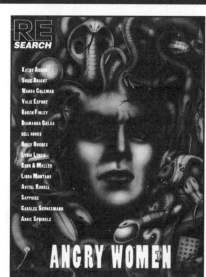

Featuring:

- ◆ Eartha Kitt
- ◆ The Cramps
- ◆ Martin Denny
- ◆ Amok Books
- ◆ Norton Records
- ◆ Perrey & Kingsley
- ◆ Mickey McGowan (Unknown Museum)
- ◆ Phantom Surfers
- ◆ Lypsinka
- ◆ and others . . .

Enthusiastic, hilarious interviews illuminate the territory of neglected vinyl records (c.1950-1980) ignored by the music criticism establishment. Genres include: outer space exploration; abstract female vocals; tiki "exotica" (featuring bird calls and jungle sounds); motivational (*How to Overcome Discouragement* and *Music to Make Automobiles By*—made for factory workers); promotional (giveaways like *Rhapsody of Steel,* produced by U.S. Steel); lurid stripping and belly dancing (which often included instruction booklets); easy listening; and experimental instrumental (which used Theremin, Ondioline, Moog, whistling, harmonica, sitar, accordion and organ). Lavishly illustrated, with reference sections, quotations, sources and an index, this is a comprehensive guide to the last remaining "garage sale" records. Volume 1 (Volume 2 scheduled for Winter 1993): 8½x11", 208 pp, over 200 photos & illustrations.

$17.99

"This book will change your life." —MIRABELLA

"Alfred Hitchcock's *Music To Be Murdered By* is just the tip of the iceberg. *Incredibly Strange Music,* a catalog of the wackiest discs ever made, goes where few audiophiles have ever gone." —ENTERTAINMENT WEEKLY

"It's not the artistry (a suspect word to the RE/Search people) that went into making these records but rather the collector's enthusiasm for the object and its meaning that is the leitmotif here. No matter whether it's Mickey McGowan, proprietor of the Unknown Museum in Mill Valley, Calif., getting hot about bird recordings or women's studies academic Lynn Peril speaking with cautious avidity about her sexploitation music collection, these people transmit heat and light about a hunk of American ephemera which nonetheless retains cosmic significance for them." —PUBLISHER'S WEEKLY

RE/Search #13: Angry Women

Featuring:

- ◆ Karen Finley
- ◆ Annie Sprinkle
- ◆ Diamanda Galás
- ◆ bell hooks
- ◆ Kathy Acker
- ◆ Avital Ronell
- ◆ Lydia Lunch
- ◆ Sapphire
- ◆ Susie Bright
- ◆ Valie Export
- ◆ Wanda Coleman
- ◆ Linda Montano
- ◆ Holly Hughes
- ◆ Suzy Kerr & Dianne Malley ◆ Carolee Schneemann

16 cutting-edge performance artists discuss critical questions such as: How can you have a revolutionary feminism that encompasses wild sex, humor, beauty and spirituality *plus* radical politics? How can you have a powerful movement for social change that's *inclusionary*—not exclusionary? A wide range of topics—from menstruation, masturbation, vibrators, S&M & spanking to racism, failed Utopias and the death of the Sixties—are discussed passionately. Armed with total contempt for dogma, stereotype and cliche, these creative visionaries probe deep into our social foundation of taboos, beliefs and totalitarian linguistic contradictions from whence spring (as well as thwart) our theories, imaginings, behavior and dreams. 8½x11", 240 pp, 135 photos & illustrations.

$18.99

"In this illustrated, interview-format volume, 16 women performance artists animatedly address the volatile issues of male domination, feminism, race and denial. Incendiary opinions of current issues such as the Gulf War and censorship and frequent allusions to empowering art and literature make this an excellent reference source. These informed discussions arm readers verbally, philosophically and behaviorally and provide uncompromising role models for women actively seeking change." —PUBLISHER'S WEEKLY

"This is hardly the nurturing, Womanist vision espoused in the 1970s. For the most part, these artists have given up waiting for the train of sexual equality . . . The view here is largely prosex, proporn, and prochoice . . . Separatism is out, community in. Sexuality is fluid, spirituality ancient and animist. Art and activism are inseparable from life and being. The body is a creative field, the mind an exercise in liberation. This is the 13th step, beyond AA's 12: a healing rage." —THE VILLAGE VOICE

See page 6 of our catalog for *INCREDIBLY STRANGE MUSIC* CDs

RE/SEARCH BACKLIST

RE/Search #12: Modern Primitives

An eye-opening, startling investigation of the undercover world of body modifications: tattooing, piercing and scarification. Amazing, explicit photos! *Fakir Musafar* (55-yr-old Silicon Valley ad executive who, since age 14, has practiced every body modification known to man); *Genesis & Paula P-Orridge* describing numerous ritual scarifications and personal, symbolic tattoos; *Ed Hardy* (editor of *Tattootime* and creator of over 10,000 tattoos); *Capt. Don Leslie* (sword-swallower); *Jim Ward* (editor, *Piercing Fans International*); *Anton LaVey* (founder of the Church of Satan); *Lyle Tuttle* (talking about getting tattooed in Samoa); *Raelyn Gallina* (women's piercer) & others talk about body practices that develop identity, sexual sensation and philosophic awareness. This issue spans the spectrum from S&M pain to New Age ecstasy. 22 interviews, 2 essays (including a treatise on Mayan body piercing based on recent findings), quotations, sources/bibliography & index. 8½ x 11", 212 pp, 279 photos & illustrations.

$17.99

"**MODERN PRIMITIVES** is not some shock rag parading crazies for your amusement. All of the people interviewed are looking for something very simple: a way of fighting back at a mass production consumer society that prizes standardization above all else. Through 'primitive' modifications, they are taking possession of the only thing that any of us will ever really own: our bodies."
—**WHOLE EARTH REVIEW**

"The photographs and illustrations are both explicit and astounding . . . This is the ideal biker coffee table book, a conversation piece that provides fascinating food for thought." —**IRON HORSE**

"**MODERN PRIMITIVES** approaches contemporary body adornment and ritual from the viewpoint that today's society suffers from an almost universal feeling of power-lessness to change the world, leaving the choice for exploration, individuation and primitive rite of passage to be fought out on the only ground readily available to us: our bodies."—**TIME OUT**

"In a world so badly made, as ours is, there is only one road—rebellion."
— Luis Bunuel

"Habit is probably the greatest block to seeing truth." — R.A. Schwaller de Lubicz

RE/Search #11: Pranks!

A prank is a "trick, a mischievous act, a ludicrous act." Although not regarded as poetic or artistic acts, pranks constitute an art form and genre in themselves. Here pranksters such as Timothy Leary, Abbie Hoffman, Paul Krassner, Mark Pauline, Monte Cazazza, Jello Biafra, Earth First!, Joe Coleman, Karen Finley, Frank Discussion, John Waters and Henry Rollins challenge the sovereign authority of words, images & behavioral convention. Some tales are bizarre, as when Boyd Rice presented the First Lady with a skinned sheep's head on a platter. This iconoclastic compendium will dazzle and delight all lovers of humor, satire and irony. 8½ x 11", 240 pp, 164 photos & illustrations.

$17.99

"The definitive treatment of the subject, offering extensive interviews with 36 contemporary tricksters. . . from the Underground's answer to Studs Terkel."
—**WASHINGTON POST**

RE/Search #10: Incredibly Strange Films

A guide to important territory neglected by the film criticism establishment, spotlighting unhailed directors—*Herschell Gordon Lewis, Russ Meyer, Larry Cohen, Ray Dennis Steckler, Ted V. Mikels, Doris Wishman* and others—who have been critically consigned to the ghettos of gore and sexploitation films. In-depth interviews focus on philosophy, while anecdotes entertain as well as illuminate theory. 13 interviews, numerous essays, A-Z of film personalities, "Favorite Films" list, quotations, bibliography, filmography, film synopses, & index. 8½ x 11", 224 pp. 157 photos & illustrations.

$17.99

"Flicks like these are subversive alternatives to the mind control propagated by the mainstream media."
—**IRON HORSE**

"Whether discussing the ethics of sex and violence on the screen, film censorship, their personal motivations, or the nuts and bolts of filmmaking from financing through distribution, the interviews are intelligent, enthusiastic and articulate."—**SMALL PRESS**

RE/Search #8/9: J.G. Ballard

A comprehensive special on this supremely relevant writer, now famous for *Empire of the Sun* and *Day of Creation*. W.S. Burroughs described Ballard's novel *Love & Napalm: Export U.S.A.* (1972) as "profound and disquieting...This book stirs sexual depths untouched by the hardest-core illustrated porn." 3 interviews, biography by David Pringle, fiction and non-fiction excerpts, essays, quotations, bibliography, sources, & index. 8½ x 11", 176 pp. 76 photos & illustrations by Ana Barrado, Ken Werner, Ed Ruscha, and others.

$14.99

"The RE/SEARCH to own if you must have just one . . . the most detailed, probing and comprehensive study of Ballard on the market."—BOSTON PHOENIX

"Highly recommended as both an introduction and a tribute to this remarkable writer."
—WASHINGTON POST

RE/Search #6/7 Industrial Culture Handbook

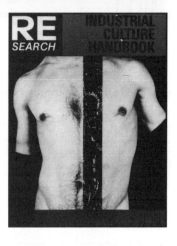

Essential library reference guide to the deviant performance artists and musicians of the *Industrial Culture* movement: *Survival Research Laboratories, Throbbing Gristle, Cabaret Voltaire, SPK, Non, Monte Cazazza, Johanna Went, Sordide Sentimental, R&N,* and *Z'ev.* Some topics discussed: new brain research, forbidden medical texts & films, creative crime & *interesting* criminals, modern warfare & weaponry, neglected gore films & their directors, psychotic lyrics in past pop songs, *art brut,* etc. 10 interviews, essays, quotations, chronologies, bibliographies, discographies, filmographies, sources, & index. 8½ x 11", 140 pp, 179 photos & illustrations.

$13.99

". . . focuses on post-punk 'industrial' performers whose work comprises a biting critique of contemporary culture . . . the book lists alone are worth the price of admission!"—SMALL PRESS

RE/Search #4/5: W. S. Burroughs, Brion Gysin, Throbbing Gristle

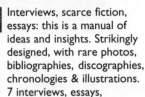

Interviews, scarce fiction, essays: this is a manual of ideas and insights. Strikingly designed, with rare photos, bibliographies, discographies, chronologies & illustrations. 7 interviews, essays, chronologies, bibliographies, discographies, sources. 8½ x 11", 100 pp. 58 photos & illustrations.

$12.99

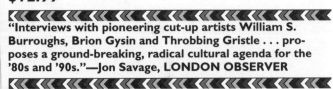

"Interviews with pioneering cut-up artists William S. Burroughs, Brion Gysin and Throbbing Gristle . . . proposes a ground-breaking, radical cultural agenda for the '80s and '90s."—Jon Savage, LONDON OBSERVER

Trilogy: High Priest of California (novel & play); Wild Wives (novel) by Charles Willeford

1953 San Francisco *roman noir*: the first two novels by Charles Willeford surpass the works of Jim Thompson in profundity of hard-boiled characterization, simultaneously offering a deep critique of contemporary morality. Unusual plots, tough dialogue starring anti-heroes both brutal and complex, and women living outside the lie of chivalry: *"She wasn't wearing much beneath her skirt. In an instant it was over. Fiercely and abruptly."* Plus the first publication of a play. 304 pp. 5x8". 2 introductions; bibliography; 15 photos.

$9.95

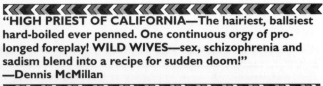

"HIGH PRIEST OF CALIFORNIA—The hairiest, ballsiest hard-boiled ever penned. One continuous orgy of prolonged foreplay! WILD WIVES—sex, schizophrenia and sadism blend into a recipe for sudden doom!"
—Dennis McMillan

"Willeford never puts a foot wrong.' —NEW YORKER

RE/SEARCH CLASSICS

The Confessions of Wanda von Sacher-Masoch

 Finally available in English: the racy and riveting *Confessions of Wanda von Sacher-Masoch*—married for ten years to Leopold von Sacher-Masoch (author of *Venus in Furs* and many other novels) whose whip-and-fur bedroom games spawned the term "masochism." In this feminist classic from 100 years ago, Wanda was forced to play "sadistic" roles in Leopold's fantasies to ensure the survival of herself and her 3 children—games which called into question who was the Master and who the Slave. Besides being a compelling study of a woman's search for her own identity, strength and ultimately—complete independence—this is a true-life adventure story—an odyssey through many lands peopled by amazing characters. Underneath its unforgettable poetic imagery and almost unbearable emotional cataclysms reigns a woman's consistent unblinking investigation of the limits of morality and the deepest meanings of love. Translated by Marian Phillips, Caroline Hébert & V. Vale. 8½ x 11", 136 pages, illustrations.

$13.99

"As with all RE/Search editions, *The Confessions of Wanda von Sacher-Masoch* is extravagantly designed, in an illustrated, oversized edition that is a pleasure to hold. It is also exquisitely written, engaging and literary and turns our preconceptions upside down."—LA READER

Freaks: We Who Are Not As Others by Daniel P. Mannix

 Another long out-of-print classic book based on Mannix's personal acquaintance with sideshow stars such as the Alligator Man and the Monkey Woman, etc. Read all about the notorious love affairs of midgets; the amazing story of the elephant boy; the unusual amours of Jolly Daisy, the fat woman; the famous pinhead who inspired Verdi's *Rigoletto;* the tragedy of Betty Lou Williams and her parasitic twin; the black midget, only 34 inches tall, who was happily married to a 264-pound wife; the human torso who could sew, crochet and type; and bizarre accounts of normal humans turned into freaks—either voluntarily or by evil design! 88 astounding photographs and additional material from the author's personal collection. 8½ x 11", 124pp.

$13.99

SIGNED HARDBOUND: Limited edition of 300 signed by the author on acid-free paper **$50.00**

"RE/Search has provided us with a moving glimpse at the rarified world of physical deformity; a glimpse that ultimately succeeds in its goal of humanizing the inhuman revealing the beauty that often lies behind the grotesque and in dramatically illustrating the triumph of the human spirit in the face of overwhelming debility."
—SPECTRUM WEEKLY

The Torture Garden by Octave Mirbeau

 This book was once described as the "most sickening work of art of the nineteenth century!" Long out of print, Octave Mirbeau's macabre classic (1899) features a corrupt Frenchman and an insatiably cruel Englishwoman who meet and then frequent a fantastic 19th century Chinese garden where torture is practiced as an art form. The fascinating, horrific narrative slithers deep into the human spirit, uncovering murderous proclivities and demented desires. Lavish, loving detail of description. Introduction, biography & bibliography. 8½ x 11", 120 pp, 21 photos.

$13.99

HARDBOUND: Limited edition of 200 hardbacks on acid-free paper **$29.00**

". . . sadistic spectacle as apocalyptic celebration of human potential . . . A work as chilling as it is seductive."
—THE DAILY CALIFORNIAN

The Atrocity Exhibition by J.G. Ballard

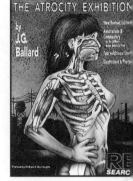

 A large-format, illustrated edition of this long out-of-print classic, widely regarded as Ballard's finest, most complex work. Withdrawn by E.P. Dutton after having been shredded by Doubleday, this outrageous work was finally printed in a small edition by Grove before lapsing out of print 15 years ago. With 4 additional fiction pieces, extensive annotations (a book in themselves), disturbing photographs by Ana Barrado and dazzling, anatomically explicit medical illustrations by Phoebe Gloeckner. 8½ x 11", 136pp.

$13.99

SIGNED HARDBOUND: Limited Edition of 300 signed by the author on acid-free paper **$50.00**

"*The Atrocity Exhibition* is remarkably fresh. One does no read these narratives as one does other fiction . . . one enters into them as a kind of ritual . . ."
—SAN FRANCISCO CHRONICLE

RE/SEARCH BACKLIST

RE/Search #1 & #3

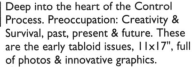

Deep into the heart of the Control Process. Preoccupation: Creativity & Survival, past, present & future. These are the early tabloid issues, 11x17", full of photos & innovative graphics.

◆ **#1** J.G. Ballard, Cabaret Voltaire, Julio Cortazar, Octavio Paz, Sun Ra, *The Slits,* Robert K. Brown (editor, *Soldier of Fortune), Non,* Conspiracy Theory Guide, Punk Prostitutes, and more.

◆ **#2** DNA, James Blood Ulmer, P'ev, Aboriginal Music, West African Music Guide, ~~OUT-OF-PRINT~~ echnology, Monte Cazazza on poisons, ~~Durtti Column~~, Seda, German Electronic Music Chart, Isabelle Eberhardt, and more.

◆ **#3** Fela, New Brain Research, The Rattlesnake Man, Sordide Sentimental, New Guinea, Kathy Acker, Sado-Masochism (interview with Pat Califia); Joe Dante, Johanna Went, *SPK, Flipper,* Physical Modification of Women, and more.

$8.00 each.

Louder Faster Shorter — *Punk Video*

One of the only surviving 16mm color documents of the original punk rock scene at the Mabuhay Gardens. 20 minute video featuring the AVENGERS, DILS, MUTANTS, SLEEPERS, and UXA. (This video is in US NTSC VHS FORMAT.)

$20.00

Search & Destroy:

Incendiary interviews, passionate photographs, art brutal. Corrosive minimalist documentation of the only youth rebellion of the seventies: punk rock (1977-78). The philosophy and culture, BEFORE the mass media takeover and inevitable cloning.

◆ **#1** Premiere issue. Crime, Nuns, Global Punk Survey.

◆ **#2** Devo, Clash, Ramones, Iggy, Weirdos, Patti Smith, Vivienne Westwood, Avengers, Dils, etc.

◆ **#3** Devo, Damned, Patti Smith, Avengers, Tom Verlaine, Capt. Beefheart, Blondie, Residents, Alternative TV, Throbbing Gristle.

◆ **#4** Iggy, Dead Boys, Bobby Death, Jordan & the Ants, Mumps, Metal Urbain, Helen Wheels, Sham 69, Patti Smith.

◆ **#5 OUT-OF-PRINT!**

◆ **#6** Throbbing Gristle, Clash, Nico, Talking Heads, Pere Ubu, Nuns, UXA, Negative Trend, Mutants, Sleepers, Buzzcocks.

◆ **#7** John Waters, Devo, DNA, Cabaret Voltaire, Roky Erickson, Clash, Amos Poe, Mick Farren, Offs, Vermilion & more.

◆ **#8** Mutants, Dils, Cramps, Devo, Siouxsie, Chrome, Pere Ubu, Judy Nylon & Patti Palladin, Flesheaters, Offs, Weirdos, etc.

◆ **#9** Dead Kennedys, Rockabilly Rebels, X, Winston Tong, David Lynch, Television, Pere Ubu, DOA, etc.

◆ **#10** J.G. Ballard, William S. Burroughs, Feederz, Plugz, X, Russ Meyer, Steve Jones, etc. Reprinted by Demand!

◆ **#11** The all photo supplement. Black and White.

$4.00 each.

SEARCH & DESTROY SET:
Issues #1-4 & 6-11 only $39.00.

INCREDIBLY STRANGE MUSIC CDs

Incredibly Strange Music CD & Cassette

On this CD you will hear a rousing version of the "William Tell Overture" whistled by the blind virtuoso Fred Lowery; an unbelievably off-key instrumental interpretation of the hit song "Up Up & Away," played on an out-of-tune sitar-with-strings arrangement; a song from an album titled *From Couch to Consultation,* "The Will to Fail"—a hilarious toe-tapping Tin Pan Alley tune about the Freudian "failure complex"; and a humorous parody of *Blackboard Jungle*-style juvenile delinquents titled "Sweet Sixteen." Energizing instrumentals include a vivacious, frenetic track performed on the xylophone ("Minute Merengue") and a rapid-fire guitar instrumental version of "Flight of the Bumble Bee." The album ends with a song called "A Cosmic Telephone Call," a 7-minute excursion into the mind-altering and hilarious world of Kali Bahlu, a self-styled guru, done with a weirdly atmospheric sitar accompaniment.

CD: $12.00, Cassette: $9.99

"In the new *Incredibly Strange Music, Vol. 1,* the editors push *way* beyond the cheesy TV-celebs-do-pop-faves LPs beloved by garden-variety music cultists. Less a practical guide than a treatise on the philosophical underpinnings of such ephemera. *Incredibly Strange Music* is best augmented by its forthcoming companion CD which collects other Bizarro-world stuff never likely to come your way in any other form." —ROLLING STONE

The Best of Perrey & Kingsley CD

Two fantastic, classic LPs (*The In Sound from Way Out,* and *Kaleidoscopic Vibrations*) combined on one hard-to-find, currently out-of-print CD available exclusively from Re/Search mail orders.

$16.00

BOOKS DISTRIBUTED BY RE/SEARCH

Body Art

From England, a glossy 8½ x 11" magazine devoted to tattoo, piercing, body painting, tribal influences, pubic hairdressing, et al. Outstanding explicit Color/B&W photographs, instructive text—a beautiful production. Approx. 48 pgs.

$17.00 EACH

ISSUE #1:	Finally back in print! Mr Sebastian, Scythian Man.
ISSUE #2:	Pubic Hairdressing, Out of the Closet, Shotsie.
ISSUE #3:	Africa Adorned, Tanta, Nipple Jewelry.
ISSUE #4:	Tattoo Expo '88, Tribal Influence, Male Piercings.
ISSUE #5:	Female Piercings, The Year of the Snake.
ISSUE #6:	Body Painting, Celtic Tattoos.
ISSUE #7:	Female Nipple Development, Plastic Bodies.
ISSUE #8:	Tattoo Symbolism, Piercing Enlargement.
ISSUE #9:	Tattoos, Nipple Piercing, The Perfect Body.
ISSUE #10:	Amsterdam Tattoo Convention, Cliff Raven.
ISSUE #11:	Ed Hardy, Fred Corbin, Beyond The Pain Barrier.
ISSUE #12:	Tattoo Expo '90, Genital Modifications.
ISSUE #13:	New Orleans Tattoo Convention 1990.
ISSUE #14:	Krystyne Kolorful, Paris Tattoo Convention.
ISSUE #15:	The Stainless Steel Ball, Bodyshots: Richard Todd.
ISSUE #16:	Tattoo Expo '91, Indian Hand Painting, Nail Tattoos.
ISSUE #17:	Body Manipulations, Women Talk Piercing, Expo '91
ISSUE #18:	National Tattoo Convention '92 & Tattoo Expo '92

Please list an alternate title for all Body Art selections.

PopVoid #1: '60s Culture. edited by Jim Morton

Edited by Jim Morton (who guest-edited *Incredibly Strange Films*). Fantastic anthology of neglected pop culture: Lawrence Welk, Rod McKuen, Paper Dresses, Nudist Colonies, Goofy Grape, etc. 8½ x 11", 100 pp.
$9.95

TattooTime edited by Don Ed Hardy

♦ **#1: NEW TRIBALISM.**
This classic issue features the new "tribal" tattooing renaissance started by Cliff Raven, Ed Hardy, Leo Zulueta & others.
$10.00

♦ **#2: TATTOO MAGIC.**
This issue examines all facets of Magic & the Occult.
$10.00

♦ **#3: MUSIC & SEA TATTOOS.**
Deluxe double book issue with over 300 photos.
$15.00

♦ **#4: LIFE & DEATH.**
Deluxe double book issue with fantastic photos, examining trademarks, architectural and mechanical tattoos, the Eternal Spiral, a Tattoo Museum, plus the gamut of Death imagery.
$15.00

♦ **#5: ART FROM THE HEART.**
All *NEW* issue that's bigger than ever before (128 pgs) with hundreds of color photographs. Featuring in-depth articles on tattooers, contemporary tattooing in Samoa, a survey of the new weirdo monster tattoos and much more!
$20.00

Halloween by Ken Werner

A classic photo book. Startling photographs from the "Mardi Gras of the West," San Francisco's *adult* Halloween festivities in the Castro district. Limited supply. Beautiful 9x12" hardback bound in black boards. 72 pgs. Black glossy paper.
$11.00

SPECIAL DISCOUNTS

Special Deluxe Offer (Save $80!) Complete set of RE/Search serials plus reprints and complete set of Search & Destroy.

Offer includes Re/Search #1 & 3 tabloids, #4/5 Burroughs/Gysin/Throbbing Gristle, #6/7 Industrial Culture Handbook, #8/9 J.G. Ballard, #10 Incredibly Strange Films, #11 Pranks!, #12 Modern Primitives, #13: Angry Women, #14: Incredibly Strange Music, Vol. 1, Search & Destroy Issues #1-11, The Confessions of Wanda von Sacher-Masoch, Freaks: We Who Are Not As Others, The Atrocity Exhibition, Torture Garden, the Willeford Trilogy and Me & Big Joe.
Special Discount Offer: $215 ppd. Seamail/Canada: $235. AIR Europe: $322. AIR Austr./Japan: $361.
**FOR *Bob Flanagan, Super-Masochist:*
ADD ONLY $10!**

PRICES FOR THE SPECIAL DISCOUNT OFFERS INCLUDE SHIPPING & HANDLING!

Special Discount Offer (Save $45!) Complete set of all RE/Search serials

Offer includes the Re/Search #1 & 3 tabloids, #4/5 Burroughs/Gysin/Throbbing Gristle, #6/7 Industrial Culture Handbook, #8/9 J.G. Ballard, #10 Incredibly Strange Films, #11 Pranks!, #12 Modern Primitives, #13 Angry Women and #14 Incredibly Strange Music, Vol. 1.
Special Discount Offer Only: $125 ppd. Seamail/Canada: $135. AIR Europe: $191. AIR Austr/Japan: $215.
**FOR *Bob Flanagan, Super-Masochist:*
ADD ONLY $10.**

Special Reprints Offer (Save $20!) Complete set of all RE/Search Classics

Offer includes the Willeford Trilogy, Freaks: We Who Are Not As Others, The Torture Garden, The Atrocity Exhibition, and The Confessions of Wanda von Sacher-Masoch.
Special Discount Offer: $58 ppd. Seamail/Canada: $60. AIR Europe: $85. AIR Austr/Japan $96.

Subscribe to RE/Search:

REGULAR SUBSCRIPTION:
You will receive the next three books published by RE/Search which will include either our numbered interview format serials or Re/Search classics. **$40.** Overseas/Canada: **$50.**

INSTITUTION SUBSCRIPTION:
Sorry no library or university subscriptions. Please place individual orders from this catalog.

SUBSCRIPTIONS SENT SURFACE MAIL ONLY! NO AIRMAIL.

Do you know someone who would like our catalog? Write name & address below.

_____
NAME

_____
ADDRESS

_____
CITY, STATE, ZIP

PLEASE SEE PREVIOUS PAGE FOR SPECIAL DISCOUNTS

◆ ◆ ◆ ORDER FORM ◆ ◆ ◆

HAVE YOU ORDERED FROM US BEFORE? YES   NO   circle one

_____
NAME

_____
ADDRESS

_____
CITY, STATE, ZIP

VISA   **MasterCard**™

Order by mail or phone: Phone orders may be placed Monday through Friday, from 10 a.m. to 6 p.m. Pacific Standard Time.
Phone #415-771-7117

Check or Money Order Enclosed (Payable to RE/Search Publications) or

VISA/MasterCard # [_____]

Exp. Date [_____]   Signature: _____

**MAIL TO: RE/SEARCH PUBLICATIONS
1232 PACIFIC AVE
SAN FRANCISCO, CA 94109**

TITLE	QUANTITY	TOTAL
Subtotal		
CA Residents (add 8½% Sales Tax)		
Shipping/Handling (except Special Discounts)		
Add $3 UPS (Continental U.S. only)		
TOTAL DUE		

SHIPPING & HANDLING CHARGES

First item $4. Add $1 per each additional item. For UPS add an additional $3 (flat rate per order). You must give a street address—no PO Box addresses.

INTERNATIONAL CUSTOMERS. For SEAMAIL: first item $6; add $2 per each additional item. For AIRMAIL: first item $15; add $12 per each additonal item.

ATTENTION CANADIAN CUSTOMERS: WE DO NOT ACCEPT PERSONAL CHECKS EVEN IF IT IS FROM A U.S. DOLLAR ACCOUNT. SEND INTERNATIONAL MONEY ORDERS ONLY! (available from the post office.)

SEND SASE FOR CATALOG (or 4 IRCs for OVERSEAS) FOR INFORMATION CALL: (415) 771-7117

PAYMENT IN U.S. DOLLARS ALLOW 6-8 WEEKS FOR DELIVERY

AUG, 1993

216

Jack Marshall's *Soundsville!*, Capitol Records.

Skip Martin's *Scheherajazz*, Somerset.
Album cover credits: cover photo: George Pickow, cover art: Will Dressler.